Acclaim for Chris Andoe's *House of Villadiva*

"With *House of Villadiva*, Andoe is officially one of St. Louis's great storytellers, and that says something."

—**Crystal Hubbard**, award-winning author of *Catching the Moon*

"Through Andoe's masterful and intimate storytelling, we become temporary inhabitants of his world—a world which is at once real, fabulous, and stranger than fiction."

—**Geoff Story**, *A Gay Home Movie*

"This book is a crack pipe!"

—**Patrick Collins**, Columnist at *Out in STL*

"Chris Andoe writes like he talks, which is a very good thing, because he's one of our city's best talkers. And the object of his fascination—whether he's three martinis into a happy hour or three thousand words into a written chapter—is the ensemble cast that is LGBTQ St. Louis, in all its pettiness and pageantry, glory, and weirdness. Sometimes he only records the drama; other times he spritzes gasoline on the flames. But all of it captivates him. Readers of this book can count on feeling the same way."

—**Nicholas Phillips**, *St. Louis Magazine*

"These stories, in their chronicling of the profound and the profane details of the city's queer community, roar out of the gate and never let up in their intensity, although they're not all rollicking tell-alls; many of the book's most affecting moments present themselves in quiet scenes and observations. 'This city saves your spot at the table,' Andoe notes . . . and you'll be delighted he's saved a spot at the house table for you, too."

—**Amanda E. Doyle**, Author of *100 Things to Do in St. Louis Before You Die*

"*House of Villadiva* is a compelling read. The writing is solid and engaging, and when you've finished, you really believe that you know Chris Andoe, the man. And you believe that there is hope for tomorrow."

—**Ken Busby**, Cultural Czar of Tulsa

"In *House of Villadiva* Chris Andoe delivers a revealing look into a slice of St. Louis. Part memoir, part history, Andoe offers a view of some of St. Louis' most contentious and pressing issues from the vantage point of his inner circle, set to the backdrop of the drama, flair, and even magic of the city's LGBTQ community. His meticulous recounting of conversations drops readers right into the fray, and proves Andoe's ability to remember every tooth on the gears that make the city's LGBTQ world turn."

—**Ryan Lee Schuessler**, Editor of *The St. Louis Anthology*

"I've long said that Andoe is in the top three of my favorite writers in the world and he did not disappoint. The story selection, the descriptions of character and settings are simply perfection. All I can say is you better get ready. It'll be the must read of the season."

—**Darin Slyman**, Darinslyman.com

"Andoe is a master storyteller. His pacing and word choice lead to many laugh out loud moments. What resonates more, however, are the entries that deal with universal experiences such as failed personal relationships, career angst, and our innate need to connect with others. An impressive collection of tales peppered with an array of memorable characters!"

—**Donald C. Miller**, Author of *Coming of Age in Popular Culture*

"Since first meeting Chris Andoe at a Chicago protest twenty years ago, I've come to know him as a soulful writer and a passionate ambassador of St. Louis. In *House of Villadiva*, Andoe paints a fascinating portrait of his beloved city. A place that seems part New Orleans, part Savannah, and part gritty 1970s New York."

—**John Aravosis**, AMERICA blog

"Chris Andoe's stories continue to help document St. Louis' most recent LGBTQIA+ history. These tales provide firsthand accounts of colorful and beloved personalities as well as life-changing events and milestones."

—**Steven Louis Brawley**, Founder of The St. Louis LGBT History Project

"St. Louis hold on to your hat, tea will be spilled tonight."

—**Robert Julian Stone**, Author of *Postcards from Palm Springs*

"If Truman Capote and Hunter S. Thompson had a love child it would be Chris Andoe"

—**Colin Murphy**, Editor in Chief of *#Boom Magazine*

"Chris Andoe's *House of Villadiva* really does have it all, offering a vibrant cast of characters and a voice that feels like your sassy gay uncle is whispering in your ear. Truman Capote would love to listen in, along with St. Louis native Tennessee Williams. I was charmed by this audacious volume from the start. Bravo! "

—**Scott Alexander Hess**, Lambda nominee, Author of *River Runs Red*

"My brother Chris comes from a long line of American storytellers. If you look up our father's side you'll first see a passenger on the Fortune, the boat after the Mayflower, and then scroll down 100 years past generations of hunters and traders with the Indians and you'll find a very literate Cherokee chief whose granddaughter walked the trail of tears at 9 after her mother died en route to Oklahoma, and that little girl's great-grandson was our grandfather, a storyteller second to none except for our grandmother who Chris learned almost as much from her storytelling as how she listened to us or didn't listen. With Grandma, you had to get it going and bring it or she was gone. Chris brought it in this book with lucid and vivid storytelling that actualizes in your mind."

—**Joe Andoe**, Author of *Jubilee City*

HOUSE
OF
VILLADIVA

HOUSE OF VILLADIVA

Chris Andoe

CAHOKIA PRESS

House of Villadiva

Published by Cahokia Press

Author Note: Some names of people and places have been changed, and due to the short story format, events don't always line up in perfect chronological order.

ISBN (black and white hardcover): 9781662906596
ISBN (color hardcover): 9781662906596
eISBN: 9781662906602

Dedicated to Kage

Contents

Preface

I only know St. Louis through Andoe's eyes, and from that view it's somewhat like an ungentrified version of its downriver sister New Orleans. The massive Mardi Gras celebrations, the pageantry, the rich eclectic history, the mosaic of distinct neighborhoods, and the eccentric inhabitants. A brilliant blue metropolis with a focus on art in all forms that has attracted such an island of misfit toys who find their tribe has been waiting for them.

In *House of Villadiva* you'll meet an unforgettable array of characters, many of whom you'd enjoy encountering at a dinner party and would find that you are fast friends after the first cheese course. And others you are thrilled are not your neighbors or even in your orbit. Whatever the anecdote, you feel you're in the room. The realism of life on life's terms in every story draws you in and evokes emotions.

This is a book of lessons learned, lessons refused and laughter enough for bellyaches! Short concise stories of people, places, events, and even the paranormal.

The main difference I see between Andoe's first book, *Delusions of Grandeur,* and *House of Villadiva* is the growth in his writing. *Villadiva* brought out a more cohesive storyteller voice, well-curated with an arc bringing the reader merrily along on a wild ride to a satisfying conclusion.

What's consistent in Andoe's work is a profound and passionate understanding of the city which is his muse. Neither sensationalizing or papering over its many problems, Andoe instead makes an airtight case that St. Louis is unique and fascinating.

I'll leave you with this quote from these pages:

"Some cities have no memories. Some are just nice, sedate places without roots, while others have transient populations and ephemeral cultures. In such cities, clean slates are easy to come by. St. Louis is not among them. Ours is an opera of larger-than-life characters with long histories of collaboration and conflict. Ours is a haunted city that writhes, a passionate city that burns."

Paul Emery
New York

HOUSE

noun

*a family or family lineage, especially a noble or royal one;
a dynasty*

2020

Adorning the grand stairway at Villadiva—the deliciously pretentious name for the historic St. Louis home I shared with my husband Kage, our burly young rugby coach roommate Marcus, and our witch-in-residence Zeeke—were framed articles and magazine covers.

When the discussion of *Out in STL*, the glossy magazine where I served as editor in chief, inevitably turned to print being dead I would often reply, "But you can't digitally replicate the gravitas of a cover."

Print's decline is not where *I* took the conversation, but there was always someone who felt compelled to alert me to that reality.

Of course, print wasn't practical, but neither was the ornate but rickety 110-year-old Villadiva, with its stained-glass windows, scalloped arches, uneven floors and questionable wiring. Practicality had never been high on my list of priorities. It certainly wasn't practical to leave financial success in the Bay Area or all I invested in my longtime marriage, but we'll get to all that soon enough.

My favorite *Out in STL* cover was in a position of honor, eye level near the base of the banister. For our "Where We Live" issue, my beautiful friend Cody, who like Kage and Marcus was Black, is pictured in aviators, sitting shirtless with a local celebrity on the windowsill of a glorious ornate turret looming over one of the city's queer intersections. You can't tell from the photo but the shadow of Bastille, the LGBTQ bar across the street where a group of regulars stood watching our spectacle, was ominously creeping up the face of the building. The iconic image, snapped when the brilliant golden sunlight magically glistened on Cody's muscular chest, was captured in the nick of time, minutes before the turret was eclipsed.

I showcased my twin *Riverfront Times* Mardi Gras covers. St. Louis had the second-largest Mardi Gras in the nation and for years I hosted parties during the celebration in the turret mentioned above. *Riverfront Times,* commonly referred to as the *RFT,* was the city's dominant weekly paper and a sister publication of *Out in STL.* The 2019 cover was "The Mad Beader of Mardi Gras" and 2020 was "The Maven of Mardi Gras."

Another *RFT* cover was for my feature on the provocative internationally-known blue-faced queen who was a constant irritant of the queer establishment, including the owners and drag queens of Grey Fox Cabaret, the bar five doors down from Villadiva.

Lowest on the wall was "Meth at the Melrose," a story which centered around the ten-unit apartment building two blocks away where me and Kage, along with a big group of friends, lived before Villadiva. Just two of the original cast remained, one being Jordan Jamieson, who I took to calling "Ms. Jamieson" after telling him that underneath his manly exterior he's essentially Thelma Harper, a southern grandma from the 1980s sitcom Mama's Family. The other remaining tenant is a story for later, and what a story it is, but I can tell you he was disgruntled about the magazine piece.

The low wall position was appropriate considering the Melrose sat at the base of two hills.

This book is a collection of stories about the colorful characters I've covered and cultivated, and the ones I feuded with. It's a tale of a complicated city of houses, and by "houses" I mean tribes. A metro built atop the ruins of North America's largest prehistoric city north of present-day Mexico where the continent's two mightiest rivers converge. It's a story of my tumultuous relationship with this place I couldn't stay away from.

The long table in Villadiva's mahogany-trimmed dining room was where I conducted interviews and where I wrote. There, beneath the coffered ceiling and ostentatious crystal chandelier, I learned of the inner workings of St. Louis, particularly Queer St. Louis. Topics like ambition and history and activism and machinations mixed with scandal and sex and ghosts and murder.

From my preferred spot at the table, I faced the arched entrance to the largely-unused (except for parties) parlor. Left of the fireplace was a gold-framed poster for my 2015 book *Delusions of Grandeur*. Opposite that was my most prized possession, a dreamlike oil painting of my dog Brawny by my brother Joe. On the imposing mantle was a framed movie-star quality black-and-white photo of my late dad in his early twenties, circa 1956. Dad manages to become part of these stories himself.

I sat down at the table to brainstorm on how I would even open such a saga, or such a hodgepodge of intertwining sagas. So much stems from the Melrose, that building down the hill, nestled in the shadows of the valley where an audacious social experiment went awry.

"I know how to open this story," I thought to myself.

Standing before the judge in a packed Downtown St. Louis courtroom as my neighbor stood defiantly nearby, I began explaining the severity of his obsession.

"Your honor, on October 14, 2017, the respondent admitted in writing to cutting open his flesh, bleeding onto the scraps of a shirt we'd given him, and summoning Satan to curse us."

But no, let's instead start at the beginning.

2014

A piece of thread loops over and under as it becomes part of a tapestry, and my journey has been similarly circuitous. Since leaving my hometown of Tulsa two days after high school graduation, twice I've lived in Oklahoma City, twice in San Francisco, and three times in St. Louis at five different addresses in the historic Tower Grove South neighborhood, including a lovely hilltop home two blocks from Villadiva. A home I was heartbroken to leave when my then-partner wanted to return to California. I worked for my San Francisco employer twice, and I'd recently returned to my St. Louis employer, Marquette Realty, for the third time.

Revisiting the same cities and offices as I have, I understood the saying, "You can't go home again." For instance, I distinctly remember how every familiar face at my San Francisco workplace was notably older, more tired, and less fun after our four years apart. Socially, friends I saw every weekend had new groups and new routines. And then sometimes you think you miss a place when you actually miss a time. My heart aches for places I've lived or frequented, but it's often aching for the way I experienced them in that moment and at that age.

My personal office at Marquette Realty, the room in which I was first hired at 23, had been mothballed for nearly four years. It looked the same, aside from being plundered of equipment and supplies. My desk was as I left it, my artwork was on the wall, and my business cards were in the drawer—unusable due to a defunct email address.

One of only two offices with a door aside from those of the brothers who owned the company, a few cubicled employees asked for the suite during my absence. They were denied without explanation, but likely were not surprised. The other doored office, with its glazed brick wall and handsome, albeit dated paneling, belonged to Stan, an accountant and college roommate of one of the owners. Stan had been dead for 15 years.

While things aren't the same when you come back to a place, St. Louis culture lends itself to returning. Even if you now lived far away, or maybe you died—the population is half ghosts, after all—this city saves your spot at the table. Still, there are "you can't go home again" moments. The second time I returned to Marquette Realty someone I'd worked well with for six years saw me as the prodigal son and was now bitter. So much so that she quit in dramatic fashion soon after my third return.

I bond with cities and workplaces like a lesbian does girlfriends, and that carried over into my writing. While I wrote for several outlets and lived from coast to coast, I maintained my *Tales from the Emperor* column in the St. Louis based LGBTQ magazine *Vital Voice* for a decade before heading up *Out in STL*.

Paul Hagan, the New York-based editor in chief of *Metrosource Magazine*, in 2015 described my work as follows:

Chris's writing—in particular his chronicles of the goings on in and around St. Louis—had the urgency of an embedded journalist in a war zone. He had clear enemies and fervent allies who agitated for their downfall. He opened doors to people with multiple aliases and secret identities, sinister perpetrators of long cons, and drag personalities who embody every aspect of the word legendary.

While I was known as a writer, property management paid the bills. The fact I even had a day job felt like a dirty secret, like I wasn't legitimate as a writer since it wasn't how I earned the bulk of my income. Plus, I felt the need for a firewall between my parallel livelihoods, witnessing the way seedy characters attempted to retaliate for stories they didn't like.

I had left the Bay Area after the collapse of my marriage of a dozen years. Damon, my husband, had fallen for a younger man, which induced a midlife crisis but was also liberating.

It was our second time in the San Francisco area and I hadn't wanted to leave our lovely Tower Grove home to begin with, only doing so as part of my continual effort to make amends for losing everything in the 2008 Financial Crisis, an event that forever changed his perception of me, from someone who could do anything, to someone who was financially incompetent.

The tinge of isolation I felt in the City of San Francisco, where I at least had a coterie of friends, magnified when we migrated across the bay to Oakland, where I had no real network, and where I often sat at home while he ran off with new associates.

Living in New York was something I had intended to do since I was 15, and I considered it to be the unfinished business of my life. The silver lining of the separation was that I had nothing left to lose (I even quoted Janis Joplin in the closing of my way too personal notice to my Berkeley employer—a letter they used against me when I tried to file for unemployment to fund a few extra months in New York).

The decision to make that leap also allowed me to deliver one of the best lines of my entire life when my dismissive husband came home and I announced out of the blue, "At this point in our lives you need to be single and I need to be in New York."

Being 19 years my senior, Joe was more like a father than a brother in many ways. His oldest child was only nine years younger than me. I didn't ask Joe if I could move into his Chelsea artist loft that sunny afternoon as I walked Brawny on the Oakland waterfront. I called to *announce* I would arrive. I was euphoric.

After years of trying to hold my relationship together I had just learned Damon was telling his mentor, a thorn in my side for seven years, that he was staying with *me* out of obligation. The punch in the gut was quickly numbed by the epiphany I had no obligation to this life of unbelievable work stress, crushing rent, loneliness, and a distant husband. A life where I didn't feel I belonged anywhere. A life so stressful, I was shitting blood.

I called to tell Joe I was free, and that I was coming. He responded with an enthusiastic green light.

The euphoria of being liberated was followed by a crash upon my arrival, and New York was not the kind of place you went to lick your wounds and regroup. With several real estate recruiters telling me, "Nobody in this town will hire you without Manhattan experience," my savings dwindling, and the only regional job prospects being in places like Philadelphia and Hartford, I had another epiphany. This was an opportunity to downshift, return to St. Louis, and finish my long-delayed book, *Delusions of Grandeur*.

Evil Stepmother

Like my brother Joe, Ray David was about twenty years my senior. He had taken me under his wing and welcomed me into the House of Villa Ray and his lavish Saturday night dinner parties when I first moved to St. Louis at 22, some 17 years earlier, and I considered him to be my gay dad. And like with Joe, I don't recall actually asking if I could move in with him.

Merely existing rent-free in Manhattan was costing $100 a day, so when my savings dwindled to about $3,500, I pulled the plug on New York and told Ray I was moving to St. Louis and would occupy what he'd long dubbed "The Christina Suite" on the second level of the palatial Villa Ray for a while, correctly assuming it wouldn't be an issue. While drinking, Ray would often refer to me as Christina. Referring to fellow gays as "she" and "her" was an old-school form of gay camp. You might call a guy "she" if you felt sisterly affection, as in having all your sisters with you, or if you didn't, as in "she's a bitch."

While living in the spacious villa wasn't an issue, what was an issue was Ralph, the sour and dreadful man Ray was dating whom I promptly dubbed Evil Stepmother.

The first time I laid eyes on her she was on the ground planting Ray's Doris Day rose bush, and, peering up sweaty and flushed, gave me a rather disgusted look.

There was always tension when Ralph was around. One evening at Clementine's, Soulard's (Soulard was the city's French Quarter) gay bar known for serving the strongest drinks, Ray attempted a reset, re-introducing me to Ralph. Sitting by my side as the loud music gave us a bit of conversational privacy, Ralph began asking questions.

"So, what are you doing here? What are your plans?" It was clear by his pointed tone that he saw me as a threat, even though my relationship with Ray had never been anything other than platonic.

"I'm going through a divorce and starting over. Ray is one of my best friends and I'm staying with him until I get reestablished." I replied.

"Ted and Lenny think you're taking advantage of him," Evil Stepmother said, delivering a sucker punch I did not see coming. Ted and Lenny were to Ray what Ray was to me. We were three generations of the same house, and to hear they said that was devastating. They had known me as independent and successful for all these years, and at the first hiccup . . .

The drinks were strong, the music was loud, and I was processing what was said. I have no memory of how I responded.

Somehow the conversation moved on in yet another unexpected direction.

"I just want to have sex, and Ray doesn't want it. I don't care if I'm topping or bottoming, I just want to fuck. And I'm oddly attracted to you," Evil Stepmother said, in what was a stunning and most unwanted advance.

Again, I don't know how I replied. But I do remember driving them both back to the villa shortly afterwards and saying to Ray, who was in the backseat, "So, I hear Ted and Lenny say I'm taking advantage of you."

Looking at Ray in the rearview I could tell he had no idea what I was talking about, leading me to believe if the comment had been said at all it was an aside Evil Stepmother initiated. That would make more sense, as Ray wasn't the type to speak ill of anyone or stand for others speaking ill of his friends. Meanwhile, Evil Stepmother stared at me in disbelief, jaw agape.

"How dare you?" she said.

"You didn't tell me that was a secret," I flippantly replied.

Cody

I'd first laid eyes on Cody when I was still in California. A friend in St. Louis, who knew Cody would be my type if not for the age difference, was dating him and sent me an incredibly sexy and memorable photo of a tattooed, dark-complected, shirtless, lean and muscular Cody in mirrored sunglasses. Like most new romances, theirs quickly faded, and maybe a year later when I moved to Villa Ray and saw Cody on the apps, I reached out.

Born and raised on the dangerous streets of North St. Louis, Cody was cool, masculine, quiet and confident. His mother was a postal carrier, and he often complained about how she didn't venture past her part of town, and how she didn't cook—and I found him amusing when he railed about it.

"She always wants us to come over and when we do there's nothing to eat! I think she should at least make some dinner, especially with boys in the house."

Unlike his provincial mother, Cody had a hunger to expand his horizons, meet a variety of people, and explore. Despite his young age I found him to be elegant, somewhat worldly even, as well as street smart.

I'd only been in town for a few days and didn't yet have a job or a car of my own, so Cody took me out in his flashy buttercream-colored Chrysler 300, which he drove without a seatbelt while texting. Being 14 years older, I was careful not to act parental, but I was terrified for us both as he drove across the Mississippi to Cahokia Mounds, site of the largest prehistoric city north of present-day Mexico, which he had never seen.

Back at the villa we made out on the bed. From the floor Brawny gave two demanding barks, and I stopped to lift him up. Cody smiled, "You and that dog."

Cody worked at a regional airport refueling airplanes, and would shower when he came over afterwards.

"I'd like to bathe you the next time you come over," I said.

He was a little surprised at the suggestion, but agreed. As he sat in the bubble bath, talking about his day, I bathed him by candlelight.

I was falling for him hard, but couldn't stop thinking about the age difference and what was best for him. In the middle of sex one evening, I just stopped and laid back.

"Is there a problem?" Cody asked.

"I feel like I'm not acting in your best interest. When I look back on some of my best moments in life, they were when I discovered something new with someone. Like learning San Francisco with my ex, when we both had the same fresh eyes. I feel like you need to find love with someone closer to your age."

While true, all of that was only part of the story. I hadn't even been away from Damon for six months. I had no income, maybe $2,000 left in the bank, nothing to offer, and I was so preoccupied with rebuilding my life I wasn't confident I could regularly perform sexually.

Cody would become one of my closest friends, and my attraction to him never faded. He wound up dating guys even older than me, and in retrospect I see that I had a rigid idea about what relationships should be.

I still believe the timing wasn't right. I had no foundation on which to build anything yet. I needed a full year of being single to reset, regroup, and to focus on the biggest project of my life. Had I pursued a relationship with him at that time it would have likely failed, and he may have not remained in my life at all.

Not long after I ended our brief romance, I reached out to make sure he didn't feel rejected, and to let him know I very much wanted to be part of his life.

"I know you want what's best for Cody," he said.

The Christy

My first utility bill arrived and was less than $20. I sat down to write out the check as if it were an event, and I felt so empowered. Despite earning the best money of my life in California, I hadn't directly paid bills in seven years—I never even knew how much money we had—and it felt good to do so.

The Christy was a striking, 1920s-era, three-story Tudor-style apartment building overlooking a pleasant park and a winding boulevard. Although it had its charms, it represented starting completely over—from the bottom. I had lived in that same building fifteen years earlier, as a struggling 23-year-old, after my phone sex addicted boyfriend ran up thousands in 1-900 number charges (How 90s is that?) and we could no longer afford our fashionable flat in Soulard. Careful to not reveal a trace of desperation in the wake of that financial disaster, I suggested to my bosses that the Christy really needed an on-site manager to run properly, and I volunteered.

So even at 23, the building of small apartments in the unassuming Bevo Mill neighborhood wasn't a place I aspired to. It was, however, a key reason I was able to survive and take hold in St. Louis. And it was there for me again.

Ray enjoyed my living with him. Before I moved away in 2010, we went out every Saturday night, and more often than not I'd sleep in the Christina Suite as to not drink and drive. Now he drank far less and came home much earlier, but we still enjoyed one another's companionship. Evil Stepmother aside, we had a great dynamic, so I didn't *need* the apartment and didn't intend to actually live there, but I thought having my own place somewhere was critical to my sense of self. It kept me from being truly dependent. If anything, it might be a good place for guests or for a rendezvous. And, since I negotiated it into my compensation, utilities were the only added expense.

I did my best to remain cordial with Evil Stepmother, despite the strain. One warm evening I went out to the deck to sit with her and Ray, who was on the phone. As Evil Stepmother played on her iPad, I initiated a conversation, which she ignored. Surely she wasn't intentionally ignoring me to my face, I thought, so I tried again, which confirmed that's exactly what she was doing.

I was through.

I went upstairs and packed, messaging Ray.

"I just can't deal with Ralph. I really appreciate you letting me live here, but I'm moving to the apartment," I wrote.

Although he'd been on the phone, he witnessed the incident.

"Are you sure this is what you want to do? I'm so sorry. I don't know why he acts like that," Ray replied.

I also messaged Damon to let him know.

"I think you should stay at Ray's, for what it's worth," Damon said.

In retrospect I think he wanted me to keep things as simple as possible in the event he and I got back together, and I returned to California. That seemed to be the driving motivation behind all of his advice, which was somehow lost on me at the time, in part because he was locked in a lease in a no-pets building. The moment I witnessed him enthusiastically signing that lease, any fleeting thoughts I had about our separation being temporary faded.

"At 39 I think it's time I live in a space where I'm not subjected to the unwanted opinions of hateful old queens," I replied, in what was intended to not only refer to Evil Stepmother, but to Damon's loathsome mentor Benny Babbish, who had to sign off on nearly every decision we made for seven years. If Damon picked up on that, he didn't show it.

Life at the Christy was simple and focused. I took Brawny for four walks a day in the park. I went to work, ate quick and easy meals, and spent nearly all of my free time working on my long-delayed book. I'd never been more driven, or more dedicated to anything.

Since Dad died in his very early forties, and I was nearly that age, I felt a sense of urgency, like I was running out of time. I turned down parties. I turned down dates. I turned down enticing offers of sex. Nothing was more important.

As "The Barbara Walters of St. Louis," as some called me because of my revealing interviews (Okay, nobody called me that but they should have!), I also maintained my column as well as my blog. The column was important since the publishers of *Vital Voice* were backing the book. On several occasions I worried the blowback from my pieces would be too much and might jeopardize the project, but the magazine's petite and fashionable publisher Darin Slyman always took things in stride.

I saw his name on my Caller ID one day, and answered. Darin always referred to me by my last name, which he regally pronounced as "ON-doe."

"ON-doe. Question. The piece you wrote about the queen who's been run over by seven different men, was that in reference to Dennis Milton? Because he's on the phone threatening to sue me."

My stomach dropped. That one, which I titled "Speedbump Sally," had come out months earlier, and I thought I'd gotten off scot-free.

Nervously, I replied, "Yes, it was."

With a big sigh he replied, "Ugh. These bitter old fags. I'll deal with it," and hung up.

Jasmine and the Original Sin

There was a nightlife photographer named Spike and I just knew he was bad news, but aside from his widely-witnessed history of domestic violence, I had no proof. Nothing added up. He and his partner, both barely thirty, boasted about their three-story house in a stuffy upper middle-class South St. Louis County suburb (an unlikely location for two young and hard-partying barflies), they drove a flashy car with expensive rims, and had a motorcycle, but Spike only worked here and there in restaurants, and his partner had some basic office job, as far as I knew.

Spike had a real racket when it came to getting free drinks. He would order the cocktail and then make a big show of photographing the bartender. When served he'd wink and walk away as if the publicity was payment. This worked every time at a few Grove (the main LGBTQ nightlife district) establishments, including Sensation, where he had several violent altercations on the patio with his partner and his former partners—including one who hanged himself.

The truth is I brushed off the inconsistencies and even the violence until the first *Vital Voice* event I attended after my aborted New York adventure.

I had followed and been friendly with Spike for years, and when I'd come to town, he was often my group's personal paparazzi. I spent a few days in St. Louis when I was en route from California to New York, and we met for lunch where he wept about how much my friendship meant to him, which I found surprising but touching.

With that fresh in my mind, I approached him enthusiastically as he was taking photos at the rooftop event venue, 360, forty floors above Busch Stadium.

"What are you doing back here?" he said coldly.

"I decided to come to St. Louis and finish my book," I said. "Hey, I've been following your work at Tim's new restaurant. I'm looking forward to trying it out."

"So, you came back to eat at a restaurant," he said, staring off into the distance.

It was clear the show he'd put on the last time we were together was to lay in the groundwork in the event I found success in New York. Now he was treating me like something stuck to the bottom of his shoe.

He ran around with a short, heavyset, glittery and made-up woman named Jasmine. Jasmine was a lesbian, which was always hard to remember because she struck me as a straight girl who hung around gay guys.

I didn't personally know her but followed her on Facebook, and one morning saw that the two had a messy and catastrophic falling out.

Even though Spike lived in South St. Louis County and she lived 40 minutes east in Belleville, Illinois, she acted as his personal chauffeur. At 4 a.m. one morning she had just gone to bed after a night of partying with him when he messaged her.

"I left my backpack in your car and need you to bring it to me."

"I'm in bed," Jasmine replied. "You can come get it but I'm drunk and I'm not driving all the way back right now."

I'm sure there were drugs in the backpack. An argument ensued, and Spike took to Facebook to rail about how betrayed he felt over Jasmine, his best friend, stealing from him.

When she woke to the poisonous posts, she tried to defend herself on the threads, but he'd delete her comments.

"Jasmine, you just need to let this go," he kept telling her privately, while leaving the accusations and the other comments up.

She instead posted her own update with her side of the story, and their friendship was over.

I sent her a succinct question: "Are you ready to talk?"

Jasmine Tells All

People don't often know what's interesting about what they know. They're too close to it, and it's all become normalized in their mind. Interviewing can be like trying to find the designer garment at a thrift store. You slam back hanger after hanger, trying to locate something of quality.

Going through an exhaustive inventory of Spike's skeletons over drinks at Sensation, the Grove bar that was among their favorite haunts, Jasmine rambled, "He was arrested for this, he fucked so and so, the house is actually his mom's, he was fired from here, everyone thinks his ex is dead but he isn't, he stole from . . ."

"What? The ex who hung himself is alive?"

"Oh yeah, he's living with family in California. I was there the night he hung himself in the garage. He had been texting Spike with questions like, 'What color rope should I use?' and Spike told him to use the green one, not thinking he'd really do it."

Jasmine, Spike and a couple of others returned to find Desmond's lifeless body hanging from the rafters. The police arrived and cut down the body as word of the suicide spread like a shockwave through the community, but the paramedics were able to resuscitate Desmond. He lingered in a coma for days, and when he came out of it his family took him to the Sacramento area.

"Desmond wanted no part of St. Louis after that, and Spike forbade us from speaking to or about him. We were explicitly told to not tell anyone he was alive."

The weekly *Vital Voice* team meetings, which took place around a giant granite-topped kitchen island in the office, were where Darin handed out assignments to the other writers, and asked me what I was working on.

"Do you remember when Spike's boyfriend Desmond hung himself three years ago? He's actually alive, and living in California," I said.

"Wait, what? Desmond is ALIVE?" Darin exclaimed. "But I remember when he died!"

I asked my Facebook followers to tune in for a major announcement at 8 p.m. where I told Desmond's story, including the history of domestic violence, and then that he was alive. It was quite the reveal.

Tim Beckman, the co-owner of Sensation, whom I had good relations with, had a soft spot for Spike and fiercely objected, slamming the story as one-sided.

I curtly replied, "Well, Tim, the other side of the story has been told for three years, and that side of the story is he's dead. And he isn't."

For her part, Jasmine was reviled and shunned by most of her Grove drinking buddies, whom we dubbed "the Snake Pit," after what they saw as an unforgivable betrayal of Spike.

I got the revenge I sought with her help, and didn't feel like I could abandon her.

That vindictiveness over Spike's disrespect was the original sin that bound me to Jasmine, who would be the source of perpetual strife and drama for years to come.

The Best Show in St. Louis

When Darin bought *Vital Voice* in 2009, which was then a newspaper as opposed to the glossy lifestyle magazine it would become, veteran writer Colin Murphy was basically part of the package. Colin was also who discovered me through the stories I'd post to Facebook, and convinced Darin to add me to the roster.

After a very public disagreement about a feature on polarizing bar owner Fancy Slovak, which included drunken late-night rants from Colin, Darin and Colin officially parted ways.

Colin posted: *Done and done. But I have a legacy; a body of work; a dedication to community and you just have a superficial bullshit sheen everyone sees through. Sick of it. It's on. War.*

And it was indeed war.

Within months Colin Murphy and his associate Colin Lovett founded *#Boom*, an LGBTQ news site more in line with the original news-focused *Vital Voice*.

When a piece Colin wrote for a national outlet went viral, *Vital Voice* served him with a cease and desist, saying he was in violation of a non-compete clause. That led to legal wrangling which ended with an agreement that *#Boom* couldn't profit off any *Vital Voice* client for 24 months.

I say Darin got me in the divorce. I returned to St. Louis not even knowing what had happened due to my own bi-coastal turmoil. I messaged Colin asking if the *Vital Voice* meetups were still at the same time, and got a curt message that he was no longer with them.

Vital Voice vs. *#Boom* was like Coke vs. Pepsi, Chevy vs. Ford, or Mac vs. PC, only far more personal.

Vital Voice had the big events and brought the glitz and glamour—flying in famous entertainers for rooftop soirées, sponsoring fashion shows, etc. They also had me, covering local public figures like full-blown celebrities. If two drag queens fought, I covered it as if it were Bette Davis vs. Joan Crawford.

#Boom, on the other hand, focused on news, ran everyone's press releases and put a priority on community service. They didn't rock the boat.

It seemed everyone in town had to pick a side.

We'd compete for breaking news, throw shade, and sometimes toss a wrench into the other's plans. The community, by and large, loved the drama of it all.

Low Tide at Villa Ray

Ray taught me much of what I knew about entertaining, and his signature event was his legendary New Year's Eve party. Of all the years I knew him, regardless of where I was living, I may have only missed it twice.

In the 1970s the tall, slim and handsome Ray was a big fish at Herbie's, the main gay disco in town, where he had his own reserved booth. Many of his friends from that era, mainly Black women, moved to Los Angeles to work in music, and at least one worked with Rick James. Some had moved back but even the ones who didn't would return for parties at Villa Ray, and all were fun, glitzy and told wildly entertaining stories.

There was a core group of about twenty of us who celebrated year after year. It was easily one of my favorite traditions.

With that history in mind, December 31, 2014 will go down as the saddest New Year's celebration in Villa Ray history.

In attendance were only Ray, Evil Stepmother, a very nice but subdued friend of Evil Stepmother's, Ms. Jamieson—who was still living in the country—and myself. Planning the events took a great deal of effort, and I don't think Ray had the bandwidth to juggle that and Evil Stepmother, who didn't really get along with anyone.

All of the typical decorations adorned the villa. The buffet was set, the crystal chandeliers were illuminated, but the whole thing felt like a deathwatch, and in a sense it was.

We didn't know it, but 2015 would be a major year for exits and entrances.

The War Room

Our group chat, "The War Room," began as a way to exchange information about local conman Dustin Mitchell, who had everyone convinced he was an attorney—some even after he made headlines for posing as one. The Mitchell exposés were part of what made me a household name in Queer St. Louis, as they'd garner thousands of comments from people sharing their personal stories. It seemed he had pulled a con on everyone, and I was like Dorothy after dropping a house on the Wicked Witch.

We expanded to uncover the crimes of others in our community's seedy underbelly. The crimes were real—many of those people wound up in prison—but our reputations took a nosedive as everyone felt they could be targeted next. The blowback was especially intense when we began focusing on Spike and his associates ("The Snake Pit"). St. Louisans are fiercely loyal to their drinking buddies and Spike was in the Grove nightly.

They say once a dog kills a chicken, once it gets that taste of blood, it will never stop killing chickens. Jasmine had her taste of blood and she was out to wield the War Room's power against anyone who got in her way.

"We should go to war on so and so," she'd exclaim, and was usually shot down by the group. But she used the fear of the War Room to bully, especially at the end of the night when the bartenders would cut her off.

One day I got a message from an employee of Sensation, asking if I'd call him.

"I wanted to see if you had an issue with us," he began. It turns out that when on drunken rampages, Jasmine would threaten everyone with "A Chris Andoe story."

I was mortified and did what I could to reign her in, which wasn't much.

As rational as I may be portraying myself here, she knew how to pull my strings.

"LOOK WHAT SO AND SO SAID ABOUT ME!" she'd say while sending a screenshot to the group, lacking any context. More often than not I'd run to the offending post and get in the big middle of it, later realizing her presentation of what went down was misleading at best—and that she had been the instigator.

Being Jasmine's friend meant being in constant conflict with strangers.

Meeting Menashe

I broke away from the *Vital Voice* team and roamed around the 2014 Pride Festival, stopping to get a drink. Working a liquor booth was a Facebook acquaintance named Menashe, and he greeted me enthusiastically.

"Here hon, you don't need to pay," he said in his deep booming voice as he handed me a bucket of fruit punch. Menashe was a Jewish guy in his early thirties, naturally lean and fit with a long thick salt-and-pepper beard.

And that punch was something. At the end of the day I was sitting next to a tree by the library when a group of homeless people chatted me up, and I shared the punch with them. When they passed the drink back it was empty, which I thought was rude at the time but now see was for the best.

Menashe had a short fuse and was prone to fly off the handle. I took him to a friend's BBQ one afternoon and the host's dog kept mouthing his phone charger cord. After stopping him several times Menashe, sitting at a table of eight near-strangers, exploded, "WOULD YOU STOP? GOD DAMN IT!"

Everyone sat in stunned silence and then the host, staring intently, replied, "You're an intense person. I like it."

Alton

My favorite part of the St. Louis region stretches from Alton, Illinois—22 miles due North of the Arch— and up the Great River Road to Grafton, alongside the Mississippi and Illinois Rivers and miles of limestone bluffs.

I found Alton while exploring the Mississippi, and so many things drew me to the picturesque place, including the dramatic topography with streets as steep as San Francisco, historic architecture, and the fact it's considered one of the most haunted towns in the nation. One reason for that, I believe, is when they deconstructed the Civil War Prison in 1865, which was the site of over 1500 deaths, they used its limestone to construct every basement in town.

But the area had a terrifying reputation long before that. Native American legend was that a giant monster, which they called the Piasa Bird, flew over the rivers and devoured men. The Illini painted a large mural of it high on the limestone cliffs near present-day Alton, and in 1673, while exploring the river, Father Jacques Marquette saw the painting, which struck terror in his heart.

He recorded the following description:

While Skirting some rocks, which by Their height and length inspired awe, We saw upon one of them two painted monsters which at first made Us afraid, and upon Which the boldest savages dare not Long rest their eyes. They are as large As a calf; they have Horns on their heads Like those of a deer, a horrible look, red eyes, a beard Like a tiger's, a face somewhat like a man's, a body Covered with scales, and so Long A tail that it winds all around the Body, passing above the head and going back between the legs, ending in a Fish's tail. Green, red, and black are the three Colors composing the Picture. We have learned that the great-great-great-great-great-great grandfather of Miss Jessica Beetner smote this monster. Moreover, these 2 monsters are so well painted that we cannot believe that any savage is their author; for good painters in France would find it difficult to reach that place Conveniently to paint them.

My friend and gentleman caller Adam visited from New York, and on his last day I took him to Alton before making our scenic, meandering journey to the airport. We parked on a brick street in the Christian Hill Neighborhood of classic Victorians and had lunch in the car while overlooking the river far below.

As we were winding our way through the district, I saw a grand, weathered and dramatic cement staircase rising some 40 feet up a steep ivy-covered slope. I had no idea what was up there and didn't have time to explore, but I was sure that it was wondrous.

Blind Lust in Bevo Mill

About a dozen blocks from my Bevo Mill apartment at the Christy was the home of my childhood friend Francis and his wonderful wife Edie. I had known Francis since he was a year old, and when he was about 21, I encouraged him to move from Ottawa, Kansas to St. Louis with $20 to his name, and I was proud of the prosperous life he created.

Around the block from Francis was a guy with the last name of Dickery, who we knew from the infamous dinner parties at Villa Ray in the 1990s and many New Year's events since.

Francis and Edie would have me over once a week for dinner and there was sometimes a Dickery update.

"He was driving up the alley the other day, saw me in the garage and stopped to drone on about nothing for thirty minutes," Edie once said.

But the conversations around the infamously dull Dickery got much spicier when an attractive young straight guy named Scout moved in two doors down. About 24, Scout was excited about owning his first house and spent a lot of time working in his backyard. While back there, Dickery would take photos of him through the blinds, which he'd then post to Facebook.

"This is the hot guy next door!" he'd post, along with things like "Outside again," and "SO HOT!"

Many in the community were aghast at the invasion of privacy and the lack of judgement, but things escalated when Dickery came home from the bars at 3 a.m., saw Scout's light on, and decided life was like a porn movie.

Dickery called Scout, and Scout answered. "Hey Scout, this is Dickery. I know it's really late but I saw your light on and (playfully laughing) I just wanted to say I think you are *so* hot and I've been taking pictures of you through the blinds and posting them to Facebook."

I'm sure Dickery thought a steamy sex scene would ensue. Instead, it was a frantic call to Francis. "Am I in danger? Should I call the police? Should I *MOVE*?"

Francis assured Scout that Dickery was harmless, and fortunately Dickery was embarrassed enough that he never photographed or came on to him again.

The entire ordeal was so cringeworthy I really tried to pretend I knew nothing of it.

Meeting Kage

It was a dreary late-January Saturday. I had no plans, and needed a break from writing.

"Have you ever been to Alton and the Great River Road?" I asked Menashe. "I'm in the mood to head up there."

He hadn't, and was typically down for anything.

In Alton we went to a famous burger place called Fast Eddie's, and noticed how many handsome men there were.

"Guys in Alton are hot!" Menashe said. "Let's see who's on our phones."

We opened our respective dating apps and center square was a smiling, friendly looking Black guy. Kage. I struck up a conversation and told him our next stop was Riverview Park. I had mapped the mystery staircase and found that's where it led.

"If you'd like to meet in person before we go to Grafton we could catch up at Riverview Park in thirty minutes," I offered.

At the top of the stairs we found a beautiful park atop a bluff 150 feet above the Mississippi, complete with a quaint gazebo where we stood waiting for Kage. He described himself as a bear in his profile, so I was expecting a bigger guy, but Kage approached and was quite lean. He was a bit thrown off himself because I had a beard, which I did not have in my photo.

It was cold, cloudy and windy and the three of us stood in the gazebo trying to ignite a conversation like three scouts trying to start a fire. It's fair to say it wasn't love at first sight for either of us, but when I said my goodbye, he indicated that he was interested in joining us on the day's adventure.

We had only been on the road for a few minutes when I held his hand, and he didn't resist. We stopped to explore a large abandoned mining cave, when being the ideal wingman he was, Menashe wandered off.

Kage was shorter than I was, with a really solid build, thick shoulders and a nice chest. At the mouth of the cave, I kissed him, and, something I can't explain to this day, I aggressively pushed against his chest with both hands, as if we were going to fight. He did the same in return, and we continued kissing. Other things may or may not have been revealed to one another in that moment.

After that adventure we agreed to meet at the bear bar, JJ's Clubhouse, that evening. The first thing he said to me upon arrival was, "I just want to let you know I'm *not* going home with you tonight."

I thought that was odd, but didn't take it as something set in stone.

My friend Brian, who sent me the sexy photo of Cody a few years earlier, was there and feeling good. Kage was sitting on a barstool while Brian stood talking to us, and he kept resting his hand on Kage's knee. I kept removing it.

Kage mentioned the first name of his ex while telling a story, and I thought I might have known who he was talking about. "Jay Goodwin?" I asked.

Kage looked as if he'd seen a ghost, and I instantly regretted asking the question. "Yeah, how do you know him?" he asked.

"I went out with a guy a few times and it didn't work out, but we're still friends and he's dating him," I replied.

It was clear he still had feelings for Jay, and not long after that awkward exchange, he said his goodbye. That was that, I thought.

JJ's was very Gotham, sitting beneath a highway and sandwiched by elevated railroad tracks. The Metro train practically ran across its roof. It had rained while I was inside, and on my way to the car, which was parked on bare dirt beneath the tracks, I saw a fat drunk girl resting against a concrete pillar holding up the interstate. I got in the car, put it in reverse, and felt my front-end sink into the earth as if the ground was made of pudding. Fuck.

"I need your help," I said to the drunk girl sitting on the ground. "My car is stuck and I need you to sit in it with your foot on the gas while I'm pushing."

"I can't do that! I'm drunk!" she exclaimed.

"You're fine all you have to do is sit there!" I said as I pulled with all my might to help her up. My plan, however, only succeeded in getting the car deeper into the mud.

I called AAA, and the driver arrived about an hour later, sat in his truck filling out paperwork for what seemed like forever, and then said, "You need a different kind of truck to get that out. If I drive up there, I'll get stuck too."

I have no clue why it took him so long to determine that, but I returned to my car to wait for the next truck. I woke to an officer knocking on the window with the tow truck driver standing nearby.

"Sir, have you been drinking?" he asked.

"I left the bar *three hours* ago," I said.

"If you drive this car, I'm giving you a DUI," he said.

"Am I able to steer while he's pulling me out of the mud?" I asked.

"If you drive on the city street I'm giving you a DUI," the officer replied.

I helped the tow truck driver get the car to high ground, got out, and walked away as the Sunday dawn approached. It had been a rough night but I was profoundly grateful that I hadn't been able to drive, and for the officer's warning.

Musings on Menard Street

In 2015 the primary gay bar in Soulard was Bastille, inheriting that ranking after the closure of the historic Clementine's a year earlier, which was at the other end of the tree-lined block of historic brick homes opening right to the sidewalk.

My eccentric friend Lydia owned a stunning three-story Mansard-roofed and turret graced building across from Bastille on Menard, where her shop Metropolis Vintage and Costume was located. I befriended her in 1997 after buying vintage furniture for my apartment, which was two blocks away.

In 1997 her daughter was 15 and I was 22, and those seven years were everything. Suddenly I'm 40 and she's 33, and the age difference means nothing and I somehow could never wrap my mind around that. Even stranger was when I was in the midst of drunken Mardi Gras madness above their family's costume shop and the daughter cornered me with, "Has my mom been drinking?"

Not only was I confused by the dynamic between her and me, but it felt like she was the parent, and her mom and I were high schoolers busted at a party. "Ummm, I don't know," I falsely replied (I had never once seen Lydia overdrink, for the record).

Bob, the brash owner of Bastille, was one of the biggest characters in a neighborhood of big characters. It wasn't uncommon for him to say something like, "A guy walked in here yesterday and offered me THREE MILLION DOLLARS for this bar and I told him to FUCK OFF!"

When bars could no longer allow smoking but casinos were exempted, Bob tried to get his bar classified as a casino. While his personality might remind you of that of a heavy drinker, Bob had been sober for ages. His drink of choice was milk.

The heart of Bastille, however, was a bartender named Peyton. He was Bob's polar opposite: quiet, humble and attentive. Peyton controlled the music videos and, while socializing with each and every patron, would sometimes put on a show with a fun little dance. He also held court with the patrons sitting at the tables on the sidewalk, where he'd smoke.

Lydia was famously abrasive, often bickering with people who parked in front of her shop, and Bob was nearly as polarizing. The two tried to get along, but I thought of them as frenemies.

I stopped in to visit her and she filled me in on the latest Soulard news.

"So, there's this woman from Chesterfield (an upper middle-class West St. Louis County municipality synonymous with pretentious suburbia, and Lydia delivered "Chesterfield" with incredulous disdain) who moved here and decided to throw a ball in Soulard and Bob helped her out, putting it all together, and then when he got there, they didn't have a table for him and he was livid," Lydia said.

2015 was the first Mardi Gras after the closure of Clementine's, which had been the epicenter of queer Soulard Mardi Gras. My dear friend Auntie M would toss his coveted custom beads from the balcony in a towering hot pink wig alongside other wildly costumed performers and shirtless muscled-up guys.

With Lydia's corner now the heart of everything, I asked if we could continue the bead tradition there, and she graciously agreed.

Kage had called a few days after our JJ's night to explain why he left. As I suspected, he still had feelings for his ex and thought they'd likely get back together.

It was a long and rambling explanation, and while I didn't know it at the time, vocalizing everything made him realize he was actually over the ex after all. Having understood the opposite, I thanked him for his call and explanation, and prepared to hang up and go on with my life.

"Why do you need to go?" he asked.

"You called to tell me all the reasons we wouldn't be seeing one another, so I didn't think there was much more to say."

Mardi Gras was that coming Saturday, and Kage was scheduled to work a split shift—valet parking in nearby Benton Park in the morning, then elsewhere in the late afternoon. I gave him the address and told him to meet us at Lydia's shop during his break.

It was him, me and Auntie M tossing beads to the masses filling the intersection from the iconic turret. Kage was dazzled by the experience and in the middle of it asked, "Hey, why am I the only one not dressed up?"

Being over a costume shop, getting him up to speed was no problem. I presented him with a mirrored shirt and the most expensive Mardi Gras mask they sold.

Midnight Annie's Final Performance

While on the topic of Soulard, the following is the story about the night Clementine's, the neighborhood's main gay bar, closed. This version was edited by Ryan Lee Schuessler and included in Belt Publishing's St. Louis Anthology.

I woke up on Wednesday, September 24, 2014, grabbed my phone from the nightstand and checked social media like I always did. The first post I saw was from a friend announcing that the bar where I spent my Friday nights, Clementine's, was closing after the coming weekend. I was floored, and hoped it was just a rumor. The historic corner bar and restaurant, famous for their strong drinks and colorful characters, was one of my favorite things about St. Louis. It was the LGBT community's embassy in Soulard, and for me symbolized permanence.

Entombed in the wall of the establishment were the remains of Midnight Annie, a drag queen who long frequented and performed at the bar. While laughing and drinking there with my friend Big Ray, I sometimes pondered having my own remains interred beside her, forever being part of the action. She passed in April 1995 at the age of 73, two years before I first moved to St. Louis, but I felt like I knew her after hearing so many tales of her antics. Her shows sounded like pure madness. She'd often sit down on stage, wearing her salt-and-pepper bouffant wig and sequin gown, and begin kicking up her heels and howling at the moon.

All morning I tried to get confirmation as I began working on the article. Bars were always rumored to be closing, and there'd been embarrassing retractions in the past. One bar, Slovak's, even had an emotional closing gala, only to open up for business as usual the following day. The LGBT magazine I wrote for, *Vital Voice*, had to balance the desire to break the story with the need to get it right, and our publisher decided we weren't running the piece until we had a quote from one of the owners.

Rather than covering it as breaking news, I crafted the announcement like a eulogy, recalling the storied past of the place, how it was a cornerstone of the community, was the oldest surviving LGBT bar in St. Louis, and how there was no more prestigious spot to be during Mardi Gras than on the grand balcony above the entrance. In 2012, I was so determined to grace that balcony that I loitered around the guarded entrance to the upper floor, and the second the bouncer's back was turned, bolted up the stairs. I strolled in like I was supposed to be there, tossing beads into the crowd below for ten or fifteen minutes until I sensed suspicion from the krewe, and nonchalantly made my exit.

The article was essentially written when I arrived at Clem's and spoke to the bartender, who'd just learned the news himself in a letter from owner Gary Reed. It was then I got word that *#Boom, Vital Voice's* bitter rival, just broke the story with a brief announcement and a quote from the same bartender. We ran our piece twenty minutes later. I began working on gathering and documenting every story I could from the patrons during the remaining days. I knew my Friday night group, but there were so many people I didn't know. People who were there during the day, or on different nights. I needed to meet and talk to as many of them I could in a desperate attempt to immortalize this place before it was too late. With a pen in one hand and a cocktail in the other, I lived, breathed and drank the moment. During those final days, I was embedded at Clem's.

"It's like Cheers, when I'm down and out there's always someone here to lift me up. That's the one thing that scares me to death: Where am I going to meet my friends? Where will us fading flowers go?" said Josie, a heavyset man of 52.

That first night the news was so fresh and most everyone was in disbelief, while some were angry. A festive, slender man of about 60, named Johnnie, was excited about my interviews, and told me who I should speak with.

"See the guy with the hot pink goblet? That's Miss Davey. He's been coming here every single day for years and they keep that goblet just for him. One day I asked Jan, 'How do I get my own goblet?' and she said, 'Well, you've gotta come here every day!' You need to talk to him!" Johnny said, but returned a moment later, "He's too upset and is afraid of what he might say. Give him a little time."

I spoke to a big, gruff, bearded man named Dennis who, in his booming voice, told me Clem's was his first gay bar, then a frail, petite man walked through the door and Dennis shouted, "HEY HOWARD!" and pulled him in. "This is Howard, he was here for the grand opening!"

I greeted Howard, who told me he was 79 and lived on the east side. "I always stopped here to get my bridge drink," he said. I suggested he grab a cocktail and then come back to talk.

"You're giving him too much time, he might die in the next five minutes! He's about a hundred and forty!" Dennis joked.

Later, at the tables on the old brick sidewalk out front, Dennis and his buddies agreed to tell me more stories if I'd smoke a joint with them. A group of six men shared tales about Clem's, reminisced about other bars that came and went over the years, and recalled the tales of Midnight Annie. Legend had it that she got the name back in the 1940s when she'd bribe a jailer to let her "entertain" inmates in the middle of the night.

"Oh, I remember Midnight Annie," one man began. "She was a trust fund baby and when she'd get an installment, she'd blow it in no time. Once she sauntered into a Cadillac dealership and bought two Cadillacs. One for her and one for her trick! That's just how she was. God, I still remember her sitting at that bar drunk as hell, with her lipstick going up her wrinkled face and her wig on crooked. She had this trademark high-pitched sound she'd make, and when she'd do it everyone around the bar would mimic it. Like a bird call."

Many of the stories about St. Louis's gay world came out of East St. Louis, because gay bars were less likely to be raided there. Some of the bars sounded a lot like speakeasies.

"Those early days were revolutionary," began a silver-haired gentleman named Beaux. "There were bars that were straight by day and gay by night, and Helen Schrader's started out that way. Helen had been a notorious madam with 50 women working for her during her heyday. When one of her first girls, Alice, got old she worked the front door at the bar. You'd knock and Miss Alice would slide a little slot open and look at you. If she knew you, she'd let you in. If she didn't, she'd tell you to go away."

Stories also came in online. My friend Dan posted a memory on Facebook, and it really struck me because it was about a passing generation.

"One really busy night many years ago I had sex right there on the counter of the bar, maybe 400 in the bar at the time. Surprised? It brought back memories of the first owner, Wally Thomas. He sold it in '85 but it stayed a gay bar. People don't want to let go, but the past *has* to go. The past, the bars, the buildings, the people all have had their time and now need to go. And they will—no matter what is said.

That place leaves far greater a legacy than I ever will. As one person said: "The old heart of Gay St. Louis will cease to beat. I see the passages. The old gay ghettos, the book stores, the peep shows, the gay bars, their time has passed. My tribe, my people, my places, become part of yesterday's mist. Museum pieces that fade and collect dust. And so does yours truly."

While Monday would be the last day, Sunday afternoon was when the community at large came to say their goodbyes. It looked like Mardi Gras as the crowd spilled out of the bar into the street, where a BMW blasted music for the hundreds of people.

I had only been back in town for a few months, having moved to San Francisco to try to salvage a long-beleaguered relationship, and then to New York to get over it. My heart, however, was always in St. Louis, and I was so thankful to be on the ground during these final days of Clementine's. It would have killed me to miss them.

Steve Potter, a public radio personality, was so moved and inspired by the stories Clem's fading flowers shared with *Vital Voice* that he came out on the air, discussing his first visit to the bar decades earlier.

As the world opened up, gay bars nationwide were going the way of the dinosaur, especially those serving an older clientele. But this haunted town had such a memory, and rather than disappear, Clem's would simply take its place in the local folklore.

I almost didn't go to closing night, and Big Ray didn't plan on going either. It was a Monday, I'd spent every waking hour there since Wednesday, and I thought it would be too sad. Around eight, however, I decided I would always regret not going. Since I was going, Big Ray came out as well. I walked in, and on the glowing dry erase marquee near the pool table I wrote, "Going down with the ship."

The bar was crowded but not overly so, and the characters there were the ones who really loved the place. Spirits were higher than expected and the camaraderie was simply incredible as old friends hugged, laughed, and made toasts. Miss Davey, the daily regular who had his own hot pink goblet and had been too upset to be interviewed earlier, came up and gave me a hug.

"I'm really sad, but I'm going to be ok," he said, smiling.

When owner Gary and his late partner Jim bought the bar in 1985, they held their first drag show. Midnight Annie was the headliner. Unbeknownst to her, they promoted the evening as "Midnight Annie's Final Performance" to make it more of a draw.

"Would you quit telling people this is my final performance?" an exasperated Midnight Annie kept admonishing.

I was less than a foot from Gary when, in the final hours, he took the mic, and the quiet, introverted man who'd hardly said anything over the years gave a rousing farewell speech. The whole place stopped to listen. He spoke about how much times had changed since the bar opened in 1978, and changed for the better. He spoke of the historic old brick building which was erected in the 1860s. He said all drinks were on the house until the last bottle was dry, and then he brought up Midnight Annie.

"I always say my only child was a 73-year-old drag queen," he began, "and she's leaving with me. Ladies and Gentleman, next to Jan is Midnight Annie!"

I'll be goddamned if he didn't have Midnight Annie's dusty urn—complete with the yellowed and water-stained label—sitting there on the bar with a cocktail.

The crowd erupted with cheers and applause.

On that final evening, there were people in attendance who'd come to see Midnight Annie's final performance back in 1985. After a 30-year wait, she and Gary Reed finally delivered with a closing number the city will never forget.

The Clem's Diaspora

Soulard was a neighborhood of corner taverns, and its inhabitants were passionately loyal to their specific home bar. Since Clem's and Bastille were rivals, a vocal Clem's contingent vowed to never frequent Bastille—the only other official queer bar in the neighborhood at the time of Clem's closing. Many of those people, along with a few Clem's employees, instead migrated a block west to Nadine's Gin Joint.

For the first few months Nadine's seemed like Clem's unlikely heir apparent, especially on the spacious covered patio on Sunday afternoons. The scrappy and colorful owner Nadine Soaib, with her trademark dyed red hair, worked for Gary Reed years earlier, and Gary became a regular of her bar.

A local legend, Nadine had run with the original founders of Soulard Mardi Gras at the tail end of the 70s through the 80s. Her third-floor apartment back then was above Soulard Mardi Gras founder Hilary Clements' place. (Lydia's costume shop moved to its permanent home next door around 1990). It featured a mirrored ceiling, a saltwater aquarium, and in the backyard was an enclosed hot tub.

"The hot tub was *notorious*," Nadine recalled when I interviewed her in 2020. "Oh my gosh the parties we would have there. It was enclosed with plexiglass and would get really steamy. In the winter we'd run up and down the backstairs naked."

Nadine said back then the city was selling derelict buildings in Soulard for $1.00 per square foot. Baby boomers like herself bought and rehabbed them.

After the closure of Clem's the flavor of Nadine's Gin Joint, which had been predominantly straight, changed overnight and Nadine warmly welcomed all the new customers, going so far as flying rainbow flags.

But Soulardians aren't just loyal to their home bars, they are loyal to their bartenders. When Nadine let one beloved longtime Clem's fixture go, a chunk of business walked away for good. Another stumbling block was that many of the new patrons just assumed Nadine's was a gay bar, and when she mentioned that she was not a gay bar, but a bar that welcomed everyone, that didn't sit well with some, who felt disrespected. A short-lived disgruntled waiter sought to add fuel to the fire with complaints that Nadine wouldn't let him work shirtless, and that she objected to him getting a second job as a janitor at the bath house.

All that being said, Nadine's had a sizable new group of exiled Clem's patrons who stuck by her through the rough parts of the transition. Perhaps it was one of those loyalists who created fliers for her bar and placed them on cars parked at Bastille's intersection. Bob, Bastille's owner, was already salty that a mainstream business was competing with him, and this stunt only inflamed tensions.

"When I heard what he was upset about I called him," Nadine told me years later. "I said, 'I don't know anything about the flier but if you send it to me I'll try to get the bottom of it,' and Bob sighed, 'I'll see if I can locate one, but I gathered all I could find and took them down to New Orleans to burn at the grave of Marie Laveau.'"

From then on Nadine was convinced Bob had cursed her.

One night at Bastille, I asked Bob point blank if he had, and he just smiled.

Meeting the Family

The first members of Kage's family I met were his older brother Joel (5 years younger than me), and Joel's wife Jenna. There were three boys in Kage's family and they all had significant others who were white—so that aspect of our relationship wasn't novel.

It was a celebratory evening at a loud South Grand bar called Upstairs Lounge, and we were doing our best to have a conversation. Despite the difficulty hearing one another, everyone was happy and loose.

Later in the night, I was dancing with Jenna when she leaned in, pointed to Kage and said, "He's good."

I wasn't sure what she meant and gave a puzzled look.

"He's a good person," she shouted over the music.

It would be another week or two before I met his parents at his nephew's birthday party. Jenna already had 5 kids when she met Joel, and Joel already had 2. Together, they had a son named Roman. Their household could have been a classic big family sitcom. There was much joy, laughter and comedy.

I remember one morning when Kage was checking his messages and looked surprised.

"Mom's on snapchat now!" he said in reference to the messaging app popular with teens and young adults. "She downloaded it to keep up with the kids, but I don't know how that's going to work out. Jenna said all the kids have been doing is sharing pictures of the dog's butt."

Kage's parents were perfectly cordial, but I gave his mother plenty of space because Kage warned me she didn't approve of homosexuality for religious reasons, and that she hoped he would change. She never accepted his ex.

Jenna's mother, who I'd regularly see at family gatherings, was also religious and proper, to the point of complaining about "upper male nudity" (shirtless men) on television. Nevertheless, we hit it off and would often sit side by side and chat about the West Coast, mainly Seattle—where she once lived—and San Francisco.

I think seeing how close I was with Jenna's mother, and more importantly how happy Kage was, inspired his mom to reach out. I noticed she made an effort to engage with me, and she specifically invited me to an upcoming family function.

The world is so full of damaged and traumatized people, and everything about the happy and carefree Kage, not to mention his warm and successful siblings, told me he was raised in a loving and stable home. He was more comfortable in his own skin than just about anyone I'd ever known, and I knew that didn't happen by accident. I appreciated his parents for the outstanding job they did.

I became close with his mother, and she'd even check on me when things got heated over social media due to an article or a feud. "I don't like the way they come for you," she'd say.

And many times over the years I reflected on the profound simplicity of the one thing Jenna told me about Kage that first night: He's good.

Alton Giants

Me and Menashe became regulars at Bubby's, the lively LGBTQ bar in Alton where Kage and his friends hung out. It was a fun getaway for us both, since controversy followed me through St. Louis bars, and Menashe, who didn't drive, needed a change of scenery. It was also a place where Menashe could pretend to be single, which he wasn't.

Alton was known for Robert Wadlow, the Alton Giant—the tallest person in recorded history, who lived in the town from his birth in 1918 to his death in 1940—and similarly I felt the characters in that town were giants.

I was a big name up there, with bartender Jason Brooks first asking Kage, "Why didn't you tell me you were dating the Emperor?" in reference to my *Tales from the Emperor* column, but I didn't feel like that. I felt like a sophomore surrounded by seniors. The regulars were everyday blue-collar types (with some exceptions, like local public radio personality Steve Potter) but they seemed so cool, especially Brooks, who was about my age.

While not overly puffed up like my teen crush "Marky Mark" Wahlberg, Brooks had a similar vibe, having been a white kid from a majority Black part of North St. Louis County. Watching him run the bar was hypnotic, the bounce in his step, his flow, the loose, calm way he handled himself with his trimmed beard, Cardinals jersey, strong hands and backwards ballcap.

I was also struck by how people up there were nice, and how they went out for the sole purpose of having fun, which stood in contrast to too many St. Louis scenes, which were downright sinister by comparison. While the relaxed and friendly atmosphere was part of the local culture, Jason and others who worked there also enforced it. They were quick to speak up if they saw anyone being disrespected, regardless of the person's station.

Me and Menashe would often grab Brawny and head up on a Friday night and stay at the home of Bubby's bartender and Kage's longtime friend George, who lived in a large old Victorian where their close-knit group of friends would play games and eat. In the morning George would serve a big classic breakfast, and sitting at the booth in his kitchen, I would look through the lace curtains and admire the charming historic homes along the steep brick street.

When we couldn't stay the night, me and Menashe would drive back the long, dark Route 3, which ran along the river levee, and talk about anything and everything or listen to loud music.

One landmark was a massive power plant off in the distance, in South Roxana. It was bitterly cold and we decided to make a detour and check it out. Sitting in the parked car we watched flames shoot out of what appeared to be some massive, evil city skyline, transfixed in the moment.

Autonomy

Mom was in her early 40s when Dad died, but looked 10 years younger.

Despite several offers, she never remarried. The main reason she would give is that she didn't want to answer to anyone. After my 14-year relationship where there was consistent tension, I could relate. I enjoyed doing what I wanted and not being in trouble. Sex was just one small part of that. Damon even got angry when he thought I spent too much time writing.

I had quickly grown to enjoy my simple, peaceful solitude in that sunny third-floor apartment overlooking Christy Park, and often said I'd never marry again.

When I began falling for Kage, who also enjoyed his freedom, I thought about how giving up our autonomy shouldn't be necessary in order to enjoy one another's companionship.

One evening our conversation turned to the sexual fluidity that seemed somewhat unique to the Alton area, inspiring me to dub the town "The Bi-Muda Triangle." He told me the story of a party he'd attended there during his previous relationship. It was a mainstream gathering of mostly straight men and women in their twenties and thirties, but devolved into an orgy. Everyone was messing around with everyone, regardless of sexuality, and off to the side was Kage, a very sexual person, hanging back because he was in a monogamous relationship.

While honorable, that's not what I would want for him. How often does the typical person find themselves in such a situation in the prime of their life? And they're going to sit it out to adhere to some heteronormative ideal? I didn't see the point. For me, loving someone means wanting them to live life to the fullest.

And then there's the Puritanical notion that being sexual means one is bad. Some of the best people I've known were whores and some of the most sadistic were basically celibate. I'm for people choosing whatever works for them and I do understand the many benefits of monogamy, but I was looking for emotional fidelity and was unconcerned with sexual exclusivity, provided one was safe, of course, and not consumed with finding sexual partners.

"You know, not all relationships have to be strictly monogamous," I replied, and he seemed surprised and intrigued.

What drew me to Kage was his radiant light, his smile, and his peaceful vibe. I wanted to enrich his life, show him the world, and make sure he was never a wallflower at a party again.

Panic Attack

One morning I was scheduled to show someone several units, including a new listing with a vaguely familiar address. When I arrived, I discovered the reason the address sounded familiar: it was next door to the longtime home of Damon's mother, sister Larissa, and her two sons.

I'm not talking "next door" in a suburban sense. I'm talking maybe a three-foot gangway between buildings. So close, Larissa once overheard a tenant crying to God about her struggles, prompting her to pay her neighbor a visit and offer help.

The front doors were so close together you could say they were going steady.

For more than a dozen years I'd been part of that family. Those boys were little more than toddlers when I met them, and when the relationship ended, they didn't even remember a time when I wasn't their uncle. They had to look almost grown by now.

And then there was his mother. I say Damon was like the rigid school teacher you could never please, who was always watching you in judgement. While I got along with his mom famously, his traits that made me the most uneasy were the ones he inherited from her. I had not seen her or anyone in the family since the split.

I shuddered to think of the things he must have told them, and all I knew in that moment was that I needed to get out of there.

I sat in my car a few doors away, hoping to intercept my prospects before they approached the property, but they came from an unexpected direction and were standing out front. I engaged them from a healthy distance to avoid being heard inside. Composing myself the best I could, I apologized to the Kardashian-esque young woman in big dark sunglasses standing beside her attractive boyfriend.

"I'm sorry I'm not able to get you inside this unit this morning, but you're scheduled to see three others so we'll begin with the flat on Utah," I said as I pivoted towards my car.

The immovable Kardashian tilted her head skeptically. Standing as if her heels had taken root in the yard, she asked, "Why can't we see this one?"

I was in a rare flight mode. My heart was racing and my anxiety was ratcheting up by the second. This bitch better get with the program or I'll leave her standing there, I thought.

I retreated another few steps.

"Maintenance didn't turn in the keys. I'll see to it you're rescheduled."

Reluctantly, she and the boyfriend moved on. I really don't know what would have happened had she insisted on debating the point, but I imagine I would have simply told them our morning was canceled and gone home sick.

While I rarely spoke with Damon about anything, much less something as personal as a panic attack, I felt compelled to write to him about it. He replied that he was sure the family would have been fine, and then shared a difficult moment of his own.

"Remember when we first got together and I'd ask what you would be doing had we never met, and you'd say you'd come find me? Something came on television that reminded me of that, and I don't know what came over me but I moved all the furniture out of the apartment as I cried," he said. "I then snapped out of it, and put everything back."

Since the morning I drove away as he stood on that Oakland sidewalk, I tried to avoid looking back, dwelling or second-guessing. A dozen years were crammed into a trunk stuffed so full, the latches were struggling under the pressure. When I arrived to meet the Kardashian, it felt like the trunk had exploded all over the yard.

I think Damon's trunks had been exploding for a while.

The Other Half of Alton

At Bubby's one evening, a middle-aged man and a drunk woman walked in, and the hot mess woman promptly toppled over. After a few people helped her up and confirmed she was unhurt, the man began a narrative that would run on a loop all evening long.

"Oh, God. I own half of Alton and if JILL MOON at the Telegraph gets a hold of this it will be ALL OVER the papers!"

Throughout the night, each time I'd pass him I'd hear the snippets. "I own HALF of Alton . . ." He'd hold his hands over his head with dread. "Jill Moon . . . ALL OVER the papers!"

I had never heard of Jill Moon but she sounded quite interesting. Was she running a local Page Six? I looked her up on social media and saw that she was close with my friend Steve Potter. I sent her a message introducing myself and telling her the above tale.

She had no idea who that man even was.

Unlike the hysterical man, being in the papers was right up my alley. Moon would later run a feature on my book, and also get me and Kage a modeling gig for a bridal show, which included our photos in the paper wearing tuxedos.

The photos turned out great, and someone on the paper's social media commented, "Where did Alton get all these fancy pants people?"

Nobody Liked Gassy

As part of the ongoing feud with Spike, he recruited a local hothead known as Gassy to come after me and several of my associates.

Despite the fact that Gassy was banned from nearly every LGBTQ bar after physically assaulting patrons, we were Facebook acquaintances and I never had an issue with him prior to the falling out with Spike, although he long loathed Jasmine.

Once, he was a guest DJ at the Grove bar Slovak's, and when he saw Jasmine walk in, he became so enraged at the mere sight of her he flipped over the entire DJ table.

Playwright and textbook author Donald Miller penned an outrageous and raunchy *Vital Voice* column and ran Facebook profiles under the pseudonyms Penelope Wigstock and Penny Gosling, and his true identity was an amazingly well-kept secret. Spike, who knew the identity from his *Vital Voice* assignments, told Gassy to release information, but because the respectable suburban father wasn't known in the Grove bars, the overhyped outing—billed as payback for the "Desmond is Alive" announcement—was a dud. They might as well have said, "The person behind Penelope Wigstock is JOHN DOE!"

Everyone was like, "Who?"

Gassy then upped the ante by sending crazed notes to the university where Miller worked, but nothing ever came of that. He also made all kinds of menacing posts directed at me.

Well, one day I was tipped off that Gassy was having a clandestine birthday party at a Benton Park bar that evening, and he swore his guests to secrecy. I arrived hours early and asked the bartender if she'd deliver a card to him in the middle of his festivities. She did.

Sitting at the head of a long table, surrounded by "friends" who mostly despised him but still attended for whatever reason, he opened the card, which read:

Dear Gassy,

You're a horrible person and nobody likes you.

Signed,
Everybody

He. Lost. His. Shit.

And for some inexplicable reason, despite the ongoing feud with me, he blamed a mild-mannered upscale businessman named Thomas Fortenberry for the whole thing, read him for filth and blocked him.

Shortly after all this he followed a man he was dating down to Memphis (after mercilessly berating him online about being ugly during their numerous fights), where he remains as of this writing.

The last I really saw of him was on a news link someone sent me. He was featured for covering Memphis in ribbons to honor police officers. He started a Facebook group to raise money for more ribbon, and would berate the fuck out of the group's members in classic Gassy fashion.

When you joined this group did you really think just joining it or liking stuff was going to do anything to help? Really? WE ARE HERE TO RAISE MONEY FOR RIBBONS! EITHER DONATE, VOLUNTEER OR QUIT TAKING UP SPACE WITH YOUR USELESS LIKES THAT DON'T DO A GODDAMN THING!

It was mostly crickets, but one woman chimed in, "I don't even know how I got added to this group!" I donated $5 to the GoFundMe just so I had access to post what a shitbag he was.

Going above and beyond to show appreciation to law enforcement was nothing new for Gassy, though. Aside from his famous temper, he was best known for getting busted while performing oral sex on a small-town sheriff on the side of a country road.

Just like his ribbon project, it was all over the news.

The Manuscript and the Seven Stages

After years of work, including one year where I focused on little else—coming home to the little third-floor Christy Park apartment and writing all evening day in and day out—I had a completed manuscript. The feedback I was getting was great, but I felt I needed to extend far outside my bubble for different perspectives.

Friend and theatre guru Joan Lipkin once told me she stopped writing local reviews because the St. Louis Arts Community is really too tight-knit to be critical, and I was ready for criticism. Or so I thought.

I reached out to Robert Julian Stone, a Palm Springs via San Francisco writer I admired, having become aware of him from his work with the *Bay Area Reporter.*

He agreed to review the manuscript as long as I was prepared for "brutal honesty."

Deep down, I felt confident he would love it, and figured he would offer tweaks here and there. After a few days he replied, beginning:

"I've read to page 48 and can already tell you there are way too many characters here."

The original manuscript covered my entire life, culminating with my 40th Birthday at the Lemp Mansion. He suggested I cut all the pre-St. Louis stories, the equivalent of a third of the book.

I went through the seven stages of grief, canceling all plans in order to process this feedback and decide what I would do. In the end, I did cut the early stories, and the book was so much better for it. I'm incredibly grateful for that essential critique.

The Lost Chapters and Kristin Ecker

With the early tales from my Oklahoma days cut from *Delusions of Grandeur*, I set them aside for a yet-to-be-completed prequel. The following is how that book opens:

Sweet and Sour

It was just before 2 a.m. and I was in line outside a Tulsa after-hours club with my friends Donald, Madge, Kyle, and about half a dozen other lanky gay teenagers when Kyle pointed out that notorious coke dealer Mike Sweet was getting head in his old, beat-up Chevy truck across the side street.

"Guys suck him off for cocaine," Kyle said seconds before a Dodge Daytona whipped into the parking space where he was standing, nearly taking him out. "Dear GAWD! If I'm to die by getting run over *PLEASE* don't let it be by a Chrysler product," he snarled.

Despite the fact Mr. Sweet was widely feared in town as some sort of macho drug lord, I thought it'd be cute to throw pebbles at his truck. In my 16-year-old wisdom I figured he wouldn't know who did it, or even where the stones came from since it was dark, many people were in line, and I was partially hidden by other vehicles, including the Chrysler product. I tossed one every few minutes while trying to look nonchalant. Finally, he climbed out of his truck and strutted over to our group.

"WHO THE FUCK'S THROWING ROCKS?" Mr. Sweet demanded.

About forty, he was old enough to be any of our fathers, and with his rugged look he did have a dad vibe. While I'd heard a lot about him, from his day job in the oil fields to the countless rumors of how dangerous he was. I'd never seen him before and took note of his bald head, thick mustache, broad shoulders and his pronounced belly.

Everyone else in our group was timid and tried to avoid his gaze, but I was too amused with myself and it showed. After dressing everyone down, he focused squarely on me, getting in my cocky, teenaged face.

"What the FUCK is so funny, little BITCH?" he demanded before rearing back and slapping me.

He then calmly returned to his truck to resume his evening.

I was wrecked.

That night I learned the world operates differently at 2 a.m. Outraged as I was, nobody was about to make a fuss or get the police involved. Nobody's really innocent at that hour. The club wasn't supposed to let anyone under 18 through the doors to begin with, and like all my friends, I'd snuck out to be there. And of course I did start the whole thing. Now it was done and the show would go on.

The next time I saw him was about six months later at Oklahoma City's infamous and sprawling gay hotel, the Habana Inn. I was on my way to the hotel's dance club on the opposite end of the complex, cutting through the labyrinthine corridors with their twists and turns, past illuminated windows, opened doors, and poolside courtyards filled with campy revelry, when I came across Mike Sweet leaning against a corner in boots and a cowboy hat. He confidently greeted me with a big smile like we were old friends, while looking me up and down approvingly.

I froze in my tracks, not because I was afraid, but because I was taken by the turn of events. The chemistry between us was intense as he gently put his strong hand on my hip, still smiling.

"So, you're not mad at me?" he asked flirtatiously.

"No, I'm not" I said, blushing.

We then went upstairs to his room.

*   *   *

Tailgating outside of the Factory one of those early 1990s nights was fellow teen Kristin McDougal, who was crying over getting shorted on a catering job when I introduced myself and sought to comfort her. We went nearly twenty years without seeing one another, aside from one Tulsa Christmas reunion at a drag show, but when her husband was stationed 140 miles from St. Louis, we reconnected.

Kristin (married name Ecker) was not only a mother to her two teenaged boys, she became like a mother to many in the local gay community. I was amazed by how quickly she navigated the local social scene.

Her first time visiting me in St. Louis, she rattled off half a dozen names of gay guys she was meeting for coffee, lunch, dinner, or drinks.

With the most bizarre sleeping schedule of anyone I had ever met, Kristin was up at crazy hours. On the rare occasion I'd wake at 2 a.m. and not be able to go back to sleep, I'd give her a call and we'd discuss all these St. Louis characters, and maybe a few from ancient times, as well as life in general.

Whatever comfort I gave to her outside that Tulsa after-hours club came back a thousand-fold, as her calming presence helped me navigate many trying chapters.

The Proof

I received notification that the proof copy of *Delusions of Grandeur* had arrived, and I went to UPS to pick it up. Holding that first copy in my hands was the closest I would get to holding my firstborn. It was magical, and I admired the glossy cover and artwork, and how all those stories had materialized and become immortalized on actual paper.

The first place I took it to was Villa Ray.

"Oh, it looks great!" Ray exclaimed. I turned to the inscription page.

Dedicated to Big Ray

Ray David was the reason I was able to survive in St. Louis to begin with, taking me under his wing just after my arrival. I felt about Villa Ray the way one feels about a parent's house. It was the family home.

Time was pressing, and after just a few minutes I was off to pore over the proof and note errors. The release event was only ten days away.

The Release

I don't think anyone in town could generate buzz or bring the razzle dazzle like Darin, and he secured the swanky second-level bar at Brennan's in the Central West End for the release event. Tickets were $30 per person, and sold out.

Copies were stacked high on the author's table, where I signed each one after a reading. In the middle of it all, I received a message from infamous conman Dustin Mitchell.

"I'm coming up," he announced, testing the waters.

"Okay, see you in a minute," I replied.

People had often assumed that I loathed Mitchell, but the fact was, I had nothing personal against him—even after he famously framed me for a hostage crisis only months earlier. I found him fascinating and couldn't get enough of his crazy scams.

I think Mitchell loved that I was giving him so much publicity. He just wanted to recruit and rewire me so it was the right kind of publicity. He sometimes played like I was writing fiction loosely based on him, and that he was in on it.

When Darin saw Mitchell enter, the blood drained from his face and he bolted out the door, remaining at the sidewalk tables until Mitchell departed.

The entire venue was buzzing about Mitchell's presence, with news of it igniting social media. He posed for a photo cheek to cheek with me and signed the proof copy I used for the reading: *Celebrity is as celebrity does.—Dustin Mitchell*

I donated that copy to the St. Louis LGBT History Project.

Mitchell wandered the party for maybe ten minutes, sitting by himself on his phone for a moment, and then excused himself for a date.

After the event, a big group of us went to eat next door, and there was Mitchell with a young guy we all knew. The man was hoping for a discreet rendezvous, but selected a poor place for one—a glass-sheathed restaurant on a buzzing West End corner next door to the biggest queer event in town.

Dickery, the guy who had been taking photos of his neighbor through the blinds, came along and was inspired to tell his own stories to the table, which really brought down the energy level. The wide-eyed Dickery was the worst story teller. Simply the worst. He told me only one entertaining tale in the twenty years I knew him, but to his credit, that one had me rolling. It was about his drunk hairstylist who nicked him bald in a spot, pulled out an eyebrow pencil to fix it, and then suggested they forget about the haircut altogether and go to Bastille for cocktails.

Unfortunately, he didn't share his one entertaining story that evening, instead sticking to the classic Dickery storytelling formula of no beginning, ending, or point.

"We're going to the Drunken Fish," Mitchell said as he approached the table. "Come over after dinner and I'll buy you a drink."

I knew that was going to be far more entertaining than the dinner had been.

The Infiltrator

I didn't learn this until about five years later, but #*Boom* sent one of their people, who would later have a child with cofounder Colin Lovett, to the release to observe, report, and return with two copies.

Colin & Colin were waiting at Coffee Cartel, located at the same Central West End intersection where we were dining on one corner and then drinking on another.

"Darin publishing a book at the height of the media wars, we knew we were probably in it. Our spy came in carrying two books and I asked, 'Are we in it?' and she replied, 'Oh yeah.' We opened it up and there we were on the FIRST FUCKING PAGE!" Colin Murphy later laughed. "I said 'I gotta go home and read this thing.' Then as we were walking to the car, we kept passing all the gays carrying the book and we'd give them serious side-eye."

A Wish at the Drunken Fish

The Drunken Fish was right across the street from the restaurant, occupying the same space that was the first glitzy gay disco back in the 1970s, where Ray David held court in his reserved booth. The layout was essentially unchanged, and me, Kage and Ms. Jamieson met Mitchell and his date at the mezzanine bar.

One of Mitchell's tactics was flirting. I knew his type was skinny pretty boys at least 15 years younger than I was, but if I didn't know that I would have been thoroughly convinced he was captivated by my irresistible beauty.

Mitchell pulled me aside. "I'd like you to work on my campaign for governor," he said, and he was serious. I don't remember how I responded to that, only that the shots kept coming as Jasmine kept messaging.

I told her at the beginning of the night that the plan was to spend the entire evening in the Central West End, because she had a habit of upending plans by demanding everyone rush off to wherever she happened to be. At this point she was at a South City piano bar and was badgering us to join her.

I wish I could explain why I didn't just say no. All I can say is I was drunk and Jasmine was relentless.

We left what was a fascinating discussion to go to a quiet bar we rarely patronized, and as soon as we walked in, we saw our nemesis, *#Boom* contributor and temperamental drag queen Margie Werther. She spoke in a hushed tone to the notoriously moody bartender—who had run warm and cold with me since the days he worked at Clem's—and then she left.

This was supposed to be a big night but there we were at a dead dive bar, all because Jasmine was interested in some woman who was supposed to show up. Trying to make the best of it, I brought in a few copies of the book for the handful of people I knew sitting at the bar.

The bartender, who I'd long heard had a severe meth problem, accused me of coming behind the bar, and he snapped.

"This is MY BAR; you better get it straight! Write a chapter about ME! Write a book about ME! I'll give you something to write about. Don't you EVER come behind MY BAR!" he railed on a loop, never pausing.

I returned to the table and sat down, thinking he would stop, but he just continued ranting at the same volume and with the same intensity until we left. We could even hear him as we walked up the street.

Tale of Two Cities: Book Tour in Oklahoma

After the St. Louis release, I took the show on the road with the first event being in Tulsa. Many have complicated relationships with their hometown, and I'm no exception. I left it at the earliest opportunity and never asked much of it since, but when I requested assistance in finding a venue, Ken Busby, a family friend who was known as "The Cultural Czar of Tulsa," hit it out of the park by securing the Penthouse Bar and terrace at the historic Mayo Hotel.

My family really pulled though as well, with all three of my brothers along with their friends and most of my grown nieces and nephews in attendance. I know Tulsa is where my family is based, but I forget what influence the House of Andoe has in that city. Or how many of us there are. Had our family been all who showed up, it still would have felt full.

I shared local tales, including those from the Bamboo Lounge, which was Tulsa's oldest gay bar. It was a total dive and I loved it, as did my nieces and nephews. Below is one of the excerpts I read.

A crude and crass guy sitting at the bar reminded me of Moe from the Simpsons. I asked about the sex maze that was rumored to be out back.

"Oh, they had to take that out after the raid. The place was shut down for a while and has been slow since it reopened," he said.

His whole world appeared to be that bar, and he seemed to assume it was a major economic engine for the city. He got riled up talking about the raid, arrests and shut down.

"And now the city's complaining about being broke! Well, they shot themselves in the foot when they raided this place, I tell you! They lost a lot in sales taxes!" he ranted. "This town can fall in the lake for all I care."

He asked where I lived and when I said St. Louis, he raised his eyebrows.

"Well I bet you have some stories to tell!" He then turned to the man sitting next to him and exclaimed, "St. Louis! Why, he's probably seen more cock than you and me could even dream about!"

I imagine mine was the saltiest act to ever grace the elegant Mayo Penthouse.

After that it was on to Oklahoma City, a hundred miles down the turnpike.

As teens, me and my friend Donald Cole went to Oklahoma City looking for the Habana Inn, the LGBT hotel and entertainment complex, and got hopelessly lost. Donald was staring intently out the window as if he was looking for landmarks.

"What are you looking for?" I asked. "We don't know this town."

"I'm looking for a sign that says The Habana," he replied.

Queer bars in Tulsa were unmarked, so the idea of a big sign visible—from the interstate no less—was ludicrous.

"Oh right. They're going to have a *sign* that says THE HABANA," I derided.

Right on cue we spotted the giant Habana Inn sign, and I felt like I was in a mighty metropolis. Almost a quarter of a century later that same sign now featured my name in lights.

I've always said Oklahoma City was one of the easiest places to make friends, and I had many there. On one end of the spectrum was my old partner in crime Donald, who lived with his longtime partner in Nichols Hills, the Beverly Hills of Oklahoma City, where they'd throw lavish cocktail hours for us. On the other end was Floyd Martin, known as "The Mayor of Gay Oklahoma City," who held court at Tramps, a bar behind the Habana known for serving the strongest drinks.

I long said Floyd was the best storyteller in Oklahoma, and he was such a character, he required handlers to keep him out of trouble when he went out. His "chief of staff" was a guy named Shane Morter who chauffeured him around and creatively regulated his drinking, mostly by giving him weaker drinks as the day or night wore on. He may have regulated other substances as well.

Shane and his partner had escorted Floyd to events I threw around the country, including in St. Louis, and bankrolled him on those trips.

"Is he going to make it to the signing tonight?" I asked Shane around 3 p.m. as we stood poolside at the Habana watching the big, suntanned Floyd wearing pearls and large sunglasses as he waded in the shallow end with an enormous cocktail.

Shane and Floyd were an odd pair. Floyd was heavy, fun, folksy and good natured while Shane was well-proportioned and pretentious with a wit that cut to the bone. In regards to my inquiry, he slightly squinted and tilted his head while observing Floyd, as if he were making an appraisal.

"I'll have them put almost no liquor in the next few," he replied. "He should be fine for tonight."

The Shane Shuffle

Unfortunately, Shane regulating Floyd could be the blind leading the blind, because Shane was a hot mess in his own right. Years after the book signing, he hit a downward spiral with his addiction, which is quite a tale.

For about a decade he and his partner, who had an MBA and a very good job, would party like it was the wildest Saturday night of their lives seven nights a week. They'd crash for a few hours, put in an eight-hour day at the office, and do it all again. They somehow maintained that lifestyle until it finally caught up with them. Jobs were lost, health deteriorated, they lost the house, which by then was overrun with bedbugs, and moved to a low-rent apartment near the Habana.

April of 2020 Shane messaged numerous friends, asking to borrow a wheelbarrow. It turns out he needed the wheelbarrow to dispose of a dead body.

Someone was doing drugs with him and overdosed. Shane panicked and shoved the body inside the sofa where it remained for a few days while he continued to have visitors and carry on like normal. He then wrapped the body in a shower curtain and stored it on his patio for a week or so until finally dragging it to the dumpster.

He was arrested, and I don't know exactly how this news leaked out but it was the worst kept secret in town. Finally, someone broke the ice by posting a meme of Shane with the caption, *You might be high. But you'll never be Shane Morter asking to borrow a wheelbarrow high.*

After that it was on, with everyone in town chiming in and fighting amongst themselves about anything and everything. What was so interesting to me about the Facebook thread was nobody in the hundreds of comments played the victim. They were all scrapping as equals. Hollow threats to sue were as extreme as it got. Had it been St. Louis, Shane would have had an army of defenders who would have said those speaking out were bullying him to suicide, and that being against Shane's actions meant they were against an entire demographic of people. Someone would have wailed that the conversation should be deleted at once because it's disrespectful to the unidentified deceased. Someone would have tried to get others in the thread fired. Someone would have claimed down was up and wrong was right.

The contrasting simplicity was remarkable.

And as if Oklahoma City wasn't stirred up enough, *Tiger King* had recently come out and since Floyd had been publicly feuding with Joe Exotic for years, the producers of the next season interviewed him.

Me and Kage visited Tramps a month or so after all this went down and a woman named Barb, who I only knew from Facebook, came up to introduce herself and chat about everything.

"See that guy over there? He was at Shane's apartment sitting on that couch when the body was stuffed inside and he kept asking, 'What's that smell?' Now we all say that to each other all the time," she laughed.

"Do you think he'd talk to me?" I asked.

"Probably not. He was kind of a co-conspirator."

Sure enough, later in the night over the loud music and chatter, I'd hear an occasional, "What's that smell?"

In addition to being a great storyteller, Floyd was quite the comedian. In reference to his upcoming television debut, he posted to Facebook:

I am scared. I am going to be in Tiger King 2 *on Netflix, and the internet can be relentless. For instance, this guy I know asked to borrow a wheelbarrow on the internet and people like to never shut up about that.*

Jet Setters

As part of my "Tales from the Emperor" column and blog, I bestowed "Emperor's Awards" annually for years. One recipient was artist Colby Adams, who I recognized for his incredible drawings. That got the attention of the Telegraph's Jill Moon, who featured him on the front page. Months later, when he learned Kage had graduated from college and needed a job, he got him hired in the corporate office of the commuter airline where he worked. And as an example of how everyone's stories intertwined in St. Louis, a year or two earlier Thomas Fortenberry, the gentleman Gassy blamed for my sinister birthday card, helped Mr. Adams prepare his resume for the position he applied for at the airline.

The job meant we had standby travel privileges on multiple carriers. Suddenly it was quicker and cheaper to get to Miami than Tulsa. But not only was the concept of standby flights totally foreign to us, Kage had never even been on a plane. Mr. Adams was kind enough to accompany us on our first standby flight, which was to Los Angeles en route to San Francisco.

Mr. Adams was still in his 20s and was definitely going places—no pun intended. He was already in an executive position and was as likely to be in Europe any given weekend as St. Louis. It was fascinating to watch how he masterfully maneuvered non-revenue travel. The first thing he would do is learn who was working the flight and how they connected with people he knew. Tall and handsome with a mop of full-bodied chestnut hair, he was warm, elegant and engaging with the crew, and before we knew it we were getting complimentary food and drinks for the duration.

In LA he made sure we were set for San Francisco, and then he took an hour detour to watch the sunset over the Pacific before returning home. California was battling wildfires and as we took off just after sunset, we could see a bustling Los Angeles below while a mountaintop burned like the Eye of Sauron above it all.

Kage was able to add an additional person to his travel benefits and chose our friend Cody, who I briefly dated in 2014. Often mistaken for brothers, Cody and Kage were always a fun combination. We knew he'd make good use of his ticket to the world, and in the first few months we introduced him to Fort Lauderdale and New York. My niece Lilly lived in a high-end condo right off Wall Street, and allowed us to stay there while she was in Italy. We took Cody to a leather bar where he lost his shirt, and then he left with an attractive gentleman caller.

I had set my alarm because he had an early flight home, and when I woke I found he still hadn't returned. I messaged him and he replied he was on his way to Lilly's. I began to drift off again and then my eyes popped open.

"Do you have a shirt? You can't come into the lobby without a shirt!"

Fortunately, the trick had given him a tank top to wear. I could picture Lilly returning to scandalous reports from the association.

Provincetown and the Priest

Ray took Evil Stepmother on a vacation to Provincetown, spurring her to post about what a treat it was because she would have never been able to experience it without Ray's generosity.

Days later she broke up with Ray via text, explaining that she fell in love with a man who had just left the priesthood, and while she was terribly sorry to do it, she must follow her heart.

Ray was the type to see the best in everyone, but the veil was finally lifted.

Well, when Evil Stepmother told the priest that they could now be together he replied, "I've just left the priesthood! I'm not looking for anything serious."

Evil Stepmother was wrecked, but even with egg all over her face she was just as shameless as ever. She told Ray what happened, pointedly leaving the door open to get back together.

Fortunately, the spell was broken, and she would be getting no encore performance at Villa Ray.

The Marvelous Ms. Pauly

It didn't seem like any time at all until Ray met the sparkling and fun Ms. Pauly, and he couldn't have picked someone more different than Evil Stepmother.

Sadly, we met under a wet blanket.

I was invited to Villa Ray for the introduction, and went out to the deck to find that Ted and Lenny, the patriarchs of our multi-generational tribe, had inflicted their bitchy little friend on us all. His name was Ronald but I referred to him as Ol' Pinch Face, because of the unappealing way his face was pinched as he surveyed everything and everyone who, in his mind, was beneath him. And everyone was beneath him.

I do not exaggerate when I say that every word and facial expression he conveyed in my presence was specifically delivered to express his superiority. We must at all times understand that to be in our presence, Pinch Face was slumming it.

Nevertheless, since he was only in his mid-20s when we first met, I held out hope with each subsequent encounter that maybe he had matured as he aged. Maybe as the lines grew on his face and his hair prematurely thinned, he would shake some of that awful pretension and simply be a semi-pleasant guest. But it was not to be.

At the time, Ol' Pinch Face was a school teacher in Alton, so I mentioned the connection when introducing Kage.

"Kage lives in Alton as well," I said.

"Oh, I'm sorry," Pinch Face replied.

We're all like ingredients in a tossed salad, but people like Pinch Face are the pungent anchovy dressing. They fundamentally change the flavor of everything they touch, as he very much did that summer evening.

I soon got to spend time with Ms. Pauly under better circumstances, and quickly determined she was the best thing to ever happen to Ray David. I had never seen him so relaxed and happy.

They initially bonded over their shared appreciation of the 1967 cult classic *Valley of the Dolls*, and found that was only the tip of the iceberg as to what they had in common.

The similarities came to a screeching halt when it came to clothing. You could hardly get more conservatively dressed than Ray, and could hardly find someone dressed flashier and more outlandish on a daily basis than the glittery, faux fur-draped Ms. Pauly, who could've given Liberace a run for his money.

I began taking Brawny to the villa for lunch with Ms. Pauly, where we'd laugh and tell stories, and where Ms. Pauly would model her latest fashions.

Leaving 'em Wrecked!:
Tim Beckman's EXPLOSIVE Exit Interview

Tim Beckman, the festive, outspoken, and oftentimes controversial co-owner of Sensation, decided to sell his half of the bar to his business partner Rose Dynasty and retire. He planned to go out with a bang, inviting the entire community to come out and roast him. And to prime the pump, we agreed that I'd run a spicy interview where he'd offer opinions on everyone and everything.

It was designed to be inflammatory, but it became the campfire that burned down half the city.

Because he was a business owner, he'd bit his tongue on certain topics like the state of the drag scene and on the rapid evolution of the art form, which for decades was synonymous with terms like "female illusion," but had morphed into something much broader and now included female entertainers performing as females ("bio queens"), which many older gay men didn't understand or like. Now that he was retiring, he offered his candid take on that and on the state of the craft in general:

"When I came out, drag queens were everything. You would go to a show and you would see entertainment that transported you to a different time and place and it was usually what a person needed to let go of the trials and challenges of daily life. Today, it is all about the fight to be number one, or to see who can be most different and break norms. It's disappointing.

"My older queens that set the stage back in the day are now trying to still be relevant with trying to stay the same as they were back in the day. I watch older queens no longer dance and stand there with their boobs out, maybe shaking a little hip for a dollar. I have seen the same queens perform the same number at different venues in the same costume. I have seen new queens that you can tell are about the money and act like old queens and just stand there. Same queen, different song, same act. Be original and bring yourself to the stage.

"I will be the first to say that I like traditional drag. As much as I love someone like Siren, I hate the beard. However, I have the utmost respect for the fact that she breaks the mold. She does her songs, her way, her beliefs and answers to no one but herself. I love that in a performer! And for doing that, I say kudos!"

Stirring the pot, I made sure to ask his thoughts on Margie Werther, the *#Boom* queen I'd been feuding with over the Spike saga, knowing he didn't like her. Setting up his quote (I'm quite embarrassed about it now) I wrote:

He also took particular issue with Margie Werther, a local queen known for being hateful and bitter.

"Some of you younger queens need to find out who you are and invest in your craft. There is a queen out there who has to make a negative post almost every day with some kind of drama. This makes me not want to go see you or the show you produce. Put out some positive vibes. If you are confident in what you do, negativity is not needed."

When pressed, he elaborated: "Margie Werther, definitely not my favorite person in St. Louis. She's too big for her britches and likes to read folks for things that don't concern her. She acts as if she's above everyone else around her. I truly like Colin and Colin, but when I learned they added Margie to their blog roster, they lost my support. She's publicly stood out against anyone who doesn't believe her beliefs. I am still in shock that Just Johns, *I adore John, by the way*, chose her as the bingo replacement, but then Margie will do anything to attempt to make a name for herself. In my own words: highly forgettable, mouthy, nosey, thinks-her-shit-don't-stink queen."

And as for the bio queens: "Don't get me started. That is only a fag hag that wants attention. This is a craft, an outlet and an art form for the gays and straights that appreciate it. Not for you to get attention."

Beckman ran down the list of infamous local characters. Of one known for soiling himself because he allegedly snorted cocaine cut with laxatives, he said, "Nothing more than a coked out, shitty—*literally*—bad breath wannabe Republican who is just repugnant. He is probably the most disliked and least respected of anyone in the LGBT community and is so tight, he could screw his socks on. Except when it comes to coke, he would sell his mother for that."

When we got around to discussing Gassy, things got interesting.

"Gassy and I have known each other many years. I met him years ago back in the Gay.com years and there was a time we were actually friends. Then he got into that whole party kids dress-up mode crap and was a DJ at Sensation at one point when I was just a bartender. Well, one night I kissed a Black friend of mine and Gassy was standing at the end of the bar. He called me a 'nigger lover,' in which time I proceeded to punch him in the face. When he went down, I kept punching as my friends were trying to drag me out of the bar. As they were pulling me out, I wouldn't let go of Gassy's shirt, and he was yelling that he was choking. My friends were yelling at me saying 'Let him go Jim, he is choking!' My response was 'Good!'"

Beckman continued, "I was about to be fired when I told the previous owner what had happened and had witnesses back up, then the owner fired and barred him instead. You may want to call him bitter about that time. Skip ahead a few years, and we had called a truce and although we were not friends, we were calm with each other, but later he hated me again over some stuff with Rose and not being allowed back in the bar. He unfriended me because of you and the Snake Pit, and I haven't heard from him since."

Despite his strong opinions, Beckman had good things to say about most every current and former bar owner in LGBT St. Louis, even some with controversial reputations, but the well of goodwill ran dry when it came to Fancy Slovak, whom he had feuded with for years and in this interview referred to as a "psychotic bitch."

"Fancy Slovak, just a hateful old bird. She always wanted to play like she was everyone's friend, then as they walked away she'd slam them. She's only nice when she needs someone and if you say anything negative about her, you're a bully. She wouldn't know the truth if God himself slapped her upside the head with a bible. She never cared about anything except money. The more she had, the more she spent. She would let her employees' checks bounce just to not let go of her money. I agree that she had an amazing place for the community when it was needed, but she also milked the people for everything she could get out of them. She loved playing games, *opening then gonna have to close*, with the community. Only this last time, she was called out on her game and lost her business. She cries all the time and plays the 'woe is me' card and everyone in sight is a bully when they point out her mistakes. She's a greedy old maid who likes both dick and pussy or whatever she can use to try to get back on top."

I asked about the rumor that, while working for neighboring bar Honey, Fancy tried to convince Honey's landlord to rent her the space instead.

"Oh yes, they gave her a shift or two a week and told her if she could build up her shift as she claimed, they would give her more shifts. She thinks her name had this huge following which didn't and doesn't happen. It's true the owner of the building wanted to sell, because he offered it to Rose and I two or three different times. But Fancy, who had no money, went behind Lisa's [Honey's second owner] back and tried to make a deal with the building's owner, and asked him not to let Lisa know. Lisa found out and fired her immediately. Of course she cried woe is me on Facebook all while claiming Slovak's would rise again!"

Vital VOICE wasn't immune from Beckman's strong critiques and ran them as well.

"*Vital Voice*. I miss the original publication. Granted, it has come a long way and the layouts and ads and overall look is amazing. However, they had went in an awful direction—from being local, with local stories and local pictures, to stories you can read in the Advocate or whatever. One thing I love about *Vital Voice* is that Darin promoted Jimmy. I've had a crush on that man for years, and at the same time am so proud to see how far he has made it. He's an amazing person with an amazing personality and one of the few in St. Louis that I have always gotten along with and always had a good time around."

About Darin Slyman: "Love him and he is a super person. Does way too many selfies and so many posts from out of the country which says he charges way too much for an ad!" Beckman laughed. "But (in reference to his expansion to Kansas City) he's a good person, I just feel he has made it a priority of going larger instead of remembering the area that supported him."

And about me: "The plus is there is no one that can tell a story like him. Reading one of his stories does not even compare to hearing him read one, because he becomes part of the story and you can see it in his expressions and hear it in the inflection of his voice. Very animated. I have also never met someone that is hated as much as loved. He is a person that you either hate or love. I am on the love side, though we have had differences of opinion. I give him kudos for using everyone or everything at his disposal to get a story and he digs deep for research. His stories are most always jaw droppers or stories that really make a person think. His downfall is when it causes harm, like the Snake Pit stories. Granted the story needs to be told, but then when it's repeated over and over in order to destroy someone, it becomes a bit obsessive. He's charming and even when he doesn't care much for you, he'll smile and talk to you anyway because there may be another story there, like with Dustin Mitchell. He has an entourage in cities across the US and it wouldn't surprise me if I ever see him run for a political office in the future. In fact, I almost can guarantee something will happen where he becomes more famous. I forgot to add, that when Andoe likes someone, he really treats them good. When he moved back to California, I was literally crowned with his crown as the temporary emperor. It was great, and a few years later, I had the privilege of putting that same crown back on his head where it started."

I asked what he will and will not miss about life in the Grove.

"Well, I can tell you that I won't miss all the demands of the gay folks. They are a very fickle bunch and if you don't agree with one thing, then you have a whole group boycotting you. I won't miss being nice to people I don't like. I won't miss feeling like I have to filter my views and opinions. I won't miss going to City Hall to renew licenses, I won't miss Restaurant Depot, I won't miss struggling in bad times, I won't miss expectations as a person in the gay community to donate to everything and everyone that needs money but doesn't support you," he began.

"I *will* miss some of my daily people who are like family. I will miss my mornings in the office with Rose where we talk about our goals, dreams and future projects. I will miss being part of big events that make Sensation stand out big above everyone else. I will miss the energy that Pride brings to the bar. I will miss the feeling of fulfillment when you do something big for charity. I will miss EFA [St. Louis Effort for AIDS], because those people are amazing, I will miss my staff because they love me so much. I will miss the Christmas parties, because I usually planned them and loved watching the employees let loose and have fun. I will miss the ability to take time off whenever my heart desires, and I will miss seeing the new direction that Sensation is heading in with new leadership. I think new blood and energy are exactly what is needed. Most of all, I will miss the many friends that I may not have met had it not been for Sensation."

After a few paragraphs highlighting all that was good about his experiences as a bar owner, I announced his upcoming roast.

Tim's being sent off with a roast on the Sensation Patio Stage Friday, October 16th beginning at nine. The combustible panel of roasters include myself, Michelle McCausland, Jasmine "Gotcha," Anthony Webster, and Spike Turner. Following will be a show with entertainers Rose Dynasty, Chasity Valentino, Makena Knight, Kitty Litter, Nadia Louis, and Khrystal Leight.

Send me your comments and critiques about Tim and I'll try to use some of them in my roast.

The Blowback

Beckman's interview nearly brought down both *Vital Voice* and Sensation. The younger drag performers, which included women, trans and non-binary entertainers and allies, were outraged over his comments about bio queens, but nobody whipped up the frenzy like *#Boom's* Margie Werther. Not only did Beckman call her out by name, but I wrote it (Margie was Pro-Spike) and *Vital Voice* published it (Margie absolutely loathed Darin to the point she'd be as hateful as possible to him whenever working the door at Just John).

Margie called for boycotts of all involved and told her followers to throw away every *Vital Voice* issue on the stands. An outside observer would have assumed the entire piece was about her, the way she capitalized on it, and even in the moment I knew she was well within her rights to do so.

It reminded me of when I was a boy and would pull honey bees off roses by their wings and flick them in the air. Most of the time they'd fly away, but once or twice one held on and stung my ass.

Sensation was flooded with threats of protests and worse if they went on with the roast, and I decided the only way to take the wind out of Margie's sails was to give her my head on a platter. I officially resigned from *Vital Voice*.

It worked instantly. It didn't calm Margie, but it deprived her of oxygen. The controversy was over.

Beckman's farewell party went on without incident, but the roast component was scrapped. The highlight of the show was when a defiant Rose Dynasty, in clear reference to all the attacks against Tim and the bar, performed "Not Ready to Make Nice."

Despite the caterwauling, many loved the interview—even if just for the attention it garnered. Photographer Mark Moore posted the following:

"Everyone, and I mean everyone mentioned in that piece is damn near a household name now!"

The Opportunist

Beckman intentionally chose roasters who had conflict with one another, and we had instructions to roast one another as well as him. Since the roast didn't happen, I decided to share a zinger or two over Facebook.

As Beckman says his goodbye, we should stop and think of all the history in this place, and how we all left parts of ourselves here. The entire building is doused in the sweat of Tim and Rose. The basement is coated in Akasha's Aqua Net, and of course the patio is splattered with the blood of Spike's exes.

Spike's allies were incensed, and seeing an opening for attention, Dickery decided to switch teams and join them. He'd always been a wallflower and I believe he saw this defection as his moment to shine.

"What's with all the hate?" Dickery began in his post denouncing me. "If you don't like someone move on, but why post things like this?" he said while linking to my roast comment. In his thread he railed about how terrible I was for the community.

This was so out of the blue. He'd long corner me at parties and demand my undivided attention and was now saying I had been a problem for too long and he was going to speak out.

It was so random, in fact, that after a few days of nonstop posts about me, which I did my best to ignore, I reached out to his ex-partner and close friend Larry. "I hate to bother you with this but Dickery has been railing on me for days. Is he okay? I'm just worried something else may be going on."

"I don't know why you're asking me. I don't know and I'm not involved," Larry replied.

Finally, I had enough, and I sent Dickery an enraged message.

"This is day SIX of your rant over a joke I wrote for a roast. Seriously. And do you have any idea how much shit I have on you? Do you know the young straight guy who you secretly photographed when he was in his own backyard and then called and propositioned at 3 a.m. was so freaked out he almost moved? Do you know that your entire neighborhood association knows all about it? What a fucking shitshow lapse in judgement! And I never said anything because you were my FRIEND OF TWENTY YEARS and I decided it was none of my business.

"You were on my jock, posing for book promos when you wanted to bask in the spotlight, but when you saw you'd get more attention by denouncing me, you took it. I hope I never lay eyes on your weasel face again."

Dickery cropped a screenshot of the last line and posted it. "This is what happens when you stand up to Andoe."

When I discovered what he had done, I wrote a blog post laying out the whole story. I didn't call him out by name, but the title of the post was, "Rhymes with Trickery." I posted it with the caption: *You've seen the carefully cropped screenshot. Here's the full story.*

Among the first to write to me about it was Larry. "Did you have to write all that? It was so vindictive!"

"Larry, I asked you for help deescalating this *days ago* and you said it was none of your business!"

Larry negotiated a truce where both sides would remove everything they posted about the other, but the nickname "Trickery" stuck, and bitter Ol' Trickery would tell people for years to come that I had ruined his reputation.

In this situation, I was the bee.

Enrichment from Enemies

Ol' Trickery was in his 50s at the time but developed a penchant for dating guys in their very early 20s, and when the relationship inevitably soured, he'd resurface and claim I was somehow involved.

I had no hand in the breakups, but I always heard about them. One young man was dumped after calling Trickery the worst thing possible: boring. That really touched a nerve, and while the guy was at work Trickery packed up the young man's shit and delivered everything to his mother.

Over lunch at Villa Ray one weekday, Ms. Pauly pulled up a YouTube video the young man posted. As tears gushed from his swollen eyes, he wailed, "I'M SORRY I CALLED YOU BORING!" and me and Ms. Pauly laughed so hard we cried.

After some social media buzz about one of his breakups and my alleged role, I wrote the following blog post.

Enrichment from Enemies

Years ago, I managed a low-rent apartment building where two women feuded for a decade. Ms. Kelly, the first-floor corner tenant, was old, wiry and irritable. Her arch nemesis, Miss Donna, reminded me a lot of Divine (of John Waters fame) and lived upstairs and one unit over. Donna not only had the upper floor, but also had the upper hand in the feud—a feud which mostly consisted of Ms. Kelly complaining to and about Donna, while the brash and bosomy Donna flippantly pretended to be unaware she was irritating Ms. Kelly—or that it was accidental. A perfect example was the time Ms. Kelly kept yelling up at Donna's unit from the back of the building, and was "accidentally" soaked by a bucket of Donna's mop water.

One day Donna was found dead in her apartment, and Ms. Kelly was devastated. Her feud with Donna was familiar, comfortable, and part of her routine. She mourned her, and she missed her.

I've thought about that dynamic over the years, how everyone in our lives has a role to play, and sometimes the right role for someone is that of an enemy or nemesis.

One that comes to mind personally is someone I've known for twenty years, but who turned against me suddenly after taking offense to a joke I wrote for a roast.

It turns out that our current standing works out much better for us both than the friendship ever did. While the joke backlash (it wasn't about him, but a fellow roaster) was the first I knew he had anger towards me, I later learned he'd been complaining about me and the attention my stories garnered for a long time— despite posing for photos with the book, buying a $30 ticket to the book launch, and cornering me whenever he saw me out.

I was his friend because of mutual friends, but thought he was insufferably dull. And when he saw me out, it wasn't enough to say hello. He had to pull up a bar stool and lock knees, making sure his face blocked out any distractions which might prohibit me from giving the undivided attention he found so hard to come by.

After our falling out he got into a romantic relationship, and weeks after it ended he came out with a bizarre story about how I had used a series of fake profiles to manipulate them into breaking up. I found the story entertaining, although I was frustrated that a couple of seemingly intelligent mutual friends claimed to believe him. He reconciled with the young man, and when they broke up again he posted twenty-five (or so) reasons why the relationship didn't work. I saw that as vindication, since I wasn't on the list, but those who defended his original story said I was a bully for pointing out the blatant inconsistency.

Despite the back and forth, if I look at the dynamic from 30,000 ft it really is a win-win. His tall tales about me sabotaging him at every turn make him interesting to his friends, which is quite a feat, and I no longer have to feign interest when seeing him out. We never worked as friends, but we've settled into our new dynamic nicely.

I'm almost always open and receptive to mending fences, but sometimes you look at a situation and think, "You know, I'm good."

Getting to the Island

Ms. Jamieson was so excited about coming to St. Louis for New Year's Eve. The 2014 event at Villa Ray had been somber, but now Ms. Pauly was the lady of the house and big plans were being made to restore the gala to its legendary status.

Earlier in 2015 when Ms. Jamieson would come to town she'd sleep on the sofa at Menashe's, where he and his lover Scott would fight right in front of her while she constantly tried to walk on eggshells around their very unstable pit bull. To top it off, when Ms. Jamieson would settle in to go to sleep, Scott would rouse her and try to convince her to get up and entertain him.

I asked Ray and Pauly if Ms. Jamieson could use the Christina Suite, and that became her regular home away from home. Expectations were through the roof between the party and the following debauchery at JJ's Clubhouse, but record flooding occurred in the preceding days and with the Mississippi to the south and east, the Missouri to the north, and the overflowing Meramec to the west, the city was beginning to seem impassable.

On December 29, 2015, Ms. Jamieson posted to Facebook: *Question: If I-44 closes just west of 141 due to flooding, how the hell else can one get to St. Louis? I don't want this water fucking with my NYE plans!*

One of her friends from central Missouri replied, *Oh, I'm sure you'll find a way to Whore Island!*

Magic at the Monocle

Kage was rarely sick, but he'd been down with a cold for several days and was clearly suffering. I came home from work on a Monday afternoon to find him in a cocoon of blankets on the sofa and asked how he was feeling. After a long, deliberative pause he said slowly, "I think I'm going to feel better on Wednesday."

That's one anecdote I long felt defined him. Even when feeling his worst, he tried to have an optimistic outlook. Another revealing quote was in regards to plastic surgery. A group of friends discussed what they would have done if given the opportunity and Kage, who was only half paying attention due to his video game, threw out, "I wouldn't have anything done. Plus, I look like my family, so I feel like changing my appearance would be disrespectful to them."

While both anecdotes serve to define his unique character, what I found the most profound, and what meant the most to me was how he never once met my anger with anger. He was never once defensive. If I was frustrated about something, he reacted compassionately with the goal of understanding and working through it.

I treasured that so much that I worked diligently to not take advantage and ruin it. I decided early on to let nothing fester, address things as they arose, and let things go when they had been addressed.

One evening during the fall of 2015, maybe nine months after we began dating, we were at the Monocle, the Grove's most upscale venue, with a small group of friends. I'd gotten cozy with Ms. Jamieson on a settee and was watching Kage, about a dozen feet away, play the role of social butterfly as he bounced around the bar visiting our people. His eyes were bright and his smile radiant.

I pointed my martini glass in his direction and told Ms. Jamieson, "I'm going to marry him."

Kage was in motion at that moment but locked eyes with me for a couple of seconds. I didn't think he had heard, but he had, and later that evening he said yes.

The Melrose

<hr>

As part of my daily duties, I went to perform a move out inspection at the Melrose. My employer bought the ten-unit 1920s-era property when it was presented to them at a fire sale price many years before Tower Grove South enjoyed its current cachet, and it had long been a bit of a neglected stepchild. Despite its handsome tile-lined roof, attractive brickwork and iron-framed balconies, it had a sad and shabby appearance due to the tired old aluminum storm windows in various states of disrepair, peeling eaves and sparse landscaping.

The tenant I was meeting, a Muslim cab driver, had his front door open and I ascended the stairs to a glass knobbed French door leading to the living room. The threadbare mauve carpeting was stained, the kitchen and bath were makeshift, and there was significant plaster damage in the bedroom. Still, I found the place charming with its rounded doorways and cozy shaded balcony, which overlooked the neighborhood. With windows on three sides there was an abundance of light, and I felt it had a treehouse vibe, nearly hanging over the alley with a view of pitched rooftops climbing Oak Hill. Finally, I liked how the layout allowed one to make a full circle through the apartment. The place had potential.

I noticed the building's potential years earlier, when a large corner unit was available. It featured a grand stairwell and a breezeway dining area with a midcentury Americana lantern light fixture similar to the one hanging over my mom's kitchen table. At the time I imagined filling the room with tropical plants, and entertaining friends with the windows open on both ends. It seemed the type of place one could settle into, and probably had.

"Tower Grove South is very desirable. You should invest in rehabbing those units," I relayed to my boss. Based on my recommendation, they ordered a complete renovation of the vacant unit. New kitchen, new bath, and refinished hardwood floors.

Once the restoration was completed, I negotiated the unit as part of my compensation package (that was the last straw for my resentful co-worker who saw me as the prodigal son. She walked into the conference room where a meeting was taking place, tossed her office key on the table and said, "I'm outta here.")

While far less impressive than most places I had lived, including the house up the hill I left years before, I was rebuilding my life and it represented progress. It was an upgrade from the little third-floor apartment I'd worked into a negotiation a year and a half prior, when my employer let me return even though they weren't looking to hire anyone.

At that time, they figured I was just passing through town (a reasonable assumption considering I had a California driver's license and a New York phone number), and before offering me a job, one of the owners asked, "Will you at least commit to staying for two years?"

The household consisted of my fiancé Kage, our dog Brawny, and our two cats. But my plans were bigger than moving into a new place. The Melrose, situated in one of the gayest neighborhoods in St. Louis, would be my boutique project. Here, as units became vacant, I would oversee renovations and assemble a cast of characters, an intentional community, and embark on an exciting new chapter in life.

The first tenant I moved in was "Maestro of Memes" Jordan Jamieson. "Ms. Jamieson," as I called her, was a nervous gay white guy from Rolla, Missouri, about a hundred miles southwest of St. Louis, whom I met online and bonded with over our investigation of local conman Dustin Mitchell. In our group chat, Ms. Jamieson would debunk Mitchell's prolific and fraudulent claims in real time through investigations that included reverse image searches. When Mitchell checked into a glitzy Vegas hotel with a picture of his feet and floor-to-ceiling windows overlooking the strip, it took Ms. Jamieson five minutes to determine the image was from an advertisement.

She'd also proved to be fiercely loyal during the blowback I'd endure from my sundry controversies.

Ms. Jamieson had just graduated from college and was interested in moving to the city. I helped get her hired at Marquette Realty and rented her the big corner unit I'd admired long before, which came available after the downstairs neighbor's 20-something drug-addled son Max apparently broke in and stole the tenant's drums. I assured Ms. Jamieson we were working on getting the bad tenants out, but it may take a few months.

Her first day on the job, I heard Max yelling from the back of the building.

"HURRY, SHE'S NOT BREATHING!" he screamed from the back door to the basement he and Ms. Jamieson shared, a scream which reverberated off the narrow canyon of red brick walls lining our end of the alley. An ambulance arrived, and I thought, "Oh God, I need to prepare Ms. Jamieson for this so she doesn't have a panic attack."

Ms. Jamieson already thought city living was absolutely terrifying.

So, it was 5 p.m. on her first day at work, and her anxious country ass was sitting in her little sweatbox of a vehicle in a crime-ridden part of town, waiting for an appointment.

My call came in as her appointment arrived, and it went straight to voicemail. Before pulling away for the drive home, she listened to my message.

Attempting a comforting, non-alarmist tone, I began, "Hi Jordan. I just needed to tell you that it looks like someone might have died in your basement. Ms. Nettle's derelict son was getting high with some woman down there, and the ambulance is here now. I just didn't want you to be surprised."

The tales of the Melrose were already unfolding.

This new endeavor was a bold departure from my firewall policy and posed risk, but based on nothing whatsoever, I felt confident it would all be fine.

Making the Most of the Melrose

A pessimist would think, "I once lived in a fine home atop that hill, and now I'm in a little apartment at the base of it," but I am an optimist. "I'm back in Tower Grove. I just upgraded to a nicer apartment in a better neighborhood, and I'm going to make something of this place."

Fortunately, Kage was an optimist as well, in addition to being a grateful man in general. It struck me how when discussing his parents, he'd say, "They always provided for us." Something most people take for granted.

Being 8 years younger and not having the same baggage of living up to former glories, he was even more excited about our new home than I was.

It was about a third larger than the apartment on Christy, had a proper dining area (no room for a table at Christy) and our own private entrance, as opposed to a common door three and a half flights down, and finally, a balcony big enough to hold seven during parties, we would find out.

And to top it all off we were in walking distance to the park, bars, coffee and restaurants, and numerous friends, several with pools.

Scrolling through Facebook shortly after we moved in, I saw a post from Kage.

I'm sitting at the window of our new apartment watching people walk by and I really appreciate Chris for getting this place for us. I love it here.

My heart melted. I've moved people to exciting new cities. I've presented grand homes to partners. I've gotten people life-changing jobs, but I never felt more appreciated than I did in that moment.

Jasmine Hits Rock Bottom

Monty, a good friend of Menashe's, owned a two-family flat in the Grove that had been in his family for generations. He lived on the first floor, and the second-floor was vacant.

Jasmine was tired of living 40 minutes away in Belleville and wanted to move to the city. Menashe made the introduction, and Monty agreed to rent to her.

It was a disaster from the start.

The Grove was the worst place for a lesbian alcoholic. She soon lost her job and would stay out all day and night while her dog Pearl whined, barked, and relieved herself on the rug.

Jasmine hated carrying keys, so she left her door unlocked. Monty noticed the door was ajar one evening and thought it was an accident, so he locked it.

At 3:30 a.m. a drunk and belligerent Jasmine beat on his door. "I'M LOCKED OUT! LET ME IN!"

He told her he found the door ajar and closed it for her.

"I don't like carrying keys and leave it unlocked on purpose. Just leave it alone!" she scolded.

"That's a security risk. If someone got in they could go down the back stairs and get to the basement or my place. You have to lock your door."

Jasmine simply refused to lock her door when she left, so Monty made locking it a habit. Every night she'd return at closing time and beat and kick his door, demanding to be let in. Sometimes he wasn't home due to working overnights, but other times, especially after the first few instances, he'd simply ignore her until morning. Adding to her anxiety in the moment were the sounds of Pearl barking and whining. Jasmine would eventually fall to the tiled porch floor and continue yelling, knocking, and sometimes clawing at his original (circa 1910) wooden door with whatever she could find before passing out.

This was embarrassing for all of us, but especially Menashe. In a group chat it was revealed she was a few months behind on rent and I said, "Jasmine if you can't afford the place you should just move out."

Angry and defensive she replied, "He wants me out? You know he can't just kick me out! I have rights! He has to take me to court!"

"He rented to you as a friend, and this is how you're going to be?" I asked, incredulous.

Later that evening she was too drunk to find the War Room chat and thought we had removed her. She sent me a threatening message declaring war, saying she would use screen shots she saved against me.

When she woke the next morning, she had no memory what had transpired, but it was too late. I was done. Jasmine turned on a dime from threatening everyone in the Grove with a Chris Andoe story, to regaling those same people with tales of what a villain I was. The two narratives dovetailed nicely for her, making for a seamless transition from friend to foe. She was able to make amends with many of the associates she lost when she turned on Spike, who had by then fallen out of the scene.

A fun aside about her landlord Monty though. He was one of the seven men who ran over "Speedbump Sally," who I wrote about in the *Vital Voice* article. Long story short, "Sally" was a belligerent drunk and when you'd try to leave her she'd apparently throw herself in front of your car. Somehow her history of being run over was inadmissible, so she received at least one enormous monetary award.

Refocus and Regrets

In 1993 I was desperate to get a sofa moved to a new apartment. I had to surrender the keys to the old place the following morning, so I had a matter of hours to get it out. Me and my friend Donald wandered Oklahoma City's Habana Inn—the center of the LGBTQ community—and one person I hardly knew found someone with a truck he could borrow and dropped everything to help us. Two decades on, when seeing this man out I'd buy him a drink.

I observe the type of people who blow through friends like Kleenex, getting what they can and discarding them. I like to think I'm the polar opposite of that. But one thing that I realized with the passage of time is that I had been so protective of Damon that instead of letting blame fall his direction, I shifted it to others, and even onto myself.

The most glaring example was our 2008 financial collapse from our Oklahoma City venture, and all I wrote about that in *Delusions of Grandeur*.

The disaster is what made me a writer. In processing what happened, how we lost everything, I painstakingly crafted the tales of how things played out and how my former mentor—a man who gave me my first real estate listing at 19—failed us.

The farther removed I was from Damon, however, the more it occurred to me that my employer and his team had been happy with my performance. They were unhappy with Damon, and that was the root of all that went wrong.

Damon wasn't even slated to be part of the business, but when a job offer was rescinded after relocating from San Francisco, they agreed to hire him. But there was no him and me. There was only us. Negative feedback about him was negative feedback about the two of us. There was no daylight.

As this came into focus, I was filled with regret about what I had written. I was the ungrateful person I despised. I sent my former mentor the following message:

Dear Rand,

Damon and I have been over for two years and it's taken that long for the dust to settle and for me to see the world as it is, and not through a distorted lens. His chronic, severe depression corroded my spirit and enveloped me until finally I broke free, moved from SF to NYC, then returned to St. Louis to get my bearings and rebuild.

While you're admittedly difficult to work for, you hired and invested a great deal in me and then hired Damon when he had no other options. You not only did right by me, you went above and beyond—like you always had, since giving me my first listing at 19. I sincerely apologize for blaming you for my financial collapse. You didn't deserve that.

Today I'm happier than I've ever been, and soon will be married to the most joyful man I've ever known. Life is good, and I'm filled with gratitude.

I want you to know that I appreciate your role in helping me launch my career and being a friend and mentor. Again, I'm sorry for my total lack of appreciation over the past nine years.

I hope you're well.

Chris

Rand replied:

Hi Chris,

I am glad things are looking up for you. I have always considered you an exceptional person.

I have no hard feelings and just wish it could have worked out better for all involved.

Beers or cocktails sometime.

Wedding Day

The morning of our wedding I posted a photo of the dramatic Riverview Park Stairs along with the following thoughts:

When I first saw these stairs, I didn't know anyone in Alton and I didn't know where these stairs led. I was just out exploring, roamed deep into a scenic and historic neighborhood atop the bluffs, and came across them.

Months later I took my friend Menashe, wanting to share this special, secret place I found, and asked Kage to meet us there for our first face to face visit.

I was struck by these stairs the first time I saw them, sensing there was something wondrous waiting at the top. And indeed there was.

It was hard to imagine that less than two years earlier, I didn't know a soul in Alton. Now this town I loved was buzzing in preparation for our early evening wedding.

Menashe had stayed at Kage's friend George's big Victorian for a few days, baking and decorating the cupcakes and cutting fresh flowers for the arrangements. Kristin and her husband Brandon came to town, and the entire wedding planning team met at Bubby's to transform the backyard for the reception, setting up tables and chairs, and making floral arrangements in mason jars. It was a sunny and perfect day in the 80s, with a good balance of sun and shade in the tree-lined yard. The group then surprised us by bringing in a big lunch they had prepared.

While we didn't think anything of the same-sex aspect, ours seems to have been the town's highest-profile same-sex wedding to date. A co-worker at the realty company received regular updates from her daughter-in-law, whom we didn't know, because she was an Alton native and followed local chats.

After setting up for the reception, we were walking to the car to go to the hotel for a nap. Jason Brooks called Kage to the side. Jason had been a bartender there and saw Kage every weekend for a decade. He saw him at his wildest, as an often-shirtless player on the scene, and observed his evolution.

Kage walked to the gate, where Jason was standing. "I just wanted to say I'm really proud of the man you've become."

The soon-to-be-setting sun at Riverview Park was gorgeous, showcasing the emerald green grass, picturesque white stucco gazebo, wide river dotted with sailboats and lined with miles of limestone bluffs. The golden sun also was kind to my handsome Kage with his freshly shaven head, neatly trimmed beard and pressed white shirt.

Rather than hiding for a big entrance, we excitedly greeted our guests, many of whom came from across the country. Dozens of friends and family members mingled and I was talking to our friend Denny Fiske, who was holding Brawny, when he stopped me mid-sentence, softly pushed me aside, and asked in wonderment, "Who. Is. That?"

My statuesque niece Lilly, accompanied by her elegant gentleman caller, arrived in a pink taxi wearing a gold sequin bodysuit, gold heels, gold choker, and big gold sunglasses in what is now known as the single most dazzling entrance in the history of Alton.

Kage was also stopped by a friend asking who she was. "Oh, that's just Chris's niece from New York," he said before hurriedly resuming his story.

Kage's longtime friend and fellow karaoke enthusiast Shondra sang Anita Baker's "Giving You the Best That I Got," and Sarah, a former roommate and one of his best friends, married us. Brawny was our ring bearer. The ring was affixed to his collar, and Ray released him from the end of the aisle. By the time he reached the front row, though, he pooped out and took a seat below Kage's mother and grandmother.

We forewent the big entrance at the park, but made up for it at Bubby's, coming out on the second-level deck to see about a hundred guests surrounding candlelit tables as fireflies dotted the trees. Our tribes came together as one, including some relatives I hadn't seen in many years.

Local media was in attendance including Jill Moon, who spent a good deal of time talking to my brothers Bill and Joe beside the fountain. She caught up with me a bit later.

"Amazing wedding! Now, I want to meet your brother Joe."

"You've been talking to him this whole time!" I exclaimed.

Many stayed late into the evening, mixing with the bar's regular patrons for the drag show, which would be my niece Claire and my cousin's daughter's first.

With his collar wide open and shirt sagging from the sweat and humidity, Kage laughed and smiled as we hugged and tried to savor this fleeting moment.

I have to say, from beginning to end, it was the most beautiful day of my life.

The Fiat Fuck You

Before I left the Bay Area I offered to sign for a car for Damon. I couldn't have a car in Manhattan, much less a Jeep Cherokee, so I told him he could either keep the Jeep (we shared one vehicle), trade it for something new, or I could drive it cross country and then sell it, which would save the expense of the rental car since I wasn't putting Brawny on a plane.

He researched cars for several days and decided he wanted a Fiat hatchback, and he wanted it brand new for reliability reasons. I'm a car guy, and specifically a big car guy. If I knew how to work on them, I'd own a 1985 Cadillac Fleetwood. A Fiat would be at the absolute bottom of my list.

We took one for a test drive and the car seemed flimsy, and even though I wouldn't be driving it, I had concerns.

"My worry is this seems like a novelty vehicle, and I'm worried you'll tire of it quickly," I said, but he assured me it's what he wanted.

When it came time to do the paperwork, he sat back and said for me to just put it in my name. I found that odd, but figured he was self-conscious about his credit after having to do a short sale on the last house, which was in his name.

Because his payments were a little higher than they should have been due to the balance owed on the Jeep, I agreed to pay for his car insurance as long as he had the car.

Within months I was in St. Louis ready to buy a car of my own. After deliberating between the big flashy cars I liked, and the desire to be smart and practical, I decided on a two-year-old Lincoln hybrid. He saw the photos from the test drive and blew up my phone while I was at the dealership.

"I really think it makes more sense for you to take the Fiat. It's already in your name, and we could ship it to St. Louis."

"See! He's already sick of that stupid car," I thought to myself, but replied much more diplomatically.

"I don't want to take your car, Damon. You picked it out, it's your taste and you should have it."

While I did think he was tired of it, I thought he also didn't want "us" to be saddled with two vehicles in the event we got back together, which I didn't see happening.

I bought the Lincoln and was happy with the purchase for years to come, even long after it was paid off.

The Fiat was a distant memory until it fell on my back a few days after the wedding. It was a Wednesday morning and I was at my desk when I received an email from Damon.

I'm no longer driving the Fiat. Where do you want it?

My stomach dropped, and I knew a few things at that moment.

He wanted me to melt down and to beg. He wanted to see panic.

No amount of begging would change anything. He likely already had a new car.

This, of course, was punishment for getting remarried, especially for having the big wedding he and I did not have.

He wanted an opening for a fight where he could unload and say things he didn't feel he'd had the opportunity to say for years (mostly because I was careful to never give such an opening).

This premeditated stunt was designed for maximum emotional impact, and to financially cripple me.

With all that in mind, I prepared for the next move, which was to close the door on any future attempt to soften what he had done. To take away any future revisions about how something was misunderstood. To flatten all the air pockets out of the bag.

"Congratulations on your new car! If you'll garage the Fiat for three weeks I'll come out and get it." I replied, knowing full well he would refuse.

"I'm not going to do that. Where do you want it?" he replied.

Good. He was on record. I imagine he thought I'd tell him to surrender it to the dealership, ruining the very good credit I rebuilt since 2008.

I went to work reaching out to Bay Area friends for help. Here's the thing, though: You don't weigh Californians down with heavy shit. It's considered rude.

I've oft repeated a quote from a St. Louis native living in Los Angeles, whom I met at a party on the eve of my first move to San Francisco: "It's a lot easier to make friends in California, but if you ever get a flat, you'll want one of your St. Louis friends."

What I had was far worse than a flat, and I was calling.

A Hard Sell and a Hard Place

A dear friend and former client in San Francisco, Kathy Looper, offered to leave the emergency room, where her daughter-in-law was having pregnancy complications, to deal with the car, but I couldn't let her do that.

The most logical people to turn to were Michael and Teresa.

Me and Damon used to take weekend trips to the midcentury Andiron Inn along the Mendocino County coast, hours north of San Francisco. The owners would host happy hours in the cozy lobby, and that's where I first took note of the striking straight couple in their late 40s/ early 50s. They lived in Oakland, and we had nice conversations about the Bay Area. When I was checking out, I decided to ask the owner to give them our contact information, and we ended up becoming close, even attending holiday dinners with them when we couldn't get back to the Midwest.

After I moved along, Damon continued that tradition, and I was glad he had them.

I'd hardly communicated with them in years, aside from the occasional Facebook like, and this was a complicated and tense situation. Asking for a favor of this magnitude was awkward for all involved.

"We'll have to talk about this," Teresa said, but Michael contacted me later to say he'd been in touch with Damon, who would bring the car over.

After that, there were logistical questions, mainly about whether the vehicle was street legal. I asked, and days passed with no response. I should have simply taken that as a no, figuring it wasn't and he didn't want to get in the middle of a potential conflict regarding that disclosure. My plan, however, was to fly out and drive the car back—and I wasn't about to drive a Black man across seven states in a car with expired tags. He finally answered that no, it was not street legal.

I made arrangements to pay nearly a thousand dollars to ship it back, and decided that we'd keep it for a few days beforehand and do some scenic drives. This was considered our honeymoon, after all.

We had the marvelous fortune of staying at a friend's Castro cottage while he was out of town. We walked around the corner to meet my local friends at the bar, each of whom warmly included Kage.

The next morning we enjoyed an hour-long walk through the city to the Ferry Building, where we took a ferry to Oakland. From there we took an Uber up the hill to Michael and Teresa's craftsmen home. They were at work, unfortunately, so I didn't get to thank them in person, but their son gave us the keys.

Nothing felt right about driving that car. We needed to take it to San Francisco, and I was out of practice driving in the intense traffic. The vehicle felt like a little tin can, very foreign to me.

I often remark about Kage being an optimist, and in that moment he said, "It's not all bad."

"Tell me one good thing about this car, Kage."

"Well, everyone who sees you in it will know you're gay."

The Leg Trap

It's hardly an exaggeration to say Damon could not have selected a worse car for depreciation than the Fiat 500. The loan balance was about $20,000 and despite the low miles, the trade-in value was a mere $6,000. The car was black and I viewed it as an ominous cloud. I even had bad luck when driving it, which included getting my first speeding ticket in years.

Even more so than a dark cloud, I saw it as a leg trap I had been ensnared in. Desperate to be free from it, strategies consumed my mind.

In the meantime, I got it properly tagged, and despite the pain I made the payments.

We attempted to trade it in on a new vehicle for Kage, throwing in his car and some cash. I hoped this plan would work, but the salesman returned and said we were just too upside down. We needed to come up with $10,000 more to escape that goddamned vehicle I hated since I first laid eyes on it.

I didn't have that $10,000.

I once heard someone say the difference between a law-abiding man and a criminal is like the difference between ice and water: it vanishes when the heat is turned up.

I thought of that quote while driving away from the dealership that evening and seriously weighing the option of wrecking the car with me in it, asking myself insane questions like what's the safest way to total a vehicle.

Keys were often left in the car with the windows down, begging a thief to take it. I parked it as close to the corner as possible, hoping it would be hit.

One day Kage raised his concern.

"I'm worried that you're throwing out to the universe that you want bad things to happen to that car, and maybe the universe isn't precise. I worry something bad might happen to the car with you in it."

The following morning our downstairs neighbor, Mr. Green, pounded on our door.

"Someone stole my car last night!" he said. It had been parked on the street directly in front of our shared porch.

I'd felt for some time that Mr. Green was a bit psychic. That morning I believed he sensed that I had some indirect, non-criminal involvement. I also felt Kage was on to something regarding the universe's shoddy aim.

Malice

I was a deeply flawed husband to Damon. I can make excuses about our agreements and our understanding, and those arguments would technically be truthful, but the fact is I lived a double life the majority of the time we were together.

On our first date, in the middle of making out, he began weeping hysterically and said, "Please don't leave me. Everyone leaves me."

Then and there I made a promise I had no business making, and contacted another guy I was seeing to break it off. I held my end of the bargain, imperfect as it was, staying with him during periods of unemployment and depression. When, in the best physical condition of his life, at his happiest, and earning the best money of his career, he fell for someone else and told his mentor he was only staying with me out of obligation, I felt my own obligation had been fulfilled.

For his part, he had grand ambitions to change me from the very beginning. Much like someone buying a house with the aim of gutting it, I was merely a vessel to someday house his ideal partner. An idealized partner with few similarities to me.

And for whatever reason he enjoyed ruining my special moments. If I got a big promotion, he'd explode about the raise being too small. If I wanted to sit on a cliff overlooking the Pacific to watch the solstice sunset, or burn regrets at a New Year's Eve beach bonfire, he'd accompany me, but rather than settling in on a blanket, he'd stand with his arms crossed until I aborted the outing.

One thing I feel completely confident in saying is that I was never intentionally cruel to him. Even when he was cruel to me, I still saw that 22-year-old guy crying on my bed. I saw the lonely little boy forcing a smile in school photos. I was protective of him in my own way.

After that Wednesday morning stunt with the car, though, I decided I would say everything I hadn't said over the years. I set about writing the letter like I was methodically sharpening a sword, or brewing a toxic potion.

For several days draft would replace draft as the message was boiled down for maximum impact. I knew all the pressure points, all the triggers, and I left nothing on the table. I knew wherever he was when he read the screed, he would collapse like an imploded building.

I saw Kage's spirit as a radiant light, and it felt awkward sitting beside him on the sofa going about such a dark task. Never before had I crafted something more malicious or with more evil intent.

And in the end, I didn't send it. Partly because of my moral compass, but partly because of cowardice.

Damon had been itching for a fight for years, and time and again I didn't take the bait. I was proud of that discipline. This letter would open Pandora's Box, and nobody on this planet knew how to make me feel like a failure the way he did. He'd gone through my personal messages for years, he knew where every body was buried. Yes, my letter would have literally brought him to his knees, but I shudder to think of the return fire.

Keep Talking

If someone stopped me on this street, I discussed the Fiat. If I saw someone at the club, I discussed the Fiat. If they called me on the phone . . .

It was all consuming. Mostly, I was thinking out loud in the hopes a solution might occur to me. My mind is geared towards problem solving, whether it's my own problems or those of others.

When I hear someone's problem, I think of ways I can help. Over the years I've made life-changing introductions, helped friends relocate, gotten people rent-controlled apartments in San Francisco, and coached several through career changes.

Someone I helped lift out of a hard time years earlier called to check in on me. After hearing about the $10,000 ransom required to free me from the Fiat, the old friend said, "Dude, I've got the money."

The friend credited me with providing him the solid foundation to build the life he now enjoyed, and said he was happy to help. And it wasn't a loan. It was a gift.

The money arrived within days, and we promptly returned to the dealership to trade Kage's car, the Fiat, and the $10,000 for a new vehicle for Kage.

The friend wanted to remain anonymous as far as the book, or even among mutual friends, and honoring that wish was the least I could do.

The abandoned Fiat was intended to devastate me financially and ruin my hard-earned credit. It felt like I was dangling from a cliff with the Fiat chained to my leg, not knowing how long I could hold on.

This friend not only saved my financial life, he saved my dignity.

SOCIAL HOUSE PRESENTS:

WIGS KNOCKED BACK

June 11th
9pm

Tawdry tales from critically-acclaimed author

CHRIS ANDOE

215 E. MAIN STREET | CARBONDALE

Clyde Russell Joins the Cast

Clyde Russell, a beefy guy in his early 30s, was a Facebook friend from Anna, Illinois, an isolated rural town of 5,000 people about a hundred miles southeast of St. Louis. I came to notice him engaging on Ms. Jamieson's posts, and when I asked her about him, I learned they had a very brief long-distance fling when they were young.

I traveled to Carbondale, a college town not far from Anna, to headline a storytelling event and book signing. Joining me was Kage, Ms. Jamieson, Menashe and a half a dozen others. Clyde was enthusiastic about our visit and rented a room at the same hotel.

Standing about 6' and weighing about 250, Clyde had a solid build and a manly vibe in his plaid shirt, jeans and construction boots. After spending a little time with him I remarked, "He's basically like a burly blue-collar straight guy, except he likes sex with guys."

Just about everything that could go wrong with my event did, chief among them the club's air conditioning going out. It was a 98-degree day, and since the club announced via Facebook that there was no air conditioning, the audience basically consisted of our crew and four locals, including Patrick Dilley, a dear friend and professor who'd written a blurb for my book. I'm not sure how many would have attended otherwise since the promoter who lured me there ghosted immediately after I scheduled the gig.

I moved the show from the stage to the unusually spacious, furnished foyer, which I could make feel like a full house while taking advantage of a slight breeze. The only downside was the occasional, puzzled patron walking through my set.

Afterwards the group went bar hopping and it was like we all had known the easygoing Clyde forever. At one bar, he and Ms. Jamieson got into a debate about which one was better at performing a certain sex act, with each adamant they possessed a special gift in this arena.

An outgoing and nice-looking gay friend of Clyde's happened to be at the otherwise straight basement bar, and I asked him if he'd let Clyde and Ms. Jamieson perform the act on him, and then tell me who was better. Surprisingly, he was down from the start, and several of us left for the hotel, where the contest would be held. The others in our group continued bar hopping.

Each contestant got five minutes, then an opportunity to make a three-minute "closing argument." Clyde went first and his performance seemed solid, but I saw a look of anxious doubt wash over him while watching the judge groan and squirm during Ms. Jamieson's performance. As an aside, Ms. Jamieson was like a relative to me so it was a bit awkward watching her go to town on this stranger, all flushed and intense. Actually, the entire scene was oddly buttoned-up, for what it was, more clinical than orgy.

I sent everyone out and sat with the man to debrief. I thought it was a foregone conclusion Ms. Jamieson was the victor, but that was not the case.

"But you were groaning and squirming!" I said.

"I was groaning in pain and squirming to try to move away!" the man said. "He was nibbling!"

It turns out Ms. Jamieson thought the nibble was her ace in the hole. She was forced to retire her trademark move after the Carbondale carnage.

101

Clyde's parents had recently passed away, leaving him alone in what we gathered was a ramshackle house in the middle of nowhere. We were finally able to evict Ms. Nettles, the tenant below Ms. Jamieson, after her derelict son fired a gun in the front yard. The rehab of the apartment had just started, and we decided to offer it to Clyde.

He was thrilled about the opportunity, and I updated him with photos as the new kitchen went in, and as the floors were refinished. He shared everything with his Southern Illinois friends who seemed happy that he was getting out.

The evening before his arrival, me and Kage went to check on his apartment and Ms. Jamieson came in through the back stairwell she'd soon be sharing with Clyde. The cleaning service skipped windows, so I lifted all the blinds and went about the task of cleaning them myself. I wanted to make sure the unit looked perfect for his arrival, so all he had to do was set up and decorate.

Pulse Nightclub Massacre

It was while we were in Carbondale that we learned of the Pulse Nightclub Massacre, where 49 people were killed and 53 wounded at an Orlando LGBTQ bar. I wrote the following blog post on June 13, 2016.

Mourning in Our Own Ways

Mass shootings have become so commonplace we can become numb to them, even when they hit close to home. Sunday morning I was reading the coverage in an academic way, trying to learn the what, when, where, and why of the story.

Then I clicked on the video of Christine Leinonen, a mother looking for her son. She had been standing behind the police tape for probably twelve hours.

"They said there's a lot of dead bodies in the club," she said as she started to break down. "And it's a crime scene, they can't identify anybody, so it could be hours and hours . . ."

I began to cry and have been crying on and off ever since.

Why was nobody standing with her? I wanted so much to be there to hug and support her, but felt helpless.

I've not been a fan of candlelight vigils because I didn't believe they served a purpose, especially when not coupled with what I consider real efforts to make change. But when Jason Brooks invited me to speak at the vigil at Bubby's last night I had a change of heart and decided there was indeed value in coming together as a community to mourn.

While at the vigil with my partner, a woman standing at a table invited us to join her. "I'm here by myself. You're welcome to join me."

In her reaching out I sensed she needed companionship. I wasn't able to comfort Christine Leinonen, but I could keep this woman company. And so I did. After conversing for a while, she told me she didn't come out much, but after watching the news she wanted to be with people. I thought about how sad it would've been had she not found anyone to talk to and left alone.

But that's the thing about LGBTQ bars. They're often a place where you can go and find friendly people to talk to, and a place to belong.

Outwardly I'm mourning by expressing anger that politicians are using our tragedy to target other minorities. I'm railing against the NRA. I'm trying to think of ways to make things better. But I'm still weeping with everyone else.

I can't think of any bigger LGBTQ anthem than "We Are Family" and the line that keeps ringing in my ear is the one about giving love in a family dose.

We're all different, we all express ourselves differently, but we're all in this together. Let's be there for one another, give space to mourn and vent, and then let's press onward.

Sounds of the Melrose

Clyde's bedroom was below Ms. Jamieson's and next to Rick's. Rick was a short, cute gay guy pushing 30, but with the persona of someone who was maybe 21. We all knew he was a hot mess, yet we felt protective of him like he was a little brother. Not that he needed protecting. He was banned from several bars for fighting. I sought to turn his negatives into a positive by branding him "The Testosterone-Fueled Bad Boy of St. Louis," which gained traction.

Clyde heard a lot of action from two directions, which was incredibly novel having only lived in one isolated rural house his entire life. He'd excitedly update the Melrose Resident Association Chat with every grunt, moan and bang. Of course, Ms. Jamieson and Rick heard plenty from his direction as well.

The basement Ms. Jamieson and Clyde shared was where Ms. Jamieson's washer and dryer were located. Nobody else got around to getting their own, so the miserly Ms. Jamieson let us use hers for $20 a month. From the laundry area you could hear every squeak from Clyde walking above, as well as Ms. Jamieson's main-level front door. One day I was loading the dryer when I heard Ms. Jamieson talking to someone directly above.

"MS. JAMIESON! WHAT THE HELL YA DOIN?" I yelled through the floorboards.

It turns out she had a new tenant from a different property stop by to pick up a key, so my caterwauling was a little awkward for her.

My niece Emily, an Oklahoma native attending culinary school in St. Louis, was often found sitting on the balcony above her apartment, which belonged to her best friend Opal. I'd stop below to chat while walking the dog and would inevitably see either a trick or a food delivery guy going to Clyde's, who didn't work for months upon arrival. He instead funded his celebratory lifestyle on the money from his mother's small life insurance policy until it ran out.

The building was L-shaped, with Clyde and Ms. Jamieson at the corner, my niece on the far west end, and me and Kage on the north end beside the alley, one unit above and over from Rick, with whom we shared a basement and back stairway. Rick's porch was below our balcony, and we overheard him and his buddies talking and laughing.

If Rick became aloof, we knew that meant he'd gotten back with his on-again off-again boyfriend Angel, a petite young Latin guy of about 22 who brought out the worst in him. There was no question Rick was crazy, but nobody could pull his strings like Angel, and their fights often culminated in Rick slicing open his arms and being admitted to the psych ward. His friends thought Angel pushed him that far intentionally, but regardless of whether it was intentional they were not a good fit. Rick knew none of us approved of Angel so he'd withdraw when they'd briefly reunite.

Directly below our unit was a 30-something straight Black cook named Mr. Green, who had a hot-headed girlfriend who always accused him of cheating. We could hear every word of her violent psychotic episodes. We never complained, and in turn he never complained about all the noise from our place, particularly the after-parties during the wee hours on Sunday mornings.

My God, the things he must have heard.

Fallout on Flora

When we were still living at the Christy and Rick was living in the southern suburbs, we invited him to join us for a big Halloween party on Flora Place, a grand boulevard of fine homes north of Tower Grove Park. When we picked him up, Angel was in tow.

We were already wary of Angel but at that time kept our opinions to ourselves. It turned out that Angel had dated the roommate of the Flora Place homeowner until the man learned Angel was already in a relationship with Rick. The roommate even had a call with Rick little more than a week prior and commiserated about how Angel had played both of them.

At the party the roommate, an artist-in-residence of sorts, made a beeline for Angel and asked, "What are you doing here? You need to leave. Now."

Angel made his way to JJ's solo, where we met up afterwards. At JJ's, Angel kept pestering Kage about borrowing his cape. He was insistent and obnoxious.

"No! This isn't even mine! I borrowed it from my dad."

I told Kage if he let Angel run off with it he'd never see it again. Just months later Angel ran off with his sister's car, totaled and abandoned it, and then went into hiding because he was afraid of how mad his family was.

Shaking his head at Angel's antics, Rick said, "She's always trying to do the most."

Get it Together

Jasmine's landlord Monty, frustrated by her alcoholism and her refusal to carry a key, shared a photo of Jasmine passed out on the porch one morning, using a four-pack of Charmin as a pillow. I shared it to the Melrose Chat and Rick posted it to her wall with the caption:

Hey Jasmine I stopped by to visit but you were busy. LOL! Get it together girl!

Rather than blaming Monty, since it was clear from the angle it was taken from his door, or blaming Rick, she singled out Kage, which didn't make sense.

"I'm going to press charges against Kage for trespassing. And it's a sex offense to take pictures of someone when they're sleeping so he's going to be classified as a sex offender!" she vowed.

Since Kage was Black we figured she thought threatening him with the law would be more intimidating. We lost no sleep over her flimsy scheme.

When Monty finally got her out, he found a phone in the apartment that wasn't hers and tracked down the owner who said it had been stolen weeks earlier at a nearby club. When word got out about the allegedly stolen phone, Jasmine somehow convinced, guilted or badgered the woman to issue a statement that it was all a misunderstanding.

Only Jasmine could pull that off, or even have the nerve to try.

The Rigid Ms. Jamieson

Ms. Jamieson could be quite rigid. I held a reception to welcome her to town her first evening at the Melrose and she nearly skipped it because she didn't want to stop unpacking until everything was put away perfectly.

"I can't relax until everything is done!" she said.

"Okay. If you decide to join us we have a dozen people here celebrating your arrival," I replied, which guilted her into making an appearance, even though she was manic.

A Chinese student named Feng, who was also a new Melrose resident, was in attendance. Rick convinced Feng to rent the apartment and then dumped him before moving in because he reconciled with Angel. Feng was like a deer in the headlights during his short time at the Melrose, and in the kitchen he and Ms. Jamieson bonded over how terrifying it was to live in the neighborhood.

"Have you looked up the crime rate?" Feng asked, cringing.

"Oh yeah, and I hear gunshots all the time" Ms. Jamieson replied. "I'm having a security system installed first thing tomorrow."

Feng and Ms. Jamieson later chatted over the apps, leading Feng to creep up the back stairs for a rendezvous. Months later in the Melrose Chat, Rick made it known he was aware with some pointed shade.

Fortunately, during the party I was able to pull Ms. Jamieson away and got her talking about her excellent credit score instead. That was always a favorite topic of hers.

"It's gone up by about a hundred points!" Ms. Jamieson began before explaining her credit strategies.

Another anecdote is from her first night at the sprawling bear bar JJ's Clubhouse when she first moved to town. She met an attractive cowboy from Tulsa of all places, and they were cuddled up for the bulk of the night. When we were ready to go, she opted to stay since she had a sure thing.

Menashe and Jasmine were riding with us, and Jasmine insisted on breakfast at Uncle Bill's Pancake House, a staple of the after-bar set, but my least favored option. I hadn't been there in ten years.

We had finished eating and were waiting for our check when the text messages began pouring in. Just before closing time at JJ's, another suitor swept in and took the cowboy home. Oh, Ms. Jamieson was fit to be tied, just beside herself with the unfairness of it all. Unable to snag anyone at the sidewalk sale (guys gathering outside after closing and going cheap), she vowed to sleep in the club's parking lot "out of principal [sic]."

In her mind, the Society of Drunk & Promiscuous Homosexuals would read all about it in the morning paper and feel such collective shame they'd never leave her trickless again, and of course, the cowboy would be plagued by guilt.

"Ms. Jamieson slept in the parking lot!" They'd exclaim. "This is a time for the community to undergo some serious introspection!"

We waved again for the check, and noticed that a giant cockroach was standing on Jasmine's plate, looking at her like, "what?"

We rushed out, and because we were in a hurry, and Jasmine and Menashe would not leave without a cigarette, Kage allowed them to smoke in his new car. That three minutes spared us from a shooting in the parking lot just after we departed.

We found the JJ's lot empty upon arrival. It turns out a motorist saw Ms. Jamieson on the clearance rack and couldn't pass her up.

Melrose Mardi Gras

2017 was the Krewe of the Tawdry Turret's third year at the Opera Box.

"You should have a big event up here, maybe even charge for it," Lydia said during one of my visits to her costume shop, which was very unlike her to suggest. While normally a bundle of nerves, she was uncommonly loose that day. I decided to just add our inner circle, including the Melrose, and it turned out that was more than enough to manage.

Luckily my old friend Kristin, who I met in Tulsa as a teenager, was present and I dubbed her "Mama Mardi Gras" because she helped with the babysitting. Tasks included getting Rick to pull up his pants and put away his dangling penis, and alerting everyone when my drunken niece Emily flailed down Russell with a crowd of strangers.

Clyde was beside himself with worry as he barreled through the throngs of revelers looking for her. We found Emily with a bindi on her forehead, and there was much drunken speculation that she may have gotten married to an Indian gentleman while on her adventure.

Cody, dressed in a white faux fur coat, was standing in the turret windows when his infamously hotheaded estranged husband Jasper Greeley spotted him.

Jasper was a short, bald, tan, muscular guy in his 40s—about fifteen years older than Cody and two years older than me—with already-dated tribal tattoos on his arms and torso. Cody had moved to Denver with Jasper for about a year, during which time the bipolar Jasper would instigate fist fights with him, lose the fist fights, and then call the police on Cody.

"If you love a Black man, you don't call the police on him," I said to Jasper one night at JJ's during an altercation.

"You wanna know what my issue is with you, Andoe?" Jasper began while standing inches from my face that night at JJ's. "Whenever we fight, Cody tells me he'd still be with you if you hadn't broken it off."

"I was too old for him," I replied pointedly, without blinking.

Cody, who enjoyed skiing and other outdoor activities, loved the Colorado mountains but the marriage was terrible and he missed his friends. He returned to St. Louis just in time for our 2016 Melrose Christmas Party where he and Kage danced and carried on shirtless. The two were like brothers.

From the Mardi Gras street below, Jasper yelled something rude before chucking a full can of beer at Cody, which Cody caught in mid-air and chucked right back at him. Cody was so pissed he acted like he was going to walk out of the second-story window as if it were a doorway, and probably would have had several of us not pulled him back.

Being in the most iconic window in all of Soulard, the turret was widely photographed in local media, including a wonderful *Riverfront Times* shot of Auntie M and his wildly costumed troupe tossing beads to the masses. Behind them in the shot was Emily in a haunting pose, her alabaster face staring out of the darkness like a specter.

I dubbed her, "The Lurking Lady."

The Day After Laundry Day

Ms. Jamieson's birthday fell on a Friday, and the Melrose invited her to Friendly's, the bar a few doors down, for drinks.

"Thanks, but Friday is my laundry day, so I'm staying in," she replied.

We already knew she was unlikely to deviate from her routine, even on her birthday, so we had planned a shindig at our place for the following evening. The lovely custom cake read, *Happy Day After Laundry Day*.

Oversharing

Ms. Jamieson was terrible about oversharing on Facebook. The main issue was her venting about flaky men in the dating scene, particularly ones who "ghosted," which is when someone you've been chatting with or seeing just flatlines with no further communication.

She seemed to believe that if she vented about it enough, those who ghosted would feel regret and apologize, when of course that's not how the world works. But it's how she wanted it to work. Ghosting was all the rage with Millennials. It wasn't going anywhere, but there was no convincing Ms. Jamieson that society would not change to suit her. I stressed that she would have to adapt, and the first step was to not ruin one's own brand and perceived desirability by constantly talking about being ghosted.

One afternoon she was telling me about a date she had the day before.

"We was sitting there and DJ walked by and I pointed him out and said, 'I don't like him because we was dating for a few weeks and then he ghosted me and I hate when people ghost me,'" Ms. Jamieson recalled as my head fell in my hands.

"Why would you tell a date that?" I groaned.

After a dry spell, Ms. Jamieson fell hard for a guy she met at a massive bear event that took over an entire downtown hotel. It seemed the feelings were mutual, because the guy was flying in from Wisconsin to see her a few weeks later.

"I decided we're not having sex while he's here. I want to build something with him."

"What? You met him mid-gang bang!" I exclaimed.

And that was a true story. The guy was getting fucked in a bathroom stall by Clyde when Ms. Jamieson wandered in, took a turn and fell in love.

Her mind was made up. The guy came to town, and each evening I'm sure he could hear the Price is Right losing horn as Ms. Jamieson strapped on her CPAP machine at bedtime. He flew home, and he ghosted.

Ms. Jamieson was just itching to tell the world about it and to shame him, but I worked overtime coaching her on how to present herself.

"The best thing to do is act relaxed and post about positive things going on."

She took my advice for several days, but I didn't realize that each day she didn't overshare, the pressure was only building, and when she blew, it was going to be a mess.

Then one Sunday morning I opened up Facebook to the notification: "Jordan Jamieson was live. 3:48 a.m."

My stomach dropped.

"Fuck."

The Video

The scene opens with a puffy, red-faced Ms. Jamieson chowing down on potato chips for several minutes while mean mugging the camera without saying a word until finally growling, "Well I see nobody gives a FUCK I'm on Facebook Live!"

And from there it only gets worse. Still crunching and munching, she begins sobbing, snot running down her lip, as she tells her audience about being ghosted again, getting loud and wailing, "AND I TOLD HIM I HATE TO BE GHOSTED!"

It goes on and on, until she runs out of chips and stays on camera as she retrieves a corndog from the freezer, microwaves and then gnaws on it live, still sobbing.

One of her friends was doing his best to comfort her before saying, "I am jealous of that corn dog though!"

Kage's Presence

I was working on getting my real estate license for the fifth time and I was grouchy. The first time was in Oklahoma City when I was 19, second was in St. Louis when I was about 25. Third was in Oklahoma City when I moved back in 2006. Forth was when I returned to St. Louis for the second time in 2008. I didn't expect to return again, so I hadn't maintained it and doing the online coursework all over again had me in a foul mood.

As I was sitting at the kitchen table working on the class, I noticed that Kage was sitting in there with me, playing on his phone. It occurred to me he had been doing that regularly.

I remember once seeing my sister-in-law sitting at the table while my nephew did his homework, and I thought about how nice that was at the time. As a child I had a desk pushed against my bedroom corner, pre-internet, of course, and it felt so isolated and non-conducive to learning. Learning and working were unpleasant things one did while being sequestered from the world.

My closest sibling was nearly a decade older, my dad died when I was only 18 months, and I envied nuclear families with homes full of fun and life. And then as an adult, even while in a relationship, I grew accustomed to doing many things alone.

But Kage's companionship warmed my soul. My favorite part of the day was when he would get home from work. As he was peeling off his clothes, he'd excitedly tell me a story, and that would often lead to him bowling over in laughter.

Midnight Chat

One weeknight I woke up and couldn't go back to sleep. I checked the Melrose Chat and Clyde was the only one active, so we chatted for a few minutes and then I suggested he come over to chat in person.

Sitting in the darkened apartment we discussed the contrast between his old life in Anna and the life he had in St. Louis. He was the most chill, even-keeled guy, and always expressed gratitude for the opportunities we'd given him and spoke about how much he loved his life now.

A week or so earlier he was at one of our parties and he and I found ourselves alone in the kitchen as he was telling a story about his mom when he stopped himself. "Sorry. I know everyone probably gets tired of me talking about my mom" he said.

"We don't mind at all," I replied. "I have a feeling your mom wants me to do this for her," I said as I gave him a hug.

He had been alone, but found his tribe.

Kage woke to our laughter, stumbled into the living room confused, and sat with us for a few minutes. Clyde then made his exit, and we got a few more hours sleep.

The Peanut Gallery

The apartment wasn't the home I longed for, but we were still able to throw some memorable parties there. I remember Kage and Cody having a dance-off in the living room, seven smokers on the balcony, conversations around a full candlelit buffet in the kitchen, and Clyde dragging a trick off to our bedroom for a XXX throwdown.

"Oh my God, that is so tacky. Why is he doing that here?" neighborhood friend Chris Kerr exclaimed.

For my part, I wandered in with a guest named Mark. There was a sofa in the bedroom where we sat and watched the show while discussing the scene as if it were behind a screen, or somehow anonymous.

We were snapped out of that illusion when our incessant chatting was interrupted by the bear who was getting fucked.

"Quiet in the Peanut Gallery!"

Rick's Heart

Rick had a heart condition his entire life, and his doctors said it was time for an aortic valve replacement.

"Dude, it's weird to think I could die during this," he said.

Since he was going to be out of work I decided to throw him a benefit, and asked "Queen of Controversy" Janessa Highland to emcee it. I felt that she was the appropriate choice since both she and Rick were people I first paid attention to after hearing bad things.

In Rick's case it was how he was banned from bars for fighting, and in Highland's it was how she upset the apple cart with her blunt takes on the status quo after moving to town from Springfield, Missouri.

We held the event at Bar PM, which featured an entertaining show and a silent auction that raised nearly two thousand dollars.

The surgery went well, and for a moment Rick felt like he had a new lease on life.

"I really thought I would die," he said. "Now it's kinda weird, and I'm wondering what to do with myself."

Home Sweet Hovel

I shake my head when I think about how I cleaned Clyde's windows before he moved in, and gave him a giant painting. Nothing I imagined as far as how he'd reside in the renovated corner apartment came to pass. He used the massive painting to block his bedroom window. He didn't decorate, his mattress was on the floor, and he didn't seem to know how to clean.

Walking Brawny, I came across Clyde sitting on his front steps.

"So, I know this will probably come out of my deposit or whatever but the other day I needed to open a bottle and used the countertop and chipped it."

"That's a brand-new kitchen!" I exclaimed, stunned by his lazy disregard.

"I know but I couldn't find the bottle opener and I wanted to open the bottle!" he said.

What bothered me most was how dark he kept his place. It was like a cave, regardless of how nice it was outside.

"That bird needs fresh air and sunlight," I repeatedly said.

He inherited the talking bird from his mother and loved it a great deal, but didn't see the need to give her a bright window now and then.

"I'm on the first floor and don't want people seeing in!" he'd reply.

His windows were 10ft above street level and there was no way anyone could see in on a sunny day, but there was no getting through to him.

The Change

It was Pride Weekend of 2017. We were taking an afternoon nap in preparation for a big evening out when I woke to Rick passionately kissing me. I nudged Kage with my elbow to rouse him, and he nonchalantly rolled over to face the scene as if it were an everyday occurrence.

"Dude, I'm rolling," Rick said. "I've got to go, but leave the back door unlocked. I wanna come up later tonight."

We hadn't been sexually involved with Rick since we had been neighbors. There had been just one minor rendezvous at the Christy a year or so prior. We were at JJ's with our lesbian friend Sarah (who later officiated our wedding) when we got separated from her and Rick suggested we go back to my place. In our celebratory state we figured Sarah went home, despite living forty minutes away, and we left. After about half an hour Kage's phone blew up with irate messages. Of course she was livid that we had left, but she had also fallen in a pothole puddle on the club's lot and nobody helped her up. She had a skinned knee, and was as pleased as a wet cat. Our interlude came to an abrupt end when she finally arrived at our door, pounding furiously.

"Sometimes you've got to deal with the big lesbian at the door," I said, which became one of our new sayings.

Back at the Melrose after the night's Pride festivities, Clyde saw that Rick's door was open and stopped in. By this point Rick had several guys over and things were getting playful. They engaged Clyde for a few minutes, but he wasn't their type and they sought to get back to regular programming.

"Chris and Kage's back door is open," Rick said as a way to lure him out.

"It is?" Clyde replied, intrigued.

We had been in bed for maybe fifteen minutes when we heard the door open. Although Rick was famously flaky, we figured it had to be him. We heard heavy steps through the kitchen, and then the hall. It was Clyde.

"Rick tastes good," he giggled as he stood there drunk.

All the lights were out, but there was enough street light pouring in from the glass block bathroom window to illuminate his proud smirk. We were dubious about his claim.

He unzipped his pants and clumsily fell backwards onto the bed.

Kage jumped up.

"No, we're not doing this. Go home," he said.

"I'll go home in a minute; would you just get me off first?" Clyde asked.

"No," Kage said while turning on the light. "Go home, Clyde."

"Well, can I at least make a drink?" Clyde asked.

"No!" Kage replied.

Clyde lumbered out the way he came in, grumbling all the way, and Kage locked the door behind him.

When Kage woke the following morning, he'd received several angry messages from Clyde.

"I can't believe you'd kick me out! You wouldn't have kicked Rick out!" Clyde said, followed by various comments in the same vein.

The argument with Kage continued in the morning.

"I bet you two had sex after I left," Clyde said accusingly.

"Chris is my husband and I don't have to explain what we do!"

When Clyde deescalated, he made a startling revelation.

"I kinda expected that at some point we'd be a triad."

"That was never our intention," Kage said.

After some back-and-forth Clyde also admitted he had been trying to be someone he wasn't since first meeting us.

"I've been putting on this fake persona of who I thought you guys wanted me to be, pretending to be happy all the time. Pretending to be the manly straight guy who happens to like guys, like how Chris describes me. Pretending I don't have feelings."

Clyde said he needed some space, and was going to take time to sort things out. In less than 24 hours he was back, saying he was over it.

"I was picking up on something that wasn't there, and I'm fine now. Please don't pull away from our friendship. It was nothing."

Ms. Magali's Grand Departure

It was around 2003 when my boss Peter, an elegant gay Swedish businessman running a San Francisco property company, abruptly promoted me to a regional manager position after several external hires in a row backed out upon receiving better offers. I was young, about 28, and clearly not ready, but I seized the opportunity.

By far the largest and most complicated property in my portfolio was the historic Cadillac Hotel, which contained over 150 rooms for formerly homeless people above half a dozen commercial spaces. It sat in the heart of the city's gritty and congested Tenderloin Neighborhood, where at any time of the day or night you were likely to see homeless encampments, prostitution, drug deals, people injecting heroin, and people urinating and defecating on the sidewalk.

Managing the property for decades was Magali, an older, impeccably dressed Cuban woman who had a mythical reputation within the organization. Employee turnover for this type of housing was high, with similar models going through new management teams annually. My friend Wes managed a neighborhood building and was stabbed in the chest by a tenant.

For the most part, corporate policy was to leave Magali alone and pray to God she never left. Magali and the Cadillac were semi-autonomous, mostly reporting directly to the hotel's hands-on owners, Leroy and Kathy Looper. (Kathy was one of the people who offered to help me deal with the abandoned Fiat).

I knew that my first order of business was meeting with Magali and making sure she was happy and cared for, so I scheduled a lunch at the famed Cliff House, perched high above the sparkling Pacific and so historically significant, even Mark Twain wrote about it. While Magali was a woman of few words, it was clear she appreciated the way I dealt with her, and the two of us became friends, even doing happy hours on occasion.

Not only was she never attacked by a tenant in all those years, the tenants were wary of *her*. In *Delusions of Grandeur,* I recalled a story about one of the times we had to go to court together for an eviction. The tenant was a big, tough-looking ex-con who hadn't paid his rent, and was making excuses for his lack of payment by citing things he claimed were wrong with the room. The judge pressed him on why he had never reported any of this to management.

The nervous and frustrated tenant stumbled and fumbled before loudly exclaiming, "Your honor, I be AFRAID of Miss Magali!"

When I left after a few years to run an operation in Oklahoma City, she came to visit, and when I then moved to St. Louis, she visited again. I returned to San Francisco for another four years, where I again oversaw the Cadillac.

The gentleman who succeeded me did not have the same regard for Magali, and when Peter retired to Puerto Vallarta the institutional reverence long afforded her all but vanished. After her supervisor came at her the wrong way one too many times, she submitted her notice. She was retirement age anyway, but the problem was she had to leave the manager's unit she'd been occupying all those years, and the average rent for a studio apartment in the city was more than her entire monthly retirement income.

Born in Cuba, raised in New York, having lived in Puerto Rico, Miami, and then thirty years in San Francisco, moving wasn't a radical notion, and was something she knew would come at some point. Most San Franciscans, having witnessed the relentless purge of long-term tenants, knew the day would come that they would have to leave. San Francisco was a city for the young and affluent.

She messaged to say that she had quit and would be considering where to move to next.

"If you think you might be interested in St. Louis, I could get you a nice one-bedroom in a lovely neighborhood for $600," I casually tossed out.

I expected her to possibly consider the offer. Maybe reply with an, "Okay I'll think about it," or tell me about all the cities under consideration. Instead, she simply said, "Okay, let's do that."

At the time, there were frequent news stories of pets dying on airplanes, and she was worried about her two beloved cats. I spoke to Kage, and we volunteered to fly to San Francisco, rent a car, and drive her and the cats cross country. Three ten-hour days.

I arranged a dinner at the Cliff House for the evening before our departure, and included the surviving Cadillac owner Kathy Looper, who was like a mother to me. The landmark was not only historically significant, but it was personally relevant. I took Magali on several occasions, and once dined there with Kathy Looper and my old boss Peter. I thought of all the history, and how Leroy Looper had since passed away, Peter retired, and how Kathy would be saying goodbye to Magali after so many years. I thought we'd enjoy one last Pacific sunset together.

Even though Mark Twain's Cliff House story involved fog, I failed to consider the possibility. It was so foggy, you could see the crashing waves below and make out a solitary silhouette on the beach, but nothing more. I wasn't in the moment as much as I wish I had been either, with some anxiety over a three day drive with cats in the car. But it was still magical, and I'm glad we went.

The next morning we arrived at the Cadillac in a small SUV, and walked in the grand two-story lobby. Rhonda, a young woman who had worked the day shift at the front desk for over five years, gave me a hello pregnant with emotion.

Magali was Queen of the Cadillac, the Leona Hemsley of the Tenderloin (similar intimidating façade but much kinder). Her staff was at her disposal for anything she needed. One evening I was out drinking and decided to stop in with some friends to visit. The elderly Filipino desk clerk was alarmed at the intrusion, and waving his hands said, "No, no, no! Nobody see Miss Magali!" and shooed me away.

Magali was standing with her best friend Jazz and several trusted employees as tenants, scattered about, watched teary-eyed.

"You're so kind to do this for her," one woman said.

It struck me because I certainly didn't see it as an act of charity. She was a friend I enjoyed, and I was always pulling people to St. Louis. But in the Tenderloin, there was a sense of being stuck. Despite being in the middle of everything the city had to offer, it was a containment zone, of sorts. A place of last resort for those with few options, filled with formerly-homeless housing and related services. Even though Magali was not in the same boat as her residents, she did reside at the property, and she had been unsure about where to go. It must have seemed novel for two much younger unrelated men to show up in a shiny new vehicle and whisk her off to a new life far away.

For the tenants and the employees, Magali was an institution, as permanent as the pillars holding up the lobby ceiling. One by one they respectfully said their goodbyes, and it felt like a president leaving the White House for the final time as she made her way out. Even the people on the street, all who knew and respected her, stopped to watch the procession.

I had left the city twice feeling forever young, knowing that Peter was at the helm and that Leroy, Kathy and Magali were at the Cadillac, and they always would be. I felt confident my place was waiting should I ever decide to give it a go for the third time. But the generations before me were vanishing, and I was no longer that young man swinging from the trees. Everything about this departure felt final.

We pulled away from the waving people of the Cadillac knowing the curtains had closed on our San Francisco.

Clyde Crosses the Line

It was a late summer night and Clyde noticed Rick's door was open.

"Hey, can I hang out?" Clyde asked as he walked in, smelling pot in the air.

"Sure. Just playing video games," Rick replied.

Clyde was drunk, Rick was high, and the two sat on Rick's small sofa staring at the television. Clyde said, "Just keep playing," as he leaned over and began to undo Rick's pants.

"Naw, naw, I'm good," Rick said as he pushed Clyde back.

Clyde sat upright for less than a minute, and then lunged back to Rick's crotch, aggressively unbuttoning his jeans.

"I SAID NO!" Rick said as he shoved the much larger Clyde with all his might, injuring his own wrist and Clyde's neck.

"Geeze!" Clyde exclaimed. "You always boast about being this proud whore and I guess if I'm the only person in the building you're not attracted to, it's whatever."

Both shared identical versions of the events the following day. We were taken aback that Clyde seemed to feel entitled to have sex with Rick, and he became irritated when we expressed that.

Rick insisted he did not want a big deal made of it, but also stressed that he was traumatized and did not feel safe around Clyde.

"I don't know man, that messed me up," Rick said.

Mysterious Meeting

On June 19, 2017, I received the following email:

Hi Chris,

Nick Phillips here w/ the Riverfront Times. Our EIC Sarah Fenske suggested I reach out to you.

I'm managing a special project and I'd like to ask your advice on some things. Could I buy you a coffee or tea either tomorrow evening or anytime Wednesday? Can meet you anywhere that's convenient.

Thanks!
Nick Phillips

I had no idea what this could be about, but speculated it involved my Dustin Mitchell reporting. I told him I was more of a cocktail guy, and he suggested the Gin Room on South Grand.

Phillips was an attractive, conservatively dressed, presumably straight white guy of about 35. He'd been living in Guatemala until recently and we spoke a bit about our backgrounds before he told me why we were there.

"The parent company of the *Riverfront Times* wants to launch a glossy LGBTQ magazine. I'd like your thoughts on what the community would like to see and if you'd be interested in playing a role. Maybe a guest column for the first issue," he said, and then asked what I'd write about.

"I'd like to write about Alton," I began. "It's the most bisexual town I've ever experienced, so much so I've dubbed it 'The Bi-Muda Triangle.'"

Phillips was excited about the idea, and asked if I might be interested in the role of Editor in Chief, while clearly stating he wasn't in a position to officially offer that.

"Oh, you don't want me. I'm far too controversial," I said.

"What do you think Darin Slyman would say about us launching this magazine?" he asked.

"He'd probably say, 'Bless your heart!'" I laughed as Phillips blinked with surprise. "He's fatigued with the community and says there's no money in it. He's launched a new fashion magazine and is focused on that. *Vital Voice* is on hiatus, and will come back as an online publication once the fashion magazine is established."

Phillips said he would be in touch, and I called Darin to fill him in on the meeting.

"He asked what you'd think about it and I said you'd probably say 'Bless their hearts,'" I told him as we both laughed.

Since writing about the LGBTQ community was what I did, and there was no work with *Vital Voice* for the time being, I told Darin and his business partner Jimmy that I would like to be involved with the new magazine, should it materialize, and they gave me their blessing.

Out in STL Debuts

After several delays which made me doubt that a first issue would come to fruition, things kicked into gear, and on September 20, 2017, *Out in STL* was on the stands. Nick Phillips was the interim editor in chief for the first issue, and I was a contributor.

I was in Soulard that afternoon and stopped by a short-lived gay bar called The Stable to get a copy. I was so excited, and I took a photo of the magazine to post to social media, and then sat at a quiet table by the window to absorb it. Or at least I hoped it would be a quiet table.

"Hey, whatchyou got there?" said a flirty day drunk.

"It's a new magazine and I've got a feature in it. I wanted to read it before I left," I said, making a show of continuing to read but being mindful to not come off as rude.

"You know you're quite handsome," the red and puffy day drunk slurred.

I was only relieved from him when someone else began an unwanted conversation.

"That's your magazine? You should run a piece on my restaurant. We have concerts and . . ."

"I could put you in touch with our ad rep if you'd like," I said.

"But if you write it as a story, I won't have to pay," the pushy man said with a smirk, as if he felt savvy and pleased with himself for the thrifty workaround.

My attempt to peruse the magazine wasn't going well, and then the Facebook notifications began blowing up.

Darin and Jimmy brought the shade, which I hadn't anticipated since I'd gotten their blessing to work on the project. What I didn't know was that in the interim, they had a meeting with publisher Chris Keating about the possibility of selling him *Vital Voice*, and it ended with Darin accusing him of fishing for information, and then storming out.

"Or you could support LOCAL business instead of some STRAIGHT GUY from CLEVELAND who just wants to make a buck off the community!" Darin commented on my photo.

The two went on about how the publication was a corporate product and not of the community. Then I was floored when they suggested readers instead support *#Boom*.

"Darin there is nobody, and I mean nobody who has done more damage to your standing in the community than Colin Murphy. The Grove got so bad you could hardly show your face without getting spat on. And do you realize everything you're saying about *Out in STL* is what *#Boom* has been saying about *Vital Voice* for years? And I've spilled a lot of ink defending you."

After some back and forth they dialed back, and even complimented the cleverness of the title of my piece on Alton, "The Bi-Muda Triangle."

Everyone was glued to that thread, including the publishers watching from the wings to see if the community would reject the magazine. They determined I was who they needed steering the ship.

The realignment of alliances was disorienting. After a decade firmly in the *Vital Voice* camp, it seemed they'd become frenemies, and Kitty, the *RFT* ad rep dedicated to *Out in STL*, was best friends with Darin's biggest nemesis, Alan Cobb. Alan was a longtime critic and thorn in the side of *Vital Voice*, and Darin long blamed Alan for steering business away from his magazine.

I was now going to Just John, which long felt like the belly of the beast for us at *Vital Voice*, complete with *#Boom's* snarling Margie Werther guarding the door. I would go there to socialize and work on projects with people who'd been my adversaries for years.

When I was announced as editor in chief, Alan texted Kitty to say something to the effect that I was the worst possible choice and that I was an enemy of Pride St. Louis.

Navigating the Weirdness of Alton, Illinois— Out in STL, September 2017

I consider Alton, Illinois, the undiscovered Sausalito of the Mississippi River. It's a picturesque town about 22 miles north of the Arch, a place with dramatic topography and grand vistas. It also happens to have mysteries below the surface. And a Historic Museum of Torture Devices.

The museum's proprietor is Janet Kolar, Alton's hearse-driving (and hearse-racing) "Mistress of the Macabre." A couple of years ago, I was writing a Halloween feature for the *Vital Voice* and I wanted to profile her. My interview requests went unanswered, so one Saturday afternoon I stopped by the Mineral Springs Antique Mall, where her museum is located. Inside the lobby I passed several shops packed with glassware, then turned down a long, dimly lit corridor leading to the museum. The gates were foreboding—and padlocked. I began to leave.

"Who are you looking for?" asked a nearby shopkeeper.

"Janet Kolar," I replied, "but she's not here."

"Oh, she's around. Just have a seat and she'll be back by."

So I downshifted out of my city rhythm and settled in. Before long, she arrived. I introduced myself, asking if this would be a good time to talk.

"I'm here and you're here," she replied serenely, "so this is a good time."

What followed was part discussion and part seance—and one of the most fascinating interviews of my life.

That anecdote speaks to the way one should approach Alton. Unless you downshift, settle in and observe, you'll miss the story.

That's especially true at Bubby & Sissy's, a bar that hosts several highly attended drag shows each week. After I began dating my husband, who is from Alton, I became a semi-regular at the bar. While the employees and owners are "family," the patrons, at first blush, seemed largely straight. But as I met people, I heard stories about the times some of them fell into what I call the "Bi-Muda Triangle"— a realm where long-established sexual preferences can momentarily fade or vanish altogether. I realized there was something about Alton that lowered the barriers between queer and straight.

Treva Swain works the door at Bubby & Sissy's. She talks about girls crowding in for bachelorette parties only to make out with women by the end of the night. Then there's the trans woman who sometimes arrives with a boyfriend, and sometimes a girlfriend. And then there were the shows in which entertainer Trixie LaRue randomly assembled a group of mostly straight men from the audience and within minutes had them all dancing through the crowd in their underwear.

Drag Show Director Teighlor Demornay says that at Bubby & Sissy's, labels are not central to one's identity, and self-exploration and experimentation are common.

"Our bar's famous for our tagline, 'An open-minded place,'" Demornay says. "So people know it's safe for them to lower their inhibitions and be themselves."

Sarah Edington is a regular who makes the 40-minute drive from St. Charles just to enjoy the vibe, which to her feels more welcoming than anywhere else.

"In most bars, bi folk get open hostility," she says. "But Bubs is friendly to us."

In Alton, the relative openness to bisexual activity extends past the confines of one bar. Native Brian Ray, who doesn't even frequent Bubby & Sissy's, estimates that 90 percent of his sexual encounters in the area have been with men who identify as straight. Similarly, Chris Keidel, the openly gay owner of the burger bar Bottle & Barrel, spends much of his time with straight male friends. "And that leads to me hanging out with a guy having a great time, and every now and then, it leads to something much more fun with someone no one ever suspected would be in a same-sex relationship."

You might think you know LGBT St. Louis inside and out. You may have even visited Alton, utilizing all the navigational tools at your disposal, and found nothing out of the ordinary. But when exploring the town's Bi-Muda Triangle, it's important to understand those tools are of little use.

Here, you can't even rely on your gaydar.

Colin Murphy Extends an Olive Branch

Having read the entire exchange where he was called out by name, Colin Murphy extended an olive branch, asking if we could start anew. While only five years older, I felt he was like my media father. I said I would like us to have a clean slate.

About a month after the first issue of *Out in STL* debuted I was formally named Editor in Chief, and received a message from him which meant a lot to me:

Congrats on joining the exclusive club of editors for STL LGBT publications. It's a small but storied group and we stand on the shoulders of giants who prepared the ground since 'Mandrake' launched in 1969-70. Always defend and encourage your writers when possible, edit gently, but without fear; make the hard choices and keep your community at heart, and when you fuck up, correct, apologize and move on. Lastly, if you thought writing put a target on your back be prepared for double criticism. I know you have a thick skin so you'll be fine. Best of luck.

"Thank you, Colin," I replied. "As I've always said, you're the one who gave me my first break and I'll always be appreciative of that. I'm glad we've buried the hatchet."

Before the media divorce, *Vital Voice* was a powerhouse and was the center of gravity in regional LGBTQ media. I knew that *Out in STL* couldn't come close to that unless there was a consolidation of talent. I made the case to publisher Chris Keating that we should acquire both *#Boom* and *Vital Voice*. Because of the disastrous meeting he had with Darin and Jimmy, he wanted to pursue *#Boom* first, and had me invite Colin and Colin to the *RFT's* Downtown office.

I simply told Murphy that the meeting was to discuss ways we could work together, so they were floored when, sitting across from us at a big conference table, Keating said, "We want to buy *#Boom*."

Even I was surprised, not expecting him to just cut to the chase.

"What would that mean for us?" Murphy asked. "What would keep you from firing us?"

"*#Boom* is nothing without you guys. What we're wanting is your talent," I replied. "And I've already told Keating that a non-compete clause won't fly because you'll never stop writing," I said with a laugh, in reference to the lawsuit with *Vital Voice*.

"You do your homework," Colin Lovett replied.

"I wrote the book."

"We know," he deadpanned.

"Well, I'm frankly shocked," Murphy said. "We've been around for years and have an established reputation. If anything, it seems *#Boom* should be buying *Out in STL*. We are beloved in the community and I think many would not be happy with us becoming a corporate product."

After some back and forth, Lovett asked, "Are you open to changing the name to *#Boom*?"

I didn't really know Lovett, but long held the position that he was overrated. An assessment, in retrospect, that was based on nothing. I think my bias against him was due to feeling he was the son Murphy took in the divorce. This meeting was the first time I engaged with him, and I was impressed with his performance.

Keating looked at me, and I said taking their name was something we could consider.

Colin and Colin agreed to talk it over and follow up. Another meeting was scheduled, and the day it was to take place, Keating asked me to attend on my own. I had vague numbers and was tasked with hammering out the rough outlines of a deal. I knew Colin Murphy would likely be offended by Keating not being present, so I sent him an email giving him a heads up. He replied a few hours later with a flimsy excuse about not being able to attend, which I forwarded to Keating with one comment: *The shade!*

Within days Keating instead bought a paper in Cincinnati. Not only was there no longer the money or bandwidth to pursue *#Boom,* the *Out in STL* budget was cut as sales fell short of projections. The window of opportunity to make something big happen had closed.

Out in STL Editor's Letter—December 2017

Out to Prove LGBTQ Media Isn't Dead

Twenty years ago, I was living in Oklahoma City and decided to spread my wings and move to a larger metropolitan area. I wanted to be within a comfortable day's drive of my family in Tulsa, and I had a few options, none of them ideal.

There was no adventure in moving to Dallas. It was full of insufferable Oklahomans who acted like their 200-mile move was akin to conquering Paris. Kansas City seemed pleasant, but was also too similar to my hometown. And Denver, the capital of the state that had recently passed the homophobic Amendment 2, didn't sound like a welcoming place.

But there was a mysterious dark horse 500 miles to the northeast, the last eastern metropolis: St. Louis. And nobody had anything good to say about it.

"Oh, it's awful," began a friend who had traveled to the city on business. "The best way I can describe it is it's like Gotham City. It's really old and crumbling, with soot-stained buildings, crowded rowhouses, smokestacks . . ."

Everything I heard only piqued my interest. This was the adventure I was looking for—and without knowing a soul in this city, I made it my home. I've since wandered around, living from San Francisco to New York, but this place has remained my muse, inspiring my book and pulling me back time and again.

Some cities have no memories. Some are just nice, sedate places without roots, while others have transient populations and ephemeral cultures. In such cities, clean slates are easy to come by. St. Louis is not among them. Ours is an opera of larger-than-life characters with long histories of collaboration and conflict. Ours is a haunted city that writhes, a passionate city that burns. Ours is a saga to keep a writer like myself busy for a lifetime.

Now, two decades on—after first being discovered by venerable journalist Colin Murphy, then ten years working under the direction of Darin Slyman (the Miranda Priestly of St. Louis)—I'm deeply honored to be chosen to take the helm of this audacious magazine.

The industry consensus is that LGBTQ media is dead. Out in STL, however, is making a bold bet: that if we deliver a high-quality product that reflects and connects us, LGBTQ media can thrive.

I'm betting my reputation on it.

Magali in the Media

Magali wasn't in town long before she was interviewed by the *Riverfront Times*. The editor asked if I had any leads for their feature on people who had recently made major life changes. I gave her a few options and she chose Magali.

We weren't sure when the piece would come out as we gathered for a release party for the latest *Out in STL* issue at Evangeline's, a French Creole bistro in the Central West End. Magali found herself seated next to Alex Braun, whom I dubbed "The Queen of Camp" due to his love of game shows, retro furniture, and his vintage vacuum collection. In time she would grow to like and care about him, but she initially found him dull and irritating.

"Andoe should have put *me* in the book because I'm the Queen of Camp!" Alex Braun said. "I'm sure he'll put me in the next one or in the magazine," he rambled on.

The *Riverfront Times* editor arrived and I asked her when Magali's piece was dropping.

"Oh, it came out today!" she said, surprised I didn't know.

I walked over to the stand by the door, picked up a copy and opened it to a large, distinguished photo of Magali sitting proudly on her front steps. .

Ms. Braun was mid-sentence when I walked over and presented the opened issue to Magali, and I'd never seen her so excited as she balled up her fists and did a little dance in her chair.

She then turned and patted Alex on the knee. "Someone will write something about you someday."

Bouncer

Despite earning a decent full-time wage at a factory, Clyde was having problems making ends meet. We figured he blew his budget on tequila and junk food.

Because of his imposing size, the owners of the neighboring bar Friendly's decided he would make a good weekend bouncer. A one-minute walk from the Melrose, the sports bar's patio felt like our own yard, and Brawny was so loved and at home the owner let him walk up and down the bar top greeting everyone in his nonchalant way.

Clyde accepted the weekend position, but when he was still struggling despite the added income I asked if he'd be interested in being an on-site manager.

"The Christy hasn't had anyone on site for some time, and if you were interested, I could probably get you a rent-free apartment in exchange for keeping the grounds clean and handling lock outs," I told him.

He seemed simultaneously intrigued and hurt. Intrigued by the possibility of getting free rent, but hurt that we would be okay with him leaving the Melrose.

"When Rick was having money problems you threw him a benefit!" he said, as if needing heart surgery and spending too much on tequila and pizza were somehow equivalent crises. But everything always went back to how unfair life was.

The fact was we thought him getting away from the building would be best for all involved. He was fixated on us and was struggling to deal with his emotions. Maybe he'd broaden his horizons if he had that mile buffer.

In classic Clyde fashion, he latched onto the tentative offer as a new vehicle for manipulation. When he felt things were going well, he'd take it off the table altogether.

"Free rent would be awesome but I wouldn't want to leave everyone at the Melrose," he'd say. "It's too much fun here."

When there was conflict with Kage, however, he'd toss out the possibility as a way to get attention. Tension would arise, for instance, when Kage would pick him up for a planned activity, like Pokémon in the park, and Clyde would pass out in the car within minutes because he was drunk.

"I don't know why I'm trying so hard to stay here, I know Kage is ready to be rid of me," he'd say, practically demanding we assure him that wasn't the case. "Is that building bouncer position still available?"

"It's a resident manager position," I corrected.

He'd used the term "building bouncer" several times and it hit me like fingernails on a chalkboard.

Clyde's communication style could be described as convoluted and manipulative. Nearly everything he said or did was to lay the groundwork for the response he desired, or an argument for not getting that response.

When he first arrived, we'd given him a key to our place, and whenever we'd have the slightest disagreement, he'd insist on returning the key. If we refused it, he'd drop it through the mail slot with a note saying he wasn't comfortable having it.

He'd also leave group chats for the same reason. When things blew over, he'd hint about getting the key back and would outright ask if he could re-enter the group chat, at which time he'd audit everything he had missed, often objecting to the characterizations of why he left.

The final time he returned the key I told Kage we were done playing the game. We never offered it to him again. The fact we had a key to his apartment (since I had a building master) but he didn't have a key to ours grated on him, which he'd reveal through passive-aggressive comments.

When we started having my niece Emily feed our cats when we were away instead of him, he once again brought up The Christy.

"Is that building position available? I'm not really part of anything here anymore. I don't have keys and nobody needs my help with anything. I might as well move."

"Clyde please don't mention this position again unless you're serious. I'm sticking my neck out for you," I replied.

After some thought he said he was honestly interested, and I arranged an interview with my boss for the following week.

Clyde arrived at the office and seemed to have put a lot of work into making himself presentable.

"Hey, Clyde! You look really nice!" I said.

His demeanor was quite odd. He did not make eye contact and was blinking excessively. This carried through the awkward interview where he sat stiff as a board and did not smile.

When asked if he had any questions, he asked, "So if I need to help with lockouts, will I get a master key or something?"

Ms. Jamieson came to my office later to ask how it went.

"For years I worked so hard to maintain a firewall between my day job and everything else. Today I sat through that interview watching Clyde ask my boss about a master key—because of course that's his focus—and I thought to myself, 'Well, I'm in a real pickle.'"

Yell Mail

Clyde developed a habit of doing the opposite of anything we told him. For example, he was cat sitting one weekend and Kage said, "You can have anything you want except the cookie dough in the refrigerator."

Sure enough, Clyde got into it. When confronted, Clyde said, "I woke up in a haze and thought it would be okay."

"That was the one thing I asked of you." Kage replied.

"I know. I wasn't thinking. I'm sorry."

We had returned on a late Sunday afternoon and Clyde was passed out in our bed from the night before. The cats hadn't been fed and the place was a disaster.

The following weekend, he and Kage were at JJ's and Clyde became enraged over something trivial and tried to punch Kage, who was faster and avoided the blow. Kage went to his car to leave and Clyde ran after him and jumped in the vehicle.

Kage put it in park right in the middle of the road, pulled the key, and got out.

"You're not riding with me." Kage said.

"You promised me a ride home, so you're taking me home."

Someone who saw the scene offered to give Clyde a ride, which resolved the immediate crisis.

When something like this happened, and things like this were becoming common, Clyde would apologize profusely upon waking up the next afternoon.

"Oh my God guys, I'm so sorry," he'd say. "We're alright now, right?"

If we didn't give him instant absolution, if for instance we said something about not wanting to discuss it, Clyde would keep pressing or would start a fresh argument.

After the JJ's incident, Kage wanted space. Clyde was working the door at Friendly's and was beside himself with anxiety and grief. He left his post to walk the short block to the Melrose, where he messaged me from the sidewalk.

"Please, Chris. Will you at least give me a hug?" he asked. I went down and hugged him as he shook and wept.

"You need to give Kage some time. It's going to be okay, please just leave him alone for a while."

He shook his head much like an upset little boy before going off to bed, and turned to go back to work.

I was upstairs for no more than three minutes when Clyde put his mouth at the mail slot in our door and at the top of his lungs shouted, "I LOVE YOU KAGE! PLEASE TALK TO ME! I LOVE YOU!" until I rushed down, mortified by the spectacle, and finally got him to move along.

A Better Fit for the Christy

The boss didn't seem too impressed by Clyde's interview, which was a relief considering the direction things were headed. I had sold him on the need for a resident manager, though, and mentioned talking to a current Christy tenant who had his own cleaning business and had asked for work in the past. The tenant was named Sam, and he was a Black man of about 60. I called him in for an interview and we offered him the position.

Sam was grateful for the opportunity and did a solid job. When Magali mentioned needing a housekeeper, I asked Sam if he'd be interested. The two hit it off, with Sam cleaning her place regularly and even driving her to doctor appointments and to the store, all while refusing payment.

"Chris has been so good to me and I want to pay it forward," he'd tell her.

"You know, my father would always help people and he'd say he thought if he helped others, then maybe someone would help his kids when they needed it," Magali replied.

She may have inherited her father's karmic surplus, but she also earned plenty of good karma of her own. She had donated to animal welfare organizations throughout her working life and did countless good works as the director of the Cadillac Hotel.

The following is an excerpt from a piece I wrote for *AmericaBlog.com* in 2015, which discussed the need to save the endangered hotel amid San Francisco's runaway gentrification.

In the 1960s two visiting brothers from Ohio checked into the historic Cadillac Hotel and had to extend their stay due to an epic blizzard in the Midwest. They never got around to going back, and both still lived at the hotel when I sat behind them at one of the monthly jazz concerts in the grand lobby a few years ago.

"Now and then I still think about going back," one said.

Not long after that concert the brother who told me the story passed away, and the state decided the other was incapable of living alone and needed to be institutionalized. Owner Kathy Looper and her manager Magali Echevarria went to bat for that vulnerable old man, who was frightened and alone, and agreed to personally look after him so he could stay in his home.

In my younger years I remember forcing things that weren't a good fit or weren't meant to be. Bringing Clyde to the center of my livelihood simply to get him out of the Melrose was a devil's bargain if there ever was one, and even considering it was a lapse in judgement. Despite the lackluster interview, I believe I could have managed to hire him had I gone all in, and I'm thankful I had the wisdom to drop it and refocus instead.

Me and Sam were the totality of Magali's support system, and he enriched her life a great deal. Had I pushed Clyde's hire, Magali would have missed out on knowing Sam, and when the great pandemic ground his business to a halt, he would have fared far worse having rent to worry about.

There had been a fork in the road: push Clyde's hire or refocus. I shudder to think of what that wrong turn would have meant for Magali, Sam, and my career.

Pie in the Face

Most every gay man who had been on a "dating" app in St. Louis knew of the Pie Guy. He'd often start with normal banter and then ask, "Ever been pied in the face?"

His sexual fetish was to throw pies, which were actually shaving cream in pie tins, into a kneeling man's face and masturbate to the scene. I was tipped off to his actual identity and messaged him with a proposition. I would allow him to pie me in the face, and even throw in a few buddies, if I could interview him while keeping his identity a secret.

He was alarmed that I knew who he was and begged me to not out him (which was never my intention).

"It's past time I stop doing this, it's gotten out of control. My partner has no idea. Please don't print my name . . ."

He was far too freaked out to even consider my proposal, and actually moved far away from St. Louis shortly thereafter. He missed out, because Pride hosted an event at Sensation where community leaders got pied in the face for charity. And since I was running *Out in STL,* I was now officially part of the pied establishment.

Unlike the media duos of "Darin & Jimmy," or "Colin and Colin," me and my fellow *Out in STL* editor, Melissa, were not close personal friends. We were packaged together by Nick Phillips and *RFT* Editor in Chief Sarah Fenske, and while I found her to be brilliant and sophisticated, we were very different people. I was drunk and irreverent, while she was sober and reverent, for starters. It didn't even occur to me to ask her to attend.

Generally speaking, I'm comfortable being alone, and it often felt simpler to just drop in solo, mingle, and head out rather than rounding up a group for an afternoon event like this. Sometimes I regretted cutting corners. This was one of those times.

Unlike me, the other community leaders had tables of supporters. I took a seat with Colin and Colin and the *#Boom* team, which was new territory. We'd been on the opposite sides of the LGBTQ media wars for years, and now there we were having pleasant, if not still strained chit chat.

Regardless of how tense things between the camps were at any given point, one person who was always gracious and above the fray was Colin Murphy's elegant husband Kurt. I'd normally run across him at Pride events and he'd stop and warmly engage, as if nothing had changed since our first meeting back when we were all on the same media team.

I hadn't seen him since the big reconciliation and he arrived towards the end of the pie event. By that point I had put in my time, been pied on stage by Colin Lovett, and was itching to leave anyway, but his addition to the mix was just more than I could handle.

Very similar to how I felt about the things I had written about Rand, my former mentor in Oklahoma City, there were things I included in the book that I sincerely regretted, mainly my insinuations that Colin Murphy was in love with Colin Lovett. I was not in the headspace to address that with him, nor was I capable of sitting beside him pretending to ignore the elephant in the room.

As he sat down, I said hello and hugged him.

"It's great to see you, Kurt, but I have to get going."

"Why do you have to go?" he asked with a look of concern.

It was clear he very much wanted me to stay, and understood why I was leaving.

Full Disclosure

The more strained our relations grew with Clyde, the more time he spent with the girls on Opal's balcony.

"He comes over and the first thing he does is fixes himself a drink, and then before he leaves, he fixes himself another for the walk back," Emily said. "Sometimes it seems he makes excuses to come over when all he wants are the drinks."

Clyde was a decade older than the girls, so constantly hitting them up for liquor hardly seemed appropriate, although not at all surprising. Clyde could not maintain a liquor supply because if he had a bottle, he would drink it. He had no shut-off. We once took him to a movie, and when he learned there was a bar in the lobby, he made a beeline for it every fifteen minutes and was obnoxiously drunk by the time we left.

One day something in the Melrose chat tipped me off that the girls knew far more about our personal life than I ever imagined.

"What exactly have you told our niece, Clyde?" I asked in a message from a Colorado hotel room.

"What do you mean?" he replied.

"I take it you've just let it rip and held nothing back, finding it perfectly reasonable and appropriate to tell the family about our sex life?"

"I moved away from Southern Illinois to get away from prude ideas about sex. You're being very Southern Illinois right now," he replied.

While he played dumb, Clyde wasn't mindlessly oversharing about debaucherous Saturday night parties. He was spinning tales that he was a third in our marriage, and any indication from us that he wasn't, like our frequent trips without him, was actually evidence of our mistreatment and abuse.

One thing that flowed more than the liquor on that balcony was Clyde's crocodile tears.

Moon Over the Melrose

Managing Clyde's erratic behavior while keeping up appearances was a daunting task. There were the internal Melrose perceptions, trying to keep things from being awkward for my niece and Opal, and there was the way our house was being represented to the community.

Over social media Clyde loved to coyly tease out that there was trouble at the Melrose and when I told him that wasn't cool, he'd reply, "All you care about is your reputation!"

In our Melrose chat one day, he came at me directly in a way he never had before. "Whatever Ms. Emperor, you think you run things but I could snap you in two . . ." he began.

We had plans to attend Darin's annual rooftop soiree at the fashionable Moonrise Hotel in a few days, and after Clyde's meltdown in the chat and the tense days that followed, it was just assumed he'd not be joining.

And then he messaged me the afternoon of the event.

"Am I still invited to the party tonight or no?" he asked.

Of course, in retrospect I should have said no, but in the eye of the storm I was trying to keep a lid on the shit stew that was bubbling. I was also trying to avoid additional meltdowns.

"Sure," I replied. "Jack and Ron are driving as well, if you'd prefer to ride with them," I said, assuming that would be more comfortable for everyone.

"I'll ride with you guys if that's ok," he replied.

We had a full car and everyone was upbeat and chatty, aside from Clyde, who sat quiet and pouty. I did my best to rope him into the discussion but he didn't bite.

My Damon PTSD was triggered because he would similarly make things awkward on purpose, and would sometimes go to events he wasn't interested in simply to ensure I didn't get a night off from the awareness he was unhappy.

We had a prime table, arguably the best table, at the end of the rooftop veranda near the stage. Darin joined us, as did a group of our Alton friends. Clyde, however, was sitting as far from us as he could at the other end of the rooftop, near the spinning moon atop the hotel's marquee. Kage checked on him three or four times and managed to bring him to the table, but he'd quickly return to his solitary perch after a few minutes.

After a quiet ride home, he took to Facebook with a faux inspirational message, accompanied by photos from the rooftop.

Sitting alone on the rooftop of a hotel tonight, I really considered jumping and ending my life. But I decided there are still things to live for, and I hope that helps anyone else in a similar situation.

Everyone knew he was there with us.

He was continually straddling the line between being part of the house and defaming it, just as much as if he'd dangled on the precipice of that rooftop, straddling the line between a glamorous event and certain death.

And he did not have the grace or talent to walk a tightrope.

A Plea to Clyde

Clyde ,

Life with Damon was like living under a dark cloud, in a house full of fun house mirrors. He worked to define me in the ugliest way possible, yet refused to let me go. He'd bring up random memories from the past, often good memories, and re-frame them in a horrible light. He'd accompany me to activities just to make sure I didn't escape his brooding punishment for even an evening.

He had little when I found him, a severely damaged kid crying on my bed, and I navigated him through a career change, got him hired at my company in San Francisco, and nurtured him until he was making six figures with the federal government.

To get out from under that dark cloud I gave up everything: The $175k household income, the waterfront loft, the guarantee of a secure retirement . . . all to live free on my brother's sofa. And I've never looked back.

Kage is like the warm sun I've missed for most of my adult life. We love and nurture one another and our friends. We address issues as they arise, and then wash our hands of them and move on. I could die broke with him and never for a second regret my decisions. I have given up everything to start fresh and build a healthy, happy life free of blame, resentment, passive-aggressiveness and toxic brooding.

You have been an incredible part of that new life, our awesome, laid-back neighbor who does his own thing on his own terms, and who is always down for fun times. But it's like the person we knew is now possessed by the man I chewed off my arm to be free of.

You've missed few opportunities to be passive-aggressive. You've re-framed some of our best times in an ugly light.

If I gave up everything to be free of this bullshit, why do you think I'd accept it from you?

We are not emotional prisoners to your shifting expectations and judgement. We are not willing to maintain an unhealthy friendship where you want to hang out with us, but also claim we're harmful to you and are untrustworthy.

You need to get your fucking shit together, and fast. We love you and want to be in your life, but we refuse to be abused, derided and defamed.

Chris

Where There's Smoke

Ms. Jamieson dragged two tricks home from JJ's one Saturday night. They'd just sat down in her living room when they heard Clyde's smoke detectors going off.

As Ms. Jamieson got closer to her back door, she could smell the smoke, and when she opened it, the stairwell was like a chimney and smoke billowed into her place.

"'Oh shit,' I thought, before running down the back stairs to his back door," Ms. Jamieson recalled. "I pounded on the door and there was no answer. I remember I have a master key, so I unlock his door and smoke is just coming out thick and heavy. I walk in and see the smoke coming out of his stove. The stove top was blackened. I open the oven door and see a completely black, charred pizza, turn off the oven, throw the pizza on top of the stove, and look for Clyde. He, of course, was in his bed, passed the fuck out. I yelled several times and started shaking him. Finally, after about two minutes or so, he woke up. I told him that he almost had a fire in his stove and that I turned it off and prevented his apartment from catching on fire. He was still out of it, so he probably didn't understand what I was saying."

Ms. Jamieson apologized to her gentlemen callers, but nobody was in the mood for sex any longer so they all just went to sleep.

"We messed around in the morning, though," Ms. Jamieson said.

"I don't find morning sex to be nearly as good," I replied.

"I don't either, but I felt obligated."

After that, Ms. Jamieson was concerned about the risk posed to us all by Clyde's binge drinking.

"Had I not come home that night, it's possible I wouldn't have had a home to come back to and he would be dead and Chris and Kage and the other tenants of the building would either be dead or homeless!"

THE CURSE

One Sunday morning we woke to find Clyde had gone on Facebook Live during the wee hours of the morning. The video was about being entangled in the evil Melrose. It was a rebuke of the house, and it was a direct, unequivocal message to our enemies and detractors that they had been right.

"There were so many warnings and I was so stupid not to listen. I was so stupid," a drunk Clyde said from his living room where he was sitting in a tank top. "There's a lot I can't say right now because of where I am, but I vow that my story will be told. It will be told."

I was bombarded with messages and decided to respond with what I thought was a restrained blog post that essentially said we helped someone move to town and he got feelings for us, and was now out for revenge.

The thread grew quickly and then a local witch named Thorne chimed in.

"I knew he was crazy when he begged for help reversing a curse."

"What?"

Thorne posted over a dozen screenshots of an exchange where Clyde was begging for help.

"Why do you want to reverse it?" Thorne asked him.

"When I cast it I didn't know that when you curse someone, you're cursed as well. I don't have time for that negativity right now," Clyde responded, and then explained how he went about casting the curse.

"I took a shirt they'd given me and I cut it up. I carved three lines in my shoulder and bled onto the scraps, and then I summoned Satan to curse them."

Clyde sent Thorne photos, including one of the three lines he had carved in his arm.

The thread exploded as everyone in Queer St. Louis tuned in.

That afternoon we were attending a birthday party for Kage's nephew Roman, who was turning eight. It was a warm, bright day and over a dozen family members were celebrating when our sister-in-law Jenna pulled us aside.

"You need to see this."

She handed over her phone and in her Facebook feed there was a public post from Clyde.

If your landlord's husband uses his building key to come in your apartment and demand sex, is that illegal or naw?

Just then I received a text from Clyde: "This will only get uglier if you don't remove the post."

"How much worse can it get from summoning Satan?" I asked.

"It wasn't a curse to harm you it was just to let you see how you make others feel."

"What are your plans, as far as our living situation?" I asked.

"What do you mean?"

"Surely you don't plan on continuing to live at the Melrose after airing a video about what an evil place it is, and then publicly accusing Kage of sexual misconduct."

"Are you telling me to move out?" Clyde asked.

This was a minefield, and I was careful to choose my words wisely when it came to landlord-tenant matters.

"No, I'm not asking you to move out. I'm saying you've ruined the Melrose, so why would you want to remain there after this?"

"Don't be so dramatic," Clyde said.

A major trigger for me was when someone sought to normalize abusive behavior. Part of that stemmed from a physically abusive relationship I endured in my very early 20s. If you don't make a big deal of the abuse the first time, it only gets harder to make a big deal of it the twentieth. Clyde was telling me that this was the new normal, and to not accept it was silly and dramatic.

"I WAS PULLED AWAY FROM A CHILD'S BIRTHDAY PARTY BY MY SISTER-IN-LAW AND SHOWN A PUBLIC POST ACCUSING MY HUSBAND OF SEXUAL ASSAULT. THIS WILL NEVER BE NORMAL OR ACCEPTABLE, CLYDE. I WILL NEVER ACCEPT THIS."

The Melrose Chat, which Clyde had recently left, lit up. When Rick saw what Clyde had posted he said, "Oh fuck. That's not cool. And he's got no room to go there after what he did to me, but I'm staying out of it," and Opal said she would try to get Clyde to remove the post.

"Clyde said he would remove his post if you would remove yours," Opal said minutes later.

There's a scene in *The Color Purple*, when Shug is sitting by the pond, painting her nails. Celie had recently discovered secrets her abusive husband had been keeping for years, and Shug knew the situation was beyond tense. A little boy walks by and she asks if he's seen Miss Celie.

"She's gone to shaaaave Mister," the boy says.

Shug's smile turns to a look of concern, and then she begins to run towards the house.

After the party, Kage was sitting beside me in silence as we monitored social media. Opal messaged me.

"Clyde's here on my balcony. You two should talk."

"Trust me on this, Opal, you do not want me over there. It won't be good."

"Please think about it. The door is open and we'll be up here."

I don't think I'd ever been so enraged, and shouting via text was profoundly unsatisfying, particularly when Clyde was downplaying my anger. I wanted to make him understand the severity of his actions. How he'd permanently ruined everything.

I also knew Kage would tell me not to go.

Without comment I stood up, slipped on shoes, and calmly descended the stairs. In that moment I picture Kage in the role of Shug, initially not sure why I went downstairs, but then hearing his inner voice say, "He's gone to shaaaaave Mister."

As Opal said it would be, her door was wide open and I climbed the stairs and walked through her living room to the screen door to the balcony where she sat facing Clyde, who was sniveling and wiping away tears.

"Please step inside, Opal." I said, and then I grabbed her empty chair and flipped it around, sitting with my chest pressing against the back.

Words gave Clyde too much to latch on to, and too many places to hide. I needed to communicate with him the way an extraterrestrial communicates. I sat face to face in total silence, looking at him with the coldest expression of hate I ever attempted.

He went from sniffling and avoiding my gaze to returning my expression. His face became hard and his nostrils flared as we sat staring at one another in silence.

"Is there anything you'd like to say to Clyde?" poor young Opal timidly said from behind the screen.

"There's nothing I want to say to him," I began in a tone of total disgust as Kage turned the corner below and ran up the sidewalk, "other than I wish he was dead!"

Clyde lunged from his seat. "I WISH YOU WERE DEAD!" he shouted as he reared back to punch me. I threw my arms behind my head and lunged towards him.

"DO IT, MOTHERFUCKER, DO IT!"

With that, Clyde flinched as if to say "geez" and fell to his seat. I stood up to leave as Opal followed me, crying hysterically.

"Don't go, this is ripping us apart! We have to fix this!" she wailed.

In hushed tones I tried to comfort her while remaining firm.

"I'm so sorry Opal, I'm sorry you're in the middle of this. Clyde is a very sick person and this is beyond repair."

"No!" she wailed, both hands and forehead against the wall as she convulsed while Kage stood at the base of the stairs trying to make sense of the scene.

The Melrose as a community was over.

Revenge Porn

We went to JJ's on a Saturday night and ran into a couple from Carbondale who asked about everything that went down with Clyde.

"Oh yeah, he told us you were in a triad," one began, "and he sent private photos all the time."

The guy pulled out his phone, opened his Clyde chat and scrolled. It was *Backstage at the Melrose*.

Kage sent Clyde a message demanding he stop sending private photos of us. At first, he denied he ever had, but when confronted with proof he became defensive.

"You shared photos I was in before! I'll be waiting on your front porch so we can discuss this," Clyde said.

"There's nothing to discuss. Stop sharing our pics," Kage replied.

"If you got something to discuss, talk to me face-to-face like a man. Not over text like a little girl. I'm out here and I'm not going anywhere."

We closed down the bar and rather than parking out front like we normally did, or turning at the alley beside our end of the building, we turned on to the alley from the top of the hill at the opposite end of the block, switched off the headlights and creeped down to the rear parking pad. From there we tried to make as little noise as possible, closing up the car and entering through the back. We succeeded in remaining undetected.

I gently opened the door to the balcony and could smell his cigarette and hear bouts of crying. He still had no idea we were home, but he'd soon get suspicious since the bar had been closed for an hour. He walked out to the sidewalk, looked up, and saw that our windows were dark.

"I'm posting your pics to Tumblr because of your dick move tonight," he wrote, followed by a screenshot of the first one he uploaded, followed by more. "I can post whatever I want."

Better Call Paul

I was beside myself with anxiety about Clyde's instability, and decided to call my friend Paul Emery. I had yet to meet Paul in person, but he had invested a great deal of time helping me edit and publicize *Delusions of Grandeur*.

From his home in New York, Paul listened to the entire saga, and then offered his advice.

"Clyde is a psychopath. In accusing Kage of sexual misconduct and mentioning the building key, he's already telegraphed his next moves. The only thing a psychopath respects is authority, and what you have to do is file for a restraining order. You need to get this all on the record before he does, otherwise you will have the entire legal system to contend with, and that's going to be overwhelming."

Initially, the advice felt radical, but I thought about how Clyde continued to escalate. The following day I went to file for an order of protection.

The Laundry Lurker

Since I did laundry in the basement directly below Clyde's apartment, I sought to make as little noise as possible when coming and going.

From the window on his back door he had a direct view down a short flight of stairs to the common door. While I was able to enter undetected, he often heard the machines start up. I'd hear the floor squeaking a foot above my head as he got up and ominously made his way from the living room through the hall and kitchen to that window, where he stood silently, waiting to watch me through the blinds.

Court

Standing before the judge in a packed Downtown St. Louis courtroom as my neighbor stood defiantly nearby, I began explaining the severity of his obsession.

"Your honor, on October 14, 2017, the respondent admitted in writing to cutting open his flesh, bleeding onto the scraps of a shirt we'd given him, and summoning Satan to curse us."

I had held out hope Clyde wouldn't even show up, but at the last minute he arrived.

Having been in court countless times to evict tenants for nonpayment, I was prepared. I had each talking point and the supporting documents, which I presented in order and then waited silently for follow-up questions.

Clyde's approach couldn't have been more different. He came with a mess of papers that didn't serve any purpose. He denied everything, and for each denial I offered evidence to the contrary.

He would seemingly conclude his testimony, and then after a substantial pause he'd throw something else out. For example, as the judge was reviewing the case and preparing to announce a decision, Clyde said, "Oh, um, your Honor. He does laundry right below my apartment several times a week!"

The judge said he was troubled by the curse, and Clyde said, "Your Honor, it wasn't Satanic like he says. It was just a Pagan ritual."

"Your honor, may I?" I said holding up documents showing the original exchange between Clyde and Thorne.

Clyde: I need your help as a witch. Please.

Clyde: No questions I just need to know how to reverse a curse. Please.

Thorne: Well, it depends on who placed it, when, why, and how severe.

Clyde: I offered a blood curse to Satan and I need to reverse it now.

Clyde: Please

Clyde: I made it yesterday.

Clyde: Please man help

The judge shook his head.

"This is a situation where two people should have just gone their separate ways," the Judge began, then turned his focus squarely on Clyde, "but you did some stupid things and here we are."

An Order of Protection was granted for six months.

Bird

Before we learned of the curse, Clyde's bird got very sick. He took her to the clinic and as he was leaving, she cried out his name. That was the last time he saw her.

Looking back on the timing, it seems she fell ill directly after the curse was cast. Of course, that's also when the pizza fire happened, so it was likely the smoke that made her sick.

The Trump Nightmare Begins

Nobody expected Trump to win, especially after he was caught on tape bragging about grabbing women "by the pussy." The day of the election, one of my bosses asked if I'd like to bet $100 on my candidate winning.

"I'll bet $500. Or $1,000," I said. The truth was I would have bet every penny I had that Hillary would comfortably win. Fortunately, he didn't take me up on the offer.

Oddly enough, I feel like I can almost predict the winner by how good the official watch party spread is. An exception was Al Gore's opulent 2000 St. Louis watch party, but he did win the popular vote.

On a winning night, the spread is lavish. For both Al Gore, and then eight years later for Barack Obama. The party spared no expense and the Chase Park Plaza's Khorassan Ballroom was filled with sumptuous buffets and bars. In 2004, the official watch party in San Francisco was so pitiful I didn't stick around, and when I returned to the Chase in 2016, my stomach sank. Most in the cavernous room were reporters, the buffet consisted of potato chips, dip and carrots, and the lights were too bright. Nothing was right, so we aborted and went to Bar PM.

Bar PM was more a bar than a watch party. The televisions weren't loud enough, but I could read the worried faces of the commentators. I paid for our one round and we went home.

I don't remember staying up to watch the returns. I only remember seeing critical states fall, and then the blur of the next several weeks.

Never in my life had I been so in the moment. If I passed a bar on my way to an appointment and wanted to stop, I would, blowing off the rest of the day.

I found myself at Bastille a few times, where I'd park myself at the end of the bar next to the tchotchke cluttered window and drink while being hypnotized by Peyton's video selections. The Weeknd's "Starboy" had just come out and I remember tripping out on the taillights of the McLaren P1. It felt like everything around me was on fast forward. I'd look up and see a friendly face engaging with me, and the next time I looked up it was someone else.

Aside from Republicans, everyone was in the mood to panic. Confident as I was that the election would go my way, I had implored everyone to take it seriously. I'd spent vacation time to work the polls. And now, after obsessing over emails and how "likeable" Hillary was, people wanted to hem and haw?

Fuck, let it all burn.

Frank Fontana and the Ladies Who Lunch

Frank Fontana was a character, and was hilarious even when he wasn't trying. About 55, he was Italian-American and quite handsome, even though he didn't see himself that way. He'd get really dark in the summer. His complexion was striking against his white hair, which was buzzed on the sides and spiked on the top.

One of his hobbies was tossing random items into the carts of other shoppers at the market, so I'd often ask for an update on his shenanigans.

"I was almost caught the other day!" he once replied.

He enjoyed standing in line behind the unsuspecting shoppers to see their reaction.

He loved to bake and his cakes were coveted and always noteworthy. For Cody's birthday party at Villadiva, he created a cake with a dildo on top. When Cody blew on the cake the dildo shot milk all over his face, to the delight of the crowd.

I became aware of Frank over Facebook, from his comments on my posts, and soon I was joining the Ladies Who Lunch, which is what I called his small club of financially comfortable older gentlemen with plenty of leisure time.

I think what I found most amusing was his off-the-cuff quips during conversation. For example, one day at lunch we were talking about a local eccentric who recently became a leather/S&M enthusiast and really embraced all his new accoutrements.

"When he got into leather, he'd change his profile pic several times a day with a new outfit," Frank began with an eye roll. "I felt like I was at a Reba McIntire concert."

The Widow Rose Dynasty

The longtime husband of Sensation owner Rose Dynasty passed unexpectedly, and I wanted to pay my respects. I knew many people at the funeral, including Tim Beckman, but Sensation was never a home bar of mine so I hung back out of respect for those closer to the family.

Someone who took the opposite approach was Glenn, an obnoxious acquaintance who unfortunately clung to me at the service

Jasmine was sitting in a crowded pew close to the front when Glenn approached and said, "Hey Jasmine! Since Trump won does that mean I can grab you by the pussy?"

Glenn was a constant source of non-stop humiliation.

I had heard Jasmine had gotten sober, and before I left we found ourselves standing in the same group. I said hello to the group as a whole, looking at her as well as the others, and it was clear she was beyond uncomfortable, with a cringe on her face and her eyes shifting from side to side.

Jasmine was close to everyone at Sensation, and I felt badly about Glenn's actions and my presence making her uncomfortable. I sent her a simple note to that effect, and she replied.

"How about we just put the past behind us?" she said.

Kage was skeptical considering she'd threatened to call the police on him, but got on board since she had taken responsibility for her past behavior and had made major changes by becoming sober. She even gave me credit for not enabling her addiction, and said my "tough love" had been important.

The Melrose had divided into camps, with Opal joining with Clyde, Miss Jamieson siding with us, and Emily, Menashe and Rick struggling to stay neutral.

It turned out Rick had been sharing our private discussions with Clyde, and one day Clyde threw Rick under the bus by sending Kage photographic evidence of the betrayal. I believe his motivation was to rub it in our faces and break our bond with Rick.

Kage loved Rick, and could hardly get out the words to tell me what had happened after receiving Clyde's text because of how hard he was crying.

Rick sent me a message.

"I fucked up, I'm sorry. I was manipulated, and the honest to God truth is I don't want anything more to do with Clyde."

While he was still hoping to make amends, when he heard that we'd forgiven Jasmine, he was not happy.

"You guys look stupid having gone through all that with her and now forgiving her. It looks bad. Don't think you can stay mad at me indefinitely and then go back to being friends. I will NEVER be a Jasmine."

Independence-Giving

Clyde and Rick celebrated their independence by shooting off Roman candles outside the Melrose on Thanksgiving Day, while posting photos and videos to social media. We took that as their declaration that they officially didn't give a fuck.

The last time Kage had chatted with him, Rick said Clyde had manipulated him into betraying our trust, and that he wanted no part of Clyde going forward. From Oklahoma, Kage messaged Rick regarding his about face, but it was Clyde who responded.

"Rick is my friend. Don't message him again."

I believe we had been a stabilizing force for Rick. I think he tried to hold it together since we lived upstairs. He even referred to us as his gay parents. With those concerns gone, Rick went downhill fast. Seemingly overnight he began running drugs from the apartment. The divide within the building radiated out into the broader community, and anyone who dabbled in hard drugs cozied up with Rick and distanced themselves from us.

"He intentionally gets friends hooked so he doesn't have to do them alone, and as a way to pay for his habit," a mutual acquaintance told me.

That seemed to be what happened with his best friend Dustin Shuab, who I was fond of. The always smiling Dustin was a Black guy in his mid-20s who came from a good home in the Illinois suburbs. His father was a firefighter and they were active in their church. You could tell he was raised right by the respectful way he behaved. I always found it odd he and Rick were so close, but they had a lot of fun together. Sometimes too much fun, like when the interracial duo tag teamed an insatiable bottom. "You're up," Rick said when he needed a break.

Weeks after the Melrose divide was set in stone, Dustin texted me from Rick's apartment. "Hey, mind if I come up?"

Dustin would often visit, even just let himself in when at the building, but I hadn't seen him since everything went down. When he came in through the back door he didn't seem like the same guy. He wasn't smiling and seemed high.

"I'd really like to suck your dick," he said.

I knew meth can make people desperate for sex and felt confident that was what was going on here.

"Are you okay? You're not yourself right now and I'm worried about you."

Dustin looked away, and then towards my crotch as he came closer. He looked oily, like he hadn't bathed recently. "I just really need some dick."

I felt bad sending him away but would have felt worse exploiting him in that moment. I hated to see him in that state, but he wouldn't be the last. Next up was Menashe.

Ms. Jamieson's Perch

Menashe firmly turned against us and sided with Clyde and Rick as his meth addiction intensified, and in social media threads he and Clyde would call our house a cult.

"The only way you can be part of that group is if you don't think for yourself. No thanks."

Menashe was particularly brutal in singling out Ms. Jamieson for public mocking. He knew Ms. Jamieson had body image issues, and so he made Ms. Jamieson's weight a constant topic.

Ms. Jamieson had French windows in her kitchen and could regularly be found standing at them while she smoked. This gave her a bird's-eye view of all the comings and goings, which often included Clyde going to Opal's apartment empty-handed and leaving with a full beverage.

Clyde never entertained, aside from the constant stream of random tricks, but one evening Ms. Jamieson notified our chat that Clyde had several guests over, including Rick and Menashe.

Not only was Ms. Jamieson's apartment above Clyde's, her stairway and foyer were next to his living room, so Menashe's deep, booming voice easily carried through the floors and walls. She could hear that they were discussing us, so she turned off the television and tried to listen.

Of course, the squeaks of the Melrose didn't take sides in the war between its residents, and Clyde's party could clearly make out Ms. Jamieson's movements.

"Oh my God, Jordan is on the stairs listening in!" Rick exclaimed as everyone laughed.

Not wanting to validate their spot-on assumption, Ms. Jamieson sat frozen in place.

Curses!

The thing about knowing someone has cast a curse on you is that you tend to believe everything bad that happens is curse related. For example, I bent over at the office one day and the seat of my pants split open.

"THE CURSE!" I thought to myself.

I managed to catch Ms. Jamieson at home and had her go to my apartment to retrieve pants.

Clyde's engine went out shortly after the curse, and then a gigantic tree next door fell, crushing both the neighbor's garage and Clyde's vehicle. Our crew was in agreement that the curse blowback was to blame.

Brawny's Vet Visit

Brawny had weight fluctuations over the years but his belly was unusually large, so I took him to our regular vet, the gay and muscular Dr. Bruce. I wondered what kind of special diet he might put him on, and how much he'd hate it.

More than any dog I had ever had, Brawny was an extension of me. I had lost the 17-year-old dog I inherited from Grandma Andoe after ten wonderful years together, and I wanted another dog desperately. I was tempted to look for one, but dogs had always just appeared in my life and I knew the right one would come to me, and he did.

I arrived to my San Francisco office and the receptionist told me of a puppy a co-worker couldn't keep. I asked for a photo and they sent me a picture of tiny Brawny, a white and tan Yorkie with beautiful blue eyes, sitting in the palms of their hands.

"What a ridiculous little dog," I thought to myself. I'd always had larger dogs, but made arrangements to meet him in person that coming weekend. It was love at first sight.

We moved from San Francisco to Oklahoma City to St. Louis and back to San Francisco together, and when my relationship collapsed, I left with Brawny and a suitcase, and thought I had made out good. He was so adorable that we were stopped on every block in New York by people wanting to admire him.

I went through some dark times in New York and feel Brawny helped me persevere. The two of us loved St. Louis, and when we first returned I took him to Tower Grove Park, where he celebrated by euphorically rolling in the grass (our NYC dog park only had pebbles), and when it was time to go he didn't want to leave. I think he thought I was going to take him away from St. Louis.

He was my primary companion during the solitary year I was working on my book, and then Kage came along and they bonded.

Now he was 12 with a weight problem, but it was nothing we couldn't figure out.

Dr. Bruce came in and I lifted Brawny to show him his belly. "Look how fat he's gotten!" I said as I handed him over.

Gently squeezing his belly, Bruce's smile fell and a look of alarm swept across his face. "Oh, that's a tumor."

I was in shock and went into some sort of autopilot. I know I told him I wanted the x-ray, and when I was alone I cried. My mind was still a blur when he showed me the images, which he tried to explain.

"How long does he have?" I asked.

"Probably three months." Dr. Bruce replied.

The veterinary office was in North County, 18 miles away from home. I did not want to be in highway traffic, so I wound through the metro streets while holding Brawny so he could look out the opened window.

It was clear now he wasn't well, I just hadn't been able to see it.

The following day I blew off my afternoon to take Brawny to Villa Ray to spend time with Pauly, where we ate lunch, cried, drank, laughed, cried again and drank some more. Ray came home from work and prepared dinner, and Kage joined us.

Processing

Initially I accepted that I had roughly three months with Brawny, but then denial set in and I sought second opinions. Money meant nothing, and I started him on Chinese medicine that was supposed to buy him time by stalling the growth of the tumor and reducing inflammation. While I doubt there was much benefit, I don't regret trying it. It gave me hope and allowed me to do something other than wait for the tumor to consume him.

Regardless of the mean-spirited Fiat stunt, I still appreciated that Damon didn't fight me on taking Brawny when we separated, which I fully expected. I remember Brawny was the last detail we had discussed in those final weeks in Oakland.

"What about Brawny?" he asked.

"I intend to take him." I said, bracing for the worst.

"I'm sad, but that dog wants his Chris Andoe," he replied.

I sent an email telling him the news.

"It's very sad but not surprising," he replied. "Thank you for letting me know, and please keep me updated."

We give these little dogs the love we'd give a child, only to lose them time and again. I'd lost many dogs, but for some irrational reason I didn't really expect to lose Brawny. Even with the Chinese medicine, reality was setting in. I told Kage that the time would soon arrive.

"I've been through this before. There will be a time he will not be able to function and will be in pain, and when that time comes I will do what needs to be done. When that moment comes, please don't second guess me. It will be the hardest thing I've ever done."

Clyde Recruits a Fighter

In the middle of all we were going through with Brawny, Clyde managed to recruit mutual friend Shawn Adams to publicly vindicate him.

I first became aware of Adams a year or two earlier when he accused an ex of date rape, which wasn't well received in the Grove where the guy was known and liked. I tried to help him navigate the situation and better manage the delivery of his message.

Always a bit of a devil's advocate, and someone with a soft spot for Rick, Adams went on a week-long tear about how we had bullied Clyde and unjustly tarnished his image.

Late one night Clyde oddly and drunkenly confessed to Adams that he knew he could manipulate him because he's quick to anger. Adams then tried to quietly dial back his defense of Clyde, and instead claimed he was actually defending Rick.

I sent him the following:

"I was good to both you and Rick, and you both spat in my face for Clyde. I nearly severed my own arm to be free of Clyde, and you spent seven days adding additional penalties. He threatened my livelihood. He told our families about our sex lives. He tried to physically assault Kage in public. He accused Kage of sexual assault. You lent your credibility to his efforts to deny all that. Clyde is maniacal and you are a pawn. Peace with Clyde means letting him into our bed. That's what this is all about. He won't stop until he gets that."

My harsh words only reinvigorated Adams's desire to stand by Clyde.

After yet another post attacking us, I wrote: "Clyde is dangerous and unstable, and whatever he does from here on out, you're a co-signer. You are bound to him, and you will own anything he does."

One never knows what words will stick when sparring, but my last warning to Adams would haunt him.

The Moment

I had been taking Brawny to the office and to my appointments for a few weeks, wanting to maximize my time with him. He was looking rough. His once lustrous coat was thin and his exposed skin had sores. I suspected the day had arrived before stopping to get lunch at Burger King. It was a warm November afternoon, the grass in the empty St. Ann park was brown, and we sat on the ground together and ate. He looked so different, but still sat upright and made eye contact with me like he always had. But when he tried a few times to defecate, he couldn't, and gave up. The tumor had finally choked off his bowls as Dr. Bruce warned would happen.

Kage's office was very close, even visible across the highway and airport runway, and I called to tell him it was time.

Still sitting in the park, a St. Ann officer pulled up beside us.

"What a cute puppy," he said, and I just bawled.

At the vet's office we made him comfortable in his bed. His head rested on the bed's raised edge and he lifted it to look when the doctor prepared his leg for the injection. "It's okay, just rest Mr. B," I said, and he did. Many dog parents reading this can empathize with the lingering feeling you have betrayed your beloved companion, even if intellectually you know you did what was best for them. Kage had never gone through this process so those feelings were especially difficult for him.

We are blessed that Brawny passed peacefully with us petting him.

Our dear friends Chris Kerr & Denny Fiske had always been so gracious when it came to their Tower Grove home, even letting me entertain guests there. They adored Brawny, and offered to let us bury him in their yard, where he had many fun times. Because of that we didn't have to leave him behind at the vet's office. We carried him out, covered up in his bed, and it felt much better than the alternative.

It was dark and had turned cold when we arrived at Chris and Denny's. We went out back and they had already dug a deep hole, but had to leave for a few minutes to attend to something. Brawny, still covered in his bed, was on a patio table near the pool, and I stepped inside to warm up. After a few minutes I went to check on Kage.

"Don't you want to warm up for a few minutes?" I asked.

Kage paused. "I'm going to stay out here. I don't feel right leaving him alone."

The Claws Come Out for Kitty

As we were preparing to bury Brawny, I received a call from our ad rep Kitty. She was at a media event pitching *Out in STL* to advertisers, surely up in her cups, when one said, "We already have a contract with *Vital Voice*," to which Kitty replied, "*Vital Voice* no longer exists."

The vendor promptly told Darin, who, along with his good friend Allyson Mace, founder of *Sauce Magazine,* confronted Kitty in front of everyone.

"Stop telling people *Vital Voice* doesn't exist!" he began, followed by a few other choice words.

In addition to the new kid on the block trying to poach his business, Darin was also aware that Kitty was Alan's best friend, and Alan had for years told business owners to pull their monthly *Vital Voice* ads and instead advertise in the annual Pride Guide. Layers of salt to go on this wound.

This was the last thing I wanted to deal with, and sure enough Darin messaged me moments after Kitty called.

"Darin, I'm in the middle of burying Brawny and can't discuss anything else at the moment," I replied.

Brawny had long been a mascot of sorts for *Vital Voice*, where he was regularly photographed holding court or relaxing on the kitchen island during our staff meetings.

Fortunately, Darin was understanding and sent his condolences.

Reactions to Brawny's Passing

Tributes to Brawny poured in from all over, which was comforting, and the reactions to the news were sometimes surprising. For instance, an 80-year-old Republican coworker stopped by my office to ask how Brawny was doing. When I told him Brawny had passed, he broke down.

"You loved that little guy so much," he said, sobbing.

Friends gave us gifts, including Frank Fontana, who made a photo album from our Facebook photos, and my brother Joe gave us the most incredible painting of Brawny. It's based on an image of him in Tower Grove Park, but is black and white, and he exquisitely captured the exact way Brawny looked at me.

A photo feels date stamped. A photo of someone deceased can have an air of sadness, a reminder of something that was fixed to a moment now gone. A fine painting, however, is timeless. It's immortal. In this case, it represents the love Brawny and I had for one another, the impression that bond left on Joe from our time living with him, and Joe's love for me.

The painting, which I believed in a sense captured Brawny's soul, will be with me as long as I live.

Fading Light

All of it had taken a toll on Kage. Generally speaking, people in Alton were nice, and because they all knew one another, they maintained civility. Queer St. Louis, by contrast, was cutthroat. The back-to-back betrayals, the intense social media condemnations, and the fact we weren't even given a reprieve during Brawny's final days—, it was corroding Kage's spirit and dimming his light.

He came home one day and I noticed how much dimmer that light was from the days he used to joyfully tell me work stories.

"He's not the same," I posted to Facebook, along with a smiling photo collage from his first day at work a year earlier. "He doesn't look like this anymore."

The light had been dimming since Clyde began melting down, but seeing him standing in the same spot where he used to perform brought it into focus.

His old friend Jason Brooks wrote to say he felt confident Kage would bounce back.

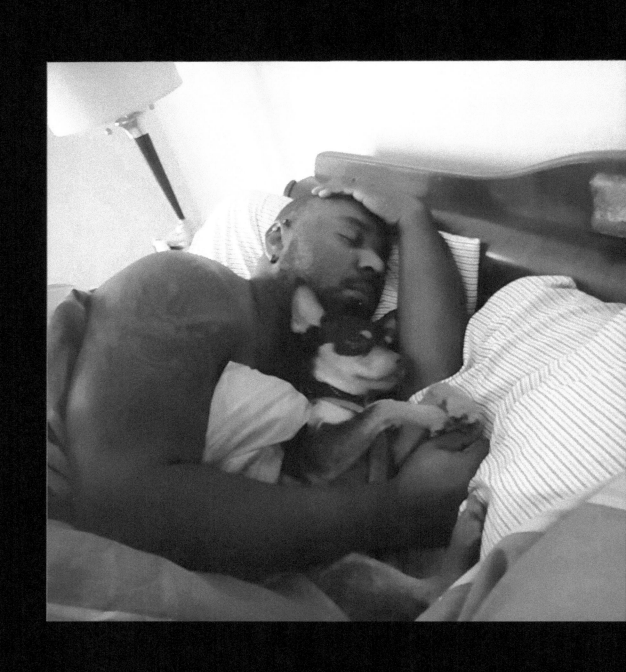

Rescue

If the time I've been without a dog over the course of my 45 years was calculated, it would likely total up to less than a year. My routine was built around dogs. After Brawny's passing I realized I didn't need to go home for lunch, but my anxiety would ratchet up in the afternoon as if I was neglecting something. I decided to maintain the routine of going home at noon anyway.

I knew the easiest way to move past my Brawny grief would be to adopt a puppy, but that didn't feel right. Rather than getting a puppy I would honor his memory by taking in a hard to adopt animal. My childhood friend Francis's wife Edie monitored rescue sites and I told her the dog needed to be at least one year old, because I noticed many breeders branding puppies as "rescues," and charging hundreds of dollars for them. I wanted a dog that was in need. She sent me a photo of a Chihuahua mix that was estimated to be one year old.

He was at a rescue in Troy, Illinois that monitored shelters for dogs on the kill list and saved them when they could. This dog was found in North St. Louis County and was deemed unadoptable by the dog pound. The rescue specified he would not be placed in a home with small children.

Both me and Kage dreamt about him after seeing his photo, and went out to meet him the following weekend. An older rescue lady spent thirty minutes explaining him before allowing us to meet. I imagine she thought we were ideal guardians and was afraid we wouldn't want him.

He was brought to a concrete-floored room that smelled of bleach, and while he excitedly ran in circles and cautiously sniffed us, he was far more interested in the shelter volunteer with whom he bonded.

"You've never picked out a dog before so I'll let you decide," I said to Kage.

"I like him," Kage replied.

He still needed to be neutered so I went to retrieve him in about a week. He seemed to somewhat remember me, but I was essentially a stranger. I walked him to the car and he was hesitant about getting in, but jumped into my lap where he melted into my legs. I didn't know if it was exhaustion, sadness, or relief. We named him Troy.

Troy was a connoisseur of softness and would find the softest spot in the entire apartment, like a folded stack of blankets, to rest. The first morning in our home he was sleeping in Kage's embrace.

A year later, just weeks before moving to Villadiva, I was perusing the same rescue's site and saw a beautiful Yorkie. She had been a puppy mill breeder for six years, and could also not be in a home with children. While I had wanted a companion for Troy, I selected her purely on emotion because she was the same breed as Brawny.

I took Troy out to meet her and the two were too interested in the smells of the yard to focus on me or one another. On the way home I was petting her when she snapped and snarled. She had a negative association with touch after all those years of forced breeding.

We seriously debated whether to take her back. It was difficult to wrap our heads around having a dog we couldn't pet. Fortunately, she played very well with Troy, and we decided to keep her and name her Madge, because that sounded like the name of an old gal who had a rough life.

There's a special bond one gets with a puppy. It's as if they become one with you. Adopting adult dogs is different, but rewarding. We would see tremendous progress with Troy and Madge, and in time Madge even let me pet her.

Ms. Jamieson's Gentleman Caller

You could have cued Cece Penisten's 1991 dance hit "Finally" when Ms. Jamieson seemed to land the most eligible bachelor in town. The sexy and successful Salam Alhamdy moved from Kansas City, and for a moment it felt like everyone was competing for his affections. But it was Ms. Jamieson he was showering with attention.

"It's going really well!" Ms. Jamieson reported. "He's got great tastes. We both wear the same cologne. It's *very* expensive, so I finance mine, but he's got a great job and makes a lot of money."

After about two weeks, however, Salam told her he wasn't interested in anything serious. Salam was on a search for a soul mate, with plans to go on many dates as part of that process. And that wrecked half of the city, including Ms. Jamieson.

About a month after the end of their brief courtship, I received a message encouraging me to dig into Salam's time in Kansas City. There was a scandalous tale of betrayal, sex addiction and community blacklisting that culminated in an Order of Protection.

It's worth repeating, I do not pursue most leads. I know which politicians, media and sports figures are on the down low getting their freak on, and I don't write about it or discuss it unless it's relevant to a greater story. And even then I normally leave it out.

As far as Salam was concerned, nobody in St. Louis had complained of any impropriety, and it seemed he was hardly even sleeping with anyone. I knew those pushing this were doing so out of spite and thought dredging it up was unseemly.

Kage was the only person I told about it. "If this gets out I hope I'm not blamed," I said.

A week or so later a few Melrose residents were on the patio at Friendly's when Kage slipped up. My phone chimed, and I mentioned that someone had a lead on a story.

"Hopefully it's not more about Salam's skeletons," he said without thinking.

I gave him a shocked look and shook my head.

"What? What's that about?" Ms. Jamieson demanded.

"It's nothing," I said, as I tried to redirect the conversation.

"You're keeping something from me. What is it?" she replied sternly.

I knew there was no chance Ms. Jamieson would drop this. The fact we clearly didn't want her to know only made her more determined.

"We don't want this getting out, but . . ." I began.

The following morning Ms. Jamieson stopped by my office.

"I called Salam when I got home and told him he needs to be careful because people are saying he's got tons of skeletons in Kansas City!"

"WHY WOULD YOU DO THAT?" I exclaimed holding my head in my hands. "You knew we didn't want that discussed! We didn't even want to tell *you*!"

"I didn't tell him it was you who told me!" she said.

We often teased Ms. Jamieson for being dingy, but we also suspected she played up being dingy when she needed cover.

I don't know if this was a case of gossip so good she couldn't resist, or if she wanted to turn the knife since Salam broke things off. Either way, I think it was a premeditated decision to ask for forgiveness rather than permission.

I reached out to Salam and offered him an interview. The weeks-long project involved dinner and phone conversations before the full spread appeared in the magazine, and during that time I discussed none of it with Ms. Jamieson.

SEX, SECRETS & SHAME

SPURNED ROMANTIC PROSPECTS DUG INTO HIS PAST. NOW SALAM ALHAMDY TELLS ALL

BY CHRIS ANDOE

Salam Alhamdy hadn't been

On the inside, however, his compul-

why they were there; everyone was wel-

that's an open book (check out his Facebook page to see for yourself). He aims to be honest with others and honest with himself. Rather than finding sex, his focus now is finding his one true love.

One could argue that Alhamdy has gone from being sexually promiscuous to romantically promiscuous. But while anonymous sexual partners are normally easy to shake, spurned romantic interests often get messy — as Alhamdy knows all too well. Few things disinfect better than sunlight, and by owning his story I think he has given us all an example of how to effectively neutralize our often complicated pasts.

While he is a single man who still enjoys sex, Alhamdy said in the past year he's had less of it than any time in his adult life. But it's not for the lack of offers.

"At the end of the night, it's not St. Louis if they don't want to fuck you." ∎

Sex, Secrets and Shame: Salam Alhamdy Tells All—
Out in STL, December 8, 2017

Salam Alhamdy hadn't been in the office more than an hour when he became fixated with setting up a sexual encounter. On that May morning in 2016, the 33-year-old was still living in Kansas City. Business travelers were always on his radar, and one was ready and waiting at an airport hotel. He fired off a few directives to work colleagues, replied to a text from his partner of two years, and then discreetly ducked out for one of his trademark four-hour lunch breaks.

By all appearances, Alhamdy, a fit and attractive young professional, had a life that was perfectly in balance: a harmonious relationship, a fashionable Midtown loft and a lucrative position in finance. He was the cook of the household, and over candlelight dinners, Alhamdy and his partner would discuss art, decor, music, politics and their future together.

On the inside, however, his compulsion was consuming him.

"I mean, I'm a project manager. Time management and milestones are my thing. But still, my erratic behavior was reaching a point where there were close calls, mostly with the boyfriend. I would show up to events late, 'long nights in the office,'" Alhamdy explains.

Instead, there was sex. What began with one-on-one action evolved into full-on orgies in hotel rooms, with the behavior getting riskier as time went on. Sometimes he even entertained extreme fetishes such as blood play.

"It would start with an app. The biggest party happened when I texted a guy in town from Chicago. He invited a couple of his friends, and his friends' friends. I think within two hours we had about twenty or so guys come in and out. Some jerked off and left, some came to watch. Others to get fucked. It didn't matter what anyone wanted or why they were there; everyone was welcome."

I first took note of Alhamdy about a year later, shortly after he'd moved to St. Louis. Seen as a mysterious, even exotic, newcomer, he ignited imaginations and generated social media buzz with his professed mission of bringing back the lost art of dating, all while looking for his ideal companion. It was reminiscent of The Bachelor, and many contestants were jockeying for position, seeing who would be the next to be wined and dined.

The St. Louis honeymoon was short-lived, with a deepening pool of spurned romantic interests telling their friends not to waste their time because Alhamdy was a player—giving every indication of budding romance, only to cut it off after a couple of dinners. Alhamdy has a fascinating ability to make anyone in his gaze feel like the hottest, most interesting man. And he offers those in his company the kind of undivided attention that's unheard of in today's distracted culture. If attention is a drug, many locals were now in withdrawal.

Soon flirtations were on the decline and cold shoulders on the rise. Then rumors of a torrid past in Kansas City hit the local bloodstream. Over cocktails, St. Louisans speculated on what exactly Alhamdy was hiding.

Aware of the whisper campaign, Alhamdy decided that if stories were going to be told, he wanted to be the one to tell them. He also felt the process would be one of personal growth. We met for dinner at the Boathouse in Forest Park to discuss what he now says was an all-consuming sexual addiction.

Alhamdy describes being in a trance-like state when in the eye of the storm, which was followed by an adrenaline rush.

"When you have that much sex, you not only lose track of time but you lose track of reality," he says. "You really do. Somehow the pleasure only became more intense. And I became more aggressive and volatile. Slowly I let go of whatever inhibitions. I didn't care what someone wanted me to do to them."

After exiting the hotel, he says, he often felt "elated."

"I didn't feel guilt," he recalls. "I felt joy. I felt connected. I knew it was a temporary high, because at the end I [know] I am doing something terrible to someone, and to myself. But for a good few hours that didn't matter. The way I felt towards the end of a relationship made nothing matter but my pleasure."

The hangover, however, was atrocious.

"By the next day guilt sets in and it's heavy. Really heavy. You feel like you're this criminal, this low grade of human filth. I thought of suicide many times. Can't tell you how many times I wished I had driven into oncoming traffic or how many times I seriously thought of shooting myself in the head. That's how bad it was."

Known for his artistic selfies, during the height of his addiction Alhamdy would avoid looking into the camera—or he'd obscure his face altogether.

"My boyfriend never knew anything was wrong. He just knew I took pretty dark pictures in which I didn't make direct contact with the camera and hid my eyes. He would ask me, 'How come you cover your eyes a lot?' I would tell him because it makes it feel like a candid cinematic shot. The truth is, I could barely look at myself."

On a flight back from Seattle, Alhamdy was looking through erotic text messages when his boyfriend, seated one row back, leaned forward and saw the contents. While nothing was said on the flight, emotions exploded at home with demands for answers and Salam's partial admissions.

"I knew there was no fixing this. He was shaking, yelling and crying, and I wanted to comfort him, but I couldn't."

The two briefly tried to live as roommates as they worked to untangle the living situation. That created situations ripe for jealousy and resentment, especially since Alhamdy hit the ground running, wasting no time pursuing a new romance. It all came to a head when he returned home to find his partner had filed for an order for protection claiming harassment, a charge Alhamdy adamantly denies.

"I walked into my apartment to find six cops with my partner, who was looking dead faced. They told me I had ten minutes to get my things and go. I checked into a hotel and sat on the phone with my best friend all night, just thinking about how badly I'd fucked up my life."

Alhamdy says he didn't challenge the order of protection, which was granted in July 2016.

Retreating to the distant suburbs as salacious tales of his double life, many of which he says were false, spread through Kansas City, Alhamdy entered a twelve-step sex addiction program.

"I'm not a religious man," says Alhamdy, "and wasn't expecting all the references to God in the program, but it did help me see and admit that I was out of control, which was an incredibly hard thing for me to do."

After the program, Alhamdy decided to make a fresh start in St. Louis. He says he has shed the duplicity that was the hallmark of his past and lives a life that's an open book (check out his Facebook page to see for yourself). He aims to be honest with others and honest with himself. Rather than finding sex, his focus now is finding his one true love.

One could argue that Alhamdy has gone from being sexually promiscuous to romantically promiscuous. But while anonymous sexual partners are normally easy to shake, spurned romantic interests often get messy—as Alhamdy knows all too well. Few things disinfect better than sunlight, and by owning his story I think he has given us all an example of how to effectively neutralize our often complicated pasts.

While he is a single man who still enjoys sex, Alhamdy said in the past year he's had less of it than any time in his adult life. But it's not for the lack of offers.

"At the end of the night, it's not St. Louis if they don't want to fuck you."

A Song for Alex Braun

Queen of Camp Alex Braun worked at Kmart for years, where he'd post about his co-workers, "the gals of Kmart," and the obnoxious people he had to deal with when working layaway.

When Kmart eliminated layaway, I composed a song for him to the tune of *Don't Cry For Me Argentina*.

Don't cry for me Layaway Rita. The truth is I'd never trust you. All through your tantrums, your zero down bitch fits, a restock promise. No cash remittance.

Christmas Eve 2018

After learning that Dustin Mitchell had been arrested in a Dallas suburb, I managed to locate the *woman* he had married and spent my Christmas Eve on the phone with her and a few other victims.

The next three months would be devoted to researching and crafting the incredible story I heard, which would knock wigs back from Texas to Illinois.

Dustin Does Dallas—Out in STL, March 22, 2018

On the morning of June 28, 2017, the doorbell rang at the luxurious townhome of Mr. and Mrs. Dustin Mitchell. The couple assumed it was a delivery, and Dustin answered the door in his pajamas to find an entire SWAT team there to arrest him.

"What's going on?" exclaimed Lacey McCullough as she watched her husband—a man she believed to be a fabulously successful entrepreneur, the president of Mitchell Judicial Group and a shoo-in candidate for Denton County Judge—being apprehended.

Detective Adams surveyed the scene in the stately foyer, reading the faces of the couple. He turned to one, then the other. "She doesn't know, does she? Ma'am, I'm so sorry."

Adams then turned to Mitchell. "Are you going to tell her, or should I?"

That morning, the Dallas-sized façade of the most infamous gay con man to come out of St. Louis, a façade held together by deceit, sheer audacity and allegedly even threats of murder, began crashing to the ground.

I shouldn't have been shocked. I know Dustin Mitchell. He and I have a strange bond.

In the 1991 horror-thriller Silence of the Lambs, Hannibal Lecter, a brilliant psychiatrist and cannibalistic serial killer, seems to develop a fondness for FBI agent Clarice Starling, and she a fascination with him. I like to say I'm the Clarice Starling to Dustin Mitchell's Hannibal Lecter.

In 2012, Mitchell was a hyper intelligent Rolla, Missouri, native who by age 31 had moved to St. Louis and spun a vast web of lies. That year, he got arrested at the St. Louis County courthouse, where he'd represented clients under the guise of being an attorney. (His arrest spurred numerous headlines, including my personal favorite from the St. Louis Post-Dispatch: "St. Louis County lawyer-entrepreneur-candidate was really none of those.") He eventually pleaded guilty to a theft charge related to a $1,000 retainer fee he accepted, for which he served four months in prison.

Upon his release, he hit the ground running, pitching one fishy business venture after another—copper bullion, discount vacations—on Facebook. I saw them streaming on my news feed and sounded the alarm on social media, in my blog and in my *Vital Voice* column. Mitchell made his displeasure known in enraged messages, but would quickly revert to his charming baseline, seeking to win me over and even offering me the opportunity to write his biography.

At one point he apparently faked a hostage crisis that triggered a dramatic police response, then tried to frame me for it after the fact. He told police I was a scorned ex-lover and should be considered the prime suspect.

"He said you're obsessed with him," said a detective who questioned me.

"Obsessed? I guess that's fair," I conceded, then rattled off several of Mitchell's outrageous scams.

My book *Delusions of Grandeur*, which came out in 2015, described much of this backstory. The back cover made mention of a deranged con man who penetrates Missouri's political scene—an obvious reference to Mitchell.

Incredibly, Mitchell attended my book signing. He was relaxed and pleasant, posing for a photo with me and the book, which he signed. Afterwards he invited me to join him for a few drinks and, in all sincerity, asked if I'd work on his campaign for governor.

When he finally moved away in July 2016, I thought he might mellow out and seek a simpler life. I couldn't have been more wrong.

A Date with Destiny

A woman I'll call "Destiny" first met Mitchell seventeen years ago at Bubby & Sissy's, a bar in Alton, Illinois. (She asked that I not use her real name.) To Destiny, the guy was fun—really fun.

"Dustin is always a good time flailing and cutting up," she says. "You just can't beat a good time with a drunk Dustin. He'll do crazy shit like singing to my boobs in the middle of a crowd of people."

In 2015 Destiny moved to Dallas, and about a year later Mitchell called with exciting news: He was moving there, too.

"The next thing I know he's saying his apartment isn't ready and he needs to stay with me for a few weeks," Destiny recalls.

Destiny claims to know Mitchell better than anyone. Though they're not far apart in age, she says he looks to her almost in a maternal way. She's who he calls when his life bottoms out. And, unlike nearly everyone else in his orbit, she was never fooled by him. Feeling certain he had no apartment in the works, she agreed to transfer to a two-bedroom unit so he could stay with her.

I spent a few hours first talking to Destiny on the phone on Christmas Eve, after being given her number by an administrator of the Facebook page "Bustin' Dustin C. Mitchell: The Conman." I had found the page while trying to determine if Mitchell was still in jail after his recent highly publicized arrest in Dallas for, again, acting as an attorney. Finding the group felt like finding lost members of my own tribe. This initial contact would lead to many more emails, calls, a flight to Texas and an interview with *The Dallas Morning News*.

Living with Mitchell, Destiny says, meant finding old business cards lying around from his many incarnations. They ranged from the pedestrian—managing an Irish pub—to the comically grandiose, like purporting to be a gubernatorial candidate. It meant overhearing arguments he was having over the phone (She and others I've spoken with now suspect there was nobody on the other end of those calls). And it meant a parade of barely legal men coming and going at all hours.

"I constantly called him out on his bullshit and he'd just laugh," Destiny says. "He never tried presenting himself as an attorney to me. His whole life is like Catch Me If You Can. He truly believes he's smarter than everyone else. He doesn't apologize for anything, and he loves the attention. He's all like 'I'm Mr. Moneybags' when he doesn't have a pot to piss in, but on some level I believe he's very self-aware. "

But also needy.

"He's addicted to attention, and the attention-seeking led to many 911 calls, normally for chest pains and anxiety," she recalls. "I got to the point I didn't bother answering calls from the hospital. I'd see the Caller ID and think, 'It's just Dustin pulling his shit again.'"

The most unsettling event at their shared Plano apartment was the night Destiny woke to Mitchell standing in her room, naked, watching her sleep. He had lost his keys and kicked the door in.

Between the damaging of property and the frequent 911 calls, Destiny decided it was time to pull the plug and asked Mitchell to move out. The two didn't talk for a few months, until he sent her a photograph of a marriage license with two names: his and that of Lacey McCullough.

"Now I know that shit's fake," Destiny thought to herself.

It wasn't.

Mrs. Dustin Mitchell

Lacey McCullough graduated from Texas A&M University School of Law in 2015. She had yet to pass the bar exam but was able to practice law under the supervision of her boyfriend Riley, who was a lawyer at a civil litigation firm. She also worked as a department manager at Nordstrom, which is where she met Mitchell.

"Dustin was at the perfume counter, and a guy was awkwardly hitting on him, which clearly made Dustin uncomfortable. I walked over and pretended to be his wife to get him out of the situation," McCullough recalls.

Mitchell's interest was piqued when McCullough told him she worked in the legal field. "I'm running for judge in Denton County," he told her. "We should keep in touch. I'm looking to make some hires at my law firm, since I'll be busy with the bench."

Then, on February 5, 2017, three weeks after meeting Mitchell, McCullough's entire life was upended when her boyfriend committed suicide.

Mitchell called McCullough, and she was nearly unintelligible, telling him the news as she wept. "Where are you?" Mitchell asked. "I'm coming over."

McCullough and her son were living in Plano with her mother, Lori McCullough-Butcher. Mitchell came right over and stayed for four days. He was by her side comforting her during a period where she was nearly comatose with grief.

"Mom was yelling at me saying, 'He was just a boyfriend, Lacy, go to work!'" McCullough recalls. "Dustin looked at her in disbelief and asked, 'Are you serious?'"

McCullough had a fraught relationship with her mother. Mitchell's supportive behavior stood in stark contrast to her mother's coldness.

But Mitchell's time at the house came to an abrupt end when he arrived intoxicated after everyone went to bed and McCullough-Butcher got up and saw him entering the room of McCullough's teenage son, Kaleb. She darted down the hall and opened the door just as Mitchell was crawling into bed with the boy.

"All hell broke loose," McCullough recalls. "Dustin swore it was a mistake, saying he thought he was entering my room, but Mom threw him out. I thought it was just a mistake from being drunk and disoriented in a dark house."

McCullough's depression over the suicide lingered, and one night she woke from an Ambien-induced sleep to find herself in the emergency room. Her mother called 911 and said McCullough had tried to kill herself with a combination of Ambien and Xanax, both of which were prescribed.

With McCullough on a 72-hour psychiatric hold, Mitchell arrived. He claimed to be her fiancé in order to see her.

"Your mother is trying to set you up. She's trying to take your son and destroy your career," Mitchell warned. He instructed McCullough to sign a power of attorney, giving him control of her affairs. She told him no but later learned he'd forged her signature and faxed it to the Plano Police Department anyway.

McCullough says she was released from the hospital after 31 hours when the toxicology report showed she hadn't overdosed—but by that time her mother had her son.

"We'll get him back," Mitchell assured her. "I'll pay for everything but only if you marry me. I'm not investing six figures in this unless we're going to be a family."

Meeting the Mrs.

When I met McCullough in Dallas, I was struck by her clear blue eyes, dark flowing hair, and tanned skin. She took me on a tour of Mitchell's stomping grounds.

As she drove through the endless north Dallas suburbs, she explained that Mitchell had been not only a dear friend but also a life raft. He was openly gay, but he'd been a rock for her when she needed him, and she loved him. His apparent financial security was comforting as well, with his $400,000 Frisco townhouse and financial statements listing assets in the millions. She recalls seeing a tax return claiming his annual income was $189,000.

In the wake of the devastating loss of her boyfriend, she was not looking for romance. She was looking for a companion, she was looking for stability, and she was looking for someone to help get her son back. She said yes, and the two were married by a rabbi in June 2017. (Mitchell, after all, claims to be Jewish.)

At first, he was doting.

"He'd take flowers or chocolates to my work and make a big show of it like he does. My co-workers couldn't believe it. But he couldn't maintain that charm on a daily basis."

The veneer began to peel in many places after McCullough moved into his townhouse. Only days after they were married, the SWAT team showed up.

But when one of the officers asked whether Mitchell was going to tell McCullough the truth or if he should, Mitchell had a ready answer. In the foyer, as he was being cuffed, Mitchell told McCullough, "This is more of your mother's shit."

McCullough believed that her mother had set him up, just as she'd set McCullough up with the overdose claim. McCullough got Mitchell sprung out of jail within six hours.

Once he was out, McCullough pushed him for answers about the arrest and charges. "It's just because I don't have a law license in Texas," Mitchell said, claiming he was licensed in Missouri. He told her you don't actually have to be licensed if you'd passed the bar exam, which she knew wasn't true.

In the preceding months, McCullough had introduced Mitchell to numerous players in the legal community. They'd attended every fundraiser, where Mitchell would hobnob, check in on social media, and of course, get his photo taken with all the power brokers. After they were married, Mitchell would boast, "My wife's going to be the next governor of Texas."

But even as his identity as a legal professional was unraveling, she still believed he was a successful businessman. They always had plenty of money and a luxurious home. When they went to Nicola's, a restaurant where Mitchell claimed to be part owner (in reality he was merely an employee), they got VIP treatment. Everything was on the house, including $400 bottles of wine.

After Mitchell was released, McCullough left town for a few days to process what happened. But Mitchell wore her down, targeting her with a running commentary about how splitting up so quickly would look bad to the judge in the custody case. "He wasn't wrong," she says, "but it was emotional extortion nonetheless."

Even while Mitchell pushed McCullough to reconcile, he went out drinking with friends Daniel and Stephanie Cardona immediately following his release. The couple didn't know anything about what had unfolded earlier that day, and, back at the townhouse, the evening would devolve into a shitshow of monumental proportions.

Mitchell attempted to perform an exorcism on Stephanie. During the unsolicited encounter, Mitchell aggressively grabbed her breast and vagina, all while wearing nothing but a dress shirt and a live snake. Mitchell then called Frisco police claiming to be the couple's attorney, saying Stephanie needed to be committed.

But if the dramatic SWAT team arrest had been the first big crack in Mitchell's Dallas façade, the second crack for McCullough appeared days later, on the day a stranger walked into their shared home.

Ten days after moving into the residence she had been told Mitchell owned, McCullough was startled by an unfamiliar man in her kitchen. "Who are you?" she asked.

"I own the house. Who the fuck are you?" the man replied.

The homeowner had taken a long-term assignment in India, but now was back. Mitchell, it turned out, was just renting a room from him.

When confronted, Mitchell was nonchalant.

"Dustin claimed he was in the process of selling the house to the man to cover medical bills and we would just buy something else, like it was the most reasonable thing in the world," McCullough recalls.

Regardless of these unsettling events, McCullough's focus was restoring full custody of her son. That seemed unachievable without maintaining her unconventional marriage with an increasingly eccentric husband.

For all that didn't add up, many more things did. Mitchell dressed in a suit every day and went to work. He had money. He had reputable business associates.

And of course, he always had explanations.

The Maneuvering Mother-in-Law

"I never trusted him from the moment I laid eyes on him," begins McCullough-Butcher, 58. She folds towels as we sit in her kitchen. "I'm a former cop, and my spidey sense was going off big time." She even invented a slur for Mitchell: her "scum-in-law."

She felt he had sordid motives.

"It was him he was after!" she says, pointing to her grandson Kaleb, who is standing nearby. His height and build belie his young age. "I saw that from the start. It's one thing to take an interest in a child, but he was just too interested."

McCullough-Butcher looks at Kaleb. "You know he's coming for you when he gets out," she tells the boy. "He's going to try to contact you."

When McCullough-Butcher had discovered the truth about Mitchell, she fought to wrangle custody of Kaleb by filing an emergency ex parte stating that her highly educated daughter was unfit, neglectful, homeless, suicidal and—in reference to Mitchell—that she consorted with criminals. She also claimed that McCullough was incarcerated in a mental institution. Two officers swiftly tracked Kaleb down and removed him from a salon in the middle of a haircut.

In order to regain custody, the couple needed to move out of the townhouse where Mitchell was renting a room and into a home of their own. They rented a spacious home in upscale Frisco's Queen's Gate subdivision. They regularly hosted chefs and business associates who came to discuss plans for Mitchell's sensational downtown Dallas restaurant, which was supposedly in development. Mitchell even interviewed potential employees at the house.

As at Destiny's place, there were also many young men who came and went.

The Southern Gentleman

Initially, Mitchell tried to engage in sexual activity with McCullough, which she didn't take all that seriously knowing he was gay. "Once or twice in the beginning he randomly went down on me and I was like 'Okay—I mean, who's going to stop that?" she laughed. He did try to initiate intercourse as well, she says, but was unable to perform.

The two quickly settled into more of a Will & Grace situation, and when Mitchell brought home a handsome 27-year-old professional by the name of Cody Lee Spradling, as opposed to the motley crew of barely legals he brought to the house, McCullough was relieved.

Mitchell quickly fell for Spradling, but the relationship only lasted twelve days—it would have been nine, but Mitchell squatted in Spradling's home for the final three and refused to leave.

Spradling spent the following months avoiding Mitchell's obsessive calls and texts, which he found disturbing, while secretly becoming close friends with McCullough. When McCullough started to suspect Mitchell wasn't really going to work each day, she asked Spradling to investigate.

"So I went to a few gayborhood bars I knew he liked, and sure enough, there he was wearing a suit and sunglasses, indoors, getting drunk in the middle of the day," Spradling laughs.

The Meltdown

Things finally came to a head in September 2017, when McCullough confronted Mitchell after discovering he had accessed her computer and sent threatening messages to people, including one vowing to "end" Daniel and Stephanie Cardona if they ever spoke to his wife again. She told him she planned to file for divorce, and asked him to leave.

Mitchell returned at 3 a.m. "I walked out of my bedroom to ask him what he was doing there. His speech was so garbled I could barely make out a response," McCullough says. He shouted at her and even pushed her, cocking back his fist to punch her, she says, but was tackled by Kaleb. At 6' tall and 195 pounds, the young teenager knocked the wind out of Mitchell, who writhed on the floor.

But when McCullough darted to the backyard, Mitchell got up and called the police to report that McCullough was trying to take his son away from him.

When Frisco Police arrived, McCullough explained to officers that she and Mitchell had only been married a short time—and that Kaleb was not Mitchell's biological son. Mitchell became enraged, charging towards McCullough while shouting, "You fucking bitch! I'll destroy this house and everything in it and make sure you never see my son again!"

The Frisco officers advised Mitchell that if he didn't leave the home, they would arrest him for public intoxication. He finally left after McCullough sprung for an Uber.

"Twenty minutes later Dustin began leaving voicemails, which I still have, saying he was on his way back and that if I cared about my son I would leave, because he didn't want Kaleb to see what he would do if I was still there," McCullough recalls. "Later that day he called again and said he would set the house on fire with me in it!"

It was when McCullough was packing up Mitchell's home office that she discovered clear evidence of his fraud. She found checks for the "Mitchell Judicial Group," evidence he represented someone on a marijuana charge—and paperwork showing he'd used the bar number of her deceased boyfriend. "I contacted his bondsman and advised her that I was absolutely unwilling to cosign on his bond."

McCullough contacted her landlord and advised her she was seeking to evict Mitchell. She got a barrage of threatening messages from Mitchell, vowing that she'd never see her son again. That's when she applied for a protective order.

In her affidavit, McCullough begins, "My husband, Dustin Mitchell, from whom I am separated, is a dangerous man."

Later in the voluminous document she states, "I fear that Dustin may be suffering from a delusion that Kaleb really is his biological child, as he posted a lengthy Facebook Live video to that effect, and that he has the right to physically take him from wherever he may be."

Part of what made it so difficult for McCullough to see the truth about Mitchell was her aversion to admitting her mother was right. McCullough surrendered. It was not only a moment of clarity and reflection, but also foreshadowing. She wrote:

"When Dustin and I first started discussing marriage, I remember my mother telling me she thought Dustin had an unnatural and unhealthy interest in my son. She told me she was afraid his only interest in me was obtaining custody of Kaleb by any means possible. I had originally thought this was absurd, however, I now fear she was absolutely correct."

McCullough's emergency protective order was granted.

The Prophecy is Fulfilled

The day after McCullough got her order granted, Mitchell filed an emergency motion of his own, stating that McCullough was mentally ill and abusive and that "their" son was in danger. In his request, he asked for possession of the Queens Gate home and custody of Kaleb. Astonishingly, the order was granted, giving custody of McCullough's son to Mitchell, who the judge believed was Kaleb's biological father.

This created a spectacle at the house, with the sheriff's department there to enforce Mitchell's order and the police department there to enforce McCullough's. Neither could figure out which order controlled.

In the midst of this, McCullough turned to another nemesis for help: her mother. "Come get my son out of here!"

The jig was up. After reviewing the filings and evidence, the judge issued an amendment to Mitchell's order granting McCullough exclusive possession and custody—even writing in boldface that Kaleb was not Mitchell's biological child.

Just over a month later, on November 6, 2017, the Frisco Police Department and the Texas Rangers again arrested Mitchell for Falsely Holding Oneself Out as a Lawyer, a 3rd degree felony. As of this writing, Mitchell sits in jail, unable to make bond, and facing multiple charges. He still calls Destiny, admitting nothing.

McCullough is currently sharing Destiny's one-bedroom apartment until she gets her own place. At the end of my conversation with her there, we discussed the fallout among Mitchell's contacts in Dallas.

"Everyone knows about it in the LGBT community and it's a big joke. The legal community, however, isn't laughing," she says. "They are humiliated and just want this to all go away. Many have photos with Dustin, and they look at me as the gatekeeper who let this happen. I brought him in. If I ever planned to work in the field again I'd have to leave DFW. This has all been a horrible reflection on my judgment."

McCullough says the FBI believes Mitchell's primary aim was to use her to give him legitimacy in the legal community, while the Frisco Police Department believes his sights were on her son.

Mitchell ran up debts well north of $100,000, she says. "It's going to take me ten years to financially recover from the damage he did in ten months. Emotionally and socially, I may never get my life back."

The only positive thing to come out of the Mitchell ordeal for those involved are the incredible friendships that were formed as a result. Mitchell went to great pains to keep the people in his life from talking to one another, but now his soon-to-be ex-wife has close friendships with Destiny, Spradling and the Cardonas.

And as easy as it is to say McCullough should have known the score much sooner, I can attest that holding on to reality while talking to Mitchell is like trying to swim upstream in roaring rapids—which is why he gets by with so much. Sitting across from him the day of the hostage standoff and again the evening of the book signing was surreal, like I was being hypnotized or transported to his reality. He can lie and justify anything, all while being confident, charming, and completely at ease.

Hannibal Lecter believed Agent Starling was driven to save people because she couldn't save the lambs as a child, lambs which haunted her. At every new development in her investigation, or in her career, he would ask her if the lambs have stopped screaming.

I was first inspired to delve into Dustin Mitchell as a subject after seeing scam after scam in my news feed. There are times I think I'm done covering him, but I always get pulled back in. The scams haven't stopped streaming.

The Night Dustin Mitchell Tried to Perform an Exorcism with a Snake in Dallas—*Out in STL, March 22, 2018*

This piece is an addendum to our longform feature, "Dustin Does Dallas," which appeared in our Spring 2018 issue.

On June 28, 2017, police near Dallas, Texas arrested Dustin Mitchell, a former St. Louis-area con man, for falsely presenting himself as an attorney. He spent six hours in jail, then his wife bailed him out.

And that wasn't even the wildest thing to happen to him that day.

A few hours later, Dustin Mitchell went out for drinks with some new friends, Stephanie and Daniel Cardona.

It spiraled into a shitshow of monumental proportions.

A Master Plan

Daniel Cardona was an attractive Elvis tribute artist in Dallas. Mitchell had become a fawning devotee on his Facebook page and invited the performer to apply for a bartending position at Nicola's, the restaurant Mitchell claimed to have an ownership stake in. Daniel went there to inquire.

"I walked in and he was in a waiter's outfit, which I thought was odd," Daniel recalled in an interview with Out in STL. "But he seemed to be in charge. It's the authoritative way he carries himself."

Mitchell interviewed Daniel in the bar area, then sent him to be interviewed with another man, who he says asked the same exact questions before offering him the job.

Mitchell learned that the Cardonas had brushes with the law, and that Stephanie Cardona was engaged in a custody battle so toxic that her attorney warned her of the possibility that neither she nor her ex would get custody of their five-year-old son.

Mitchell offered Stephanie some legal advice and offered to take custody of her son, whom he'd never met.

"Dustin suggested I give him temporary guardianship of my son, saying that it would look good to the judge," Stephanie said. She found the offer strange, but didn't give it much more thought.

On the night last June that Mitchell joined the Cardonas for drinks, however, his proposal took a darker turn.

"He was pretty sauced up when he arrived, putting on a big show about where he'd been and how much money he'd dropped," Daniel said. "He was talking about how he was a judge and a lawyer and how his wife was going to be the next governor of Texas. But then he brought up his custody plan as if we'd agreed to it."

Reportedly, Mitchell looked at Stephanie and said, "Here's the deal we have to make. When we do this, you can have no contact with your son whatsoever. You will know nothing about him."

"I was dumbfounded," Stephanie recalled. "I never considered handing my son over to him, and this was creepy. I just got quiet."

The Snake Charmer

Later, as the bar was closing and the Cardonas were leaving, Mitchell suggested they split an Uber, since they were headed in the same direction. Once in the car, however, Mitchell told the driver to take them to his townhouse.

"Instant horror movie," Daniel said.

The story the Cardonas shared about the events that followed was also recorded in sworn affidavits to the Frisco Police Department.

At the townhouse, Mitchell announced he was a clairvoyant. He insisted on examining Stephanie. He went upstairs and then returned wearing nothing but a white dress shirt with a live snake draped around his neck.

"He ordered me to a chair in the dining room against the wall," Stephanie said. "He then forced me to sit down. He began asking a series of questions and claiming he could heal me. He then straddled me and insisted that I let him help me. I didn't understand what he meant and became very frightened, and he proceeded with what he was doing anyway. He put his hand on my head, shoving it against the wall, closed his eyes and asked me 'What's happening here?' Startled by this, I replied, 'I have seizures and a little bit of depression. Let me up.' He held my head against the wall, still straddling me with his eyes closed, as though he was a faith-healing televangelist. He then opened his eyes, looked at me, and grabbed onto my left breast, and again asked, 'What's happening here?'"

This moment hit Stephanie especially hard, she explained, because she is a survivor of sexual assault and was also coping at the time with a very recent miscarriage.

Mitchell grabbed her vagina and told her she had never been pregnant.

"When I started to sob, he took his hand off my vagina and covered my mouth so that I could barely breathe. Dustin then stood, announced that the snake had determined I was possessed by a demon, and that an exorcism would be done. By this point my mind and body went into a block-it-out, shut-down sort of state and I was paralyzed by fear. With his hand still on my breast, I replied, 'I have supraventricular tachycardia and I just had heart surgery. Please let me go.'"

Daniel had stepped outside, and returned to find Mitchell on top of his wife.

"He was wearing nothing but a man's dress shirt, with a snake wrapped around his neck," Daniel said. "Stephanie looked like she was barely breathing. I yelled 'What the fuck is going on, man? She's a sex assault victim! Take it easy!'"

Mitchell screamed at Daniel to go back outside, saying he had things under control and that he was helping her.

"He looked completely insane," Daniel continued. " I insisted that he get off my wife and let her up, but he acted like he couldn't hear me until he turned and growled again for me to get out. It was pretty obvious the dude was not all there. I grabbed the cell phone off the counter and went back outside to call us a car to get us out of there. I didn't care if I was going to have to fight this huge guy to do it. The situation was completely out of control."

Daniel's phone was dead, so he ran back inside. "Dustin was walking away from Stephanie mumbling something about a demon and an exorcism and Stephanie was crying really hard. I told him we were leaving and he went outside—still wearing nothing but the dress shirt and the snake," Daniel said.

While outside, Mitchell called the Frisco police insisting Stephanie was violent, suicidal and needed to be forcibly committed. Police arrived to the townhouse (Mitchell put on pajama pants in anticipation of the arrival) and when Daniel would attempt to talk to the police and paramedics Mitchell would interrupt and say he was the couple's legal counsel and they were not permitted to speak to them outside of his presence.

"He was not my lawyer, and I later found out he was not a lawyer at all, but he had told me he had just been elected a judge in Denton County, so it felt pretty hopeless to argue. I was not ever able to tell any of the first responders on the scene that we had spent the evening terrorized by a mad man."

The couple decided that Stephanie leaving in the ambulance was the easiest way to get out of the situation. Daniel Cardona said that he now believes Mitchell was trying to get Stephanie out of the way—in the immediate term, so he could sexually pursue Daniel, and in the long term, so he could find a way to get custody of her son.

Despite Mitchell's insistence Daniel stay with him after the ambulance left, Daniel called an Uber and went to the hospital.

Like Daniel, Stephanie had concerns about not being believed due to Mitchell's standing in the community.

The Cardonas had no idea Mitchell had been arrested earlier that day, but said the officers were very familiar with him, with one saying he'd been called to the home more than once for "the exact same thing."

Dustin Doubles Down

The next time Daniel saw him at work, Mitchell acted like nothing had happened.

The Cardonas didn't tell their stories to the police until a few months later, after comparing notes with Mitchell's wife, Lacey McCullough. Daniel says Mitchell was alarmed when he learned Stephanie and McCullough had been in contact.

Closing out his affidavit, Daniel said: "When our wives became friendly, Dustin went on another tirade, forbidding Stephanie and I from speaking to her with threats of prosecution, job loss, violence, and even death. When it came to the subject of his wife and stepson, Dustin was extremely irrational and easily agitated. He claimed everything from mafia affiliation to freemason affiliation as a way to get even and punish anyone who spoke to his wife without his permission. His wife found out anyway and left him and now he is lashing out at everyone and being scary and unstable."

Daniel finished his story to the police with this: "I need there to be a record of what happened before in case something happens again. This guy is unstable."

Drug War

I heard rumblings that Rick had really been rocking the boat in the queer drug community. I was one of many recipients of a nude photo circulating of him smoking meth, along with photos of S&M scenes shot in the Melrose basement.

"So, Rick has crossed one too many lines lately," began local drug dealer Brian Ray in a Facebook message to me. "And as a leader of the Saint Louis Gay Streets or whatever we're gonna call it, I've got to take him out. I'm contacting you to find out if you know anything about any kind of security system or neighborhood watch I should be worried about at his residence? I can assure you the actual unit won't be harmed nor will any of the others in the building."

"I think there are many nonviolent ways to address the situation," I replied.

"I disagree."

"He's always driving while high. I suspect his plates are stolen and he'd certainly be fired if drug tested at work," I said.

"If this were an issue in mainstream society then absolutely by all means arbitrate, debate, handle it. But this is an issue in the streets. He's breaking rules that you're not allowed to break. There are certain ramifications that must happen.

I thought he had already been fired?"

"What's he doing? Has he? We don't speak? Do tell."

"He's stealing from people already very down on their luck, he's using his social influence to lie about local pharmaceutical representatives and hurt their business, therefore boosting his own as he is now a pharmaceutical representative. He literally picked off the customers of a former best friend, days after that guy lost his job. And not with good business tactics, or working hard, with lies. All lies."

"So he's selling drugs?"

"He's absolutely, positively, most definitely a meth dealer."

"Any downside to informing the police?"

"Well, I can't do that. But if you want to that's your prerogative. In fact, they'd be hard-pressed not to listen to you considering you live in the same building."

"Do you think they'd do anything about it?"

"It would take a minute. They would have to survey the house and eventually raid it. No, no, no, you know the landlord, right? If the apartment is raided the landlord can't re-rent that for like three years. Tell the landlord he'll kick him out immediately. Landlord has the right to enter the building when he's gone to confirm there are drugs there."

"Do you know the story of him losing his job?" I asked.

"He stopped going to work because he was convinced he'd make enough money selling meth. He quickly started doing way too much and got upwards of six months behind in some bills. He was about to have his electricity shut off when he let Ben Jones, one of my best friends, sleep on his couch because Ben is currently homeless. Ben had received $2,000 days before from taxes or something. A week later after Ben pays $1,500 to fix Rick's bills, Rick decides that Ben is shooting heroin and kicks him out. Ben was shooting meth. Meth that Rick had sold him, and he was fully aware that Ben was shooting it. Rick is irresponsible and skirts the consequences by taking from people and then convincing the public that he's the victim. He's Taylor Swift."

"He's the worst," I replied.

"Dude. Literally."

"We threw him a benefit that raised tons of money and then he stabbed us in the back to help our stalker—and tells people the benefit was to get publicity for the book."

"He lies. He lies a lot. He lies for very little reason. He lies so he has something to talk about. It is time he has some consequences."

"He plays this 'I'm a crazy kid' persona that seems to work on people. Makes people want to help him," I said.

"In person he's actually not confrontational at all. He talks all game and when amongst what he thinks are friends, he'll talk mad shit. Then call him out in person, and suddenly you're the crazy person who is a bad thing because you're crazy and when he's crazy it's not a bad thing and he's not crazy now cuz you're the crazy person."

"But it sounds like he's on thin ice. Maybe support for him is waning?" I asked.

"Well, you simply can't fuck over this many people. Ever since he's entered the world of St. Louis drugs and crime I think he's assumed that it's the Wild West and that we all just do whatever we want and it's very much not. There is an order there. And he has broken some cardinal rules."

"He's the cockiest guy around," I said.

"Which is ironic considering his five-inch dick. I mean he only dates tiny guys for a reason. Gotta feel big somehow. I won't feel an ounce of regret, remorse or guilt for the things I do to his property. He doesn't deserve those things. He did not pay for those things. He owes people a lot of money. Instead, he bought those things."

"What did he buy?"

"Not even just bought. He took Ben's camera, the only thing that Ben has, a hobby or really loves as an art, because he says Ben owed him money and never paid him rent. $1, 500 of bills Ben paid. Side note: Ben stayed there for 10 days. He would have gotten a better rate at a 4-star hotel downtown."

"Is Ben one to retaliate? Is Rick using heavily?"

"Ben will retaliate in a certain way. He will definitely not actively seek out revenge, but he will definitely jump should it arise."

"Do you know if Clyde is involved in any of this?"

"I do not believe Clyde is selling. Rick is using, very heavily. Haven't you noticed his recent weight loss?"

"I try not to look at him."

"I am so glad people are finally fucking coming around. I have known he's been this kind of shitbag for like five years. Like, I'm a criminal. I live, breathe, eat, sleep and work in the criminal world. I'm even a high-ranking criminal. But I don't lie, or steal, or cheat. It's criminals like Rick that make the law a good thing. I have a point in there somewhere. Like I don't claim to be Mary Homemaker Law Abider, but there is still wrong and there is still right. I just know he's going to use the world I live in as an excuse for his actions. And it's not one."

"He relishes fucking people over," I said.

"He thinks he'll get away with it forever. It's just fucking mean that his response when somebody calls him out for literally causing them to lose money or literally fucking up their lives is 'Well, he's a psycho.' How is it psychotic to hold you accountable for your horrible actions, Rick! He needs to grow the fuck up."

"Just Saturday someone described him as a troubled kid. I replied he is not a kid. He's about 30."

"He doesn't even look young."

An associate of Brian's forwarded images of the S&M dungeon scenes in the basement along with screenshots of conversations he had with Rick.

"Some of the guys who buy drugs from him are straight, like this one," the guy said as he sent a photo of a slim Black man balancing on a bucket with a bag on his head, álà Abu Ghraib, and another of the same man with a dick in his mouth.

"He'd make the guy suck his dick in front of his cracked-out wife and insults him the whole time."

In the accompanying screen shot, Rick wrote, "I like to humiliate them to give them the fucked-up memories."

Unverified back channel sources said the police were aware of Rick, but were waiting for him to climb the drug ladder before moving in. I have no idea whether that was true, but I didn't see any police activity at the unit.

I told my employers about the drugs being run out of the unit as soon as I learned of it. When the photos landed in everyone's inbox soon after, he was formally asked to vacate and he did without incident—aside from intentionally clogging the toilet with paper towels and leaving it full of feces.

Peyton Rescues Lydia

Lydia was leaving her costume shop when a car abruptly stopped and several men jumped out and rushed a cook leaving the restaurant next door. During the melee Lydia tripped while trying to flee the violence, her phone skidding across the sidewalk.

Peyton was standing outside Bastille and rushed across Menard to help her up. He was punched in the face multiple times, leaving him bloody and bruised.

The rumor mill was spinning as everyone shared their theories behind the attack, as well as Lydia's role.

"I was at the dentist and he had heard all about it already," Lydia relayed. "And in the version he heard, I was on the ground yelling about my jewels!"

"Your jewels?" I laughed. Lydia might wear retro costume jewelry now and then but I was never aware of her wearing fine jewelry.

Of course, it was the talk of Bastille as well. At the neighboring table I heard someone saying Lydia was a racist.

"She's always talking about her daughter, but she's got a Black son who helps her out a lot who she doesn't acknowledge as hers," the guy said.

I was amazed by all that was wrong with that story. Twenty years earlier, Lydia's daughter, still in high school, had brought home a young man with nowhere to go. Lydia allowed him to live there, and because of a disability, had looked after him all these years. She even made allowances for him in her will. It was a beautiful story that had been somehow spun into something hideous.

In that moment, though, I couldn't see any benefit to explaining all of that to drunks who were upset about Peyton's assault, so I simply shook my head.

A few months later, Peyton was called to view a police lineup.

Murder on Menard

Jade Sinclair's Monday night drag show had wrapped up at Bastille, and the performers were in the back changing when they heard screaming in the bar.

"He's just lying on the ground! He's just lying on the ground!"

Police officers and detectives came in and said nobody could leave. Jade heard someone yell that Peyton had been murdered.

"I said over and over that I wanted to go home and I was worried about Mark," Jade began.

Mark, also a Bastille bartender, was Peyton's best friend and lived two floors above Sinclair in a converted schoolhouse in Lafayette Terrace. A three-story building which could be seen from the back porch of Villa Ray.

"They called to let him know. I thought that news should have been delivered in person. It's a lot to share with someone home alone. They were my neighbors," Jade said.

Memorial Planning

Over brunch on the patio at Nadine's, my friend Tim said, "Lisa West and a few other people are planning a memorial golf cart parade in honor of Peyton."

"I'd love to help promote it. How can I reach her?" I asked.

"She's down at Bastille now if you wanna go."

Tim gave me, Kage and Magali a ride to Bastille in his golf cart, where we found Lisa sitting out front. Lisa, a lesbian in her 50s, was an incredibly kind, soft-spoken, motherly figure. She was smiling, but it seemed more of a shell-shocked grin.

Sitting in the sun on the front sidewalk where Peyton was murdered, I interviewed her and submitted the following for the *Riverfront Times*.

Uneasy After Recent Shootings, Soulard Plans a Second-Line Parade—*Riverfront Times, June 4, 2018*

After a violent week that saw beloved bartender Peyton Keene shot to death outside his workplace, followed by a second shooting last weekend, some Soulard residents are feeling a growing sense of unease.

"The only thing I ever feared at this intersection was seeing a bicyclist get hit," says Lisa West, a Soulard resident and a regular at Bastille Bar and Grill, the LGBTQ mainstay where Keene tended bar. "Now, it feels we're being targeted. It feels we're sitting ducks."

West and her neighbors Joe and LuAnn Denton decided to plan a New Orleans-style second-line parade through Soulard. "We've done funeral marches for others in the neighborhood, and thought this would be a good way to honor Peyton," West says, sitting on the sidewalk outside Bastille.

For others, though, the march is also an attempt to defy the neighborhood's recent violence.

"I see this as a protest march," says one passerby eavesdropping on West's conversation.

Some Soulard residents say they feel anxious, in part because they believe Keene's murder may have been related to a previous act of violence in the neighborhood.

West is one. "It all started with a simple act of kindness," she says.

The act of kindness took place February 8. As the *RFT* previously reported, Keene saw the owner of the costume shop next door topple to the ground as she tried to flee a fight. Keene rushed over to help the woman, and was assaulted.

Keene was later called upon to identify the suspects and, friends say, looked at a police lineup.

Neighbors say they believe two of the four men involved in the fight were employees of Harpo's Soulard. But owner John Rieker says this is not true, and that none of those in the fight were his employees. (The seven-month-old bar, which has a successful sister concept in Chesterfield, abruptly shut its doors last week.)

Then, around 11:30 p.m. Saturday, a man threw rocks at Bastille's patio. When a bouncer confronted him, the suspect left—but returned with a gun and opened fire on the bouncer. Police say the bouncer "retrieved his personal weapon" and shot back, striking the suspect in the knee.

The suspect, described only as a 25-year-old black male, left the area, but was later found at a local hospital. His condition is reported to be stable; police say a warrant has been issued for his arrest.

Police would not comment on whether any of the incidents are related. Anyone with information is asked to call CrimeStoppers at 866-371-TIPS.

In the meantime, a memorial service for Keene's life will be held at Bastille this Wednesday at 6 p.m., followed by the procession which will include family members, Soulard's ubiquitous golf carts, prominent drag entertainers including Jade Sinclair, Trixie LaRue, Adria Andrews and the House of Highland, contingents from Pride St. Louis, Tower Grove Pride, and Rudis Leather Society, neighbors, friends, and those wishing to stand in solidarity.

Keene didn't hide from danger. As the community honors and mourns him, its members are determined not to hide either.

The Memorial

Frank Fontana offered to chauffeur Peyton's family in his mint-condition 1960 Pontiac Bonneville convertible, which was adorned with a large rainbow flag covering the trunk. Beginning at Bastille, dozens of golf carts and hundreds of marchers followed Frank through the neighborhood as musicians played their instruments and bartenders stood outside their respective establishments serving shots to the passing crowd.

The community pushed Mayor Lyda Krewson to attend the memorial, and she arrived at Bastille where a stage was set up in the closed street, surrounded by floral bouquets and enlarged photos. Lisa West met her at her car and thanked her for coming.

"I'll introduce you," Lisa said.

"Oh, I'm not speaking," said the mayor.

"Oh yes, you are!" Lisa replied, taking the mayor by the hand and leading her to the mic.

I didn't know at the time the mayor's speech was unplanned but did note how mousy and disjointed it was.

Mark Rumback, who had been Peyton's partner for more than 20 years before they amicably split and remained best friends, spoke to the crowd as he wept, followed by the family and many friends. I spoke as well.

"We can get so numb to the violence that it hardly interrupts our routines," I began "So it's a testament to how much Peyton was loved that in the wake of losing him, we shut down these streets."

Despite the fact many Soulardians claimed to know who the murderer was, saying he worked in the kitchen of a nearby bar, there were no arrests.

Peyton's mother visited Bastille on the anniversaries of his death, saying she felt he was still there, wandering the streets he loved. And Lisa West still called him from time to time years later.

"I know it's silly, but I call and leave messages for him now and then," she said as a tear ran down her cheek. "I really love that guy."

Ms. Jamieson's Live-in Lover

It seemed the famously thrifty Ms. Jamieson was shoved into a crate in the Melrose basement and replaced with a big spending sugar momma when she met Dallas, a quiet young man nearly two decades younger.

Dallas didn't have steady employment, but the two seemed to eat out almost every night. When I raised concerns about her spending, knowing how much she earned and that everything was going on credit, she created two Facebook settings. Her close friends would no longer see posts that involved spending money, but everyone else would see posts boasting about what she'd bought for Dallas.

I knew Dallas had no concept of money, and when he wanted to plan an elaborate birthday bash for her, I knew Ms. Jamieson would ultimately foot the bill, which gave me anxiety.

"I want to plan a big surprise for Jordan," Dallas said. "Maybe a trip."

"Dallas, you're not working right now, so I think we should do something simpler," I suggested.

This clearly irritated him. "I'll get the money," he snapped.

I took over the planning and hosted a party at Dave & Buster's, a game-themed restaurant. While I knew Ms. Jamieson liked games, it was really about something Dallas would like. I knew if Dallas was happy, Ms. Jamieson would be happy.

The Handlebar Mustache

~~~~~~

On several occasions I saw a heavy white man with dark glasses, a shaved head, and a distinctive handlebar mustache leaving the Melrose. I never saw which door he came from, but assumed he was Clyde's latest trick.

One Summer Thursday afternoon I was showing a lesbian a few apartments in the area, and feeling she'd be a good fit for the Melrose, stopped outside the building.

"The last balcony is the unit that's coming available," I said, pointing to Opal's apartment. "It's a fun area. And the neighborhood bar is right there."

While we were pulling away the mystery man arrived, and as I returned home some twenty minutes later, I saw him leaving. I hurriedly snapped a photo, which I sent to Kage.

"Looks like this is Clyde's new trick," I began. "He's been coming around quite a bit."

The next morning Ms. Jamieson sent me a message saying she probably wouldn't be at work because she found out really bad things about Dallas, and was about to have an anxiety attack. Dallas had been sleeping around. Everything came to light when the love interest of a man Dallas propositioned messaged Ms. Jamieson.

Disgruntled Queen: "We should talk today."

Ms. Jamieson: "Oh? About what?"

Disgruntled Queen: "Your dude tried to fuck my dude last night after the gym, apparently."

Ms. Jamieson: "What??"

Disgruntled Queen: "Apparently he has no shame and has been fucking around for a WHILE. I'm pretty pissed because I met him and he was nice to my face, but was trying to snatch dick from me behind my back."

Ms. Jamieson confronted Dallas, who admitted to once having sex with the guy in question, but said that's the only time he'd cheated. Ms. Jamieson was in a tailspin, and later in the day messaged me to say she didn't know what to believe.

Meanwhile, Kage learned that Clyde was in the hospital for dehydration, a common occurrence for him due to his binge drinking, and had been admitted days earlier.

I was driving down a busy thoroughfare when it dawned on me that the mystery man *couldn't* be Clyde's trick. I pulled over and sent Ms. Jamieson the covert photograph, asking, "Do you know who this is? I assumed he was a trick of Clyde's. I've seen him around."

Ms. Jamieson: "When did you take that?"

"Yesterday when I got home." I replied. "He has a distinctive mustache."

Ms. Jamieson: "Oh. When did you get home?"

"4:22. I saw him arrive about twenty minutes earlier."

Ms. Jamieson: "Is this him?"

She sent a sultry photo of the man with an unbuttoned shirt. He was someone already on her radar.

When confronted, Dallas said he was less sure about the relationship than she was, and needed to leave to clear his head. I arrived shortly after he left to give Ms. Jamieson her paycheck and visit with her. She was not answering her phone.

"I'm at your door with your check," I texted.

Moments later she answered the door. She was on the phone with a concerned-sounding woman, and I correctly guessed she was speaking to Dallas's mother, who was only two years older than Ms. Jamieson.

She ended the call and we sat in her messy living room. Ms. Jamieson had always kept a neat house, but a cushion was missing from the sofa, a blanket was strewn across the floor, half-empty soda bottles littered the coffee table.

Ms. Jamieson sat opposite me on the sofa with her hand on her head.

"He says he's not sure about the relationship," she began. "And I don't even want to think about how in debt I am. I've put his car payment and a car repair on my credit card. I've bought him jewelry. I opened up a new card and put an old ticket of his on it so he wouldn't get arrested. We eat out almost every night."

I later learned it wasn't a mere car payment. She'd bought him a car on her credit card.

"I thought all the dining out was concerning since only you were working," I said. "Was he pushing for that?"

"No, but I know he enjoys it and I was just trying to keep him happy," she replied. "I have so much anxiety right now."

"Let's talk about it. What's the main thing you're anxious about?"

"When he left, he said he had doubts about our relationship," she lamented.

"So you're worried *he's* going to leave *you*?" I exclaimed.

"Yes."

"That is backwards. He's contributing nothing to this, and if you're going to be a sugar daddy, you can get much better for your money!"

"Oh I *don't* want to be a sugar daddy!"

"Well, that's what he wants, a sugar daddy, mother, maid combination to take care of him while he gets fucked by everyone when you're at work. That's what he's offering you. Whatever you decide to do is your decision, but you need to see that you deserve much better than this," I said.

Her phone rang, and it was Dallas.

"Hey, um, so can you get dressed and come down? My car is broken down in the street," Dallas said.

"Where are you?" she inquired.

"In the street," Dallas replied.

"What street? The street out front?" she asked.

"Yeah," Dallas responded.

"Do *not* pay for that car repair, Ms. Jamieson! You can't afford it, and you're in the fast lane to Bankruptcy Court. Your new refrain needs to be '*There is no money!*'"

I peeked through the blinds and saw Dallas's sporty little car below, which was far nicer than Ms. Jamieson's old green subcompact.

"I'm going down the back stairs," I said, wanting to avoid coming face to face with Dallas and being forced to interact.

Later that evening, Ms. Jamieson messaged saying Dallas apologized and said he does want to be in the relationship.

"This is your decision. The last thing I'll say, however, is *close your purse!*"

Of course, I knew she wouldn't. Miss Jamieson's high credit score was her proudest achievement, but I predicted that she'd be bankrupt within the year.

And indeed she was.

The Package

It was stuck in Clyde's craw that he was a laughingstock over his Satanic curse, and he was desperate for a way to settle the score.

In his group chat with the girls, Clyde sent a photo of a package with a pair of feces-splattered underwear next to it.

"But hey I did all the bad right? But it doesn't involve you two, right? So, who cares!" wrote a petulant Clyde, which was odd since Opal had been fully in his camp for months.

Upon closer examination of the photo, there were far too many stamps and they weren't even canceled out.

The long-running fixation and resentments over underwear stemmed from Clyde's spur of the moment decision to compete in a bear pageant. The event was in a matter of hours, and he planned to step out on stage before 500 people in untidy not-so-whities. He didn't even invest in shirts, much less undergarments, and I couldn't let him step out with dingy, ratty dollar store drawers.

"All those guys are going to be in really nice underwear," I said while walking to the dresser. "Here, take these. They're perfect."

Clyde competed in brand new camouflage underwear, and in the moment was appreciative. But like most things, his opinion soured as he had time to stew. He'd regularly post snide comments like, "I may not wear $50 underwear, but . . ."

The soiled underwear in the photo were the dollar store's answer to designer underwear, with some unfortunate Santa Fe pattern. From the garment selection to the uncanceled stamps, every corner was cut during this hurried and shoddy scheme.

Undoubtedly, he thought news that we mailed him shit-covered underwear would spur the community to rally around him and forget all about the curse, but his stunt only served to make him look crazier and forever alienate key supporters, including Opal, who cited his behavior as her reason for moving.

He wasn't willing to accept that hard reality, though, and continued to parade the shit package as if it were the ultimate vindication.

He even brought the fecal folly to court.

Sleeveless in St. Louis

I mentioned that Clyde did not spend a penny on clothing, which reminded me of the backstory of the shirt he used to curse us.

Me and Kage had been out shopping and saw a nice short-sleeved button-down shirt we thought would look nice on Clyde. It was road crew orange, and indeed was flattering on him.

"I wish it was sleeveless," he said more than once during the course of a night out.

He owned two or three tired old shirts he'd wear to the club, and they were all sleeveless.

The following week he posted a picture of himself in the shirt with the sleeves hacked off. Rather than being removed at the seam, it was clear he used scissors, and not carefully.

Friends made a few puzzled comments and then "Maestro of Memes" Ms. Jamieson sprang into action. She had people on his thread rolling with Clyde memes based on the movie poster for *Sleepless in Seattle*, but instead titled *Sleeveless in St. Louis*.

In the meme series the title never changed, but the subtitle varied. One that got the biggest reaction: "He liked his shirts like he liked his men. Old with gaping holes."

Clyde pretended to be laughing along, but in retrospect he was Satanic cursing along.

Emergency Call from Shawn Adams

My protection order against Clyde was set to expire soon, and he made a show of counting down the days in not-so-vague social media posts.

We were housesitting at Villa Ray when Cody called.

"Shawn Adams has asked that you call him. He said he knows you hate him, but it's urgent. He also said he fucked up."

Shawn was the former friend who Clyde recruited to come after and troll us while we were dealing with Brawny's advanced cancer and subsequent death.

I called to see what he had to say.

"Thanks for calling," Shawn said, seeming to struggle with where to begin.

"As I'm sure you've seen, Clyde has been counting down the days until the protective order is lifted. I texted to ask what that was about and he said he was going to confront you guys. He was all over the place, saying he wanted to punch you in your smug face, and then minutes later that he wanted to fix things, but if he can't fix them he might as well ruin them."

Shawn told Clyde he didn't know what he meant.

"If I can't fix things, we'll all die."

"What do you mean by that? You're not being rational" Shawn wrote.

"It hurts more than I thought it would, and I didn't know there would be this much blood," Clyde replied.

Shawn called 911.

"The operator asked for Clyde's address. I said I didn't know it, but then said, 'Oh it's on a protection order I have a copy of' and as soon as I said that I thought 'What the fuck am I doing?' and how you said I would own everything he would go on to do."

Shawn profusely apologized for all he had done in defense of Clyde and sent screenshots of the entire exchange.

"I'll do whatever is needed to try to make this right. I'm really sorry."

Clyde accused Shawn of betrayal for calling 911, and after Shawn told him he needed psychiatric help, Clyde blocked him.

Two hours after the police left that evening, around midnight, Clyde messaged Emily claiming it was me and Kage who had called 911 as part of our campaign of harassment.

Back in Court

In my experience, people rarely admit they are wrong, much less try to make things right, so I was impressed that Shawn appeared in court as a witness for Kage.

A few weeks earlier, using screenshots of the conversation between Clyde and Shawn, I had tried to get my order renewed but was unsuccessful. I think I was overconfident since I had evidence that he was counting down the days and spoke of murder-suicide, and therefore was too relaxed and composed.

Clyde was typical Clyde, bringing a mountain of garbage as evidence and randomly presenting things to see what would stick.

"Today's been a good day," Clyde boasted on social media after the hearing, which of course made my blood boil.

With Kage's order we weren't taking any chances or sparing any expense. We hired a respected attorney and asked Shawn to appear in person to testify.

For his part, Clyde was armed with the shit package.

"Your honor I have a package I believe they sent to me."

"You believe but you don't have proof?" the judge asked.

"No"

"Then I don't want to hear about it."

Under cross examination the attorney asked Clyde, "Have you sent or posted private photos of the petitioner?"

"No," Clyde responded.

"Do you have a tumblr? And is your handle tripleXcub?"

"Yes," Clyde said, his voice dropping.

The attorney handed him copies of the revenge porn.

"What does the screenshot say?" she asked.

"Shared this on tumblr after your asshole move tonight, and many more. I can share whatever I want," Clyde solemnly read.

The attorney handed the paper to the judge.

"Your honor I'm trying to move but there are no apartments," Clyde said.

The judge granted the order.

Emily's Departure

Emily decided to return to Tulsa, with plans to continue on to San Antonio. Not wanting to feel left behind and being uneasy about Clyde, Opal moved a few blocks away. The west end of the Melrose was empty.

I posted a poem to Emily's Facebook page, along with photos of her in *Newsweek* and the *Riverfront Times*.

Windows defined your time in St. Louis

Like a sunbeam you were just passing through us.

You made Newsweek documenting police from behind glass,

And the RFT as "The Lurking Lady" with your mysterious Mardi Gras sass.

The drama coursing through this city's veins I know at times made you insane,

But this moment in time will come into beautiful focus as you turn back to look, and of course it will all be told in my upcoming book.

Have a great move and enjoy the adventure!

New Melrose Resident with Backstory

The next person to occupy Emily's charming apartment was a young woman named Jamila, who was a tenant at one of our nearby buildings but grew uneasy about a neighbor. When she called to ask if she could transfer, she explained:

"Seth, the guy across the hall, has been acting really strange. He carries a samurai sword on his back and has been creeping me out with the way he's been acting. I'm feeling unsafe here. Is there any way I could transfer?"

I thought the Melrose would be a good fit, and after seeing the place she agreed to take it, with plans to move the following week. The very next night she returned home from work to find her building surrounded by police officers and crime scene tape.

Seth had mutilated his friend with that samurai sword.

RFT

RIVER

THE

Seth Herter's life in St. Louis

SAMURAI

was full of delusions.

KILLER OF

But the murder was all too real

SOUTH CITY

BY DOYLE MURPHY

The Samurai Sword Killer of South St. Louis

I remember quite a bit about meeting Seth Herter. First of all, I found him to be quite handsome: 29, 6'4", blond, strong jaw.

"Ms. Jamieson, I'm showing the apartment to a guy who looks like Evan Peters from American Horror Story," I texted.

I thought it was peculiar that his roommate Mel was a grouchy, dumpy man in his 70s.

In the middle of the showing, Mel revealed they had a dog, which was not permitted in that building. When Mel asked why, I said for starters the owners typically didn't want dogs in units with carpeting.

"They're worried about *this* carpet?" he asked in a huff.

"This carpet is brand new," I replied.

"But it's *shit* carpet!" he snarled.

And then a third person showed up out of nowhere, their affable friend Tim, who appeared to be a middle-aged construction worker.

"Hi, I'm Tim, yeah Seth's my friend and wanted me to see this place he might be getting. Nice place, looks good." He spoke a mile a minute while bouncing through the apartment.

Initially the pair's application was denied, but when Seth begged for guidance, I threw out that a solid cosigner might make a difference. Within a day he presented a cosigner who was a university official in Texas. The man, whom I spoke with over the phone, described himself as Seth's godfather and seemed intimately familiar with Seth and Mel's dynamic.

"You're very kind and sexy to be so helpful," Seth said to me as I walked him through the process.

Despite the fact he was gay, it was such an odd thing to say and made me uneasy. I was careful to keep him at a solid arm's length.

During the year and a half he lived there, Seth found himself on the verge of eviction due to noise complaints—mainly centered around his loud singing at all hours—and excessive traffic. It was also suspected that his associates were breaking the back common window to get in and sleep in the basement.

It was yet another broken window on the common back door right next to Seth's apartment, coupled with other complaints from the unit below, that spurred a May 3, 2018 maintenance visit.

The maintenance man caught Seth as he was leaving his unit.

"I need to get in for a maintenance check."

"Now is not a good time," Seth stated as he pulled the door shut.

"I'm here now, and need to check your unit."

"Looks like I left the key in the car. I'll go get it," Seth offered.

Instead of coming back with a key, he fled town in the victim's vehicle.

That evening, the police called the company and said they needed to access the apartment. What they found would rival the set of any slasher film.

Horror Headlines

Killer used samurai sword in St. Louis murder, police say—*The St. Louis Post-Dispatch*

Samurai sword used in south St. Louis slaying—*FOX 2*

St. Louis man charged with samurai sword killing, theft—*Montreal Gazette*

After conferring with the property owners, I told my editor at the *Riverfront Times* that I could get them exclusive access to the apartment on the condition they did not reveal the address or the company.

Star reporter Doyle Murphy was assigned the cover story. Interviewing Seth in jail, he learned that Seth had believed he was the Antichrist. He felt people were in his walls and furniture, and he called his ex-boyfriend Tim, the affable guy who was at the original showing, to ask for help.

When Tim arrived, Seth said the voices told him to kill him. He cornered Tim in the bathroom and stabbed him to death.

Police captured Seth outside of a dive motel 80 miles west of St. Louis.

In an interesting twist that stunned everyone, including Seth, Timothy Wilson was not the real name of the deceased, and he was 55. Seth believed he was in his 30s.

His actual name was Christopher McCarthy and he was living a double life. In the city, Timothy Wilson was the sometime lover of Herter. In the far-flung exurbs of St. Charles County, Christopher McCarthy was a heterosexual member of a long-running gospel trio.

That's a St. Louis plot twist for you.

Villadiva

With so much of my bandwidth dedicated to my creative pursuits, other areas of my life had been neglected. One was fitness—I'd put on some weight, and the others were home and financial related. I went on a diet and lost twenty pounds, sold an apartment building to one of my clients, which earned me a nice commission, and then we began looking for a house.

It seemed we were priced out of Tower Grove South unless we went for something small and plain. Much of the neighborhood consisted of generous homes from the early 1900s, but the last blocks to be built consisted of spartan post-war infill, which was all that was within our reach. I instead focused on the up-and-coming Carondelet and Patch neighborhoods along the river at the south end of the city, near Bar PM. I began to zero in on one house with a view of the Mississippi, but Kage was lukewarm on it because it did not have a front porch, which I learned was important to him.

Then a large, beautiful Tower Grove home showed up in our price range. It was on the same hill as the house I was heartbroken to leave when returning to California, and five doors up from the drag bar Grey Fox Cabaret. From the photos, I was taken by its original mahogany woodwork, numerous stained-glass windows, ornate radiators, and its overall presence.

I dubbed it Villadiva because it was the grand villa looming above the drag divas on the corner.

I tried to schedule a showing but it went under contract instantly.

Back to the drawing board, and we found a large flat-roofed Carondelet home that looked to me like an embassy with its symmetrical, formal side yard, manicured 10-foot hedge walls, and wrought iron benches facing a fountain, which had a dead bird floating in it.

While Mom isn't generally superstitious, a bird flew in the house shortly after Dad's first heart attack. That was supposed to be a bad omen, and when it happened, she went to a private spot and cried. He died within weeks of that incident.

I got word that Villadiva was back on the market, and rushed to view it. Kage was not a love-at-first-sight kind of guy. He was just taking it all in and wanting to digest the information.

"This kind of house isn't going to linger on the market," I told him. "It's twice the house we'd normally get for the asking price."

One reason for the price was its location in the less gentrified southeast corner of the neighborhood, closer to all the gunfire on the other side of Gravois Avenue. Plus, Tower Grove buyers were looking for gut rehabs. While in good overall condition, this was an old house filled with original plaster and even some original wiring.

I said it was like we had the budget for a new Honda Civic, but opted for a big old Cadillac.

Just as I predicted, the house went under contract for a second time. I worked to resume the search and move on, but Kage had decided that was the house he wanted, and nothing else would do.

He did not want to move to Carondelet or to my other riverside choice, Alton. He wanted to be in Tower Grove and have a garage, a nice yard, a porch, and basically everything Villadiva offered.

"That house is not coming back on the market for a third time, Kage," I said.

"Let's just wait and see," he replied.

It did, but getting financing was complicated. Had we selected a tidy 1000-square foot post-war infill, it would have been no problem, but we chose this big old drag queen of a house with the stage name Mona Moneypit. I pulled out all the stops and managed to arrange for private financing.

We later spoke to others who had seriously considered buying it, and they all said things like, "The first thing you'd have to do is paint all that dark woodwork."

We loved the house just as it was and were amazed by how much of the original splendor was intact, all the way down to the original matching hexagon knobs on every door in the house.

As we'd got to know Villadiva and its history in the coming years, we strongly suspected the house had derailed the other buyers intent on gutting it. The house had chosen us.

The Marking of the Territory

The evening before closing, not yet having a key to the house, we began moving things from our Melrose balcony to the backyard of Villadiva. The house being situated on a corner, the neighbor behind us faced the side street and his front porch was adjacent to our driveway.

The fact we even had a driveway was novel in Tower Grove South. Most everyone had a garage or a parking pad only accessible from the alley, while we had more of a suburban arrangement with a roomy driveway off the main street, as well as a stately garage. The neighbor, who was named Javier and probably in his early 50s, only had street parking. And we'd come to learn he was very territorial of it.

Standing on his porch with a scowl on his face and his chest puffed, Javier stared skeptically as we were unloading.

"Hi, I'm Chris and this is Kage. We are moving in tomorrow."

"I was wondering what was going on. Strange to move at night," he said gruffly.

The following day I showed up with the dogs and noticed him again standing on the porch.

"Hey," he said as I was getting out of the car. "I didn't know you had dogs. I've been noticing dog poop on my yard . . ."

I cut him off while shaking my head. "This is the first time these dogs have been here, they are on leashes, and affixed to their leashes are their poop bags," I said as I basically blew him off and closed the wooden privacy gate.

I knew the South City drill of marking territory. Letting the new neighbor know what's what, including the pecking order.

We didn't really acknowledge one another for a few months until each of us were shoveling our walkways after a blizzard. We began discussing a neighborhood security issue when he said, "You don't have to like me, but I'm looking out for—" and then a timid young Black woman approached from the street. She was stuck and needed help.

Javier joined me in digging her out and getting her on her way. Before she left, she said, "You two don't fight anymore."

We looked at one another puzzled.

"You two were arguing when I came up," she said.

"Oh, he always sounds like that," I dismissed.

Moving from the Melrose

Our dear friends John Kreisel and Jonathan Batchelor were an enormous help when we were moving. We repeated that it wasn't urgent we get everything out immediately, but they were adamant that we get it all done in one fell swoop. Years later, during an intimate holiday dinner at their Belleville home, pictured, they explained why. They both felt an evil presence.

"I walked in and was like, 'Okay, we're moving today!'" John recalled. "I was willing to do things I'd never otherwise do, like hoist the sofa by ropes from the balcony. I just wanted to get you guys out of there. It wasn't a mere haunting. The place felt swampy, like something was summoned up from the basement."

Jonathan sensed it too. "When you walked in there was the dining area to the left, and that's where it was, back in that corner. It was bad."

The dining area was where the back door to the stairwell was, so it made sense something that came up from the basement might be there. In addition to the basement, that corridor also led to Rick's old apartment, where many became addicted to drugs and were forced to sexually humiliate themselves for his sinister amusement.

When we returned to the Melrose to retrieve a few final things, John stayed at Villadiva to light the water heater.

"I thought you guys were back because I heard walking in the kitchen. When I came upstairs and realized I was the only one in the house, the hair on the back of my neck stood up."

While he knew Villadiva was haunted, He said it wasn't anything evil.

AUTUMN 2018 | VOLUME 2 | ISSUE 1

OUTINSTL.COM | FREE

NIE LEE BOWLS US OVER | STU... ...AY... RHOODS | BEAR ESSENTIA...

OUTINSTL

where we live

Where We Live: Presenting the St. Louis Area's Top LGBTQ Neighborhoods—*Out in STL, September 2018*

There was some grumbling in conservative Jefferson County when the 2016 DeSoto Christmas Parade was slated to include the county's drag bar, Rumors on Ice. Among the garden-variety homophobic comments posted to the event's Facebook page, one stuck with me: "Go back to the Central West End."

The remark amused me on a couple of levels. One: the dated idea of the Central West End being synonymous with "gay"—a concept that hit its peak in the seventies and eighties. Second, I can't help but think it would blow this troll's mind to learn that his Jefferson County community is home to more drag than the Central West End today.

While residing in concentrated LGBTQ neighborhoods was once a necessity for those wanting to live openly, these days it's more of a preference, one factor to be weighed alongside other area amenities. Still, many of us seem to cluster in our preferred enclaves, whether it's because we share similar tastes, we like living where the action is, or both.

We asked our readers to tell us what St. Louis area neighborhood was the best "gayborhood," and your top five picks have some similarities. Three are near the Mississippi River, four out of the five are in the city, all have impressive historic housing stock, all have LGBTQ businesses in walkable proximity to residences, and all serve as magnets for LGBTQ visitors from throughout the region and beyond.

Most importantly for the purposes of this poll, all of these neighborhoods have passionate supporters.

5. Soulard

Called "The Island" by many of its cocktail-loving, golf-cart driving residents because of the way the river and highways cut it off from everywhere else, Soulard is the oldest intact neighborhood in the city, as well as St. Louis' own French Quarter. The area has had a sizable LGBTQ population since at least the seventies, when several bars catering to our community opened up. At that time many of the historic brick homes were abandoned, and all were going cheap. Today, property values in Soulard are among the city's highest.

St. Louis is a drinking town, but nowhere is alcohol more central to the culture than in Soulard, with its countless corner taverns, tucked-away patios and of course its massive Mardi Gras celebration. Once, leaving brunch at Nadine's, I saw three golf carts in a row and was trying to determine which one belonged to my friend. "This one must be it," I proclaimed. "It has beer bottles in the cup holders." We then discovered all three had beer bottles in the cup holders.

Saturday mornings are the best time for shopping and socializing at Soulard Farmers' Market. Grab a cheap and delicious Bloody Mary at Julia's Market Cafe and peruse the offerings while stopping to visit with friends doing the same. Any evening of the week you can find good conversation just by walking down the street, where bars and restaurants have tables lining the uneven brick sidewalks and residents enjoy libations on their front stoops.

Of all the neighborhoods chosen by readers, none comes close to honoring its dead like Soulard. Examples include Midnight Annie, a drag queen who long performed at Clementine's and whose remains were entombed in the wall there, and the recent funeral march held for murdered Bastille bartender Peyton Keene, where hundreds marched, played instruments and rode in adorned vehicles and golf carts while bars along the route offered free shots to passing mourners.

An island in the heart of everything, Soulard is among the most interesting districts in St. Louis, and feels like home, even to many of us who don't live there.

4. Carondelet/Patch

Founded in 1767 by French-speaking settlers, and annexed by St. Louis in 1870, Soulard's scrappy and much more diverse down-river sister is seeing a resurgence with rehabbers drawn to the historic housing stock, some of which is among the oldest in the region but remains surprisingly affordable. From the workers in the industrial businesses along the riverfront to the homeowners restoring their domiciles brick by brick, this is a place where skilled people use their hands.

The community's roots in this area, at the southern tip of the city, run deep. Greg Yogi Thomas, whose family has resided in the neighborhood for generations, remembers a trans woman who lived openly on his block for much of the seventies.

"Did people leave her alone?" I asked him.

"Hell yeah they did! She'd kick your ass!" Thomas replied.

South Broadway has had gay and lesbian bars going back decades, and the two current LGBTQ bars, Bar: PM and Hummel's, flank "Queen of Country" Bonnie Blake's antique shop. Steven Louis Brawley of the St. Louis LGBT History Project believes that Blake, 90, is the world's oldest performing drag queen.

Brawley has concerns about the increasing buzz around South Broadway. "St. Louis's 'gayborhoods' have always been on the margins, and our local LGBTQIA+ community needs more recognition for its many contributions to the revitalization of historic neighborhoods such as Benton Park, the Central West End, Lafayette Square, South Grand, Soulard, etc.," he says. "Many of our pioneers and elders, including Bonnie, have settled where they feel at home, not because it's trendy or fashionable. Gayborhoods are places to work, play, and live. Sadly that is a hard trifecta to sustain."

3. Alton

While the Mississippi River that passes by St. Louis is a workhorse, filled with gigantic barges, a swift current and dangerous debris, twenty miles north it feels more like a lake, with broader width, numerous islands and recreational watercraft. Situated on dramatic bluffs rising high above it all is picturesque Alton, Illinois. Known as one of the most haunted towns in America, I've also dubbed it "The Bi-Muda Triangle" (see "Navigating the Weirdness of Alton, Illinois" on outinstl.com), thanks to the town's penchant for bisexual activity.

The area is rich with outdoor activities, from the marina on the riverfront to the famed Great River Road, where you can drive or bicycle alongside the bluffs for miles in what's been called one of the most scenic drives in America. Hiking, fishing and ziplining options are available, in addition to numerous wineries.

It was Alton's marvelous (and shockingly affordable) neighborhoods that lured Kevin Dyer to move here from Old Town Florissant in 2014.

Dyer lives in a circa 1865 elegant Italianate-style home on Christian Hill, a beautiful area defined by steep streets and sweeping views. Like the famously haunted town itself, many homes in Alton have their secrets. In the case of Dyer's home, so did the man who built it.

"This house and the one across the street were built by Alton architect Lucas Pfeiffenberger, who played an important role in local history," Dyer begins. "This house has a crawl space between the first and second level that was used for hiding soldiers from the Confederate prison to sneak them out of Alton. The house across the street, which belonged to the best friend of the man who built my house, has a secret passageway from the basement to the garden shed that was used as part of the Underground Railroad to smuggle slaves through Alton."

The ruggedly handsome Jason Brooks lives in the nearby Middletown Historic District and surveys the city's goings on from behind the white picket fence in front of his charming two-story, circa 1871 wood-frame home. On a recent Sunday afternoon, he's on his front porch, conversing with his partner and a couple of friends, when he stops to take notice of an attractive guy walking towards Schwegel's, a full-service corner grocer that's a throwback to days gone by. Brooks refers to the blocks around him as "a mini-gayborhood."

"There are so many of us that live within just blocks of each other. Seven or eight I can just think of off the top of my head within just three blocks of me," Brooks says.

When the sun goes down, the party kicks off at Bubby & Sissy's, the LGBTQ bar where Brooks works. Expect a packed dance floor downstairs, a dazzling drag show upstairs and great conversation on the patio with an amazing cross-section of open-minded people.

A 45-minute commute to downtown St. Louis, Alton may not be the best fit for those with city-centered lives or for those who require constant stimulation. But for those who can surrender to the rhythm, this captivating jewel of a town gets in your blood and has plenty to offer.

2. The Grove

In the 1990s the Manchester strip was a mile of boarded-up buildings climaxing with Attitudes, Slovak's and—who could forget—Grandma's Rainbow's End. Today, LGBTQ establishments in or immediately outside its borders include PrideCenter (the region's LGBTQ center and home of Pride St. Louis), Attitudes, Just John, Rehab, the Monocle and the behemoth JJ's Clubhouse. Many mainstream businesses and venues have also taken hold in the Grove, creating a vibrant, walkable mile illuminated by neon signs hanging over the street demarking the district's entrances.

In addition to the venues, the neighborhood hosts large street events including GroveFest and the World Naked Bike Ride. But there's more than meets the eye to this festivity factory, especially at Just John. Pride St. Louis's Todd Alan is among the many influential people who frequent Just John, sometimes even setting his laptop upon the bar and working there. He notes that Just John raises a tremendous amount of money for the community.

"Last year Thirst For Life raised $12,500, which was more than all other participating bars combined. They also have done events for Pride, Team St Louis, GLASS, GMC, Gateway Pet Guardians, Mullen

Day Foundation." Alan explains. "We are actually lucky in St. Louis to have a lot of generous bar owners in Just John, Rehab and Bar: PM."

With the area's boom in high-end housing, with both expensive single-family rehabs and big new multi-family complexes springing up in the neighborhood, some people worry our businesses might be pushed out. Only time will tell, but right now the Grove has never been hotter. Despite the fact fewer of us live within its boundaries than some of the other top neighborhoods, both commercially and in terms of influence, the Grove's Manchester strip is widely recognized as the region's most high-profile "gayborhood."

1. Tower Grove South

You would be hard pressed to find a more well-rounded neighborhood for LGBTQ people than Tower Grove South. Want a lesbian-owned social-justice-oriented coffee shop? OK! A drag bar within stumbling distance of your door? Grab your dollars! An LGBTQ-focused twelve-step program? Step right up. Endless Instagram-worthy international food options, food trucks, and an all-night diner? A buffet of options! Affirming, rainbow-flag-flying churches? Praise! A place to buy that last-minute sex toy, or get a replacement key for your handcuffs? Take your pick, and bring your trick! Neighbors who broadcast their liberal beliefs on yard placards? More good signs! Your own world-class pride festival, attracting upwards of 10,000 to your own neighborhood park? Well aren't you precious? And in the right place!

Beginning in the 1970s and increasing throughout the 1990s, many in our community migrated from the Central West End to south city, and Tower Grove Park was and remains the epicenter of our St. Louis settlement. Tower Grove South is such a multicultural liberal bastion, even its Alderwoman Megan-Ellyia Green is frequently on the streets during major protests, a fact that's even caught the attention of the *New York Times*.

Living in close proximity to so many people you know, the neighborhood lends itself to the impromptu. Walking my dog, I've been invited to last-minute barbecues, picnics, pool parties and, yes, protests. Even the dead of winter can be fun; a snow day that shut down the city in 2017 inspired a big group of us to take over Friendly's.

With all the cyclists, dog walkers, people doing yoga in the park, and fit, shirtless joggers, Tower Grove South is teeming with active residents. With all it has to offer, it's no surprise readers voted it the Top LGBTQ Neighborhood in St. Louis.

Zooming Out

In the grand scheme of things, neighborhood boundaries in St. Louis are somewhat arbitrary. While the cosmopolitan Central West End has no regular drag shows, stroll across a short bridge and you'll find them several nights a week in the Grove. Similarly, south city, which encompasses many of the highest-ranking LGBT neighborhoods, largely operates as one ecosystem rather than semi-autonomous districts—and a whopping 67 percent of respondents to our poll voted for city neighborhoods south of Interstate 64. You can happily enjoy the delights of Tower Grove South even as you live one block away in Tower Grove East—or even a bit further east in Fox Park. There are enough LGBTQ-friendly businesses, and friendly neighbors, to go around.

That said, we're glad to bestow bragging rights upon some of the enclaves where it's easiest to surround yourself with "family." And for everyone else, isn't it nice to know we can find welcoming neighbors throughout the St. Louis area—and even in Jefferson County?

Rumors on Ice owner Dave Sassman tells me that those who made a stink about the club participating in the parade succeeded in one thing only: galvanizing the local community to stand up in support of his business and patrons.

"What was funny is it really backfired on them because more people supported us, enjoyed our float and saw nothing wrong with it," he says. "We actually won 'best float' in the parade that year."

I surmise that "Central West End" wasn't merely a geographical location in the mind of the Facebook troll, but was an idea of a worldly, urbane place where those he considered "weird" would be readily accepted. But rather than sticking to the Central West End, we've made the entire region a bit more like it.

Chris Andoe is the editor in chief of Out in St. Louis and the author of Delusions of Grandeur. He's currently married to Tower Grove South, but flaunts his torrid affair with Alton.

The Villadiva Dining Room

Villadiva was designed for entertaining, and the big formal dining room was the star of the home with its coffered ceiling, stained glass windows, and antique crystal chandelier restyled and rewired by our friend Chris Kerr, the friend who let us bury Brawny in his yard.

One of the Ladies Who Lunch, Frank Fontana, gave us an enormous dining table, which is where I held interviews. Being photographed at that table was a sure way for someone to generate buzz in advance of an article or magazine feature.

I was preparing for the Out in STL Influence Awards, which burlesque star Mazie Mason (formerly known as Charlotte Sumtimes) graciously agreed to emcee along with ballroom legend Meko Lee Burr. We met in the dining room to plan, and when she got home, Mazie posted the following to social media, along with fun photos:

Last night was a meeting for the Out In STL Magazine Influence Awards at legendary "A-Gay" Chris Andoe's Villadiva. Fashion sensation Meko Lee Burr was there, as we are hosting the awards. Two improv emcee divas, one stage, this is going to be something!

Producer/Photographer Chuck J Pfoutz was in attendance to discuss entertainment.

Speaking of influence, a heart-to-heart talk with Chris Andoe a little over a year ago is the reason I began recognizing the perks that lead to enjoyment and eventual ownership of my bad girl of burlesque status. I'm enjoying a recent resurgence of that status but as a completely different being, existing in and exuding new ownership of inner power.

I've always felt comfortable with Chris because he is fascinated with characters. Takes one to know one, which makes me utterly fascinated with Chris Andoe. He's got this way . . . you know you shouldn't open your mouth and spew tea into his ears but you can't help confessing your sins. Father Andoe's Confessional. Why isn't that a YouTube show and Chris, if it ever is one, I'm fucking co hosting with you.

If you're ever invited to The Villadiva Dining Room, GO. If those walls could talk . . . and they probably will in his next book.

Chris has had mucho influence on both my mental state and career. I've evolved into a fierce, yet calm and controlled force to be reckoned with. As far as the Charlotte chatter, if it's not said to my face, it doesn't have meaning. Keep talking. I'm already interesting. You're just making me more so.

It was great to see Chuck J Pfoutz again. We met years ago when we were both starting out in the scene. He's a different Chuck, too. The success of his Maximum Exposure brand has brought the inevitable duality of love/hate that's de rigueur with, well, exposure! Maximum, in fact. It was a bonding moment if I GET IT. "When people talk shit on you, I say I don't care. She's fucking hilarious. I judge her by her art." Honestly, when it's happening to you, the hate, the social media callouts as first means of resolution, it feels like you're the only one experiencing the nastiness. Truth is most higher profile people in our Scene and beyond have as many haters and as lovers. If you want to be public, you have to learn to find healthy ways to deal.

The commonality of experiences made for a bonded, creative, and productive meeting of minds. If more people in our scene could drop the mafia-esque ruling of our city's art, think of the beauty we could create to further normalize, humanize, and show off to untapped audiences what would lead to further understanding and acceptance of our community. Imagine the combining of talent that doesn't happen because of the turf and ego wars that would ultimately lead to some mind-blowing entertainment for the people of St. Louis.

The Out In STL Magazine Influence Awards is Thursday, March 28th with further details TBA.

I didn't know Mazie Mason was in a slump when I landed her for the Influence Awards, but she said I inspired her to stay on the stage after she all but decided to hang it up. Chuck Pfoutz said something similar. He had stepped back from the community after being targeted by a full-figured drag queen named Sugar who once had her own show at the Grey Fox a few Wednesday nights a month.

By all accounts Sugar wasn't an impressive performer. To ensure she filled seats, her affluent husband would buy prizes the audience members could win.

"He basically paid people to watch her show," bartender Jack Abernathy said.

Sugar was a chain smoker, and halfway in or out of drag she'd stop, come downstairs and stand on the front step in front of all Tower Grove South humanity and light up a cigarette wearing nothing but her panties, pantyhose and gogo boots. Right there on the city sidewalk. It was a sight, and it irritated Jack to no end.

"If you're going to come down to smoke half-dressed go out back," he'd say.

"Oh, you're just being silly," she dismissed.

One day Jack had enough and posted a photo of her nearly naked ass standing in the vestibule with the caption: *This is why I can't get anyone to come into the bar.*

Many commented and shared the post, but Sugar blamed Chuck. He'd been filling the Wednesday slots Sugar wasn't using, and she saw him as a threat. She circulated a petition asking club owners to blacklist him and dozens signed.

After that, Chuck focused on producing mainstream events. Maybe a year or so after the petition, I invited him to Villadiva for an interview. He said the story I wrote emboldened him to step out again.

"I was never in a house. I never had a house leader who looked out for me," Chuck explained. "After the petition and all the hate I was just staying out of the scene, and then you summoned me back!"

I liken the thought process of decorating Villadiva to that of set design. Inspirations came from New Orleans' grand and eclectic Pontchartrain Hotel, as well as my late Grandma Andoe's house, where our family's best stories were told. We wanted it to feel settled, like we had always been here, and like it's a home that's been in the family for generations. It was a very different approach from what everyone was doing in Tower Grove, which involved opening up walls, painting everything shades of grey, and choosing modern decor.

Sparkling crystal chandeliers appropriately dimmed, bookcases lined with 100-year-old books, accent lamps everywhere, big Persian rugs. I joked that the decorating style was "Homosexual Hand-me-down" because there were pieces from everyone we knew, but it all came together to create a place where guests and subjects felt they could settle in.

We apparently succeeded in our goal of making the decor appear as if it had always been there. Our friend and eventual roommate Marcus assumed we'd bought the house furnished.

Around the corner from the dining room, beside the grand staircase, was the Wall of Fame. That is where the fruits of what was achieved at that table were showcased. A gigantic cluster of framed articles and covers climbing into the second story.

It had been about eight years since I had what I considered to be a proper home, and that house was on this very hill. Like an old diva who was holding it all together with plastic surgery, cosmetics and good lighting, Villadiva had character and was just my style.

Not only was Villadiva our home, in a sense it was the family home for our extended House. And it felt we had always been here.

Keeping Order

I thought I had bonded with Javier during the blizzard, but he was still aloof. There had been a few times a guest parked in his spot, and he came to the door to tell me about it. But other than that, we didn't speak.

While Tower Grove South was considered trendy and somewhat affluent, we were in the scrappier southeast corner and Javier had been holding it down for about twenty years. He saw his role as a protector of sorts, and would yell at loiterers and apparent drug dealers, often stopping just short of coming to blows. More than once I witnessed him grab his bat.

I took his work for granted until he disappeared for a few weeks. I don't know why he was gone, but I could feel the difference.

One afternoon I was in the yard and the dogs were barking at the privacy fence, where a big group of about ten kids aged six to 16 were walking just on the other side. The kids began grabbing anything they could find, sticks, large pieces of bark, and even a bottle and throwing it all over the fence.

I rushed through the house to cut them off out front.

"Where are your parents?" I demanded.

Immediately I thought of the scene from *Stand by Me* where the old man who runs the salvage yard is haplessly yelling, "Come back here!" at the kids as they were walking away. What the fuck happened? I was the ornery kid ten minutes ago, and now I'm yelling at a bunch of kids, knowing I'm completely powerless to do anything.

Fortunately for my ego, they didn't point and laugh, but merely avoided eye contact and kept walking.

The next time I saw Javier it was late on a Saturday night and I was walking back from Grey Fox, where I'd been up in my cups.

"Hey! It's really good to see you!" I said enthusiastically, and I meant it.

"It's good to see you too," he said, obviously surprised.

I think my sincere appreciation for his presence put us in a better place.

Photo credit: Justin Lehman

Niles

The first time I saw Niles, he was standing alone in the back bar at JJ's, and me, Kage and Clyde were sitting opposite him at the end of the bar.

"He's hot. I haven't seen him before," Clyde said.

"Go talk to him!" Kage nudged.

"I dunno," Clyde said.

"Fine, I'll go talk to him."

As soon as Kage said hello, Clyde ran over and body slammed him in a fit of jealousy. Kage wasn't hurt, but found it a ridiculous way to treat a wingman.

When *Out in STL* launched, Niles wrote expressing a strong desire to be part of it, having interned at national publications during his time in Los Angeles. I gave him an assignment but I had never seen someone so terrible about meeting deadlines.

He wouldn't communicate at all; he would just ignore repeated inquiries about where the piece stood.

"Nick was hounding me about the assignment and seemed *really* stressed. I think it's best to let him cool off for a few days before replying."

What? Who thinks like that?

Niles was no longer receiving assignments, but expressed interest when he learned we were going to rent out a room. With our menagerie of animals and our love of travel, we needed someone there to look after them when we were away.

We agreed to $400 a month, and Niles moved in. Since he worked in fine dining, his schedule was opposite ours, which was nice. The first $400 cash payment was really helpful too, but payments got smaller and more random over time.

METH

AT

THE

MELROSE

Meth at the Melrose—Out in STL, January 3, 2019

My husband sleeping by my side, I woke from a Saturday afternoon nap two summers ago to my friend and downstairs neighbor, whom I'll call Keith, passionately kissing me. My Tower Grove apartment building, The Melrose, was like a big gay frat house back then, a place where it wasn't uncommon for neighbors to let themselves into their friends' apartments. Still, this was highly unusual.

"Dude, I'm rolling," Keith said before nonchalantly turning to leave.

"Rolling," as I came to learn, means tripping on Ecstasy. My drug is alcohol, which enables me to roll past these kinds of situations without much thought in the moment.

I'd vaguely known Keith dabbled in some sort of drugs on occasion, but he held down a good job, paid his rent and, despite his bad-boy reputation, seemed more or less together. In the coming weeks that façade would fall away, along with our friendship. Keith left his job to become a full-time drug user and dealer, running drugs out of our building. As things spun out of control and Keith pushed meth, fentanyl and GHB on everyone in his orbit, our mutual friends and neighbors split into two distinct camps: those who used and those who didn't.

I began to notice friends losing weight, which I'd always considered a good thing, but they were evasive when asked how they were doing it. Soon, however, the reason became obvious.

The downstairs apartment was now a main distribution site, and I felt the crisis forming concentric circles around me. Addicts living in and running in and out of my building. Friends in Tower Grove South relapsing after long being in recovery, including a friend who lost his long-term relationship and life as he knew it after starting to use again, locking himself in a friend's bathroom and absolutely destroying it. The third circle consisted of high-profile people in the local LGBTQ scene, including a title holder in the bear community who resigned to focus on recovery and a former news reporter whose meth-arrest mugshot went viral.

I also noticed the social media innuendo about the latest young person in the community to die. It's something everyone talks about without ever talking about it. "Another gone too soon," they write. "Senseless." That's followed by dozens of comments where nobody answers those asking, "What happened?"

While I knew our community had several high-profile dealers, I felt my home was radiating destruction. A situation I had created by recruiting friends to move in had become a cancer on the city.

Meth-Induced Madness

Opioids may be getting all the mainstream headlines, and they certainly impact our community, but the crown jewel of our drug habit remains crystal. A 2015 report from the Substance Abuse and Mental Health Services Administration found that gays and lesbians were significantly more likely to have used illicit drugs in the last year than our straight counterparts. Gay men, the report found, are four times more likely to use meth than straight ones.

And while meth is initially presented as a fun party drug, it's far more insidious, as I've learned while observing its impact on the men living in and visiting my building.

It's not like the drug and the issues around it were new to the Melrose before Keith's downfall. Months earlier, a resident had an attractive trick over who was clearly high and consumed with paranoia; he became convinced a siren in the distance was a signal to the apartment building. When the guy left, too distracted to consummate the rendezvous, he hung his leather harness on the street sign out front, apparently in defiance of those he believed were tracking him. (Surprisingly, in a neighborhood rife with both package thieves and harness enthusiasts, it remained there all night. I discovered it when I left for work in the morning, correctly guessed who it belonged to, and returned it.)

Such paranoia, I came to learn, is par for the course. "Meth made me lose my mind. It takes you to the darkest places imaginable," says my friend Brandon Reid, who used for a decade and went to prison four times on meth charges before turning his life around and becoming a counselor. "You think everyone is out to get you."

Aside from learning it's not uncommon for meth users to spend three or four straight days at the bathhouse, the most surprising thing I learned while researching this piece was that meth often induces psychosis, which is similar to schizophrenia, and the drug can even be an "on switch" for schizophrenia.

"I heard entire conversations that weren't actually occurring," Reid recalls.

Longtime user Jimmy Eden, who shocked the St. Louis community this past summer by sharing photos on Facebook of the meth-related cellulitis superinfection ravaging his face, says he hears numerous voices—something Keith attempted to mock him for when they ran into each other a few months ago. Looking the newly gaunt Keith up and down, Eden replied, casting shade, "And you look like the picture of good health."

Walking through Bellefontaine Cemetery, where we'd been discussing friends he'd lost to drugs and suicide, Eden explains the various personalities of the voices—which he says are both male and female, black and white—and the things they say to him.

"Basically, my psychosis voices are all of my fears and insecurities. 'You're getting evicted, you're going to prison, you're stupid, you're disgusting, you're going to die'—which is actually the most feasible and realistic, and sadly the one I cared least about. I'm smart and logical enough to know that after the, I don't know, 50th time, that this isn't reality and these things aren't going to happen. But aside from that, it's less than fun to say the least, and completely illustrates the infinite insanity of meth addiction. Because I'd keep doing it."

During one of our interviews I experienced firsthand the paper-thin walls of Eden's 1950s south-city infill apartment, where one of his neighbors' entire conversations could be easily heard. The voices Eden hears, he says, sound just as real.

"Sounds as real as neighbors talking through walls or the floors above me. Particularly sounds like the unit above me. You have to keep in mind using heightens your senses, including hearing. And obviously paranoia. I think your mind draws from white noise, creating these sounds. Definitely much worse and many more conversations to be had when the A/C unit is on, for instance. I'd say there's about five to ten voices. But I also keep in mind the fact that I'm not that important for five to ten people to fuck with me for three days straight."

Can't Trust Anyone

"Anyone who sells it uses it. That's how they afford it. I've never been down that road because I know how it ends: prison or ratting someone out to avoid prison," Eden answers when I ask if he's ever sold drugs.

I could almost feel Brandon Reid shaking off the cold as he recalls his old life of addiction. "Meth showed me things I'd prefer not to have seen. A very dark side of the gay community, a different world you didn't even think was a world," he says. "The people you meet, dark people, it's a subculture. Everyone is up all night, and they're inside all day because they look terrible. The mentality is get them before they get you. I was conniving. I was manipulative, I'd steal and help you look for it."

I saw similar treachery play out firsthand when a drug war erupted between Keith and flamboyant dealer Brian Ray. I describe Ray as flamboyant because of his brazen openness about his profession, to the point of handing out business cards complete with prices. Keith, according to Ray, had violated every possible code of conduct among dealers and, to add insult to injury, was cocky and disrespectful to the point of trolling Ray's right-hand man over the rape and murder of the guy's mother.

The walls were closing in on Ray—he would be arrested in a raid within days if not hours of sending a cryptic message to his enemy in July 2018: "You deserve this."

A photo of a nude Keith smoking meth while holding a baggie was distributed to many who had beef or business with Keith, myself included. Additional photos of Keith's drug use, as well as images of S&M sex scenes in the common basement of the building, followed, as did screenshots of numerous conversations Keith was involved in. The one taunting Ray's associate was forwarded to my inbox: "I wonder how gaped your mom's pussy was after they lit that bitch on fire."

Someone who was a regular at Keith's admitted to me that they tipped off the authorities to Ray's operation. Ray had several meth arrests under his belt when his motel room was raided on July 11, 2018, according to federal court records. Police seized more than 50 grams of meth, including an envelope ready for distribution with a handwritten note that read: "HAVE A DOPE A$$ DAY :)" He ended up being charged in federal court on four counts of possession with intent to distribute. Prosecutors allege he'd been busted with more than 50 grams of meth on two different occasions.

On November 6, Ray pleaded guilty under an agreement with prosecutors. He faced sentencing on February 21, 2019.

But for Keith, the repercussions continued. He was asked to vacate the building within days of Ray's attack.

No Longer Fun

When Jimmy Eden began regularly using meth in 2005, he was 27 and working at Faces, the legendary East St. Louis nightclub. A veteran of the rave generation, Eden was no stranger to substance abuse. He saw "Tina," as meth is often called, as just another designer drug, akin to Ecstasy. "I'd say the appeal was the loss of inhibitions for someone such as myself lacking confidence, sexual or otherwise. And of course the numbness was huge. It made me not feel the longest. I don't like to feel feelings," Eden says.

Meth's grip, Eden quickly realized, was much tighter than expected. Thirteen years on, he still hasn't found his way out. Increasingly, he sees death as the way.

"Meth's often cut with fentanyl now, which causes shallow breathing, much like when you die. I always think, 'I hope it kills me this time,'" Eden says.

"It no longer even feels good. The psychosis voices, the visual hallucinations . . ."

One reason he does meth even though it's no longer enjoyable, Eden says, is that it's the only time he has energy. "When I'm sober I'm always tired. One thing I want to convey is the exhaustion of it all. The exhaustion of always starting over. Always having to learn a new job."

The events around my small apartment building seem like a microcosm of what's going on community wide. Some who weren't using last year now are, some who seemed to be maintaining are self-destructing, and the rest of us are witnesses to the devastation.

The golden "Barbary Lane" age of our building lasted about a year, when everyone enjoyed amazing camaraderie, when we'd gather for big meals together, and when we'd wander in and out of one another's places. We were a family. The shift was abrupt, like when a cold snap hits after an unseasonably warm fall. And like that plant you forgot to bring in before the first freeze, there's no bringing it back.

Most, but not all, of the Season One cast has left the Melrose, and new characters have taken their places. Meth would probably not be the reason anyone would give for leaving, but the party was clearly over. What was for a beautiful moment one proud tribe became two distinct and distrustful factions, and brotherhood turned to hate.

Only one member of Keith's tribe remains, and like the paranoid trick who hung his harness on the street sign, his motivation seems to be defiance. Simply holding on to the wreckage of what was, like a ghost wandering the Titanic, seems to somehow give him a sense of purpose.

Just blocks away from this building, however, there is hope for addicts. A Crystal Meth Anonymous meeting occurs every Tuesday night at 8:30, with a goal of helping people like Jimmy Eden—who does often attend—finally beat their addiction. And there are stories like Brandon Reid's: in recovery for five years, Reid is now living a healthy and rewarding life, and says the option is out there for everyone, if they're ready.

Meth at the Melrose Reaction

The piece mentioned that a title holder in the bear community resigned to focus on his recovery. That guy was bitter about the mention for years, which surprised me because he was fairly public about his journey, and I did not name him. It certainly didn't help matters that in the depths of his meth addiction, Jasmine conned him out of his car.

It was a shady sounding deal from the start. He only had a few payments left but couldn't afford them, so she offered to make the payments if they could share the vehicle, and a bill of sale was drawn up that didn't look legit at all. Once she had possession of the car, she never thought sharing was convenient, and instead suggested he use public transportation. She even suggested that since he worked for the state, the metro train would likely be free.

Well, he took that as gospel and found out it wasn't free. Considering she wouldn't share the car and he felt duped about the train, he tried to undo the arrangement, and even got his mother involved.

"You really made out on the deal!" his mother angrily said to Jasmine.

The group chat had tuned out the car drama much like we'd tuned out the Christine saga, both of which Jasmine discussed ad nauseam. At the time it seemed all involved in the car arrangement were shady, and when we'd push for specifics, like how she obtained insurance, she was evasive. But the spat over the train not being free hit us as funny, and inspired the "Maestro of Memes."

Ms. Jamieson made a meme based on the movie poster for *The Girl on a Train*, but with Jasmine in the image, and the title changed to, *The Girl Who Lied About the Train*. Under the title was the caption, "She made out on the deal."

So not only did Jasmine con him out of his car when he was on meth, the group made a big joke out of it and even pulled in his mother. Not our finest hour. In 2020, he and I talked it out (after he angrily read me for filth) and I apologized to him. I had many such apologies to make resulting from my Jasmine judgement lapses. The car saga ended with Jasmine claiming he had stolen it, but from what he told me it was repossessed by the bank because she, according to him, didn't make a single payment.

In retrospect, our group chat really was a bit scary considering how we could collaborate so quickly and effortlessly. While rarely unprovoked, one funny remark or a sloppy attempt to come for us and we'd roll out talking points, clever quips, nicknames, robust threads and even viral memes without even being emotionally invested, and then we'd forget about it. It was all very flip, but as with this case, the impact was often bigger and longer lasting than we understood. I think in our minds, or at least in mine, other houses were equally capable, and there was nothing extraordinary about the influence we wielded.

Back to the feature, Clyde and Menashe were livid. They both publicly denied having used meth, but then Menashe contradicted himself with a boastful post about all the different drugs he used. (For the record, unlike Rick and Menashe, Clyde was never an addict).

Rick was quiet publicly. He'd long since fallen out of polite society anyway and was exclusively surrounded by fellow addicts, whom he sold to. He, and to a lesser extent Clyde, did troll Jimmy Eden for his role in the piece. For years afterwards. Rick messaged him on the apps to hurl insults and I always found it comical that Jimmy didn't simply block him.

I had forgotten exactly what Rick would say, so I asked Jimmy.

"I'm a loser, worthless to society, kill myself," Jimmy began. "Pretty much anything he is. He's a deflector and projector."

When asked why he didn't just block him, he said he got off on confrontation. Jimmy dished it out plenty, as well. For instance, he had brutal nicknames for members of Rick's crew based on physical characteristics and alleged sexual kinks, names like "Brown Tooth," and "Piss Face." He also used the widely-distributed naked photo of Rick using meth as his profile picture.

On the bright side, I was happy to hear from Brandon Reid that something positive came from it.

"So, I wanna tell you, your article has been great for people. I've had several members in the gay community reach out for help."

FEBRUARY 27 - MARCH 5, 2019 | VOLUME 43 | NUMBER 8

RIVERFRONTTIMES.COM | FREE

RFT

RIVERFRONT TIMES

THE MAD BEADER

OF SOULARD MARDI GRAS

AUNTIE M MAKES THE BEADS
THAT MAKE THE PARTY

BY CHRIS ANDOE

The Mad Beader of Mardi Gras—
Riverfront Times, February 27, 2019

Wearing a top hat and sitting at my cartoonishly long dinner table, my wildly eccentric friend of 20-plus years, known to friends as Auntie M, revisits the last time I tried to interview him. That was two years ago, and part of the conversation took place over text. At one point, he replied to my inquiry, "I'm tired of texting and I'm bored."

"Wanna know why I said I was bored and ended it?" he asks playfully. "Because you asked about the famous people who owned my beads, and that question makes their value contingent on that, like that's what's important, when the beads are what's important!"

The beads are piled high on the table in front of him—some with black and white babies, some with big floppy sea creatures, some with skulls adorned with Swarovski crystal eyes, and some with stout erect golden penises. Auntie M grandly fans his open hands over the sparkling endowment, each strand of which will be bestowed upon a reveler in St. Louis, or New Orleans, or at New York's Mermaid Parade on Coney Island, or maybe even on his favorite cashier at Whole Foods.

Respecting the Alice in Wonderland quality of his storytelling, and not wanting to risk derailing this interview, I simply allow Auntie M to begin talking, and only gently steer (or attempt to steer) the conversation now and then. Each strand has a story, including the first beads he presents, which are adorned with golden babies.

"I was in New Orleans in my French aristocrat attire—you know, with the towering pink wig—and I see the hottest entertainer," he says. "He was Mediterranean and dressed in a sailor's outfit with really tight pants, and I was in love. We talked and he was the sweetest guy, and I gave him a strand of my golden king-cake baby beads.

"The next morning I'm on the balcony and there he is oiled up and dancing on stage in nothing but a G-string and one strand of beads. My beads!" Auntie M proudly recalls. "I hadn't brought any other costumes; I'd just put on the same thing, and on day three I walked past these queens who had been partying hard, probably doing all sorts of drugs, and one noticed I was still wearing the same outfit and turned to his friend and admiringly said, 'She's been up for days!'"

Nothing pleases Auntie M more than seeing others wearing his beads like heirloom pieces, especially if it happens long after he first bestowed them. In the late 1990s, Auntie M set his sights on the most coveted spot in all of Soulard Mardi Gras: the balcony at Menard and Allen above Clementine's, which was the oldest gay bar in St. Louis when it closed in 2014. Only a handful of people were permitted up there, so without any connections Auntie M showed up a few days before Mardi Gras wearing one of his outrageous costumes and carrying a bucket of his first-generation beads, which he'd made from braided garland and pearls. The beads were impressive enough that owner Gary Reed agreed to allow him to grace the balcony during the festivities, where he delighted the crowd below and whipped them into a frenzy of bead lust. The next year he returned to the perch and noticed people in the crowd wearing his beads. He was deeply honored, but also slightly embarrassed because his artistry had improved so much over that year, as he'd moved beyond repurposing Christmas decorations and begun incorporating rosary beads and better wire.

In the two decades since then, Auntie M has become one of the city's most recognizable Mardi Gras personalities. He graced the 2000 Soulard Mardi Gras poster, has been featured in countless Mardi Gras photo montages and, more recently, hosted the High Heel Drag Race. But for him, it's still all about the beads.

And Auntie M's creations have become the ultimate Mardi Gras status symbol in St. Louis. They're simultaneously exclusive and populist. They represent authenticity, street cred, and Mardi Gras glamour, perhaps because they cannot be bought. These are beads you have to earn.

Auntie M's real name is Matthew Traeger, and convincing him to let me use it here was an easier task than getting him to reveal his age, which even I am not sure of. "Those details are only known to me and Madonna's plastic surgeon, so let's just say I'm solidly Gen X territory," he says.

He lives in a flat overlooking the Missouri Botanical Garden with a yoga mat in the living room and a bed in the very center of the bedroom surrounded by a garden of blacklight-illuminated glow-in-the-dark flowers. Everything in between those two rooms—dining room, kitchen, hallway—is a warehouse of beads, wigs, hats, mannequin parts and sundry insane items. Unlike his age, I know about his day job, but he doesn't want me to say much about it. It doesn't have anything to do with beads.

He went through several artistic incarnations before settling on beads. The first time Auntie M attended Soulard Mardi Gras, for instance, he was adorned in recycled artificial flowers spray-painted in Day-Glo colors. At the time there was a popular nighttime Mardi Gras parade, and his group of similarly adorned marchers followed a golf cart topped with a blacklight spotlight.

He became interested in beads after buying strands and thinking about how much more fun and interesting they could be. Also, he saw people literally risk their lives for them. "I've seen people run and grab throw beads from between the wheels of tractor trailers in the parade. I've seen them pick up beads that were on horse shit. I mean, if people are willing to debase themselves for beads, give them something worthwhile," he says.

If I had to use pop culture references to describe Auntie M, I'd say he's part Dr. Frasier Crane and part Roger the Alien. He's almost hypnotic in his speaking style, very even and measured, although when amused he is prone to let out a hearty cackle. I've never once seen him frazzled, hurried or even distracted. Each word is thought out.

Auntie M scours the globe for beads, and when he finds something truly unique he buys in bulk—and I mean bulk. "A giant Brooklyn warehouse was being liquidated and they had all these beads from West Germany, so they'd been sitting in boxes for decades," he says. Rubbing his finger over one kitschy German bead that looked to be from the 1960s, he explains how the beads have no seam, which is unusual. He spent $10,000 to acquire all they had.

The babies he uses in his beads are manufactured for use on baby shower cakes. He orders them in bulk from a bakery supplier and then drills holes through them. "Mardi Gras is so white, not just in St. Louis either, so I began with black baby beads to celebrate diversity, and then came out with the interracial baby beads—and nothing compares to the excited reaction when I give those to an interracial couple."

He patronizes bead stores in San Francisco, Seattle, and Houston. The golden penises are imported from France. "The French just have that aesthetic down," he says. He has a favorite supplier in China. "When you open the bags these come in it smells like a toxic waste dump," Auntie M says of the gorgeous absinthe green Chinese beads. "The air quality is so bad in the industrial province where they're made. I set them in my hallway to air out for a few days when I get them. I'm sure my neighbors love me."

Sometimes beads do not cost money. That was the case at the 2002 Burning Man festival, which Auntie M attended wearing a kimono-style ensemble custom-made from metallic organza fabric by Marie Oberkirsch, an artist in Old North.

"There was this domed Arabian tent where you could create your own jewelry and the price was taking a photo wearing what you made," Auntie M recalls.

That leads to another memory, one from the Burning Man festival: "I had that billowy outfit on with a golden Italian-made mask and a headpiece from Bali, a golden ornate thing, and I was sitting in the actual effigy. That year it was all about gods and deities, and the base of the effigy had these alcoves you were supposed to sit and pretend like you're a deity, and a nerdy white couple came up and presented me with an offering of beautiful glass beads and a little bracelet, and in return I gave them one of my own strands, and as I'm handing it to them it busted apart and fell into a cloud of dust."

In the moment, Auntie M just laughed, thinking what an appropriate comment on impermanence it was, being at that ephemeral festival in the desert. "But they didn't seem to see it that way, and they just kind of wandered away with devastated looks on their faces."

And then there's New Orleans, a city so awash in beads they clog the sewer system. During his annual pilgrimage to march in its numerous parades, Auntie M collects the most intriguing krewe beads thrown on the streets there, takes them apart, and incorporates the krewe emblems into his works.

Not every supply source is so exotic. Locally, he enjoys the fine selection at Carnival Supply and Schaefer's Hobby, and he's even slummed it at (shudder) Hobby Lobby when it's had some insane sale on disco-ball ornaments.

And then there's Bass Pro. "You go past the kettle corn and all these people getting geared up to go out and kill animals, and I'm looking for tackle boxes for my beads and fishing line to string them," he says. "As far as the fishing line, I've found that 30-pound test has enough of a resistance to give the strand some shape. It's like Bass Pro is my Michael's Annex."

Auntie M feels a great deal of camaraderie with the seasoned bead traders he encounters.

"There are diehard Mardi Gras people who are really into trading really good beads. Oftentimes it's an older lady that looks part Kentucky Derby and part hooker and has so many beads they take on the form of a life preserver. Some will even zip-tie their favorites together to make sure they don't trade those," Auntie M explains.

"They talk to you about them—every strand has a story. Some are handmade, some you can't find anymore and sometimes they are wearing beads I made. One had this incredible strand containing a miniature rubber chicken. I had to sweeten the deal a bit to make that trade."

After obtaining the rubber chicken beads, Auntie M engaged with a group of nondescript people with really basic signs, like "Have Fun," preparing to walk in the parade.

"Can I walk with you?" he asked them. "I'm handing out beads." They consulted with one another and agreed. Halfway through the parade he realized they were Scientologists.

Every tribe has its corner for Soulard Mardi Gras. Ninth and Barton, around D's Place, is the single & mingle tribe. The bottom of Russell near Hammerstone's is where many of the most serious drinkers gather. Auntie M posits it's because they lack the ambition to climb the hill after the parade since the drinks are right there anyway. Frat bros love 12th and Russell around McGurk's, and 12th and Allen is a more relaxed mix of Soulardians, hippies, hipsters and drag queens.

After Clementine's closed, the center of gravity for the LGBTQ community shifted one block south, from Menard and Allen to Menard and Russell. That's where Bastille, the block's other gay bar, is located, as well as Metropolis Vintage & Costume. I've been close friends with shop owner Lydia Dane since I first moved to Soulard from Oklahoma City in 1997. We became acquainted when I purchased Art Deco chrome furniture from her, which she conveniently allowed my 22-year-old broke ass to pay for in installments.

Dane graciously offered my crew the use of her iconic second-floor turret so the bead-throwing tradition could continue. Auntie M invited a group of elaborately costumed clown entertainers to join us and I invited several colorful friends, including one who peeks at the crowd through a mock glory hole, and the Krewe of the Tawdry Turret was born. The turret has also been dubbed "the Opera Box" because of its sweeping view of the intersection, which is packed with thousands during the height of the revelry.

"It's the ideal location to continue the Clementine's tradition," Auntie M enthuses. "Such a crossroads with so many people moving around. New Orleans has Bourbon and St. Ann, and St. Louis has Menard and Russell. And being above a costume shop is perfect."

Auntie M has been in the Grand Parade many times, but preferred the intimacy when the parade used to snake through the neighborhood rather than march down Seventh Street. After twice being mobbed by the crowd, he understands why they had to move it. Still, he finds the enthusiasm lacking on the newer route. "It's like many of those watching the parade here don't know they're at a parade. They're just kind of standing there." The colorful crowds below the Opera Box are more his speed, and between stints at the turret windows, Auntie M descends to street level and mingles with the people near Bastille's drag stage on Russell.

Mid-afternoon during Soulard Mardi Gras 2017, Auntie M mingled with the crowd beneath the Opera Box. "C'mon, just flash it," a 20-something woman said to her boyfriend while lusting after a luscious strand of Auntie M's glass and wood beads, which he was gently twirling off the end of his pink skull-capped scepter. With very little prodding the sculpted man complied, the gallery of huddled onlookers was impressed, the beads were awarded, and Auntie M moved along to find the next lively exchange.

More often than not it doesn't involve any forbidden flashings, yet still results in the awarding of beads.

"It used to be everyone would flash everything. They'd be flashing right and left. Our culture is not as debaucherous as it used to be," Auntie M says. "I think a certain amount of debauchery comes from oppression. People felt oppressed all year and then went wild when given the opportunity."

While Auntie M doesn't talk a great deal about his other life, which involves a job in the mental health field, he does have many observations about psychology and our ever evolving culture. In the case of Mardi Gras, he says people seemed anxious in the George W. Bush years, like they felt somewhat guilty about partying (although both men and women did flash more than today, which he thinks was in part due to fewer cameras). In the Obama years, people seemed happier, but that's only increased with the new guy in the White House. "The new generation is just happy, and the women party hard, which is new," he says. "It used to be more the guys doing that. I think it's part of the women's empowerment we've seen in the face of Trump."

Auntie M is interested in the symbolism behind the party. Of his famous King Cake baby beads, which consist of one-inch plastic babies varying from creamy white to brown to jet black, separated by colorful glass or by wooden beads, Auntie M says, "In modern Western culture we see any baby symbols in this wholesome light, but like the penis beads, these were fertility symbols, symbols of spring and bounty and partying and sexuality. Mardi Gras, Bacchanalia . . . these were times to cut loose from the ongoing catastrophe of life."

He also notes the environmental component to his artistry. Auntie M's hope is that he's crafting beads people will actually keep rather than discard. In that one small way, penis beads could help save the planet.

The Krewe of the Tawdry Turret prides itself on throwing the finest beads in Soulard. But in addition to holding court in and around the Opera Box, Auntie M is also known for being the host of the High Heel Drag Race, which originated around Clementine's but was bequeathed to Nadine Soaib, owner of Nadine's.

As Auntie M explains, "Patty Poo" (also known as Soulard socialite Patrick Burke) used to throw a party during Mardi Gras in the late 1980s or early 1990s. It was he who organized a high-heel race, which originally went from his store to Clementine's.

The first event permitted participants to run any route between the store and Clementine's as long as they wore a wig and heels. A few rough-and-tumble contestants wore helmets over their wigs.

A tradition was born, but it was far from smooth sailing. "I remember when the race went up the hill on Allen and then back down to Clem's," recalls Auntie M. "The crowd would close in on the street to watch these guys run—many of which were just regular guys in heels. That would create a V of spectators, and the guys running back would smash into people. There was blood!"

After much trial and error over the years, the operation, which takes off at 12th and Allen, is safer and smoother now. It comprises four races. First is a relay race; anyone can participate and no heels are required, other than the one you will be carrying. The second is open to anyone in heels (minimum two-inch height, but no worries, loaners are available), and the third is racing against Tony, St. Louis' fastest high heel racer, winner of countless high heel races (they actually had to add more events so others had a shot). The final race is for full drag.

Nadine Soab is thrilled to have Auntie M run the show. "I think he's awesome in a totally freak-me-out kind of way, but probably the most sane guy I know," she says. "He's just such an incredible person. When we're planning everything he gives me all the time in the world—he's never in any hurry."

And of course, Auntie M always has special beads commemorating the race, some with high heel beads, and some with letter beads spelling out HIGH HEEL DRAG RACE and then the year.

Prime time at the Opera Box is from 10 a.m. to 3 p.m., with Auntie M making his way to the High Heel Drag Race by 1 p.m. As the sun fades, so do the cultural nuances differentiating one intersection from the next. Soulard takes on one single, rowdy flavor. The parade people, the bead traders, the drag entertainers and even Auntie M and the krewe roll out and are replaced with a tsunami of what Bastille and Grey Fox queen Jade Sinclair refers to as "the Zombie Apocalypse."

For two decades Auntie M has lived and breathed beads. I can't help but ask why. It is an answer he ponders for a day or so before replying by text.

"Making the beads is a way to stay sane and happy," Auntie M explains. "My mother would crochet all the time and it would all just pile up until she began donating it all to a shelter for children. A lot of the reason behind doing the beads is because I'm able to do something creative and give it to people right away.

"It takes it out of any kind of craft show or art gallery or anything like that. And nothing compares to the happiness you can bring to someone with a random gift. They're like, 'Oh wow. What just happened to me? I was just given this free thing at a fun event.'"

There's a social contract involved in going out in full regalia, Auntie M posits. You are signaling that you are there to engage, and to put on a show. But he sees a role for revelers as well, especially those wanting beads. "You have to be interesting and fun. We're all making an effort to entertain one another. What are you bringing to the party?"

If you're fun, interesting and engaging, you stand a chance of obtaining a fine Mardi Gras heirloom.

And if you've got your sights set on the precious Golden Penis, you better work.

Mad Beader Postscript

Patty Poo, who was mentioned as having founded the High Heel Drag Race, was thrilled with the story and attended the race for the first time in ages. Adorned in a big curly wig, she held court, posed for photos and had a ball. She passed away before the next Mardi Gras, and I was so glad she was able to enjoy that moment.

Hamming it Up

After nearly a year, the apartment where the samurai sword murder took place was ready to go back on the market. Significant upgrades had been made to compensate for the gory history, including a new kitchen, but I still knew it would be a tough sell. A woman moved out of the apartment across the hall after only two nights, saying a ghost kept lunging at her, and maintenance men working on the murder unit reported finding the bedroom doors closed when they had been left open.

For me, standing in the bathroom where the murder happened was dizzying. I thought about the odd man who was murdered coming to see the apartment with Seth and his roommate, how I couldn't figure out how he fit into their strange story. The entire party was peculiar, the stunningly attractive but childlike Seth, the frumpy and grumpy old roommate—at least 30 years his senior, the affluent college chancellor from Texas who cosigned, and then this slender little man who popped in towards the end of the showing. Very upbeat guy. And it was he who was called and who came to help Seth. He walked into that bathroom and left as a mutilated corpse.

Jasmine fashioned herself as a ghost hunter, and I asked if she'd like to investigate the unit. I don't recall why I didn't participate in the hunt, but I think I had too much on my plate, so I simply provided access to her and two associates.

According to Jasmine, the site was incredibly active, and using a black light she also found that the hazmat team failed to fully rid the bathtub of the blood splatters. The recordings were especially fascinating, including one with a creepy voice slowly and clearly saying, "It's always here."

Everyone who heard the recording agreed on what that first part said, but nobody agreed on what it said afterwards. All I could hear was, "Have some ham," which is pretty dumb. I'd like to believe it said "handsome man" in reference to one of her investigators, but it really did sound like ham to me.

One Friday night, Jasmine came to Villadiva to play the recordings for us. Our new roommate Niles stumbled in with a trick he'd picked up at the corner, and was excited to learn what we were doing as we gathered in the parlor with headphones. He jumped at the chance to listen, sitting on the floor against Jasmine's legs and donning the headphones, while his trick, a stranger to us all, sat opposite him on the other sofa, playing on his phone and looking confused and irritated.

Niles was absolutely transfixed by what he was hearing, staring wide eyed at the laptop on the coffee table while listening intently as he pushed the earpieces as close to his head as possible. After about ten minutes his trick stood up and began to walk out.

"Niles! Your gentleman caller is leaving!" I said.

Without looking up or changing his pose whatsoever, Niles flopped his arm towards the departing trick as if to say, "Go! Just be quiet on the way out!"

Convergence at Nadine's

Niles built a career in fine dining restaurants, but was burned out.

"It's all consuming," he began. "You make good money but you spend it all drinking and eating out with your friends, who are all industry people who talk about nothing but work and the restaurant scene."

He said the work was grueling, but those in that environment were adrenaline junkies and were proud of being able to survive in the harsh conditions.

He downshifted by getting a job at Nadine's. His former associates were puzzled that he'd leave his prestigious Central West End and DeMun haunts to slosh together cocktails for Soulard drunks, but he was enjoying the relaxed environment and basking in the reverence in which Soulardians held their bartenders.

"Bartenders are like celebrities in Soulard. It's crazy! Anywhere I go in the neighborhood, people recognize me and wave," he said.

I had initially organized a standing Friday happy hour to give Magali social opportunities and I called the group "The Friday Floozies." The happy hours didn't take off, but the group was sold on Sunday brunches and adopted the non-alliterative name "The Brunch Floozies."

I tried to rebrand it "The Brunch Bimbos," but it didn't stick. Floozies it was.

Like clockwork our group of a dozen or so would meet at 10 a.m., and most of us found the routine comforting, even if it derailed our afternoons—which I'll get to shortly. During the warm months we'd sit on the spacious covered patio surrounded by the tropical plants, and during the winter we'd sit along the tall narrow windows overlooking Allen Ave.

Shortly before Magali's first Midwest Christmas, she saw snow for the first time in thirty years and was so delighted. The large white flakes adorned her woven beret and popped against Soulard's red bricks.

Despite my efforts to dissuade her, Jasmine took a weekend shift at Nadine's for extra money. I was not a fan of this arrangement because I knew it would end poorly. She did not have the humor or friendly disposition to work in Soulard, and knowing her, I figured when it ended she'd pressure everyone to stop patronizing the business.

It also set up an uncomfortable situation because she and Glenn, one of our brunch regulars, loathed one another. In her defense, many people didn't get along with Glenn, including the Ladies Who Lunch, who avoided our brunch for that reason.

Glenn was infamous for having no filter, as demonstrated by his humiliating behavior at the funeral of Rose Dynasty's husband, where he asked Jasmine if he could grab her by the pussy since Trump won the election.

The situation with Glenn and Jasmine was worse than I feared, as both parties made the arrangement as unpleasant as possible. Jasmine would badger me relentlessly to ditch Glenn, and regularly said, "I'm going to celebrate so hard when Glenn is expelled from the group."

Glenn, though, was much worse. Several times he mumbled "fat cunt" when Jasmine passed by. None of us stood for that and told him to cut it out, to no avail. When, after the second or third Sunday, it became clear he'd never stop, me and Kage decided to put the brunch group on hiatus. Our stated reasoning was that we wanted to do other activities sometimes, and that the group could reconvene periodically.

While no Rhodes Scholar, Glenn knew we were pulling away from him, and he resented it.

Days after our announcement that the standing brunch was canceled, Jasmine quit Nadine's because she was tired of working seven days a week between her two jobs, which was predictable.

Around this same time, she ignited a firestorm in the community when, in her role as the director of the Pride Parade and a member of the Pride Board, she pushed to ban uniformed officers from marching in the parade and posted anti-police messages and memes to social media.

Nothing had ever divided the community so fiercely, and we at the magazine were trying to hold everything together, coming short of endorsing the uniform ban, but seeking to educate on why some marginalized communities were uncomfortable with uniformed officers marching beside them.

No demographic was more enraged than white men over 40, and Glenn was chief among them. In a fit of rage, he unfriended all friends who were also close with Jasmine, and railed over social media about the proposal and how ditching his group of friends was the right thing to do.

A day or so later, however, he began to backtrack. I received the following text:

With the mounting tensions, esp with this fiasco with the Pride Parade, I'm going to step back from the entire gay scene and focus more on my relationship with Bob. Sorry if you felt I was attacking you directly. No ill intentions.

I did not respond, and he then reached out to my old friend Kristin to say he didn't intentionally unfriend her, but that he was hacked.

The following Sunday, Glenn returned to Nadine's.

"Oh God it's Glenn. Do I have to wait on him?" Pauly asked Nadine.

As Pauly approached the table, Glenn was already talking shit to the woman sitting with him, who turned out to be his niece.

"I used to come here with a big group but I ditched them because all they did was talk about people. Plus Andoe thinks he's all that but has no talent," Glenn snarled, before looking up and smugly saying, "Hello Pauly."

Pauly, wearing platform shoes and a sparkly ensemble, took their drink order and while he was walking away he heard Glenn say, "Oh yeah he's always dressed like that. Everyone makes fun of him for how he dresses."

"Nadine I don't think I can do this," Pauly said in passing.

When the food was served, Glenn took a bite and pushed the plate away. "This is garbage."

"That's it!" Nadine said as she stormed over. "You are so full of shit Glenn. You're the reason they don't come anymore! You did not ditch your friends, they ditched you! And you wanna know why nobody likes you? Because you shit on everybody!"

Glenn sat in stunned disbelief and then the niece chimed in. "What's this all about?"

"He's an ass! He complains about everybody and everything!" Nadine exclaimed.

"No he doesn't," the niece began, but Nadine was on a roll and turned back to Glenn.

"And another thing, has it ever occurred to you to brush your teeth before going to a restaurant? You've got chewing tobacco stuck in your teeth all the time and it's disgusting. I want you to leave and never come back!"

Having had his ass handed to him, Glenn and his niece retreated, taking to social media to respond.

"I was just verbally assaulted at Nadine's," Glenn's post began, while his niece left a scathing review of how terrible the restaurant was and how Nadine was a bitch.

Nadine responded directly to the review, beginning, "You're totally wrong. Not about me being a bitch, you have no idea, but about . . ."

The following day Frank Fontana showed up to Nadine's and surprised her with one of his coveted cakes, which read: *You have no idea.*

Brunch Madness

Ms. Pauly didn't work at Nadine's because she needed the money. Her working for Nadine very much reminded me of Karen Walker working for Grace Adler. I guess it was something to do. She and Ray spent her earnings on their vacations.

For a long time she didn't even charge the Brunch Floozies for cocktails, which for me led to 5 Bloody Mary brunches (and sometimes one to go) followed by a nap that consumed the afternoon. And those brunches could get wild. It was especially interesting when a Floozie would bring a new friend or gentleman caller. If they could roll with a conversation that ranged from Satanic curses to the monthly orgies in the Queen of Camp's basement to questions about their penis, they passed the Floozies test.

One Sunday there were about a dozen of us and Magali said she needed a new laptop because hers went out. Several of us had our Amazon apps open as we compared notes and tried to figure out what she needed and how to order it, all while stopping to visit friends who wandered in and stepping onto the patio to check out the plant swap taking place. Finally, one of the floozies confirmed the item with Magali and placed the order using my phone.

Waking from my nap that evening I decided I better review the details of that order. Among the problems I found: It was somehow placed on an old Amazon account I didn't have the password for, and was charged to my debit card, not Magali's credit card. It was also en route to the Melrose rather than Villadiva or her apartment.

Nadine briefly took on a business partner who put an end to our comped cocktails, which was for the best.

Jasmine's Obsession

About once a month I had to appear in court downtown to evict a tenant, and when that happened I'd normally meet Jasmine for lunch. We'd discuss work and a variety of current events around town, but the conversation always drifted back to her unrequited love interest, Christine Elbert. Always.

"Look at this. She copied my status again!" Jasmine exclaimed holding out her phone, showing me a status she posted and a similar one from Christine.

Known as "Lesbian Jesus," Christine had helped many people get sober, including Jasmine. When Jasmine expressed a romantic interest in her, and then irritation about not getting enough of her attention, Elbert snapped the line.

"I have to enforce my boundaries, kid," said Elbert, who was about 15 years older.

Not wanting to just ditch her, Elbert attempted an arm's-length friendship, but the persistent Jasmine was always trying to wiggle her way back in.

"Many of my tenants go on to buy houses. Since you're a mortgage broker we should keep some of your cards here." Jasmine suggested. "I'm only a few blocks away, I could come by and pick them up."

"I'll mail them to you," Elbert rebuffed, leaving Jasmine flustered.

After one too many emotional outbursts, Christine cut her off altogether, which ignited the most boring feud in all of Lesbian history. If Jasmine couldn't be with the revered Christine, she'd seek to destroy her and become the new Christine. She focused on the twin goals of being with her and destroying and replacing her simultaneously.

I noticed Jasmine adopting Christine's style of speaking. For example, she began referring to her friends as "her humans," the way Christine had been doing forever. She tried to brand herself as the same type of mother figure to younger friends, especially young trans and non-binary friends, and she even painted her living room—half a mile from Christine's longtime Tower Grove home—in a similar color scheme.

She'd manipulate friends to message Christine on her behalf to say the way she was treating Jasmine was abusive and unacceptable, or she'd take the phone of an easily-manipulated friend and write her directly as that person.

With her paraprofessional background as a rent collector, she diagnosed Christine as having Narcissistic Personality Disorder, and decided Generation X was holding back Millennials by not passing the torch, and by passing the torch she largely meant validating them and handing over all titles and monikers (i.e. "Lesbian Jesus") they earned over the years, and then heading out to pasture.

She was especially bitter about the "Lesbian Jesus" moniker, a moniker that was driven by the community, not Christine herself.

"She's such a narcissist she equates herself to Christ," she repeatedly seethed.

The generational warfare claim was also leveled against her former mentor Ellen Vanscoy. After assisting Vanscoy in running the Pride Parade for years, Jasmine was involved in a plot to get her voted off the Board, at which time Jasmine would join the Board and take over the parade.

Jasmine felt Vanscoy should have validated and celebrated her ascendancy, but didn't because, of course, generational warfare.

"If Elbert's mimicking your statuses that's a pretty mild form of trolling, and one you wouldn't even be aware of if you weren't policing her page. She occupies half of your mind. I would be very satisfied to know I occupied so much room in the head of an adversary—and that I could fluster them so easily. You need to stop following her page, and stop having others follow it for you," I implored.

Jasmine typically opted to do the opposite of whatever I suggested. In this case, rather than move on from Elbert, she'd start a Narcissist Support Group in a barely-veiled effort to defame Elbert and perhaps push her to talk.

The Madness of Jasmine's Social Media

"If there's a way to manipulate a post audience, Jasmine will know how to do it. She is a black belt in Facebook manipulation"—Mac Taylor

Jasmine would send me a random photo of a smiling Christine Elbert out having coffee or going for a walk, adding the caption, "FML" (fuck my life).

The photos were so innocuous that the first few times I didn't know what she was upset about, and would stare at the pictures and wonder what I was missing. Soon I figured out she was upset about having merely seen the photos. She found images of Christine triggering and didn't want to see them in her feed, period. Odd, since she and her assistants scoured Christine's page all day every day.

"Jasmine, this is a small community. You're going to see her in real life and online," I said.

"There's a lot of people I never see!" Jasmine stubbornly replied, arguing that she would eventually succeed in having a Christine-free feed.

I subconsciously pulled away from Christine, despite knowing her longer and holding her in much higher regard. Part of it was that the grief I'd get from Jasmine was just too much.

One day I made a silly comment on one of Christine's random threads for the first time in six months, and within two minutes Jasmine sent me a screenshot of my comment. "Funny how nobody cares about abuse and bullying unless it's directed at them! I am so done!"

I've never heard of anyone with such a byzantine approach to managing their social media, and even those of us who communicated with Jasmine daily couldn't make heads or tails of it.

She had several Facebook profiles under her name which she'd alternate between, constantly activating and deactivating, sometimes on a daily basis (in addition to the fake accounts for spying). She was just as frequently changing the privacy settings on her various posts for no discernable reason. A specific post would go from public to private to public to a specific audience to deleted in a 24-hour period. And sometimes it wasn't deleted at all, but set to "only me" and then opened up again.

At one point, over maybe a two-week period, her statuses were getting hundreds of likes the minute she posted them, so it must have been a paid thing. The names on the accounts seemed to be of Indian and Russian origins.

She'd unfriend and/or block people on one profile, and then switch to the other when she wanted all of those still-connected people to see her doing something she felt was glamorous, or if she regretted having unfriended them.

"Didn't you unfriend me?" someone might say.

"Oh, no I didn't. I just deactivated my account because [insert nonsense here]."

The answers as to why she did these things were never satisfying.

"I deactivated because I needed a break and didn't want to hear the notifications all night," she'd often say.

During a birthday party for Ms. Jamieson at Villadiva, she was adamant that nobody tag her in photos because she didn't want Christine to see, and she deactivated her primary account and reactivated a secondary account, saying she felt more confident it was Christine-proof.

To reiterate, Jasmine was the one stalking Christine, as well as recruiting gullible friends to approach her to convince her to talk to Jasmine. Christine, for her part, was unwavering in her stance that Jasmine was, and would remain, part of her past and she never even mentioned her.

It wasn't until much later that I learned she also had settings for people she liked to talk trash and troll with, and other settings for those whom she played the part of fragile victim. All her trolling was hidden for the latter group, who she wanted to believe she was being bullied.

Finally, she had an app that told her not only who unfriended her, but who unfollowed her, and she measured her community standing by those stats—and assumed everyone else measured their own standing in the same way. When she was at odds with someone, she'd pressure her friends to unfriend the offending party en masse to send a message that crossing Jasmine had cost them.

One person who didn't need such an app was Ms. Jamieson. I swear she had a sixth sense about unfriending.

"So and so [someone she hardly knew and who we hadn't spoken of in ages] unfriended me!" she'd exclaim.

"How would you even know that?" I'd ask.

For my part I rarely, if ever, was aware when a casual acquaintance unfriended me. On several occasions I ran across someone in person and warmly greeted them, but noticed they seemed uncomfortable. I then looked them up and found they unfriended me at some point (almost always on Jasmine's behalf).

I think the fact I obviously didn't even notice was the best kind of "fuck you."

The Narcissist Group

I interviewed Jasmine on her sobriety. Needing a photo for the piece, I called to ask when we could do a shoot.

"The Narcissist Support Group is meeting at Pool Pavilion in the park at six if that works," Jasmine said.

"Ok that's fine. I'll get there by 5:30 to take the main shots of you alone, and then I'll take a few that show you speaking to a group and then I'll be out of your way." I replied.

"What should everyone wear?" she asked.

"It doesn't matter because the focus will be on you. You might even be the only one directly facing the camera, and the only one in focus."

The first phase of the shoot went very well. The early evening light was flattering and she appeared joyful and healthy, in stark contrast to how she looked at rock bottom when her hair was falling out.

A few group participants began to trickle in, including one petite young woman with a large dog who wanted to be sure I understood she couldn't be photographed. Based on her slouchy body language and her obvious anxiety, I sensed she had been in an abusive situation, which of course was what the group purported to be about, but I didn't expect anyone to take it seriously. She stayed about forty feet behind me as I began shooting the next set of photos, and I noticed that all the other women were oddly dressed up for a weekday evening in the park.

With the awkwardness of knowing my presence was keeping the anxious young woman from the meeting, and my confidence that I got what I needed, I told Jasmine I was done. I started to pack my camera away.

"But Kendra hasn't made it yet. She said she's only ten minutes away."

"I wasn't taking photos of the group per se," I replied. "I was taking photos of you speaking to *a* group."

"Awww, but they're all so excited about being in the shoot. Kendra will be so disappointed if you leave."

Despite being irritated by the entire situation, I waited 15 minutes (because it's never just 10) for this bleach blond Kendra woman to arrive, and then spent another twenty minutes photographing Jasmine talking to these women on the steps. Women who looked hours early for the club or fresh out of Glamour Shots. I say she was talking to them but they were all vapidly talking past one another about their own alleged narcissists, while giving the bare minimum polite nods or "uh huh" while the others spoke.

I kept glancing back at the frail young woman lingering by herself on the sidelines. Like an abused animal, even my assurances couldn't lure her closer. Not one of the dozen or so participants showed any awareness, much less concern for her.

"I've got what I need, that's a wrap" I said as Jasmine groaned about the shoot ending.

The light was fading, and the anxious young woman, who was dressed appropriately for the park, shuffled slowly toward the group.

I got what I needed that evening, but I'm certain she did not.

Ol' Hot Rod Elbert

"I don't see what the big deal is about unfriending Christine," Jasmine said. "Unless she enriches your life so much you just can't let her go," she mockingly added.

She had been suggesting friends overtly sever ties with the beloved community icon for a long time, but was increasingly demanding and irritable. Several in our group chat did block Christine to placate her, including Ms. Jamieson and Kristin, but that didn't count. She wanted *me* to denounce her.

"I don't know why nobody will just block her," she'd post to a group where the majority actually had.

"Jasmine, this is the most boring feud in the history of Lesbianism," I said. "So far you've said she won't talk to you and she trolls you by mimicking statuses. That's all you've got."

Message received, apparently. New, spicier stories debuted of Christine stalking her in Tower Grove Park and at the coffee shop. There was now even a high-speed chase.

"I'm literally shaking! Christine just chased me down Arsenal! She was right on my bumper!"

None of her close friends invested in these fantastical tales, which was frustrating for her. We actually laughed about how ridiculous they were, but she was able to recruit new people to take up her causes, including one local nut who concocted a scheme to nullify one of Christine's professional licenses.

Seeing our disapproval when telling us that scheme, Jasmine acted like this new friend was overly zealous, and she was actually trying to reign them in.

Our group would laugh for years about the ludicrous thought of the mild-mannered Christine Elbert chasing folks down Arsenal. We started referring to her as "Ol' Hot Rod Elbert."

*   *   *

The following is a feature on one of the city's prominent drag families. Janessa Highland, long known as "The Queen of Controversy," had emceed the benefit for Rick years earlier. I interviewed her and "Mother Markstone" in the Villadiva dining room.

Better Together: How Alicia Markstone and Janessa Highland Saved Each Other—and Rose to the Top— Out in STL, March 29, 2019

When Janessa Highland became show director at Martha's Vineyard in Springfield, Missouri, in 2011, she knew she was following in big footsteps. That included those of Alicia Markstone, the 2002 Miss Gay USofA at Large, who had gone from small-town Missouri to Florida to be the show director at the famed Suncoast Resort Hotel.

But when the two performers first met in person six years later, it was hardly a warm-and-fuzzy moment.

By then, Highland had moved to St. Louis, where she embraced a reputation as a villainess of sorts due to her outspoken ways. Dubbed "the Queen of Controversy," she was blacklisted from nearly every stage in town and even felt her name was too much of a liability to pass down to her drag daughter Brooklyn Burroughs.

Behind that intimidating mask, however, she was still the same starstruck kid, and when she learned that Markstone would be in town performing, she dragged Burroughs out so they could meet her. The two greeted Markstone in full drag and humbly asked for her opinion on what they were doing right and what needed improvement.

"Can I be honest?" Markstone asked. "Your makeup is horrible."

Fall of a Diva

In the year prior to meeting Highland, Markstone saw her world crumble. For decades, she'd earned her living as a full-time entertainer, but Suncoast, her employer of fifteen years and the place where her reign was unquestioned, had recently succumbed to the wrecking ball to make way for a Home Depot. Political controversies drove her from her next job at Hamburger Mary's, and nearly all those she mentored along the way turned their backs on her, or quietly slinked away as life moved on.

"When you get old, nobody wants you around," Markstone says.

The life of an entertainer is often paycheck to paycheck, and when those paychecks stopped, Markstone was left in a desperate situation. She decided to retire and return to Rock Island, Illinois, but didn't even have a way to get there until a friend set up a GoFundMe, which she found humiliating, even if she was grateful that the campaign raised the funds she needed.

Life in Rock Island was bleak. Markstone did little more than watch television and stare at the walls. "I'm fortunate that I was raised to believe suicide was the ultimate sin," she recalls. "I know several entertainers who killed themselves when they got old, and I definitely would have."

After a year of solitude, Markstone began making limited appearances. Weeks after giving Highland and Burroughs her brutally honest assessment of their makeup, she was performing in Cape Girardeau, where to her surprise, the two fans were back for more.

"Is this better?" a revamped Highland asked.

Sewing, but Skeptical

"I'd always heard about Markstone and all the legendary stories of her costume designs, including how she won nationals with her acclaimed Mary Poppins performance," Highland recalls. She asked Markstone if she could hire her to create a Mary Poppins costume for the Miss Gay St. Louis America Competition. Markstone quoted her $500. Highland agreed, and soon surprised her with payment in full.

"I've probably donated $100,000 in clothes to queens over the years, and I did it because I wanted to be liked," Markstone says. But at this point in her life, Markstone didn't trust anyone and really didn't want to like Highland. Markstone tried to be abrasive in an effort to push her away, but Highland kept her word and accepted her criticism.

Impressed by the younger performer's tenacity, Markstone began to let her guard down. Still, she expected that their business arrangement would be finite and that Highland would soon move on.

Highland won Miss Gay St. Louis America, and then it was full speed ahead in pursuit of Miss Gay Missouri America. Markstone would spend weeks at a time at Highland's St. Louis County home, helping her prepare. The preparation went way beyond designing and sewing, however. Markstone saw that what was in greatest need of alteration was Highland's attitude and outlook on life.

"She was bitter and mad and angry when she should be in her prime. She was angry too soon," Markstone recalls.

"How bad do you want this?" she asked Highland, who eventually conceded that she really wanted it.

"I'm going to tell you what was told to me when I was going after Miss Gay USofA at Large: You're going to have to learn how to eat a lot of shit," she said. Highland needed to humble herself, Markstone told her, pick her battles, make amends and, most importantly, shed her "Queen of Controversy" moniker.

"She taught me how to be a star without acting like a star," Highland says.

Highland won Miss Gay Missouri America, but rather than saying their goodbyes as Markstone had anticipated, Highland invited her to move in with her and Burroughs. Since March 2018 the three have shared a home that's a drag wonderland; they can count on one hand how many times they've so much as gotten testy with one another.

Sitting together, Highland begins telling the story of going to Rock Island to get Markstone's things. She pauses and looks at the older performer as if to make sure that it's OK to continue.

"Oh God, that," Markstone says, tossing her head back. "Go ahead."

"In the kitchen I saw . . ." Highland says, holding back tears, "A food pantry schedule. I stepped outside and cried. I was sad, and was angry that our community didn't take care of someone who spent her life taking care of everyone else."

Building an Empire

On the heels of Highland's successes, all eyes were on Markstone, and orders for custom gowns came rolling in. In 2018, the former performer launched Markstone Creations. She is currently booked out for months. A half-dozen of her gowns will be worn by various contenders in the 2019 Miss Gay

Missouri America pageant, and notables including Alexis Mateo of RuPaul fame have given them exposure. She's even expanding to the bridal market.

In January, Markstone wowed the runway at the Maximum Exposure Fashion Series, where, channeling her inner Donatella Versace, the 53-year-old followed her models wearing a black-sequin pantsuit with slicked-back blond hair and dramatic eyeshadow. The mostly straight crowd roared in thunderous applause.

"I'm used to being on stage so I wasn't nervous," Markstone recalls. Still, seeing the video afterwards made it real, and reminded her of how far she has come. Seeing her fashions come to life on the runway was also something new. "I thought, 'Wow. I made that!'"

Separately, Highland was a pariah and Markstone was out to pasture. But together, they are a powerhouse enjoying a meteoric rise. More importantly, they are family.

Highland sums it up. "Family isn't necessarily the people you share DNA with, it's those you choose to share your life with," she says. "We are strong separately but together we rise."

The Car

Pauly showed Niles the ropes at Nadine's, and grew to feel sorry for him for not having a car. "I hate that you spend so much of what you make on Uber rides," Pauly told him. "I tell you what I'm going to do. I'm going to sell you my car for $100. I just inherited a car and I don't need my old one."

Niles was dumbfounded, and for the next few weeks didn't know if it would really happen. It was probably the equivalent of an eight-thousand-dollar gift, and Pauly only had only known him for a few months.

One day, Pauly announced he was ready to sign it over, and sat down with him to plan a visit to the DMV. Ray, Pauly and Niles all went together, and with all the i's dotted and t's crossed, the car belonged to Niles. Niles didn't register the car at that time though, saying he was going to instead use his mother's address in Illinois, where he'd register it later in the day.

Keyton to the City

Niles brought a socially awkward trick named Keyton to Kage's 36th birthday party, and he sidled up to me on the loveseat. "Niles tried to get me to come over when you were out of town last week, but I told him I wouldn't disrespect your house like that," he said, in a clear attempt to curry favor while throwing Niles under the bus.

"Niles pays rent here. He can have company whenever he likes," I replied.

That uncomfortable moment quickly passed due to the celebratory energy, and everyone, including Keyton—who stayed the night with Niles—had a good time.

After that Keyton was all over my Facebook posts, and at one point in a thread, dropped that he had been in touch with Clyde.

"You've been talking to Clyde?" someone in the thread asked.

"Yeah, I've spoken with him. Seems nice" Keyton replied.

I didn't know what he was up to. Our group was suspicious, but at the same time it seemed like he was just a strange guy seeking relevance. Jasmine was abrasive and hostile in her questioning, while the motherly Kristin focused on getting the facts. After a few minutes of all that heat, Keyton blocked both Jasmine and Kristin for a few days.

Kage, in his natural "good cop" role, reached out to him with a kind word while trying to figure out what was going on.

The Friday after the party, me and Kage decided to go down to Bar PM with Cody and Niles. I posted a photo of the four of us, and Keyton replied, "WTF?" followed by numerous statuses that evening and over the coming days about how he had been sitting at home bored and if people were going to go out, they should have included him.

I'd only engaged with him once and there was nothing about him I found intriguing, so he nailed his coffin shut with those red flags.

It so happened the next big Villadiva shindig was Kristin's Going Away Party. After years of maneuvering, her husband Brandon was finally going to be stationed in Hawaii.

Keyton threw shade about not being invited on those photos as well, and Kristin responded: "You just recently blocked me. Why would I invite you to my going away party?" at which time he blocked her again.

The next time I saw him was on the patio of Bar PM on a beautiful Sunday afternoon.

"Hi Keyton!" I said warmly. The color drained from his face, he gave a half wave and nervously fluttered away. I later learned the reason for his reaction was that he had blocked me, and blocked or unfriended all affiliated with me, including Frank Fontana, who went to the gym with him a few times, and our good friend John Theodore who invested a lot of effort in showing him around town and introducing him to people.

"One of the last posts I saw from him was just after he moved to the city from the county," Frank began. "His mom pays his car insurance and was upset because she didn't know he was moving to the city, and his premiums doubled. He was furious with her for being upset and was calling her a bitch and going on a tear," he cringed.

Keyton sought to throw low-key shade at me, the House of Villadiva, and the magazine whenever possible. For instance, in the Gay Men's Social Group someone posted, "Is anyone going to the *Out in STL* event tonight" and he quickly chimed in, "Def not."

The following is a feature about the ballroom scene, which I felt was one of the most vibrant scenes in the city. The charismatic Meko Lee Burr had emceed at the first Out in STL Influence Awards, and referred to me as his godmother.

Strike a Pose: St. Louis Has a Storied Ball Scene—and its Stars Are Ready to Strut Their Stuff at Pride—*Out in STL, June 27, 2019*

It was 2001 when Mechee Harper took her nineteen-year-old friend Meko Lee Burr to Chicago for his first ball. "We ended up taking over a KFC as our dressing room," Harper recalls. "And the employees were like, 'Well, alright!'"

The underground, largely Black and Latinx LGBTQ ball culture has mostly existed out of mainstream awareness throughout its long history, although Langston Hughes wrote of drag balls as far back as the 1920s. It briefly pierced broader queer consciousness in 1990 with Jennie Livingston's powerful documentary *Paris Is Burning*, which explores the highly structured ball competitions in which contestants "walk," much like fashion models on a runway, and compete, or "battle," with other performers. That same year, Madonna introduced voguing—the highly stylized dance that evolved out of the ball scene—to the world with her chart-topping hit.

Now, the FX series *Pose*, which takes place in the New York ball scene of the 1980s, has put the culture front and center for a new generation. And we're all rooting for our favorite "house" to win.

Eighteen years after his first ball experience in Chicago, Burr remembers it as a defining moment in his life.

"Everyone was costumed and dressed up. It was summer, but there were people in mink coats for one of the categories. Everyone was elegantly going about their business, holding court at their personal tables, but I was ready to turn it up!" Burr says, his face beaming. "The loud house music overtook me and I lost control of myself. I knew some of the fundamentals of voguing and began dancing down the steps, but my family stopped me and told me I wasn't ready. I knew I couldn't make a mockery of my family. I needed more preparation."

When he returned to St. Louis, Burr began rearranging his life to accommodate that preparation. That included dropping out of Lincoln University, where he'd been studying sociology.

"I had to learn everything there was to learn," Burr says.

I first took note of Burr during a rehearsal for Chuck Pfoutz's Maximum Exposure Fashion Series, which I was writing about. The flamboyant Burr, wearing big dark sunglasses, would escort models down the runway to show them how it was done, swinging his hips side to side. Then he'd stand with the mic and coach them with a seemingly hypnotic chant, saying things like, "Walking the runway. Serving the runway. Walk!"

Months later, when I was researching ball culture, I learned not only that St. Louis has a vibrant ball scene going back decades, but that Burr is the voice of it.

Families & Houses

At only 22, chiseled model Spirit Ebony has already cemented his reputation as the leader of the younger ballroom generation, traveling the nation and winning battles. Ebony, a native of St. Louis, began walking balls at only fifteen. "My cousin introduced me to the ball scene, promising 'a whole bunch of gays' would be there," he recalls. Since his parents were in jail, and his grandparents worked nights, getting out of the house wasn't a problem.

Ebony won the very first ball he walked in, and found a family. Today he's an Instagram celebrity, accumulating nearly 100,000 followers before his last account was pulled owing to his penchant for pushing the envelope with racy selfies. After all, showmanship is in his blood.

"When those real-life parents let you go, you find your queer family," Ebony says. Of *Pose*, he says, "Pose nailed queer families." That's true even if, he says, the show conflates families and houses.

"You're going to eventually love them like your own," adds Harper, who has "adopted" ten children.

Sitting at my dining room table, Burr, Harper, and Ebony explain that families and houses are similar, but houses are primarily about the business of preparing for and competing in ballroom categories. They're typically more structured and purpose-driven, and often involve a lot of traveling for events.

Families, by contrast, are about taking care of one another. Members of a family can belong to different houses.

"St. Louis is home to several world-renowned houses," Harper explained. "The Iconic House of Ebony, the Iconic House of Mizrahi, the House of Xclusive Lanvin, the House of Balmain, the House of Ambrosia..." The three agree that St. Louis is a top-ten ballroom city, after New York, Chicago, Detroit and Atlanta, and that the talent here competes in the top tier. Members also travel to and share expertise with cities where the culture is less developed, including Memphis, Kansas City and Dallas. In Dallas, Burr says, he was the first ball commentator (or emcee) in that city's history.

All of the traveling allows for the element of surprise, which has many advantages.

"You'll go to a city and sit in your car until your category is called," Harper says. "Someone competing will be relaxed thinking they don't have to work too hard, and at the last minute you'll make an entrance, and everyone is stunned."

Harper continues, "Ballroom is 90 percent improv. You're in a battle with someone who's 100 percent unpredictable."

Status

"Ballroom is shade. I grew up in shade," says Harper. The ball scene operates on a hierarchy, with a loose caste system:

Statement: Three to five years of consistent performances.

Legend: Five to ten years. A person who has mastered categories, and has been helpful to the community.

Icon: Typically ten to fifteen years in the scene, and considered true masters of their craft. "They are held at a standard of pure opulence," says Harper.

Pioneer: At least fifteen years in the ballroom community.

And then, there's The Commentator, who functions in an emcee role for events. As Burr puts it, "They are the journalist, the historian, the gatekeeper, the sergeant at arms. They keep drama low by controlling the audience."

Burr was inspired to be a commentator after witnessing the legendary Frank Rodeo Revlon during his first Chicago ball in 2001, recalling "his charisma and his powerful voice that would make everyone jump . . . . his chant while voguing. I wanted to hit the runway. I just wanted to get on the floor. I thought, 'I want to do that.' He started a fire in me."

The following year, Burr met Revlon during a ball in town. "He said, 'A little birdie told me you wanted to start emceeing. I'm going to walk and have you call me out.'" Revlon told him he'd tap him on the shoulder if Burr "woke it up," letting him know he had what it took to be a commentator.

"I had worked him over, honey," Burr says when describing how his introduction whipped up the crowd. "I had walked the Big Boy European Runway later that night—and won. When the event was over, Frank said, 'I live for you. You're going to be the voice of St. Louis, and whatever you need, call me.'"

Running the Show

Owning the Monocle stage for a photo shoot, Ebony is posing on the floor wearing leather pants, mirrored thigh-high boots and a netted shirt—showcasing his tight, muscular chest and washboard abs. His showmanship and his use of the element of surprise are demonstrated when he shocks photographer Theo Welling by lifting his leg to a 115-degree angle.

"Holy cow!" Welling exclaims. "Hold that! Hold that! Hold that! Don't move."

The camera flashes illuminate Ebony's face while "Vogue" blasts over the speakers. There's no competition today, no battle, but as he strikes a pose, he is absolutely within his element.

Today, these three stars are running the show. Mechee Harper directs the St. Louis Awards Gala, and Meko Lee Burr runs the annual event he began in 2002, the My Bloody Valentine Ball, both of which routinely draw more than 300 attendees. Burr's event is among the longest-running in the Midwest, and offers an unheard-of grand prize of $1,000.

And this year, all three will be performing on Pride's Main Stage as the St. Louis Ballroom Collaborative.

Just as Ebony wowed the photographer, he wows competitors and spectators from coast to coast, all while proudly representing St. Louis. "I love my city."

Parade and the Poison Pill

For several years there had been tension between uniformed officers marching in the Pride Parade and the Trans Community. Neither trusted the other. Trans people were disproportionately targeted by police, and police marchers were suspicious of the trans marchers due to perennial rumblings their activists planned to shut down the parade.

For 2019, the 50th anniversary of the Stonewall Uprising, a few on the Pride Board, mainly Jasmine and local celebrity and trans woman of color Simone Shasta, began a discussion about banning uniformed officers. Stonewall, after all, commemorated a riot against the police. Going even further, Jasmine decided to make the Trans Community as a whole the Grand Marshal.

Jasmine made herself the face of the uniform ban, and the effort severely divided the community. I had never seen gay white men over forty so worked up about anything, and I do mean anything. They were fire-breathing mad about the proposal. For them, seeing police marching was a sign of progress and symbolized a progressive city. They quickly rallied around an "inclusion not exclusion" narrative.

In protest of the proposal, beloved community elder Michael Mullen, founder of Pets Are Wonderful Support (PAWS), which helps care for the pets of people living with HIV/AIDS, announced he would not accept a Pride award he was set to receive. Others circulated petitions and backed boycotting efforts.

Those most likely to support the uniform ban, which included younger and more radical elements, did next to nothing to speak out in favor of the plan. That was political. The natural supporters of banning uniformed officers were also longtime foes of Pride St. Louis—the organization behind the main downtown parade, preferring the earthier rival Tower Grove Pride which happened the same weekend and was born out of protest after Pride St. Louis left Tower Grove Park for Downtown. They were not in the business of praising Pride St. Louis and greeted news of the plan with shrugs and grumbling about how they'd likely reverse the decision.

"This is a self-fulfilling prophecy," I replied on several social media threads. "If Pride is only hearing from those against this proposal then yes, they are likely to reverse the decision and then you'll get your, 'I told you so.'"

In the middle were the more moderate parts of the Trans community, including many parents who simply wanted to enjoy their moment as Grand Marshal without feeling threatened by hostile officers.

Being on the Board of Pride St. Louis, Jasmine wasn't fully trusted by many of her natural allies, although she did have the support of a local Trans organization called MTUG, or Metro Trans Umbrella Group. Overall, she was disparaged by a vocal majority, and only quietly supported by allies.

I saw my role as supporting Jasmine while trying to get the angry older white gays to understand that some in the community had very different experiences with the police than they did. I failed on the latter.

It didn't help that Jasmine enjoyed trolling her opponents, and bragging about "banning cops."

"The talking point is you are banning uniforms, not people. Officers are welcome. They can wear shirts showing they are officers," I coached. "Banning clothing is a winning message, banning people is not."

I tried to explain to my readers that a uniformed officer was not akin to a drag queen or a leather daddy. You can exchange shade with someone in leather or a wig and be on equal footing. Once a police uniform goes on, however, there's a power differential.

What I wouldn't learn until more than a year later was that Jasmine kept talking about "banning cops" because that's exactly what she promised the Trans community she would do.

In the end, Jasmine would not stop her indulgent trolling, the older white gays would not listen to any opposing viewpoint, the natural allies of the uniform ban wouldn't do much to speak up or to show support, and the plan was scrapped.

Jasmine pinned the blame on Mayor Lyda Krewson.

Would I Lyda You?

Mayor Lyda Kweson sent a message to the Board: *Just so you know the city is requesting I investigate your permits and sponsors if you don't allow the police in uniform. I just want you to have a heads up of possibilities to come.*

This was taken as a threat. Let the police march in uniform, or the permits would be pulled.

The Board abruptly reversed the uniform ban at a hastily assembled mayoral press conference that had the feel of a hostage video. Jasmine did not stand with the mayor and the Board, but watched from across the room. Based on Jasmine's accusation, a reporter present asked the mayor if she pressured the Board to reverse the ban, and she said no. Later, when Jasmine accused the mayor of "casual blackmail" in a rant posted to the mayor's Facebook page, the *RFT* again pressed Krewson. The *RFT* headline was: *Mayor Denies Threatening Pride St. Louis Over Police Participation.*

In a 49-minute YouTube video where Jasmine told all—or at least her version, and where she mercilessly mocked her detractors while laughing maniacally, she said that prior to the press conference the mayor leaned over the table, looked directly at her and said, "You know it's a lot easier to be inclusive than to cause division."

Soon after, she was "laid off" from her position at a major downtown building, and told friends that the mayor had a hand in it. Tellingly, Jasmine would not publicly accuse Krewson of getting her fired. She told me she feared she would get sued.

Pride STL's Police Uniform Decision Reversed. Trans Leaders Devastated—*chrisandoe.com, June 18, 2019*

For the first time, Pride St. Louis decided to put the Trans community front and center in the parade in honor of Stonewall 50. Going a major step further, they attempted to ignite a discussion about Trans issues by asking police marchers to wear civilian clothing for this year's celebration. Another idea was for unarmed officers to march in MTUG (Metro Trans Umbrella Group) shirts. While many like myself enjoy seeing uniformed police in the parade as a symbol of how far we've come, other communities have very different realities. There are many marginalized people who don't call the police when they need help. This was an opportunity to discuss that.

It didn't go well.

Most in opposition genuinely felt this proposal was discriminatory and disrespectful to LGBTQ officers. They kept to those general talking points, and a few even offered a kind word to Trans friends and their supporters. Many others, however, poured gasoline on the controversy with hyperbolic, defamatory and discriminatory statements about both the Pride St. Louis Board as a whole, individual members–many who were sent hateful messages, and the Trans community.

I've been saying for over a week that proposals are often scrapped (remember the $5 entry fee?) as details are finalized, and today the Board has reversed the request after winning a concession from STLPD to attend diversity training.

Below is MTUG's official statement:

Liberation

This year, 50 years after the Stonewall riot, we were cautiously optimistic that we would finally be seen by our own community. Earlier this year, the board of Pride St Louis decided to center gender expansive and trans lived experiences by holding us up as grand marshals in honor of 50 years into our movement. When we agreed to take our place as grand marshals, we agreed to make our bodies vulnerable; we put our most marginalized community members at risk once again, especially our siblings of color.

While hesitant, we agreed despite knowing that uniformed, armed police officers who have historically and presently criminalized our bodies would be in the parade. We have strained at best, and violent at worst, relationships with police officers. There has been no indication or effort made to gain an understanding or awareness by the police of who we are and what our community needs from our police officers.

We knew that our constituency would be resistant to marching with armed officers however we wanted to work with the Pride Board and Parade team. Once the decision was made to exclude armed, uniformed police officers we finally felt seen, heard, understood and centered. Watching the backlash from white, cisgender gay and lesbian and straight community members, we realize that there is so much more work to be done. More than 50 years into this fight, we are not safe even within our own movement.

So what are we going to do now? We don't know. For right now, our leadership core is at a loss for words. We are disappointed. We are frightened. And, now quite frankly, we are much more aware of the massive targets on our backs put there by the Federal government, our state legislature, and our own community leaders.

An irony in all this is many of MTUG's natural allies sat on their hands due to their general opposition to Pride St. Louis, ceding the field entirely to those opposed to the proposal. That of course was not helpful, but will be self-serving for the masturbatory cynics who can now say, "I told you so."

Pride is a community organization that answers to the community. They held firm longer than I would have expected, and hopefully the concession they won has some impact on the lives of people in our community. I commend their efforts.

I believe in the long run some good will come from this, mainly a better understanding of Trans issues. But for now, calls for unity will ring hollow after refusing to even listen to the other side. We all limp towards Stonewall 50 battered and bruised.

And for those who have been drunk on rage, you're going to have a hangover from Hell.

Just as Expected

Once the uniform decision was reversed nearly everyone who had been angrily denouncing Pride St. Louis suddenly claimed to be ready to listen, and paid lip service to addressing the concerns of marginalized communities. It's easy to be magnanimous when you've gotten your way. But that ship had sailed.

The final version of the Pride Guide, set to go to print within hours, still had community icon Michael Mullen, who publicly turned down their award, profiled as an honoree. Jasmine caught it and made sure his section was pulled. I believe it was swapped out for a random advertisement.

After a Bruising Controversy, Metro Trans Umbrella Group Withdraws from St. Louis Pride Parade—*chrisandoe.com, June 26, 2019*

Metro Trans Umbrella Group (MTUG) has pulled out of Sunday's Pride Parade with a surprise announcement by MTUG Executive Director Sayer Johnson on St. Louis Public Radio.

"So much of the conversation has been taken over by this parade when so many in our community aren't even getting their basic needs met" Johnson said. "Pride for us is a mark of survival, not celebration."

The Board of Pride STL sought to honor and highlight the Trans community's contributions for Stonewall 50, but faced intense backlash and even threats over a request that officers marching not be uniformed this year. Proposed compromises included officers wearing shirts that read "LGBTQIA+ Officer" or MTUG shirts, but were resoundingly rejected by representatives for police marchers. In the end, a press conference was held in the office of Mayor Lyda Krewson reversing the decision.

The group was to participate as grand marshal.

Plots and Machinations

Days before the parade, *The St. Louis Post-Dispatch* reported that a man was arrested after sending a message to one of Pride St. Louis's parade organizers from a fake email account saying he would take his guns to PrideFest and "kill every gay person I can before I kill myself."

Meanwhile, plans were underway to shut down the parade with a die-in at the judge's booth, at which time Jasmine would resign from the Board in grand fashion. Her scheme was to add protesters to the volunteer list and give them official shirts, and then have them open up the barricades to allow in a flood of additional demonstrators. The police would be marching with the mayor, who would be told the die-in would not end until all officers had left the parade route.

Trans writer Terry Willits, who had worked closely with Jasmine on the parade planning, notified the Pride Board. Soon after, the Board concocted a story that because of the terrorist threat, Homeland Security was taking over event security, meaning anyone shutting down the parade would likely face federal terrorism charges.

The Board's plan, which Jasmine wasn't in on, succeeded in dissuading those planning the disruption. It would be over a year until I learned more of the backstory, which I'll get to later.

Carted Around

"Simone Shasta switched out my golf cart!" Jasmine exclaimed as she kept slamming her foot on the gas as we putted around the parade set-up. The cart worked, but it reminded me of a pedal boat. You could pedal as vigorously as you wanted but you're not going to go any faster. "I put my name on the one I was supposed to have and she switched it! This one barely moves! It doesn't even have a horn!"

Parade set-up was my favorite part of Pridefest. Each year I'd wander around and visit with friends on various floats. Riding around in the cart was novel and fun, aside from Jasmine berating every fellow board member she could find about that damn golf cart. That was embarrassing.

I didn't realize it at the time, but she had alienated many of her closest friends during that Pride season. It wasn't because they disagreed with her, it was because she was arrogant and abusive towards them, even some who had volunteered under her. It seemed to me she was drunk on the accolades from new associates who were appreciative of her public stand.

But I was exempt from her abuse. She even appointed me as one of three parade judges, which was fun. I was sitting with two radio personalities under a tent enjoying unlimited booze as we exchanged thoughts on the passing entries.

"The mayor of Dellwood is here?" I said, surprised. Dellwood was a tiny, low-income bedroom community of about 5,000 in North St. Louis County, and wasn't at all considered an LGBTQ enclave. The mayor was a nice-looking man and I quipped, "I could be the First Lady of Dellwood."

A shady gay cop named Lambert was in the parade with his local organization even after creating and circulating an "Enemies of the Police" list which of course included Jasmine, but also me and the owners of Bar PM, whom he had it out for because they wouldn't let him play with his loaded gun while drinking at the bar.

I thought it was unseemly for his organization to bring him, and as they passed the judge's tent I held a dry erase board which read: *LAMBERT LEAVE JASMINE ALONE.*

Despite all of her faults I will say that Jasmine could run a parade. I was impressed. Some parades in the past started late and had sizable gaps between the floats, but hers was a well-oiled machine.

After the parade, though, Jasmine resigned and I believe she left with our score cards, so I have no idea how they determined the winner (I had wandered off as soon as the parade ended).

The stand she took earned her fierce loyalty among many young Trans and nonbinary activists, and in reference to them she said to me, "I now have an army."

"Now to figure out how to harness that energy," I replied. "You can't keep their interest with your ill-defined war with Elbert."

I delivered that line partly as a joke, and partly as an effort to nudge her away from acting upon her worst compulsions. Maybe if that was what she intended I could prod her in a different direction. But of course her intention was to use her new followers as cannon fodder in her war against Christine Elbert. Why would I even think there was a doubt?

What good were friends or followers if not weaponized?

Awakening the Demons

One day I simply wasn't mad at Clyde any longer, and I could hardly remember why I was mad to begin with. A mutual friend posted a photo with him, and I was happy to see him out. I thought he looked good.

He had clung to that apartment out of defiance, but I saw it as a prison cell. He was entombed in the walls of his enemies. I had heard over the years that he was offered other housing opportunities. An Indianapolis-based trucker he was dating tried to get him to team drive, explaining all the money that they could make, but Clyde refused to leave the Melrose.

Between me and Kage, I felt I had been the driving force behind the war. Kage was typically an agreeable guy, and I tested the waters by mentioning opening a dialogue. In the moment Kage didn't seem opposed.

It was a Sunday afternoon. I sat alone by the front window in the parlor and called Clyde.

"I don't know what kind of game you're playing," he said before disconnecting. Later, he followed up on messenger and we began communicating.

I was seeing our entire history from the opposite perspective. *Maybe* we needed the first protective order, but did we really need two? Those orders on his record could derail housing and employment opportunities for the rest of his life (I'd forgotten the "we'll all die" comment). And maybe I was only interested in him as the one-dimensional character I found so cool initially, and made zero allowances for his emotional side. Maybe I could have better navigated the situation.

Stranger than forgetting most of the reasons I disliked him, I felt far more attracted to him than I ever had. Back at the Melrose I thought he was a cool guy, and we were both involved in debauchery, but very little was with one another.

I had completely misread Kage, because when I mentioned talking to Clyde, he was not at all on board.

"I don't want anything to do with him!" he exclaimed, expressing bewilderment that I would feel differently.

It was the first thing I recall us seriously disagreeing about. He somewhat tolerated my ongoing communication with Clyde, and seemed to be interested in hearing about the conversations, but his guard was very much up.

"Kage is going to need time," I told Clyde, but he was never one for discipline or patience. When he spotted us at JJ's he made a beeline, strutting over in one of his worn-out sleeveless shirts.

"We need to talk, Kage."

"Now is not the time or the place."

Clyde argued the point and then lost his cool.

"WOULD YOU AT LEAST STOP TELLING PEOPLE I'M A RAPIST!"

"That was your buddy Rick's story. You need to take that up with him."

With that, Clyde let out a primal yell and slammed his fists on the bar top with all his might before storming off.

Everyone knew our history, including the owner, who was nearby.

"Are you okay? Do you need us to ban him?" he asked.

"No, no, it's okay," I said.

The Task of Healing

After being blindly focused on mutual destruction for years, looking at the landscape with an eye on rebuilding was daunting. Me and Clyde were friendly with one another, but our respective groups were another matter. And as much as Clyde wanted reconciliation with Kage, he held festering resentments towards most of our friends. Shawn Adams, who testified against him, chief among them.

Conversely, I wasn't interested in reconciling with the handful of friends he took in the split, most of whom were consumed with meth addictions.

Menashe's addiction had gotten so bad that he was homeless, sometimes spotted sleeping in the doorway of the adult novelty shop on Chippewa Street, at the bottom of Tower Grove South. This was a person who once had a large wildflower garden on his terrace, flowers which he used to make arrangements for our wedding. He's someone who would prepare big meals and feed half the block. Now, he was doing things like faking a suicide to manipulate his ex to buy him a pizza, having someone post a photo of him hanging by a noose but conveniently not showing his feet. When he succeeded at getting the man's attention, he persuaded him to load his debit card with enough to buy a convenience store pizza and Frappuccino.

Clyde had offered Menashe money from time to time, but didn't feel comfortable letting him sleep at his place in light of the addiction. Another factor was how threatening and nasty he had been towards Ms. Jamieson. The two crossing paths on the shared front porch would be quite awkward.

Had Menashe been in recovery I would have enjoyed talking with him and seeing if there was anything to build upon. He was the reason I became friends with Ms. Jamieson, tagging her in one of the infamous Dustin Mitchell threads at a time when we didn't get along. "You did not just summon Ol' Lecturing Linda!" I said at the time. He was the ultimate wingman, not only helping me and Kage get together, but also stay together in the first weeks. And of course, he was our volunteer wedding planner.

Rick, on the other hand, was someone I felt numb to. After the initial outrage of the betrayal wore off, and after he moved from the Melrose, I didn't hate him, I didn't miss him, and I didn't think much about him aside from the updates I'd receive about how he continued to climb the drug dealing ladder. From what I heard he'd become the top queer distributor in the St. Louis area.

"I went to see Rick for some Adderall," a guy told me one day while we were standing in the Grove. "He's married, and his husband knows that three days a week he's at a local hotel doing business, but he doesn't know those three days are a nonstop orgy," he laughed.

"How does he stay out of jail?" I asked.

"He can afford a great attorney!" he replied.

Ms. Jamieson was among the first I reached out to in regard to mending fences with Clyde, and she agreed to let him use her washer and dryer again. During the war she had installed locks on them. Quite a statement considering they were the only two tenants who shared that basement. Before hostilities began, Clyde stopped paying the $20 a month for laundry access, and Ms. Jamieson wasn't about to give anyone a free ride.

Kristin took the cue and resumed some communication. Even though she was less than 15 years older, she had once filled a mother role for him, as she had for many.

"He kept saying he was a bad person, and he'd say it at random times," she recalled. "But I've been around a long time and I know that guys who want in often try to go through the fag hag. The entire chat for a month or so was just one manipulation attempt after another."

Before the blowup at JJ's I created a group chat that included both Kage and Clyde with the hope small talk might lead to a reconciliation, but Clyde was too pushy and Kage was too aloof. Kage wound up leaving that chat.

"I wanted to be over you guys so I intentionally broke things so it would be done. I guess I broke them pretty good," Clyde said.

I finally told Clyde I didn't believe Kage would ever be open to a friendship again, and he was devastated.

On any given day Clyde's emotions were all over the map. During the course of one conversation he could go from joyful to angry to distraught. It was draining to deal with, but I felt cutting him off altogether was too risky. I awoke the demons and now I had to babysit them.

The Apparition

On June 14, 2019, Ms. Jamieson sent the following message:

Omg. So Clyde was messaging me saying that he thinks there's some sort of entity in the basement that he's felt ever since he's started to do laundry again. He went down there like 30 min ago to burn incense and next thing I know, I hear him screaming down there in fear and he ran up the back steps and slammed his back door and then locked it. He said he saw a corpse down there and I thought he meant a literal dead body so I was freaking the fuck out. I heard him open his door again and head back to the basement so I went down there and he was sitting down burning incense and said he saw a dead woman with a dress on in the corner and she reached for him. He was genuinely terrified.

Fancy's Final Bash

Five years earlier an internal disagreement over running a piece on polarizing Grove bar owner Fancy Slovak led to Colin Murphy's departure from *Vital Voice* and a long media war the magazine never really recovered from. Now, it was the Summer of 2019 and from my hotel room at San Francisco's Sir Francis Drake, I fielded panicked phone calls about our planned Slovak feature, and wondered if history was repeating.

Fancy had announced that she was dying. She had been living in California and planned to return to St. Louis for one big final bash. Our editorial team decided to make Fancy our cover story. The frantic calls were the result of a revolt by Kitty in the Sales Department. Some of our main advertisers were longtime foes of Fancy and, according to Kitty, indicated they weren't interested in running ads in an issue with Fancy on the cover.

There had always been a strong firewall between editorial and sales, but the stark reality was we would fold if these advertisers walked. I agreed to not put Fancy on the cover, but dug in my heels on maintaining the feature. I assured everyone it would not be a puff piece nor would it be a smear piece. I wanted to accurately reflect on her legacy.

I assigned it to one of our very best writers, Patrick Collins, and the arc of the story was basically an explanation of what made Fancy so controversial, and then a humanizing, vindicating take on who she was and the positive impacts she had made. I myself would be thrilled to have such a piece written about me at the end of my life. Fancy had initially agreed to cooperate, but then said she wouldn't agree to an interview unless we sent her the professional photos we had taken of her farewell event. She badgered both me and the writer for the photos, sending texts at all hours, and eventually seemed to admit she had only agreed to cooperate so she could have the shoot.

"I just wanted the photo shoot! What don't you understand?"

In the end, we had to write the piece without interviewing her.

Jasmine and a few other friends of Fancy's previewed the piece and found it balanced. Sales took a hit but didn't crater, and there was some suspicion that Kitty intentionally slow-walked the issue.

Letter from the Editor, September 2019

If you've been around the St. Louis scene a while, what I'm about to say might make you feel really old: Many LGBTQ twenty-somethings don't know who Fancy Slovak is. The five years she's been in exile (or retirement) is a lifetime in the bar scene where Slovak reigned. But for those of us who have been around long enough to have been invested in all the excitement and drama that surrounded her, it feels like yesterday. For better and for worse.

The catalyst for the Great Media Divorce of 2014—when the team running our city's oldest LGBTQ publication irrevocably split apart—was a fierce disagreement over running a feature on her. The subsequent media war divided the community for years. In the past few months I have learned the hard way that in some corners the passions around Slovak are as potent as ever, and it felt history was repeating.

Threads binding our *Out in STL* team together were beginning to unravel as our internal debate raged. Vacations were interrupted with dire warnings that key advertisers would walk and the community would revolt if we ran a flattering piece, while others were aghast that anyone would even suggest being critical of a dying woman (Slovak has announced that she has terminal cancer). Some on our team implored us to drop the piece altogether, citing "more deserving" people.

If I had to boil down this publication's mission to one sentence, though, it would be this one: We are here to introduce our community to itself. Even if you're just hearing of Slovak, she shaped the place you live, often when that wasn't even her aim. To avoid bias, we assigned the feature to the illustrious Patrick Collins, who lived in Portland during Slovak's rise and fall and hasn't patronized bars in ages.

Speaking of introductions, on our cover is GutterGlitter's Elizabeth Van Winkle, who may be the most influential person you've never heard of—especially if yours is more of a mainstream, color-between-the-lines existence. Associate Editor Melissa Meinzer takes us to a world most of us could never or would never access as we get a glimpse inside one of Van Winkle's "no-men" kink events.

If you need a shot of testosterone after all this, I'll introduce you to the rough and tumble St. Louis Crusaders rugby team, who are more than up to the task.

Enjoy this hard-fought issue, and stay tuned to find out if the dire warnings of "the Slovak curse" make this our final edition.

Chris Andoe
Editor in Chief

Fancy's Furor

Sales and the skeptical advertisers were satisfied with the feature. Readers who didn't know Fancy found it to be a good read, and were left with a favorable impression of her. Fancy's longtime drinking buddies, however, were livid.

"Ummm, I worked there for eight years and never had a check bounce!" one posted to our link on Facebook in reference to a comment in the story. It was an odd hill to die on since the bounced checks were common knowledge. Most of the angry comments left me with the impression her allies didn't get past the first few paragraphs, if that.

"I was laughing with Kate that the only people who are mad are the drunk old lesbians who aren't smart enough to comprehend it," Jasmine said.

Fancy admittedly didn't read it in its entirety, but created a YouTube video where she wept as she decried adult bullying, and followed that on Facebook with endless memes on bullying.

"She's the QUEEN of bullying! Fuck her!" Jasmine said privately in reaction to Fancy's posts.

I'm quite critical of myself for my lack of discipline in these situations, especially when up in my cups, but I knew there was no way to win a public fight with a dying woman, nor did I want to further upset her. I'm satisfied with how I navigated the fallout.

Time and again Fancy dragged my name and her followers tried to pick fights, but I did not take the bait.

Wheels Come Off

"Why is Kage's car parked in the Grove?" Pauly posted to my Facebook when we were away on a weekend trip.

Before our roommate Niles had a vehicle, we let him use ours when we traveled so he could easily run home to care for the pets. But why was he still driving them? When I asked, he said he was out of gas. But he clearly had money to drink.

"Hey, I know I'm behind on rent but I'll have $500 for you on Wednesday," he'd say, and with the day and amount stated, I almost felt the cash was in the bank. Then Wednesday would come, and nothing. And nothing Thursday.

"Sorry about not having my shit together. My mom had an emergency," he'd say on Saturday as he left $200 on the table.

Niles was barely maintaining as it was when a handsome blond guy named Mitch appeared on his radar. Mitch lived a few hours south of town and had been in a serious relationship with a local drag queen named Natalie Sheridan, who was part of the House of Markstone. Right after the break up Niles and Mitch began talking. I didn't see how it would work since both men were tops, but Mitch came to town and stayed at Villadiva for a weekend.

Niles spared no expense wining and dining him, and their public posts raised eyebrows all over the city. On a Saturday, I believe, Nadine messaged Niles to ask why he wasn't at work. Niles replied that he wasn't on the schedule.

Frustrated, Nadine replied, "You need to stop worrying about who's going to suck your dick and start worrying about doing your job!"

She quickly apologized for losing her cool and speaking to him that way, and she also confirmed that there had been a miscommunication and he indeed was not on the schedule. Not only did Niles not accept the apology, he quit and he distributed Nadine's message all over Soulard and the LGBTQ community.

That evening at Grey Fox I found myself standing beside a sour faced Natalie Sheridan.

"Hi Natalie," I said.

"Hi" she said curtly, cutting me side eye. "You know *I* was the one who broke up with *HIM*."

"That's the word on the street," I replied.

"And this weekend he's staying with your roommate up in that . . . house," she said bitterly, as if she'd been looking for the right adjective, or decided to abort an unkind one.

Niles and Mitch then arrived at the bar, and were all over one another. When I left, they had moved to the side of the building, and I was nearly home when I heard shouting. It was Natalie, and she was letting them have it. They ran up the hill to Villadiva, hand in hand, laughing.

When Mitch returned to his small town, he told Niles he just wanted to be friends. There Niles sat broke and unemployed in the wake of the big weekend. He found another job at a restaurant comparable to Nadine's, but in a sleepy, low-rent section of South City as opposed to coveted Soulard. One could rationalize leaving the fashionable Central West End for Soulard, although it was rarely done. But there was no way to spin his current station.

I think that weekend broke him. The disappointment, the overspending, the falling out with Nadine.

Our extended group and many in the community came together at Just John in the Grove for the release of our latest *Out in STL* issue. Jasmine and Niles hung out much of that time, having gotten to know one another working at Nadine's.

I didn't see Niles for days afterwards, which was not unusual. On Friday September 20, 2019, I woke to a message from his best friend Dana, which she sent at 12:45 a.m. "I need to talk to you. I need Niles' dad's number. He's in the city jail since Wednesday. I'm the only number he knows from memory. Didn't check my voicemail."

It took another day or two to discover what actually happened. After leaving the bars, Niles totaled the car Pauly sold him for $100 after having it for a matter of weeks, and it was apparently an injury accident with Pauly's plates on the vehicle. He had lied about getting the car registered in his name.

Then I learned the $100 check to Pauly bounced.

"A week ago I told him that check bounced and each time I'd see him he'd say he would bring me the money," Pauly said. "And today I got a few parking tickets in the mail!"

I was livid. Incensed. Had it been my check that bounced I would have been so mortified I would have dropped everything to make good on the payment, but Niles was nonchalant.

I wrote to his best friend.

Hi Dana,

I'm writing in the hopes you can be of some help in getting our keys back along with written instructions from Niles on what he wants us to do with his belongings. I wrote to his dad as well, but since we're not Facebook friends I don't believe he's seen the message.

The income from the room is set aside for utilities, and Niles is already $600 behind. While I understand he's currently in a dire situation, before any of that began he was giving false promises of payment, and he also rewarded my best friends' incredible generosity of selling him a nice car for $100 by giving them a bad check followed by casual empty promises of bringing them cash. Then of course he totaled it within weeks.

I'm very glad he has friends like you and Salam, and hope he gets his life together. I just feel no obligation to subsidize his life any longer after the way he's handled his business with me and my people.

Any help would be appreciated. Basically, the keys with a note saying "Release my belongings to . . ."

Thanks,
Chris

Pauly and Ray were beside themselves with anxiety. Would they get sued and be cleaned out by the injured party? Who would have thought a generous gesture would lead to such a mess?

I was morbidly fascinated by his motives. I had assumed all along he was clinically depressed and I knew he was hopelessly disorganized, but the car situation changed everything. I felt like he might get a shoplifter's high from not paying people. Maybe lying to their faces and buying time got him off.

In addition to Dana, I turned to Jasmine and Mac Taylor for help figuring out how to navigate the situation. Mac had dated him years earlier. I also vented to our mutual friend Salam, who was sympathetic, but pushed hard for me to not go public about everything.

When Niles was released, he initially lied about the accident, saying nobody was injured, and he downplayed his neglect, saying things like, "I know I should have switched the tags sooner," and "I'm going to pay everyone back."

Regarding me being upset about how he handled the car, he told friends, "How is this any of this his business?"

Fortunately for Ray and Pauly, they were not legally liable for anything that happened since they had proof of signing over the title.

My one phone discussion with Niles was heated and he told Jasmine, "I feel threatened. I might request the police be present when I move."

"You tell him if he shows up to my door with the police there will be Hell to pay. Cause a spectacle like that in front of all the neighbors and I'll make sure the worst battles of his life look like pillow fights by comparison."

Kage played good cop and told Niles I would stay in the den. He and his dad arrived and moved him out without incident.

Niles posted that he had a substance abuse problem and was now in recovery as a way to take the heat off, but a week or so later a former friend of his told Pauly he was hitting people up for Adderall.

"You're not sober if you're hitting people up for Adderall, Niles!" Pauly posted to Facebook while up in her cups.

The Impulse Dog

When out of the blue Jasmine posted cutesy photos of her new rescue puppy I turned to Kage and said, "We're going to end up with that dog."

The older woman who had owned the pup suffered a stroke. A Facebook rescue group posted the story, and Jasmine impulsively pounced.

Jasmine was about as nurturing as a steel post, so I figured she would maximize the social media spotlight and then be ready to move on. And right on cue, maybe five days in, her tone began to shift with updates like: *I didn't know puppies could be so destructive. #RIP remote control.*

In addition to social media attention, what she was really wanting was her former dog Pearl, not an energetic puppy. I could empathize because I adopted Madge based on her resemblance to Brawny. That too was an emotional and irrational decision, because of course we can't get our former companions back.

The dog updates only soured. She was working to paint an image of a very troubled and hopelessly unmanageable animal. Many of her current followers were dog rescue people, and they rushed in to offer helpful advice. She wasn't looking for advice. She was looking for validation.

I believe that most in a similar situation would simply say it didn't work out, but that wasn't Jasmine's way. She wanted to be given a pass for getting rid of the puppy, while getting sympathy because she had no other choice due to its severe behavioral problems. It was a very tall order.

"Look what this bitch wrote to me!" Jasmine said, while sending our chat screenshots of a message that read:

"I'm an admirer of yours ever since the Pride thing. You rocked that shit. But when it comes to the dog you really need to grow up. Dogs are a lifetime commitment, and if you can't handle it, at least don't doom the little guy's chances by telling everyone he's a problem."

"Whoa," Jasmine replied to the woman. "This conversation is not working for me."

She'd privately complain about the dog and say odd things like her and the dog fought like siblings. I figured we needed to meet the creature since we'd probably end up with him, so I suggested a play date.

"When you run errands drop him off for a few hours and our guys will wear him out for you."

She promptly took us up on our offer, and while energetic, we found him to be perfectly normal.

I was sitting on the back steps when she returned through the gate. He rushed up to greet her, but when she dangled the leash he ran back and snuggled into my side, seemingly begging to stay.

The next I saw of him was in a smear video she created late one night. In the dark, 15 second clip which had the feel of a political attack ad, the dog is sitting alone on the sofa growling and snapping as she scolds him off camera.

"I just can't do this," she posted.

"What lengths did she go to in order to set that up?" I wondered. "What's going on in that home?"

The thread erupted with advice and people saying they wished they could take him but had too many animals already. I feared he'd end up in another temporary home or worse, and chimed in: "We want the dog. We will take him."

This was an enormous face saver for Jasmine, who removed the video and many of the older posts and replaced them with the happy ending. The new story was the dog preferred men, which was quite a stretch considering the original owner was an old woman.

Kage decided to name him Jett. When we went to retrieve him he was excited to see us, and to leave. Jasmine had a bag with all his things ready to go. Kage looked over the contents.

"Where are his toys?" he asked.

"He doesn't even play with toys, he just likes socks," she replied.

At the door she attempted a big goodbye but Jett wanted nothing to do with her, and even growled.

"Aww he's already protective of Kage," she said.

Jasmine's focus shifted to uncovering dirt on Niles, seeking to expose the way he had taken advantage of our group—especially Ray and Pauly.

Since everything she did somehow tied back to her Christine Elbert obsession, I surmised she was only investing in the Niles situation so I would be indebted to her, in her mind making me more agreeable to blocking and publicly denouncing Christine as she had relentlessly lobbied for.

I didn't want to take on such a debt. I was already in too deep by asking her to relay my threats to Niles about bringing police to the house. Besides, my public feuds tended to be with public figures, or with those who came for me in a public way, not everyday folks. Finally, I wasn't in the market for a messy new feud. I couldn't afford it with the Clyde saga so fresh in everyone's memory.

"Are you going to call him out by name?" she asked.

"No, I don't feel that's necessary."

"Wow it's so interesting how someone could con you and your best friends and they're not interesting enough to write about, meanwhile when I was struggling with addiction I couldn't show my face for months because I was all you wanted to write about."

Each time she didn't get her way about something she brought up the past. And each time she brought up the past, she was more innocent and everyone else was more guilty than in the last retelling.

I had apologized many times, but the goal posts were always being moved. I believe she was haunted by some of her actions in those days, particularly the neglect of her late dog Pearl, and her way of dealing with that was to make the issue our anger over her neglect as opposed to the neglect itself, which she scrubbed from memory. I once told her, "It's great you are so forgiving of yourself, except the more you forgive yourself the less you seem to forgive anyone else."

All this time I bit my tongue for the most part. I didn't see any point in dredging up the past or making her face ugly truths that she was probably not strong enough to handle, and I was also motivated by my own desire to move past it all myself. Plus, she was probably the most stubborn person I've ever met, and vehemently denied anything that didn't fit her narrative.

"It's so miserable to rehash the same things over and over. I feel like the only thing that will bring you peace is for me to wholesale accept your one-sided version of history. I was wrong in the way I handled your declaration of war. I was blinded by rage, there was tit for tat but things got out of hand. Seems you would be glad to see I'm more measured these days."

A text debate consumed my Saturday morning as she went around and around, disputing everything I said. She had no memory of anything she did during our past dramas, only the harm inflicted on her.

"This whole thing is a hideous way to spend a Saturday," I replied. "And you always do shit like this. There is always turmoil where there doesn't need to be. I reached out after the funeral to begin the process of mending, but it's never over nor will it ever be over. I don't plan on rehashing this on my only day off but what you don't see is the current sensitive and delicate Jasmine is not the person I was warring with. You were a battle tank. You were an equally capable opponent who inflicted plenty of damage. You have revised history so that you were this injured little squirrel I was throwing rocks at. You were a worthy nemesis who excelled at recruiting fighters. Niles is a nobody playing possum. We were a battle of superpowers, and during those days you owned the Grove. That was enemy territory for me."

"No, drinking Jasmine was a battle tank. Sober Jasmine has always been this way. I was sober when all that happened but you didn't know because no one cared to know that part of me."

The miserable debate raged on.

"I've more than paid for anything I've done in that saga. I'm paying for it today as we speak. I've overpaid and there's nothing more. My Saturday is destroyed. I spend a lot of time regretting things, but you are the victim in all of your stories."

"I apologize for ruining your Saturday. It seems we really are beyond repair. I don't feel we can continue this friendship. We both clearly feel things are one-sided and nothing's correcting it."

"Several times you've ended our friendship over something outside of my control—a triggering post from Menashe, someone bringing up a bad memory. That, coupled with unpredictable emotional torrents also counts as abuse. When you unfriend me, the truth is I feel a sense of peace. I get a break from worrying about being in trouble. I was always in the doghouse with Damon, so your volatile emotions hit me harder than you realize, and are disruptive to every part of my life. What I'm asking is for you to honor this latest ending and leave me in peace. You called it—our friendship is irreparable. That doesn't have to mean war or drama though."

I don't for a moment think she was sincere when saying the friendship was over. I believe it was manipulative, intended to be a "break the glass" moment, resulting in me getting more entangled, not less. Nothing about this argument was particularly unique, and I expected that we would soon make amends and continue the dysfunctional dynamic.

Triggered

"She didn't even have a toy for him!" Kage relayed to the Ladies Who Lunch while dining at Nadine's. The lack of toys didn't really register for me at the time, but was deeply troubling for Kage. I thought back to the bitterly cold night we were burying Brawny, and how at the last minute Kage ran home to grab his favorite stuffed critters.

Michael Lonergan brought Jett a bag of toys. He looked so cute as he played with one that I snapped and posted a photo—the first photo I had shared since adopting him.

Jasmine was of course monitoring my social media. Triggered, she sent the following message within minutes.

"You used Jett to jab at me. That's unforgivable. What that leads me to believe is 'here we go again she can't take care of a dog.' You know I miss him, so using him to jab me is disgusting. So have my dog and your peace. Goodbye."

"That's fucking nuts," I replied.

"Two days after I put Pearl down there was a post talking about me not taking care of her. You don't see how this is triggering for me? I can't with this. Like I said, enjoy my dog and your peace. You get both this time."

Rather than peace, we got an immediate and unrelenting onslaught of public accusations that we adopted Jett for spite.

"What kind of person adopts a dog for spite?" she railed in post after post for hours on end, from the afternoon until the late evening.

Her followers were deeply confused, posting comments like, "This was such a happy ending, I don't understand."

Finally, close to midnight and well up in my cups, I was sitting at Bar PM and answered her question with a question, posting the following to my Facebook:

What kind of person would risk a dog being euthanized for a few likes?

I deleted it after a few minutes, but she was off to the races with the screenshot.

"HE SAID I KILLED THE DOG! HE SAID I'M A PUPPY KILLER!" she railed hysterically.

The following day, a Sunday, I was working alone at Lydia's shop as part of my payment for use of the turret during Mardi Gras, and was so hungover and miserable I laid down on the floor, hidden by racks of costumes in the event a customer came in. Ms. Jamieson called to discuss the fireworks.

"Jasmine's furious. She said if you don't regret saying she killed the dog you're a sociopath."

"Miss Jamieson, why would I claim she killed the dog when I have the dog? Is this the Twilight Zone?"

"That's what I said!" Ms. Jamieson began. "I said clearly he wasn't saying you killed the dog because he already has the dog and posted the picture! But she just keeps talking like she didn't even hear me."

Later, a volunteer from the rescue reached out asking if I had time for a call. Luckily it was someone I had been Facebook friends with for many years, and she knew I cared for my animals.

"I'm just trying to figure out what's going on," she said.

I explained the situation.

"The previous owner even caught wind of the drama and was worried sick. Someone adopted her dog for spite! I called Jasmine and asked if we need to go get the dog, and she said yes."

She said yes. Somehow that last part didn't hit me in the moment. My mind was on the original owner and the horror of being told your beloved pet was in a bad environment. I thought of how I would have felt had I been forced to give up Brawny and was then told he was not in a loving home. I assured the rescue that Jett was happy and loved. I invited them to visit anytime they liked.

Maybe half an hour later, though, it sunk in. They asked Jasmine if they should take the dog back and she said yes. And what else could she say? She painted herself into a corner by that point. She couldn't then say, "Well actually he's fine. I'm just being toxic and vindictive."

I was fuming, and composed a status about what she had done, but did not mention her by name. I don't recall everything I said but I ended with:

Trying to get a pet removed from my home is a permanent stain on your wretched soul. And for her enablers, I don't give a damn how you're taking this. Your disapproval doesn't mean shit to me. My pets are family, not Instagram props.

Five Alarm Fire

As you can imagine, Jasmine lost her shit and went into full War Room mode. First, she texted the animal rescue lady demanding she issue a statement that the accusation was false.

"Oh dear. Jasmine is asking why I said she tried to get the dog removed when she didn't," the lady wrote over text.

"She's screenshot shopping," I replied, pulling over and furiously typing. "She's trying to manufacture evidence. Do not answer her in real time. It's a trap. Space out replies. Tell her you're unavailable."

I'd witnessed Jasmine's ability to browbeat people into lying for her. I think the first time I saw it was when she apparently swiped a woman's phone in the Grove. Her landlord found it after she moved out and returned it to the woman, and when word got out about it Jasmine somehow bullied or manipulated the woman into saying it had been a misunderstanding. I feared the rescue lady was no match for Jasmine's dogged persistence and might fold under pressure. Fortunately, the lady instead took my advice.

"Ok that's what I'm going to do," she said. "I'll say I'm in a bad service area."

Jasmine then switched her focus to Ms. Jamieson, who was trying to stay out of it but reluctantly agreed to mediate.

"This is a disaster!" Jasmine said. "Tell him we can both post statuses saying things got out of hand but I did not tell the rescue to take back the dog."

"No deal," I told Ms. Jamieson. "She told the rescue to take the dog back and I will *never* say otherwise."

I'd just taken on a fifteen-year commitment by adopting the dog, all to allow her to save face after an impulsive decision, and that didn't give her a moment's pause when deciding to turn on me. I knew if I walked back my report of what happened in order to bail her out again she'd immediately use the retraction to paint me as a liar and seek to inflict maximum harm on my credibility. Jasmine was not one to honor or be satisfied with a truce. She was uncomfortable with loose ends.

After some back and forth she told Ms. Jamieson she was going nuclear. She would release the contents of every chat we had been in together.

"What? But I'm in most of those chats! That will hurt *me*!" Ms. Jamieson exclaimed.

"Chris should have thought about that," Jasmine bitterly replied.

Ms. Jamieson called in a total state of panic. I sought to calm her down.

"Let her do it!" I began while pacing back and forth in the backyard as the sun was setting. "First of all, there's really nothing serious in there, just garden variety shade. Second, she threw as much shade as anyone, if not more. Third, she's such a one-trick pony that she's infamous for screenshot blackmail, let her add nails to that coffin. Finally, releasing those conversations will reveal the depth of her insane obsession with Christine Elbert, since that's all she talked about. So no, she won't release them in their entirety. She'll release carefully cropped and curated snippets that will invite scrutiny. Call her bluff."

Ms. Jamieson was disgusted that Jasmine would threaten to throw her under the bus.

When told I was not going to succumb to her demands, Jasmine said she was going to kill herself.

"I have nothing to live for anyway. I'm through," she said.

"Tell her she had a good run," I replied to Ms. Jamieson.

"Oh my God I can't say that!"

Ms. Jamieson was legitimately worried, and called 911.

About fifteen minutes later, Jasmine wrote to Ms. Jamieson, "You can tell whoever called 911 that it backfired. The police remembered me from Pride and we all just laughed about it. When I showed them all the bullying screenshots, they said they were turning them over to the FBI's Cyberbullying Unit. As I was explaining how bad it was the officer really leaned in."

She was clearly unstable, as demonstrated by the suicide threat and nonsensical stories, so I offered a proposal thru Ms. Jamieson: Both sides remove all dog posts without comment and don't discuss it any further.

Jasmine came back with a peculiar counter proposal. She would accept the deal I presented if me and Kage left several specific chats. In retrospect I should have said no, but in the moment I thought it was best to de-escalate, and it was certainly beneficial to have all of the ugliness taken down. We didn't know what she could be up to, but we left the chats.

"She said Kage is still in Confidential Conversations," Ms. Jamieson relayed. Kage looked that forgotten chat up and left it as well.

Everything was taken down.

The following morning, true to form, she put up a brand-new post saying the dog accusation was a lie. She went through many chats, deleted her comments, and then harvested and curated screen shots to turn various people against us with no way for us to show the full context. The first soldier she recruited was Keyton, that odd trick Niles brought to our party.

Having alienated nearly everyone in her life since Pride, she was assembling a brand-new group, and was scraping the bottom of the barrel.

Working the Refs

I've mentioned how Jasmine had been able to pull my strings, yanking me into messes between people I didn't even know existed seconds beforehand. Now she was manipulating her army to come after me and Kage.

The core story was that we adopted her troubled and aggressive dog for spite in order to bully her by claiming the dog was neither troubled nor aggressive, but she'd tailor each retelling to the triggers of her audience. For example, when recruiting someone with a certain disorder she'd say I did all the above *and* posted statuses mocking people with that disorder.

"If you're going to be a problematic asswipe at least hide your workplace on your profile!" one person upset about a nonexistent post wrote to me.

Jasmine's latest group had locked-down profiles, and would "block and talk," or more accurately "block, stalk and talk." Block someone, follow their every move using fake profiles or spies, and post statuses about them by name. I hated that she was teaching her young followers this was the way things should be done. Those kids seemed to think the only reason I didn't operate this way was ignorance due to my "advanced age." Jasmine was infamously ageist, believing the only role for someone over forty was to be a cheerleader for someone under forty, i.e., her.

I replied to the person who called me a problematic asswipe. While I had never met them, I knew they were an aspiring performer who hosted a lightly attended Monday night show. (Part of having a show is being able to draw a crowd. Even when this entertainer had a completely empty house they felt entitled to be paid by the club, which caused tension).

"I'm a 44-year-old man and I don't post things I won't stand by. I don't subscribe to the 'Block and Talk' strategy, which is why my page is public. If we ever speak again, I hope it's regarding something creative, and not the tired pursuits of one perpetually angry person's vendettas."

Jasmine manipulated others with her trademark cocktail of highly pressurized hysterics and guilt. Using her custom Facebook settings, she'd deftly cultivate someone by hiding her trolling posts from them, and then pointing out all of the seemingly one-sided shade when she's "simply trying to move on."

"Look at what they're saying!" she'd exclaim along with screenshots of garden variety shade where she wasn't even named—often sarcastic comments or jokes about vicious puppies, the FBI coming for us, or "Ol' Hot Rod Elbert" chasing people down Arsenal Street.

Such comments were typically buried deep in an unrelated thread just to see how closely they were monitoring. She and her team never missed a one.

She was masterful at collating, packaging and marketing her evidence, and with her multiple accounts, sundry settings and vanishing posts, the person she was selling to likely had never seen her trolling posts where she mocked her enemies by name and made wild accusations.

Granted, her job would have been infinitely more challenging had I had the discipline to not return fire at all. I was so angry that she told the rescue Jett was in a bad home, and that she would rather see everyone at one another's throats than simply admit what she had done. My way to deal with my emotions was with humor, mocking her ridiculous claims and flimsy accusations. That wasn't helpful to my cause.

But even if I had gone quiet, I still wouldn't have been out of the woods because she was focused enough to convince her audience that I was behind anything *anyone* posted about her. And she had plenty of enemies posting about her.

For instance, she told the suburban dad behind the Penny Gosling character that he was a bad father. I often became furious with Jasmine, but I never hated her. I'm pretty sure the disparaged dad did, however, and each time he lashed out she simply ignored him and packaged his posts as evidence against me and me alone.

It was a savvy move. The biggest mistake vengeful, unstable people make is they spread their fire too thin. They have too many battles happening at once or in close succession. But she was never distracted from her target. I was the threat that needed to be neutralized. (Christine Elbert was a different matter because that issue was never about an argument or a back-and-forth, but was simply about Christine's firm boundaries and her refusal to validate Jasmine's disturbing behavior).

A person with no contextual understanding would receive a volley of screenshots Jasmine claimed were aimed at her, along with her theatrics. "They are trying to bully me to *suicide* and *nobody* will stand up for me because it doesn't involve them!"

When possible, she'd toss in a screenshot of a vintage private conversation they might not like for good measure.

She had effectively rebranded herself, at least to one audience, as a fragile person who was being bullied. And it was bullshit. Jasmine was a beast. A war machine set on perpetual vengeance. It was in her DNA, and I couldn't judge her for what she was when that's the very reason I first reached out, and I accepted her all along even as I tried to steer her in healthier and more productive directions (most of the time, anyway). The newer fragile persona wasn't an about-face, as she claimed, but an effective mutation. By convincing her followers she was a defenseless victim, by eliciting sympathy and stoking their hero complex, she could activate "her army" to attack on her behalf. By the time most of them figured out the truth, they'd already served their purpose.

The first individual we knew personally to turn on us was longtime neighborhood friend Ron Tellcamp, who was someone we didn't hang out with, but were always happy to see. We were both in our mid-forties, and had probably been friendly for about fifteen or twenty years. We were the two closest friends of a cultured and affluent Bostonian named Tom Choinski who moved to town for his husband's job. St. Louis was a hard place to break into, and Tom credited the two of us for getting him established socially and helping him navigate this city's nuances. We'd both attended his elegant dinner parties at his sleek Midtown condo.

Ron began with passive-aggressive shade on Jasmine's behalf, which was unexpected for several reasons, one being he'd been verbally abusive towards her in the past. In January of 2018, for instance, Jasmine was devastated after Ron read her for filth for defending the svelte Brandon Reid, who I later interviewed for the "Meth at the Melrose" piece.

"Ron Tellcamp told me to fuck off this morning. Like I seriously can't today. I was defending Brandon Reid on the Tower Grove South page and Ron is an administrator and flipped out," a rattled Jasmine relayed at the time.

The situation brewing with Ron was reminiscent of Shawn Adams coming after us on Clyde's behalf, but the critical difference was Shawn Adams was self-aware. He'd always acknowledged his temper and his tendencies, and he was capable of eventually admitting when he'd gone off track. Shawn Adams could laugh at himself and he also had a longtime companion to ground him, which was something the emotionally brittle Ron never had.

I knew Ron was a loose cannon and whatever his rationale was for coming for us now, I sought to nip it in the bud.

"I was where you are only a couple of months ago. I'm Class of 2019, you're Class of 2020. I know Jasmine is showering you with praise for taking swipes at us, but that's not going to satisfy her for long. I gave her an entire print rebranding campaign, held up a sign in her defense as a parade judge, and adopted her unwanted dog. Look where it got me. You're going to get sucked in much deeper than you realize, and one day you'll find yourself on the other side, trying to fight back attacks from someone you've always been cool with."

Ron acknowledged that Jasmine's pattern of weaponizing private conversations was unseemly and problematic. "I don't like that receipts game," he said, but because I was a public figure, he argued that the onus was on me to use restraint.

"You are CHRIS FUCKING ANDOE LGBTQIA MEDIA TITAN to many . . . she is no one," he wrote.

It's an argument I heard often, and not an unreasonable one.

We hashed things out and I even acknowledged my part in escalating things with him, which seemed to neutralize him for a few days, but Jasmine seduced him with an invitation to one of her trademark potlucks. At one such event a year earlier, I staged a Last Supper photo with her as Jesus. Jasmine had a cocky, unfriendly expression in that shot, which I found odd, but I later made the connection that the scene had a very different meaning to her. I was simply inspired by the long skinny table. She, however, took it as a challenge to "Lesbian Jesus" Christine Elbert.

She recreated that image with almost all new friends at the table, mostly misfits like Nile's trick Keyton. I wasn't clear on the message she was trying to convey that time. Maybe that friends are replaceable with warm bodies.

After the potluck, Ron Tellcamp ramped up the shade and escalated to hate posts about me, lending his credibility to her fantastical claims. As unnerved as I was about him dragging me over social media, with Tom in mind I again reached out to try to calm the waters.

"I hope the hate threads were cathartic, but considering we share some good mutual friends I hope we can at least remain civil in person," I wrote.

I didn't ask him to remove his posts or even to stop posting. I simply requested a gentleman's agreement where we didn't make things any more awkward for friends who might like to invite us to the same gathering.

"You sound incredibly insecure and ridiculous," Ron wrote. "I pity you."

"I don't think an insecure person would extend an olive branch to someone who was actively facilitating hate threads against them, but it's clear we don't see eye to eye on anything—even on being civil. Good night."

"You know where you stand. You don't matter to me," he replied.

"I do know that very well. And in spite of that I was seeing if we could remain civil. I got my answer."

"You could've stopped attacking Jasmine. You could've taken a breath about this whole dog BS. You chose the opposite. This is 100% about you and you alone."

Tellcamp accused me of lying about the dog. I wasn't clear if he meant I was lying about the dog *not* being vicious, about me adopting him for spite, or about Jasmine telling the rescue to retrieve him. But I assumed all three, considering comments he made publicly and the fact he tacitly cosigned everything she said.

"You've known me for twenty years and you know I love and care for my dogs," I replied. "I have proof that she told the rescue to take my dog away."

His replies were oddly confrontational, like he was putting on a show. I initiated the conversation without any real understanding of how his allegiance to Jasmine had consumed him, becoming central to his identity and social standing. It felt the conversation was less about communicating with me than impressing outsiders. In particular, I suspected every word was crafted to pleasure Jasmine. With his keyboard, he was performing fellatio.

I still attempted to reason with him after he again said I was a liar. When I said I had proof for all I relayed he reiterated that he didn't like "receipts."

"I'm not lying. And the whole reason she was mad to begin with is I wouldn't publicly attack my former roommate Niles for the cons he pulled. I said it wasn't necessary. Falsely claiming the dog was vicious was bad enough. It was going to make him much harder to re-home. You know my history with dogs and all I went through with mine, especially Brawny. You know I love dogs and wouldn't adopt a dog for spite. You know that Jett is in a good home."

By this point I understood he didn't give a damn about the welfare of our pets. My repetitive argument about how I cared for my animals was to shame him. In the time we knew one another and were connected on social media I lost my Grandma Andoe's elderly Boston Terrier, and then a beautiful Golden Retriever I eulogized in a viral article, and finally Brawny. I was telling him that I knew that he knew he was defending the indefensible. I was rubbing his nose in shit.

"I'm going to say this exactly one time: stop. Walk away. My name needs to not come from your mouth again. Ever."

Ron had this incredibly bizarre tough-guy act, where he even hinted at violence, but he was the least intimidating person. He was as hard as a pile of pillows. Yet he was Jasmine's top lieutenant/ manservant, and as such, he shredded his brand and threw his professed principles out the window and posted our private exchange, ginning up a new hate thread. It took him minutes to embrace the "receipts game" he long derided. It was reminiscent of a Nine Inch Nails song about once being up above it, but now being down in it.

I wasn't upset about the contents going public per se. I remained civil and polite for that entire exchange, while he was insulting and emotional. I came off far better than he did. What infuriated me was I respected him enough to think we could have a private conversation in the first place.

In public comments forwarded to me soon after, he and Jasmine teased out a story about having received embarrassing information from Damon, of all people. I knew it was simply a sloppy intimidation tactic. For starters, me and Damon were in a relatively decent place after Brawny's passing. But even if we weren't, Damon was a serious man who was brilliant and accomplished, serving as VP of a major

California housing developer. We had been a power couple in San Francisco, and navigated major battles against our employer's enemies in City Hall. I knew how he strategized and how he fought. Strapping a hatchback to my leg and dropping me into the bay? Yeah. Whispering to the likes of Jasmine and Ron so they could dish with their sad shut-ins? Nah.

Later, Ron would learn that Kage was depressed because another friend, someone Kage really liked, publicly rebuked us on he and Jasmine's behalf. Ron then posted a meme making fun of Kage for being sad about losing the friend.

Kage was my Achilles Heel. His joy was something I cherished, and I intensely hated Ron for mocking his sadness. I hated him more than I had ever hated anyone.

In retrospect I recognize I was in an irrational state of mind, but during this episode I thought Kage would be better off if we divorced. I questioned what kind of life I'd given him if he was subjected to relentless mocking by miserable people who relished him being depressed. What kind of life was this when on any given morning he could open up his phone to find that people we've broken bread with, or even that we had agreed to father children for (that plan never came to fruition), turned on a dime and were now saying the worst things about us?

In that moment I forgot about the strength of the house, how our true friends were as unwavering as ever. In that moment I could only see Jasmine and Ron's success in undermining several peripheral friendships, and I felt the very ground our life was built on was poisoned. Maybe Kage would be better off building a life in a healthier location.

At one point in the exchange with Tellcamp he said, "You'll never come between us. You can't."
How weird.

Yes, I regrettably went after strangers on Jasmine's behalf during the course of our friendship. That is part of my history and something I have to live with. The fact she could so easily manipulate me is deeply embarrassing. But in the heat of the moment, I believed her. But even when she convinced me Christine was copying her statuses, which I actually believed at the time, I never went public. I didn't go after known quantities or turn on longtime friends, and I certainly never agreed to bear false witness.

"Why would he sign a 30-year note on a pop-up house? Why would he hitch his wagon to someone who is infamous for their fantastical dishonesty?" I pondered to Kage.

Ron spent his life building a personal brand that was the polar opposite of what he became to please Jasmine. He sacrificed his reputation for her the way Rudy Giuliani did for Trump.

I had slightly less contempt for the others she turned against us, but still enjoyed hearing about her screwing them over. Upon such a report, I posted:

If you side with someone who sheds friends like winter coats, I think it's fair to throw a little shade when you're dropped off at Goodwill.

Speaking of shade, if Jasmine and Ron's "Block and Talk" was the lowest form of shade, the highest was the ballroom standard. When someone decided to shade ballroom legend Mechee Harper, for instance, the man not only named her, he tagged her. Harper replied on his post, "Feel free to check my wall for my response. I wouldn't dare reply on such a low trending thread. Bye."

That, children, is how it's done.

House of the Saccharine Sisters

Jasmine purged from her life anyone who gave her push-back, and push-back constituted half of every conversation some of us had with her as we tried in vain to get her to move past her tiresome obsessions. She ditched at least a dozen very close friends I can think of, including someone who was like a father to her for ten years, and someone she called her best friend. On top of that, there were dozens of acquaintances she cut off because of their even casual ties to Christine Elbert or the House of Villadiva.

With her post-Pride notoriety, she preferred the company of fans who only validated, and who acquiesced to her demands that she be given the authority to dictate their social media block list, which she claimed was for her own safety. Trans writer Terry Willits said Jasmine even demanded a lesbian friend break up with her longtime partner because Jasmine didn't trust her. Given the choice between Jasmine's cult and her partner, fortunately the woman made the right decision.

Jasmine was done hearing she should move on from her Christine fixation, and that she should stop stalking her page. She was done paying lip service to working on her debilitating abandonment issues. She was ready for an all-cotton candy diet.

I referred to Jasmine and Ron's hobbled together group of random joyless and easily-dominated shut-ins and hangers-on as the Saccharine Sisters because of their over-the-top artificial sweetness. Everyone in their circle was a delicate victim with an insatiable need for affirmation, and *everyone* they didn't like was an abuser.

And of course, the alpha victim was always Jasmine. Since her name had been in the papers, she held an odd celebrity status among the easily-impressed followers who would jockey to see who could heap on the most words of encouragement each day. Some would even compete for the "opportunity" to clean her apartment.

I saw her entire rebrand—from someone who wasn't afraid of City Hall or our city's most corrupt officers to someone too traumatized to even see photos of people she didn't like in her newsfeed— as a con job for the sad, gullible and desperate.

Thinking about the vulgar amount of energy devoted to feeding Jasmine's insatiable appetite for sympathy, I was reminded of how my worst tenants in San Francisco could orchestrate the biggest armies of advocates when they wanted something, effectively trampling over everyone else.

With that in mind I posted the following reflection to Facebook:

I once managed two buildings in San Francisco which housed formerly homeless people. Each building had about 40 units, nearly all drearily facing the side of neighboring buildings. But there were a handful of coveted units facing a park, and you have not seen knives come out until you've been around those buildings when a tenant in a park front unit died. I'm not exaggerating when I say that the body would still be in the room when tenants and their army of outside social workers and pro bono attorneys would begin demanding the unit.

The caring, on-site team of social workers had educated opinions of who was in the greatest need. Maybe it was someone suffering from depression at the end of their life who was always home, and could benefit greatly from simply having more fresh air, sunshine, and something to look at in their remaining days. Regardless, in the end it was always the squeakiest wheel who got the unit. The drug-addicted sex worker who was rarely home but had a guilt-ridden father with a loudmouth and deep pockets. The sociopath. The criminal. All with their advocates banging on doors and filing papers.

The nice people didn't have it in them to whip up such a fuss, so staring at a shadowy wall was their fate.

I think about that often to this day. How it seems the worst people seem to elicit the most sympathy. Poorly behaved adults who cry about "bullying" and somehow attract a following of vacuous validators and champions. I shake my head thinking of all the energy wasted on the sociopaths, the narcissists, the monsters while countless suffer without notice.

I can hear it now, "Who are you to decide who is more deserving?"

The point is one type of person is deemed most deserving time and time again, and gets everything. You may be the type who joins the chorus of those caterwauling over the insatiable squeaky wheel, but I save my sympathies for those in the shadows staring at the wall alone.

Just as there were victims in the story of the tenants passed over for better housing opportunities, there were victims as a result of the Saccharine Sisters' manipulation. Turnover was high as members were manipulated and discarded, and in the meantime real people like Christine Elbert were subjected to wave after wave of weaponized trolls on a sugar high.

And after those trolls had fulfilled their purpose, all they had to show for it was six-to-twelve months of wasted time, diminished reputations, and burned bridges. Feuding and making amends is what's done in St. Louis, but after one was a soldier for the Saccharine Sisters—trying to get community icons banned from coffee shops, bearing false witness, targeting the jobs of strangers and even joining a smear campaign against a dog—there really wasn't a way to rehabilitate one's image short of a full-throated apology tour. And doing that would make them a target of the sisters.

Not to mention there were undoubtedly human beings in these people's lives who could have used the kindness and companionship during the months they were pissing it away on a couple of manipulators.

Kage's PR Offensive

It was exhausting and infuriating to constantly defend our record of caring for our pets. We had brand new people we'd never even spoken to, most all feigning neutrality, regularly weighing in on Facebook and asking for fresh explanations as to why Jasmine and Ron would lie about us adopting Jett for spite.

"I've been on their pages and on your page and I just don't see why they'd make these things up. I'm trying to understand and give you the benefit of the doubt but quite frankly I see a lot of mudslinging coming from your side. If what they are saying is false why not ignore it?" one such man posted.

Being a public figure, everyone felt they had the right to question my actions, and felt I didn't have the right to be offended by their questioning.

With the full-scale assault on our family, and with our pets front and center, Kage had a brilliant idea: He would post a story about each of our five animals over the course of a Monday thru Friday week.

He went in order from oldest to youngest, which would build anticipation for Jett. His long, descriptive posts were so heartfelt, giving the reader a sense for each pet's individual personality and the love we had for them.

I fashioned myself as the PR Chair of Villadiva, but Kage's project did more to make their claims look foolish than any of my efforts. I'd been consumed by anger and had been engaging with our enemies in the gutter where they stood, while Kage rose above them and created something pure and beautiful. His stories were something anyone could enjoy.

Meandering Thoughts on My Last Ten Years—
chrisandoe.com, November 23, 2019

Ten years ago, I was still picking up the pieces and trying to find my footing after the 2008 financial crisis–an event that not only cost me my fortune, but the respect of someone who was closest to me. To make up for what I saw as my own personal screw up, I did things I didn't want to do, like moving away from the city where I felt most at home.

The pain, frustration and torture from that time is what pushed me from being someone who told stories at parties to being a writer. This means if given the chance to undo that failure, I wouldn't be who I am now. And I like who I am. It also means I wouldn't have befriended all the wonderful friends I've made as I flailed from coast to coast, especially my friends in San Francisco. And I wouldn't have met the love of my life.

One thing you might not know about me is I'm scrappy AF. I can make things happen, and I can make something out of nothing. And I'm proud of that. It's a useful skill that might have atrophied had I not lost everything and not had to climb back while bouncing from place to place.

A woman is born with all the eggs she'll ever have, and since I was a late surprise, I was born from an old egg. I've always felt I should be about twenty years older than I am, and have bonded with those in that age group. When I was in the seventh grade my favorite show was *Thirty Something*, and when my friends came over I'd carefully plan the lighting scheme, dimming the chandelier and serving them sodas on a big silver tray. Entertaining in the home is one of my favorite things, and as a consequence of moving around, the divorce, etc. I haven't been able to properly do that (which has been incredibly frustrating) until the end of last year, when we acquired Villadiva. It's big, old, haunted, and needs work, and we absolutely love it.

Today, I'm preparing Villadiva for Mac Taylor's going away party. Never do I feel myself as much as when I'm preparing to entertain. The Little Liberace from my childhood is very much still here.

As I look at the past decade, I can say that I have very few regrets and much that I'm proud of and am thankful for. I've never been as true to myself as I am now. In retrospect it really seems a catastrophic failure was just what I needed.

Life at 44 (45 in a few weeks) is more fun than I ever imagined.

Trapped in the Basement

It was close to midnight when Ms. Jamieson's phone illuminated. The message was from Clyde: *I need help getting out of the basement.*

"When I originally got the message, I thought he meant that someone was actually in the basement and I got scared. He clarified that there was a spirit down there and he couldn't leave." Ms. Jamieson said.

She descended the two flights of winding stairs, anxious of what she might find, then she saw Clyde on the opposite end of the dimly-lit space, with his back to her as he stared straight into the stone wall.

"What's going on?" Ms. Jamieson asked.

Clyde slowly turned around and had an angry expression on his face.

"When I first saw him down there staring at the wall, my first thought was, 'Oh my God! This is exactly how the Blair Witch movie ended, where the guy was standing facing the wall right before he suddenly turned around and attacked the girl with the camera'. So, I hesitated at first and then called his name a few times," Ms. Jamieson explained.

"He turned around and laughed maniacally and for a minute. I thought he was going to attack me. He then said something like, 'You never fucking cared about me. I hate you,' and laughed again. I said, 'Come on. You're coming with me. We are getting out of this basement.' I grabbed his hand and as I turned to walk towards the stairs, he resisted and wouldn't move and then laughed again. I said, 'Come on, we're going now!' He then let me lead him out of the basement to the back building door. When we got outside, he walked towards the parking pad, stood there with his back towards me for a minute, and then looked back and said, 'I'm so sorry. I don't know what happened.'"

Marcus

I used to deny I had a type. I was open to a variety of guys, dated various races, but I consider my 40s to be my acceptance phase in many regards, one being that yes, I indeed had a type, which I would summarize as masculine men of color with strong shoulders, arms and chest, and a belly. Scrolling through Instagram one day I came across exactly that: Marcus.

I followed, and regularly saw his rugby pics as well as his shirtless selfies, and was struck by the cocky way he owned and embraced his body.

I finally met him at Bar PM one evening. "Hey, you're Beef 'n Beans!" I said, calling him by his Instagram handle. Marcus flashed a smile and laughed. "Yeah, I am! Nobody has ever called me that before. I'm Marcus."

He was the same height as Kage (and Cody) with a thicker build.

Marcus was one of those guys you'd never clock as being gay.

His family was in Chicago, and his living situation was less than ideal. The affluent interracial couple who owned the house, only blocks from ours, rented out several rooms on Airbnb. Marcus lived in the basement, which he had to himself, but shared the kitchen and bathroom with tourists. This created awkward moments as some guests didn't realize they'd be sharing the space.

In exchange for very cheap rent, he cleaned the rooms between visitors and walked the owners' dog on a strict schedule with the distance measured by a device. Even if he were in class miles away, he would need to take a train and bus, or Uber back home to care for the dog.

Once Niles was out, I invited Marcus to come over to see the room. He walked through the door and smiled. "Oh, this is much better than what I have now. I don't even have a window."

I offered him the same low rent amount he had been paying. He was noncommittal, and mentioned the possibility of renting his own place. One night just the two of us were in the car heading out and I sought to assure him this would be a good move.

"Our dynamic is nothing like where you're at now. We expect you to help out with housework and pet sitting as you're able, but would never make you leave school to do it. We've got a relaxed environment and you'd be more like a full-fledged roommate. You could entertain whenever you'd like."

I worried that someone would catch wind of the invitation and sabotage things, but Marcus was the strong silent type, and didn't discuss his plans. It also helped that I hadn't had a public feud with Niles.

Rough & Tumble: Sitting Down with the St. Louis Crusaders—
Out in STL, *September 2019*

Rugby involves a lot of whoring. In fact, the whoring is one reason there's such a brotherhood between players across the sport. As if that weren't intriguing enough, they even have hookers on the field (for real!), and all of this goes on under the watchful eye of "the Sir."

OK, I may have inadvertently led you to believe rugby is like a muddier version of Caligula, so I'll elaborate. A team always has fifteen players on the field, and if they're short of that number—as is often the case when traveling—the other team will "whore out" a few players.

"Is that just what the gay teams call it? Or is that across the sport?" I inquire.

"It's the term everyone uses," the imposing Kevin Hayes Jr. replies. "And they play hard, too. You'd think they'd be pulling for their own team, but when they're playing with you, they give it their all."

The hooker is the man in the middle of the scrum hooking for the ball, and the sir is the referee. But plenty of ink has been spilled over how rugby is played. My goal is to better understand what it's like to be part of the Crusaders brotherhood, so I sit down with four members of the team to discuss. In attendance were the aforementioned Hayes, 34, Robert Fischer, 28, Daniel Fanning, 29, and Marcus Watt, 25.

I begin by asking what drew them to the sport.

"Boys in short shorts. What you sayin'?" Hayes quips. "The sexiness pulls you in, but we're all just players on the field."

Fanning, who like Hayes, has a military background, says he's always been athletic, playing football in high school and enjoying cycling and volleyball.

"I found rugby through a friend. I wanted to join to get to know more people and develop friendships through sportsmanship once I moved back to St. Louis."

Watt moved to St. Louis from his native Chicago, where he played on a gay team. "I jumped back into it with these guys. Made it easier to meet people here."

Fischer, unlike the others, didn't consider himself to be athletic. "A buddy played in college, and it seemed he was always bloody, bruised and battered. I moved to L.A. for a few years, and when I returned, I was ready to try new things and came to practice. I was apprehensive at first if I could do it, but everyone was incredibly friendly, making it easier. I went to one practice, kept going, and then before I knew it, I was in a real game."

The Third Half

"The third half is what players call party time after the game," Watt says. "In Chicago, I played against a mainstream team called the Chicago Riot. I loved, loved, loved playing them. Some teams don't like playing against gay players or have issues with it, but they were always fun, always had good spirit. Even though they were straight, when we'd go to the sponsor bar afterwards, we'd have a dance off and underwear contest, and they'd bring out the Speedos and jockstraps."

Rather than getting hotel rooms, whenever possible traveling players will stay with members of the host team. Fanning hosted four players from New Orleans, taking them on a bar crawl, beginning with Third Half at Just John and ending the night by shutting down JJ's.

"Were you muddy all night?" I ask.

"Haha, no, we weren't muddy at all. The ground was dry, so we were dirty at Just John but took showers before Rehab," Fanning says.

"I picture the field being permanently muddy for some reason," I say, laughing.

Fanning replies, "It's nice when it is. Getting tackled on dry ground hurts more."

Home Bar Advantage

Just John is the sponsor and the home bar for the Crusaders, and the team feels they can really cut loose there. "It's rugby—we drink a lot, and everyone knows who we are. We go in after a game, all dirty and they're just like, 'There go the rugby boys.' It's really a family vibe there," Fischer says.

"Traveling around, you go to some teams' home bar and you can't even tell it's theirs, but Just John goes all out. We come in, and the Crusaders are all over the televisions. If we throw a party, they decorate for us and push it on social media, and the staff are really welcoming to the visiting players. They provide our jerseys and are always checking in on us, seeing what we need," Fischer explains.

Joining the Brotherhood

The guys concede that from the outside rugby looks incredibly intimidating.

"Looks rough on the field, but we're all queens," Watt jokes. But they stress that they have a need and a place for all types of guys, and increasing membership is a key part of their goals in building the organization. They've got big guys, little guys, trans guys, straight guys. And if you can only give a few minutes here and there, they'll take it. "We don't care if you're not the most talented at rugby. If you can only play ten minutes, give us your all in those ten minutes, and we'll make sure to put you in." Fischer says.

"It looks rougher when you're watching it," Hayes says. "Looks hard as fuck, but rugby is fucking fun."

The Cursed Object

I came home for lunch and in the center of the back porch was a large, rusty nail, which struck me as odd. I looked around but couldn't determine where it could have come from. I sensed that I should not bring it inside, so I set it on the deck railing.

That evening we discovered that our cat Ginger couldn't walk. Kage took her to the emergency vet and they said she had a blood clot in her brain.

At 1:45 a.m. I was woken by Troy rushing downstairs barking viciously as if someone had broken in. In the middle of this chaos, I heard my name being called. It sounded as if both Troy's barking and the voice were coming from the base of the stairs, but thinking perhaps there was an emergency and someone was at the front door, I grabbed my phone to see if there were any messages, and there was nothing. I knew I was not going downstairs.

The next day I messaged Clyde about all that had been going on, curious about his reaction. There was an uncommon delay of about five minutes before he responded, and when he did, he was uncharacteristically brief. "Wonder what that's about?"

Later that evening, probably while drinking, Clyde had more to say. "I was doing laundry in the basement last night, and for whatever reason walked to the darkest corner and said, 'If you're still here, bring him to me.'"

Over the next few days I noticed that the energy in the house was off. There was an ominous vibe.

I contacted paranormal investigator Rachel Poirier—who'd I'd been in touch with regarding a ghost hunting article I planned to write for the *RFT*—and asked if she'd visit the house, which she did the following Saturday afternoon. Before she arrived she asked if we'd like her to pass on any spirits she encounters, to clear them from the house. I told her to do so if they were negative, or if they were trapped. Otherwise not necessarily.

As she walked through the first floor with her sensing hand raised and oscillating, she told me what she was picking up.

"The original owners are here. They lived here for a very long time. They both died here. I'm seeing mourners pass through the dining room." She then looked at me with a pained, saddened face. "Ooh it's going to be hard to pass them on."

"They can stay." I replied.

"They're nice." she began. "And they like you guys and the way you're caring for the house. They don't really know what to make of the gay thing, though. They're from a different time."

Downstairs she had a full, rich understanding of the spirits, but things were different upstairs. Particularly in our bedroom.

"There's a little girl here," she began with a puzzled expression. "She's mischievous. She likes to hide things," she said more as a question than a comment.

Back in the dining room we sat down to continue our discussion.

"There's something you should know," I said "Two years ago, a former friend cut three lines into his arm, bled onto the scraps of a shirt we'd given him, and summoned Satan to curse us."

With this, she seemed to get clarity, nodding as if everything made sense.

"The man who did this is very weak minded," she began as her sensing hand drifted behind her to the northwest, in the direction of the Melrose. "He has no idea what he's done, and quite frankly, most likely needs to be blessed by a priest every week for the rest of his life. Something uses him as a vessel, it takes control of him. This is dangerous because the ultimate aim of this entity is murder."

Rachel, who had been focused squarely on me, jumped in her chair and swung her arm around, pointing directly at Kage. "And it's *YOU* he's mad at! You're the one keeping him out!"

I was startled and felt exposed, afraid of what she might say next.

"Yeah," Kage shrugged. It was a muted and casual response to such a dramatic moment.

While talking about Clyde's aims her arm drifted back to the northwest. She felt certain he brought the nail, and that it was cursed. Its aim, she said, was to bring about the end of our relationship. I wondered if that influence was why I had the irrational thought that it would be best for Kage if I divorced him in order to spare him the ridicule Ron and Jasmine ginned up.

"Would you like to visit the Melrose basement? I asked.

She excitedly said yes, but after a few minutes said she better wait until she had her team with her. She seemed afraid.

"Ok, if you'd like I can drive you past the building," I offered.

She said yes, but after a few minutes again said she should wait. She also said she worried that the little girl in our room was actually a demon.

Rachel left with the nail. She said that evening a demon came to her in the dark, and the following day she stepped on a nail at work.

The Exorcist

A friend from Pittsburgh was in town and told me of his happy hour plans in hopes we could get together. My text reply: *Ok we are waiting on a priest to expel a demon from our house and then need a nap but will try to make it.*

The prior Thursday night Kage had gone down to the Grey Fox with our new roommate Marcus. I decided to call my dear friend John Kreisel to fill him in on what's been going on, since he was far more sensitive to spirits than I was.

Rather than sitting in my regular spot at the table, I sat at the other end with my back to the corner. I told him every detail of Rachel's visit, and at the first mention of a little girl he interjected, "Okay, no, uhuh, she doesn't belong."

During our call, there was a lot of interference, including bursts of static and my own voice echoing back. These were issues I hadn't had on calls in the house before.

"I'd like to join Kage at Grey Fox, but that would mean going upstairs to get dressed, and nothing sounds more terrifying than going up there at the moment."

"I'm going to contact Father Marek to help you," he said.

Father Marek Bożek was the pastor of St. Stanislaus Kostka Church.

It was a sunny afternoon when Father Marek arrived. The friendly man with clear blue eyes and a thick Polish accent sat opposite us in the parlor and asked about what we were experiencing, listened attentively. He then said he personally didn't believe in hauntings, but that our home would be well-served by a blessing anyway.

He walked through every room sprinkling holy water and saying prayers, then he joined us for wine and cheese at the table where we discussed other things including how the two of us shared the same exact birthday. We were born hours apart.

When Father Marek said he didn't believe in hauntings I thought that didn't bode well for the effectiveness of his blessing, but it was really incredible. The house felt clean and comfortable when he was done.

Last Call for Fancy Slovak

Fancy's death was announced the day after Thanksgiving, and of course Jasmine didn't let such an opportunity pass her by. In a dramatic Facebook post she said she made Fancy a promise back in October (when Fancy's *Out in STL* feature was released) and reiterated the promise to her on her deathbed. The promise being that she'd take on the bullies and get Fancy's *true* story out.

I was quite certain she wasn't referring to the story she told me months earlier, which was that Fancy was a bully and anyone who was upset about the feature was too old and dumb to comprehend it.

If there was ever a time for Jasmine to harness raw emotions for her own ends, this was it, and I took it seriously.

Initially I instructed our social media team to not post anything about the passing, knowing it would likely become a magnet for backlash. I intended to follow the same plan for my personal page, but after a few hours Elizabeth, our social media director, suggested a simple photo of a Grove sign reading RIP Nancy, and I agreed.

In my Board of Directors chat, Mac Taylor said I really needed to post something. After several drafts I settled on the following, along with a photo of her framed feature on my wall:

Everyone knows Fancy was no fan of mine, but I'm glad she at least liked the images our photographer captured of her beautiful farewell event—one of which adorns the Hall of Fame in my home, alongside other titans of this community.

Fancy was tireless, dedicated and fun. She leaves a void that will never be filled.

The post was met with approval from community elders, and aside from vague shade about how unfairly she was judged by the community, and Elizabeth getting posthumously unfriended (certainly at the hand of Jasmine), we tiptoed past the immediate aftermath without incident.

The window of opportunity to weaponize a community's grief was short. A fact that was lost on Jasmine. Or perhaps she knew I had extensive evidence that she not only approved of the feature, but she derided those who were upset about it. Not to mention evidence of the unkind things she said about Fancy.

In the end this was just another one of her many scrapped storylines.

Dustin Mitchell's Prison Letter to Darin

On September 18, 2019 Darin wrote to say he'd received a prison letter from Dustin Mitchell, who was seeking to exploit the competition between our publications. We laughed about it and I got the sense Darin was planning to simply discard the letter.

"Post it!" I said. "People LOVE Dustin Mitchell updates and this is gold!"

Darin posted the following to Facebook:

I'm always reticent/nervous of opening the hand written mail I receive at Vital VOICE. I've had to endure many death threats and queer bashing correspondence from a lot people over the last ten years.

However, today's letter made me chuckle! That's right boys, girls and theys . . . . DM has popped right up, direct and live from prison in Texas. lol

Apparently, the darling Chris Andoe and his RFT produced publication Out In STL have upset St. Louis' most notorious conman.

The ending is the funniest. "Once i'm released, maybe we can get together for lunch?" . . . . Gurl please . . . my delicate nature is not accustomed to lunching with criminals. Though, he does have nice penmanship.

In his letter dated September 8, 2019, Dustin writes:

Dear Darin,

I thought you may be interested in knowing that I have named Chris Andoe and Out in STL Magazine as defendants in a defamation (libel) and false light invasion of privacy lawsuit. It is my understanding that Chris is now in competition with you so you're more than welcome to print a story about the pending litigation. Under Texas law he has absolutely no defense to what he published about me in 2018 and I felt that it's time he finally be held accountable for his deliberately reckless behavior. If you'd like me to send you a copy of the complaint just write me back and I'll be more than happy to send it to you.

I hope that you're well. Perhaps when I'm released we can get together for lunch. I look forward to hearing from you soon!

Yours Truly,
Dustin Mitchell

The post was a wild success. The love of Dustin Mitchell stories may be the one thing that unites St. Louisans.

Ruminations on Revenge

I parked on a residential street a block from my office to get extra steps in each day. One afternoon a man of about 50 was standing outside of his house and yelled down at me from his sloped yard. "Why do you park up here instead of in your own lot?" he asked.

Though he sounded irritated, I replied in a friendly manner. "Just getting my steps in where I can." I began before he cut me off.

"You could park down there and walk around the block! People have lived here 20, 30 years and you're pissing a lot of people off," he replied.

"Your neighbor (whose home I was parked in front of) said she likes me parking here because it looks like someone's home." I replied, but he turned and walked away, saying, "Self-entitled asshole."

Before bedtime I knew his name, where he worked, phone numbers and email addresses, which I added to a document titled "Enemies List." I didn't know what exactly, if anything, I would do with the information. I just felt better having it. The next day I decided to mail him a book on anger management.

At this snapshot in time, I had an obsessed and neurotic enemy with an army of enablers after me, a notorious con man sitting in the penitentiary vowing revenge, and more than one curse cast by a possible fatal attraction. Did I really need to be classifying new people as enemies? Probably not, but fuck that guy.

Lunch with Ms. Jamieson

Despite working together and being in chats where we discussed most everything, I hadn't filled in Ms. Jamieson on many details about what was going on with Clyde, including a possible new curse.

One evening I noticed a friend's post was showing that there were four comments, but I could only see one. I asked Ms. Jamieson who I was missing and it turned out Clyde had blocked me.

"That's odd," Ms. Jamieson said, knowing the two of us had been getting along.

"Clyde's always been an all-or-nothing type of guy," I replied. "He finally gets that things can't be like they once were, so maybe this is what he needs to move on."

The following day I suggested we go to lunch, and over fajitas I told her the entire story, including my bizarre heightened attraction to Clyde.

"That's so odd that you say that, because I have been oddly attracted to him lately too, like I had never been before," she exclaimed.

I told her about how the paranormal investigator, while sitting at my dining room table, kept motioning in the direction of the Melrose when discussing the portals he'd opened in that basement, even though she'd never been there, and wasn't told where it was.

"That's crazy," Ms. Jamieson said. "He sent me a message the other night about the basement."

Ms. Jamieson pulled up an exchange with Clyde on her phone.

Clyde: The basement is actually all ok now.

Ms. Jamieson: Well, that's good.

Clide: Ya..I know it sounds strange . . . but Chris and I have talked about it before, since he's [sic] has a lot of dealings with hauntings in his life. There was a circle of apparitions in the basement for a time.

Ms. Jamieson: Omg. I'm glad I didn't see them. Lol

Clyde: Beezlebub I thought was the ringleader . . . but it was something called Axis. I managed to send it away though. But still . . . something about that back corner. Stay away from it please

For the previous few nights, Ms. Jamieson said she was woken by voices in her white noise machine. "It was startling! Woke me from a dead sleep."

"Could you make out what they were saying?" I asked.

"No, just sounds like a man whispering."

Later that evening Ms. Jamieson sent me the results of her research on curses involving a rusty nail.

One of the comments: *Yeah, do a reversal "return to sender" spell asap. Rust, nails, barbed wire are used when you're not fucking around. The reason they're used in both protective and malicious magic is because they harm the target, so whoever is throwing this your way is trying to do you harm. A return to sender spell will reverse the curse back at them and should give you protection.*

While at my home, the investigator suggested I drive the nail into the ground at the Melrose, as close to his apartment as possible.

Ms. Jamieson was afflicted with severe diarrhea later that afternoon, which lasted for several days. Considering I didn't get food poisoning, and that Rachel said Beezlebub is the God of Shit, she grew suspicious. Ms. Jamieson posted several Facebook statuses about her toilet troubles.

That weekend I went down to Bar PM, where after a few drinks a friend asked where Ms. Jamieson was.

"Bitch she's got diarrhea!" I exclaimed. "Been posting about it for days!"

The Teapot and the Colander—*chrisandoe.com, November 19, 2019*

The sparring with Jasmine was ongoing but stale. I tried to get my point across in creative new ways including the following post, which was aimed at her enablers.

We are like pieces of a tea set. Sometimes we're the teacup, and sometimes we're the pot. But there are imposters among us: colanders posing as teacups.

When we fill the cups with our goodwill, they are warm and grateful. The colander, by contrast, is insatiable. It takes a teapot time to figure out what's going on. Soon, there's an army of teapots pouring all they have into the colander, to no avail. Filling it becomes an all-consuming obsession, and the teapots feel a sense of pride and camaraderie in their team effort.

Once a teapot runs dry, it's a threat to the colander because it signals to the full pots that their efforts may be futile. At minimum the imposter wails about being betrayed and abandoned by the teapot, but oftentimes it seeks to destroy the empty pots, sweeping their shattered pieces out of sight.

The moral of the story is to look for the holes.

Package from the Past

I came home from work to a large package, and found it was from Damon. I fed the pets and then sat down in the quiet parlor to open it. There was a holiday card with a lone blue bird on a snowy branch against a gray sky. I wondered if this symbolized him being alone (last I heard he was in a serious relationship) or if it just symbolized him not being with me. Regardless, the lonely image filled me with sadness.

Hi Chris,

Happy Birthday & Merry Christmas (& New Year too!)! I've been organizing my apartment and came across some things I know you'd like—especially the painting of Rox by Grandma Andoe [her Boston Terrier I adopted] *and the pottery from Bill.*

I hope all is well w/ you and your family. Kage too!

Kind regards,
Damon

I thought he had moved in with his new partner, but from the return address saw he was living in the same place he selected when we separated six years prior. People don't give up affordable rent in places like the Bay Area, and his Oakland apartment featured floor to ceiling windows leading to an enormous terrace for all his plants. From the terrace you could see past rooftops to the bay and the mountains of San Mateo County.

Six years normally wouldn't feel like a long period of time to me, but this six definitely did. Between leaving everything behind in 2014 to losing my original Facebook account in 2015 (and all the photos and memories that it contained), in many ways it's like my past was erased. I think, too, that writing *Delusions of Grandeur* gave me such closure I didn't need to spend much time thinking about it.

It was like these artifacts were from a past life. Having them back was almost like receiving items that had long ago been buried with a loved one. The whole thing was dizzying.

Including Magali

We were normally with our families over Thanksgiving and Christmas, but Ray and Pauly were sure to always include Magali at their gatherings. She'd arrive all done up and dressed to the nines in something velvet or silky. It was all such a treat for her. Living in crowded coastal cities, people rarely entertained in the home. Few had the space. But her gay friends in St. Louis had formal dining rooms, crystal and fine china. Every Saturday night in December there would be a party and the holiday decor would be magazine worthy.

On her Birthday the Brunch Bimbos surprised her with her *RFT* article framed and signed by everyone. In gold glittery lettering the script read, *Happy Birthday to the matriarch of the Floozies.* On the way home that day she said in her seventy years she never had friends like the ones in St. Louis, and after one of Ray and Pauly's parties, as I was helping her down their wide front steps, flanked by large cement lions, she said, "Ray & Pauly are the nicest guys. I wish everyone in the world were like them."

My Day

I spent much of my days driving my Lincoln through red brick canyons, admiring decaying structures the way others admire ancient ruins.

I might get out on the north side and climb around an abandoned mansion, or stop to appreciate a nice view of the river. Maybe even walk across the Chain of Rocks spanning the Mississippi, a pedestrian bridge once part of Route 66.

I've always been interested in houses. As a kid I built entire subdivisions out of business and index cards on the pool table. Now I spent my days looking at houses. The best part was when I found a really great place for someone, particularly a friend. When I'd see Miss Jamieson poking her nosy head out of her French kitchen windows, I felt satisfied that she was where she belonged, much like a Sesame Street character. When I thought about the tent cities, odors of urine, and the grinding noise Magali lived with beneath her windows for decades, it felt good to see how much she enjoyed her place near the Botanical Gardens. "So many trees," she'd often say when I dropped her off, still struck by the greenery years after moving in.

There were moments of stress, like any job, but much of my day was spent doing things I would do for free. It was sustainable and it preserved my bandwidth, allowing me to run a magazine and write books. I had time to think.

My favorite thing was telling stories to an interested audience, and the job gave me the space to achieve immortality through my craft. Long after my time's up, my stories would live on.

Discussing Demons

Clyde always had my full attention when he'd open up about the demons in the basement, which I found endlessly fascinating. At the same time, I knew it was a dangerous game for him, and only suffering would result.

"I do think you're too casual about dealing with demons," I told him. "I'm fascinated by it, but I'm worried for you."

"As I told you before," Clyde began, "I've met more demons in the light of day than I ever have in the darkest of nights. I don't fear what can't be seen. I'll be fine. I'm not down there brooding or calling out anymore. Thank you for caring. It means a lot."

"How did you first become interested in demons?"

"It's always been something I was interested in. As a gamer I loved playing jobs that called on spirits for enchantments and aid. That was mostly my being a nerd though, then I started to research things in Daemonology, and possessions and such. This was probably back in like 2005. It's not like I pray to them or evoke spirits or anything. I just made myself familiar with the basics. Like with a Ouija Board, once the door is open they can always see you and you stick out to them. I'm hardly an expert or anything but I know enough to commune a bit."

"Do you use an Ouija board?"

"No."

"I mentioned I used one as a kid" I replied. "7th grade. And I think that opened a door."

"It always does."

"That summer was insane. My mom's house was always creepy but was off the charts then. Once I woke to the bed shaking. Lights went off on their own. Even now she has an oven timer that hasn't worked since the 80s but goes off when I'm close to arriving."

"I have woken up a lot over the years to the sound of a loud bang," Clyde said. "Run to the front door and check outside. And nightmares have become more frequent too but less over the past month."

"What happens in the nightmares?" I asked. "And what do you hear from the basement?"

"It's normally some horror movie scenario of being lost or isolated in the woods or in a house or bad dreams of my mom. The basement I sometimes hear thuds on the vents or a pop on the floor but that could just be the vents expanding or the wood floors. I was starting to dream about you frequently a couple times a week but that was just me dealing with things in my head more than anything."

"Were any of those dreams creepy?"

"The horror film scenario dreams were. I'd wake up with such a feeling of dread and loneliness it was so intense."

Clyde regularly solicited my help in closing the portal in the basement, but I declined. He was either being insincere in order to lure me down there, or he was overconfident and we'd fail and make matters worse.

I was in Tulsa once when he sent an unsettling request.

"Bring something back that scared you as a child. There's got to be something."

Hell no.

Ms. Jamieson's Birthday Greeting

I was often exasperated by Ms. Jamieson's foibles, but she warmed my heart with kind words like the following, which she posted to Facebook:

I want to wish one of my closest friends, Chris Andoe, a very happy birthday! Chris is one of the best people I know. Not only is he smart and successful, but he's also an amazing friend who goes out of his way to help others without any hesitation. He's done so much for me and I'm beyond grateful. I literally wouldn't be where I am today if it wasn't for him. Happy Birthday, Chris!

The Coloring Book

We caught up with my old friend Molly when we were all in Puerto Vallarta for a destination wedding. Despite living two miles apart we never saw one another since she had two young kids.

"Villadiva is definitely not cut out for children," I began. "Our youngest nephew was here for five minutes while dropping off their dog and he started flipping through a coloring book on the coffee table . . ."

Molly interjected, "Well that doesn't sound . . ."

"IT WAS A PENIS COLORING BOOK!"

I don't believe I ever saw her laugh harder. That damn book was a gift from the tawdry Courtney "Glory Hole" Groves, a childhood friend who was a member of the Krewe of the Tawdry Turret and who traveled from Tulsa to St. Louis about twice a year for shenanigans. We had the book out as a conversation piece. Ignite conversation it did.

Zeeke

I'd been aware of Zeeke for several years because of his involvement with Cody. The two had an intense attraction for one another, but Zeeke was already in a long-term open marriage, which closed the door to anything more than sex. By the time Zeeke's marriage was ending, Cody was happily committed to a horse trainer named Jack and was living on his ranch about 45 minutes east of town. Cody and Zeeke missed their window of opportunity by a couple of months.

In his mid-thirties, Zeeke was devastatingly handsome, with a nice complexion, dark hair and thick beard. A native of Oklahoma who like me chose St. Louis as an Anti-Dallas, he sent me a friend request after noticing me engaging with his friends in Oklahoma City, where in his early twenties he was a dancer at Gushers, the disco inside the Habana Inn. The same club where 'Tiger King' Joe Exotic once brought in a leashed tiger.

Although we barely knew one another, he turned to me for advice when he decided to leave his husband. Not all that unusual. While Villadiva was famed for its high-profile dining room interviews, the intimate parlor hosted therapy sessions for those who seemed to see me as some sort of wise old sage.

In addition to our roots, I felt his relationship dynamic had many parallels to my relationship with Damon. A narrative had been established that Zeeke wasn't responsible or capable, and he found himself walking on eggshells. I sought to dispel those internal narratives, and help him see past them.

The relationship ended amicably, with Jeff, his husband, going above and beyond to be supportive and helpful during the transition. I got acquainted with Jeff and held him in high regard.

The two lived in a large, remote log home in a close but rural part of Illinois, which Jeff was keeping. Zeeke owned a vacant house in Belleville, which he didn't want to return to, so we offered to let him rent the guest room. We were a bit surprised he was interested, but he was excited about the change, having never lived in the middle of an urban environment, and I believe our full house was the perfect place for him at that pivotal moment.

One thing I hadn't given much thought to: Zeeke was a witch. As he was carrying his witchcraft accoutrements into the house, I thought about the ghosts of the original Catholic owners. "They're not going to like this."

Note: The following story ran more than six months after Zeeke moved in, but since it's an introductory piece I moved it up.

From Seminary to Coven: The Journey of Brother Zeeke— Out in STL, September 2020

"I like these crackers," said my roommate Zeeke Harris, 36, while happily munching on a multigrain wafer in the kitchen. "I give them as an offering to the spirits I work with. Ancient Greeks used to offer the first grains of the harvest."

Living with a witch is interesting.

At 25, Zeeke left Dallas Theological Seminary and his position as youth pastor to come out of the closet as a gay witch.

"Either I was going to be happy or my family was going to be happy," he said when we sat down to discuss his journey. "I always had a strong spiritual side, and I was looking for a faith that empowered me and taught personal responsibility."

"But how did witchcraft even get on the buffet of options?" I asked. "How were you introduced to it?"

"The Bible!" he replied. "The Bible is full of witches and witchcraft, prophets and seers. My birth name, Kiel, is a variation of the name Ezekiel, the prophet who had the vision of the valley of dry bones. Zeeke is a variation of that name too."

An avid reader, Zeeke immersed himself in Wiccan literature. "The first was *Wicca for the Solitary Practitioner* by Scott Cunningham. "In it I found peace and substance."

During a pilgrimage to New Orleans, he also became initiated in Haitian Voodoo in a wild three-day ritual. "Both Wicca and Voodoo are cultural systems of magic," he said, "but Wicca is where I found my own power."

I asked him to explain that power.

"Confidence in my own decisions and spiritual abilities. Witches are survivors. Can't drown us, can't burn us, can't crush us! The only way to heal the world is to heal ourselves first. Take responsibility for the way you treat people and the planet. Consistently working to love everybody."

House of Cards

Beneath the dimmed crystal chandelier as shamanic music wafts through the air, Zeeke prepared for a card reading in the dining room. "I do a banishing of the reading area with a silver bell, incense and a white candle," he said.

Zeeke reads oracle cards as opposed to tarot. "You have to build a relationship with the cards. Cards are like binoculars, they open the door to the event horizon. They connect to the underworld."

I asked for examples of what he's been able to reveal during the readings.

"I told a woman her daughter-in-law was pregnant when nobody had been told. I told someone their spouse was being emotionally unfaithful. I've told people they were in abusive situations. The cards lay everything bare."

When asked if he's ever read for someone who was the abuser in their dynamic he replied, "People with guilty consciences tend to avoid me."

Curses

"Cursing is when the universe calls you to be God's left hand. Sometimes you're called to tip the cosmic scale, but magic has a cost. When you curse others you also curse yourself. You must decide if the cost is worth the action."

In 2018, Zeeke was at a psychic fair in Alton when he met a woman who needed help with an abusive ex-husband.

"She had me work over an abusive ex who was causing problems with their children and who would harass her at home. He'd just walk in uninvited. I gave her red brick dust to put across the front and back doors. Red brick dust protects from evil intent. After that, he wouldn't even get out of the car when dropping off the kids. I later lit a seven-day candle and said a prayer to Saintisma Muerta, the patron saint of death, to make him think about what he had done. By the third day, he fell into a deep depression and became sick. I panicked and blew out the candle."

As far as the blowback from the curse, Zeeke said he had a few nights of restlessness and disturbing dreams.

The Coven and the Afterlife

Zeeke explained that a central purpose of a coven is to serve and protect the community.

"A coven is a gathering of witches, normally thirteen, who gather during the full moon and sometimes during the new moon. They work on spells for the community to bring peace and bring healing. Bringing protection to those who need it."

Knowing witches don't have typical western beliefs on heaven and hell, I asked what he believes will happen when he dies.

"I believe when you die you go to an area to review your life and relax, decompress and then come back" he said. And he believes you come back as many times as it takes to learn what you need to learn. "Once you've learned all the lessons you become the Mighty Dead. Ancestors of the Craft. The protectors and guides of the people walking the path."

And speaking of the dead, Zeeke's eagerly awaiting Halloween.

"That's our New Year, and there will be a full moon on Halloween this year," he said. "It will be a busy night for me I think."

Villadiva Witch-in-Residence

Having a witch live with us kind of muddied the waters on Clyde's whole Satanic curse stunt. That was the biggest news in town at the time, a core reason he was ostracized, and now we had a spellcasting, pentagram-wearing full-blown witch-in-residence. Clyde saw the irony as well.

Additionally, he was jealous of Zeeke for countless reasons including his good looks, his training, his membership in a coven, and most importantly, that he was living with us. Clyde felt like an outcast his entire life, and above all else was resentful of those who seemed initiated. Those who belonged.

While the two had never spoken, Clyde reached out to Zeeke as soon as he hit the Villadiva radar.

Clyde: *Hello there. Sorry to bug ya but I tried to add ya as a friend on Facebook the other day and saw one of our mutuals post something and tagged you in it and clicked your name and seems I'm blocked from adding you as a friend. I was wondering if maybe we had conflict or something in the past that brought this about. I know it sounds trivial but I wanted to get to the bottom of it.*

Zeeke: *I added you.*

A few days later, Clyde messaged again.

Happy Holidays Zeeke . . . I know this may sound funny and off but I need your help with something that has to do with dark magic.

Zeeke: *Shoot sir*

Clyde: *I don't want to mention names but there has been abnormal happenings in my apartment for a few months, admittedly that's why I added you as a friend. When I saw you dealt with occult happenings. I was hoping you could help me maybe. A friend noticed something here too. Something he doesn't think I can deal with alone.*

Zeeke: *What's shaking?*

Clyde: *I fear it's after my neighbor now because he had a sex dream about me and that's VERY unlike him to talk about with me or even have. So I fear the demon might be after him next with its lust workings.*

Zeeke: *What did you promise to the spirit?*

Clyde: *It doesn't matter. I revoked it and told it to go away and leave that guy I lusted for alone.*

Zeeke: *I hope it does. Doesn't mean it will leave other people alone.*

Clyde: *That is exactly why I need your help. I want to ensure this all goes away so we can quiet it. I was hoping if we could use your magic and what's left of my Wicca, we could do something good and seal it.*

Zeeke: *If you want to banish something that nasty. I'd try burning some asafoetida to banish it. That's something we could try. Asafoetida smells GROSS.*

Clyde: *I've tried sage and incense and everything from the start Zeeke and it didn't work.*

Zeeke: *Then a ritual it very well may need to be.*

Clyde: *A ritual or gathering is what I feel is needed.*

Zeeke: *Demons man, you gotta have hard and fast boundaries.*

Clyde: *It's gone now I don't feel it anymore. But . . . it started to manifest in other ways.*

Zeeke: *They always get their pound of flesh.*

Meeting the Maven

I held an *Out in STL* release party at Nadine's, and a couple we knew brought their friend Luann Denten, who I would soon dub, "The Maven of Mardi Gras" because of all the events she threw, including balls. I was telling my friends the story of the psychic medium's visit and what she said to me when Luann chimed in.

"You've got several who follow you," she said in regard to entities.

I was reminded of a Tower Grove Halloween gathering ten years earlier when a Creole woman who lived four doors down was laughing about a story and casually touched my arm and then pulled away as if she'd been shocked. "You've got some energy about you!" she said. She tried to change the subject but when pressed she said that I had an entourage of spirits.

The Maven sat down beside me and held both my hands. "You've got a magical energy, my dear." She then closed her eyes and worked on offering protection.

I couldn't get enough of talking to her and we soon became close. I decided to write about her for the Mardi Gras issue of the *Riverfront Times*, and reached out to a mutual friend for a quote.

"You do remember that it was Luann who brought you and I together? "he asked.

"No I don't! I just met her."

"You wrote a piece about the first ball, the one where there was a setup mistake with the venue, and Bob from Bastille ended up without a seat. In the piece you referred to her as "an aging socialite" and I kind of panicked because it seemed you'd heard one angry side of the story. I reached out to explain from the inside what went on, and that's how we met!"

I was mortified and ashamed. I had heard about the turmoil around the first ball when I was at Lydia's shop years earlier, and slapped together a blog post. The audience in mind were gays interested in Bob's experience. I gave no thought to Luann reading it, or even that she was an actual human being. It was among the sloppiest things I had ever written.

I thought back to my interactions since and how she never let on that we had that history. Did she realize I didn't even make the connection?

Nothing was left on the table with the apology letter I crafted. She was beyond gracious in her reply, saying few are willing to apologize and she appreciated me for doing so.

The blue-faced Maxi Glamour was a St. Louis institution and a counterculture icon. When she was featured on a reality series, I wrote the following cover story in the RFT.

RFT
RIVERFRONT TIMES

BY CHRIS ANDOE

GLAMMING THE SYSTEM

MAXI GLAMOUR, *St. Louis' "Demon Queen of Polka and Baklava," is bringing vivid drag activism to an international audience*

Maxi Glamour, "Demon Queen of Polka and Baklava," Is Going Global—*RFT October 30, 2019*

This past March, Maxi Glamour eluded questions about their plans. The St. Louis-based entertainer, guru, event planner, designer and self-proclaimed "nonbinary queer demon" was set to be honored with a 2019 Influence Award at a splashy Out in STL awards party overlooking the Arch. The award was in recognition of Glamour's work and influence in the drag community, holding drag workshops and mentoring emerging performers.

But when asked if they planned to attend the gala, Glamour was noncommittal. "I'll likely be out of town that week," they posited.

"I told everyone I was going to Paris for an artist residency program," Glamour later reveals. "And I'm so bad at keeping secrets."

Secrecy, however, was contractually required. Glamour was actually flying to Los Angeles to film season three of the hit reality show Boulet Brothers' Dragula, vying to be "The World's Next Drag Supermonster."

The Making of Maxi

As a rule, Glamour doesn't reveal their age—not because they've got a complex about it, but because nurturing the mystery is an investment in their future intrigue. However, they drop a few clues. They explained their public life began as a fourteen-year-old club kid, once mentioned being "in the scene" for fifteen years and said they've got a milestone birthday next year which they plan to spend in Norway. Their Facebook page also reveals they graduated from Fort Zumwalt South High in 2008.

"I started off just going to parties and concerts wherever they were—basements, clubs, warehouses, trailers, et cetera—the more people the better," says Glamour. "But not just people—the weirdos, the freaks, the broken, those were the people to whom I was drawn. We would congregate at shows and even malls in our most outrageous costumes that we thought were so fly.

"You remember the scene-kid days when the goth aesthetic was vibrant and glamorous, when malls were still busy and the war between preps and punks raged on? These were the days when Mississippi Nights, Creepy Crawl and Cicero's were still around. It was a different era of St. Louis nightlife culture," Glamour says. "That was my youth." And during this time, their Myspace page was lit.

"Myspace was the newest, coolest thing in the music scene, and you had to make one. Being yourself was antiquated. You needed a new identity so people online thought you were cool. There were the Jeffree Stars, the Scotty Vanitys, the Lexi Lushes—it was all about being someone, someone unique, someone you created, someone cool enough to be in your friends' top eight."

Glamour went by several aliases during this time, including Rumpelstiltskin, Alex Shaw and Xander Wright.

"So I created Maxi Glamour. It was my way to create a new identity to make coming out of the closet easier. It was my superstar identity to lose all inhibition and join the ranks of Sid Vicious, Boy George,

Marilyn Manson, Walt Paper, James St. James and all of my other icons. I wanted to be a club kid. I knew that's what I wanted in life."

The 2003 movie Party Monster, based on the true story of club kid Michael Alig, who bragged on television about killing his drug dealer and roommate, further fueled Glamour's interest in club culture.

"After seeing Party Monster five-thousand-too-many times, I read up on club culture and knew I wanted to create events. Parties that were for freaks like me. For the people that couldn't fit in with the rest of the world or didn't want to. It was centered around sex, drugs and that rock & roll lifestyle. It was an escape from the reality of the time we lived. Queer folk had no rights—we couldn't get married, we were barely in the media in the early 2000s, and it was a depressing state," they explain. "Especially in the middle of the country where time moves slower. The underground club scene shouted loud messages that enticed my young heart. Messages like PLUR—Peace Love Unity Respect, from the rave scene—really resonated, as it created a sense of welcoming. In addition, the imagery of punk and electro musicians really helped make their concerts a way to feel comfortable as a masc-ish person to be hyper-flamboyant in makeup and in weird clothes.

"I can say that music hasn't had nearly the same impact on me as it did in these days. Maybe it was the drugs. But all I knew is that I wanted to help create a space for weirdos to be and exist to show off cool costumes and rejoice in each other's presence while enjoying some art form. At that time it was all about the music, knowing the coolest bands, the most underground things going and being original."

MTV's Sweet Sixteen also inspired Glamour's desire to party like a rock star.

"I saw all these spoiled girls getting their own parties and booking B2K, Nelly and other celebrities for their sixteenth birthday party, so I decided I wanted to book something cool for my sixteenth. I reached out to local band Center Pointe and had them play at my mom's boyfriend's house. It came complete with hot-tub, swimming pool, and on this night a band to play songs for me. The next party I threw was when I was seventeen and booked Super Fun Yeah Yeah Rocketship at a mini rave in my basement. I say it was a rave, but it was just twenty people on Ecstasy waving glow sticks in the dark. That party lasted a few days and changed locations multiple times. We'd go on these party binges where we'd just party every day for days on end, drinking, smoking, fucking. It was a mess, but it was romantic."

At nineteen, Glamour left for San Francisco to study fashion at Academy of Art University—but says their dad stole their student loan money, which resulted in being homeless by the second semester.

"I didn't have a home to do homework and had to party crash," they explain, "where you'd just crash at the places where you partied."

After a year, Glamour returned to St. Louis. I asked if there was ever any resolution with their father.

"I don't really chat with him. He's not really a part of my life."

By 2012, Glamour, who's fascinated by world cultures, adopted the moniker "Demon Queen of Polka and Baklava"—two things that transcend cultural boundaries—and graduated from house parties with the production of their first event, Glamourfest, which was held at Tower Grove South's venerable drag bar, Grey Fox Pub. "It was my birthday and I had a slew of shirtless twinks hand-crush almonds for baklava for this epic event. It was very crowded, even though six people in the cast of fifteen didn't actually come. There was drag, burlesque, music, belly dancing and of course baklava."

Maxi-mizing Their Impact

Today, Glamour is seemingly the busiest entertainer of their kind in St. Louis, and a big part of that is Qu'art (pronounced like a quart of milk), an organization they founded in 2014 aiming to promote diversity and inclusivity of queer artists. Qu'art's projects and festivals, which blend intersectional and multidisciplinary queer artists on the Crack Fox stage, draw applicants from across the nation.

Then there are the smaller, community-focused activities, including cleaning up the city in drag and the monthly queer round table where people meet to discuss problems affecting the LGBTQ community. October's topic, for instance, was making social advocacy more accessible to rural Americans.

While attending RuPaul's DragCon LA this past May, Glamour was surprised to meet artists familiar with their organization, even if those artists had yet to hear of Glamour. "When I was in LA and met people who mentioned Qu'art when I said I was from St. Louis, it validated the entire thing," Glamour says. (By the time Glamour attended DragCon NYC in September, they were an A-lister, hobnobbing backstage with RuPaul's family).

Among Glamour's most intriguing projects is their monthly event Devil's Cabaret, which they describe as "Satanic, dark, hedonistic, self-loving, sideshow drag, aerial, focusing on the darker side of reality. Eroticism as an art form. Take it in. Use it."

Glamour calls themself a Satanist, a detail that has inflamed their army of "traditional values" detractors—especially around Drag Queen Storytime, an event in which drag queens read to children at the St. Louis Public Library.

The anti-LGBTQ group Missouri Mass Resistance seems to consider Glamour their top nemesis, and a member posted the following to Facebook, along with a fabulously insane photo of the blue-faced Glamour with a massive, ratted-out blue wig:

> "THIS is the St. Louis drag queen who 'performed' last Saturday, September 28th, at the Schlafly branch St. Louis Public Library. He is a well-known SATANIST who is reading to little, little children in a public library. The children are being psychologically damaged at such a young age, this should be a crime!"

With Missouri Mass Resistance vowing to protest Glamour, extra precautions were taken to ensure their comfort and safety. Glamour was handled like a head of state,—or a superstar.

"The library made me feel so comfortable and protected," Glamour says. "Becky from Carpenter branch picked me up with a security team and escorted me into the facility, driving me through a gated garage. It was lovely."

After the event, Glamour requested to be driven past the protesters. Only about ten had shown up, and only a few remained. "I saw like five people that were sad and clearly misled. They were staring off in the distance with pathetic signs that said 'one man and one woman' and all that. There were a few counter protestors, and some I recognized their faces from the Occupy Wall Street days."

During my interviews I learned that Glamour is actually an atheist. When asked about their thoughts on Satan, they replied, "It's to shock people. He's not really real."

They are a member of the Satanic Temple, which they say is for people with similar views. "It's an activist organization fighting for the separation of church and state—many people in the queer community, including myself, were physically, emotionally and mentally abused by the church."

Den of Drag Monsters

Filming reality television means being secluded from reality. For six weeks, Glamour was holed up in exurban Los Angeles, dividing their time between their eighteen-hour days on set and nights in a sketchy motel complete with fighting drug users.

"It was very difficult at first," they admit. "It was a complete social media blackout, it was like detoxing. And there was a child lock on our phones, so no porn at first. But they fixed it."

The days of shooting began to blend together. "Staring at the walls, hurry up and wait," they recount. "Little sleep. No windows." Still, there were some perks. "It was so good not seeing straight people for six weeks, though."

Proving your mettle as "The World's Next Drag Supermonster" isn't a joy ride. Punishments included things like getting mystery tattoos and eating live spiders, and fellow contestants had very sharp elbows. "They were mean," Glamour, who arguably came off as the nicest contestant, recalls. But wigs were knocked back in episode four when Glamour came to the end of their journey and read everyone for filth—a read which surprised and inspired respect from the contestants.

Once the elimination episode aired, Glamour posted the following to their Facebook page:

"It's taken me a week to reprocess my elimination. I've gone through all the feelings of being cheated, not good enough, and hyper critical of my own art. I by nature am not a competitive person. When many people are fighting over the same thing I choose to find something else that pleases me. Maybe that's my nonconformist attitude that I don't want what everyone else wants. I didn't care about the crown and I didn't care about letting everyone know I thought my art was better than theirs. I went there to be me and use the show as a platform for social change. I went in the show with a non-confrontational attitude with an attempt to diffuse any drama directed to me. Some behaviors on the show and many other shows were toxic attention seeking actions that replicate aggressive bullying found too often in our home communities. My point of being on the show was to demonstrate an outlet that deviates from that path. I wish I had thousands of dollars and sponsors to make my experience easier and get a bigger platform. I didn't, I just had the polka gods smiling down on me! And smiled they did! Looking forward to spending this next chapter with y'all and seeing where the roads take me!"

Marrying the Global & Local

With season three of Dragula broadcasting in more than 60 countries, a Boston-based talent manager lining up appearances and their new jet-setting lifestyle, Glamour has a different perspective on their art and their work.

"We validate mediocrity at times," they assert. "We validate our own mediocrity. I know what level I can be on. What I should be on."

They're also less prone to accept the status quo in their own backyard. One of many topics Glamour has been speaking on is the lack of diversity on some local drag stages.

"If you're a producer and you're not putting black people in your show, maybe you shouldn't be producing," Glamour says, in what has become their oft-repeated mantra.

"I'd like to help use the fact that most St. Louisans that are registered voters are Democrat to help encourage those queer folk to not just be Democrat but also progressive. I think St. Louis can often find itself stuck in the past. It's that whole 'Show Me State' mentality that makes people afraid of new things. Honestly, I hear more people talk about the 1904 World's Fair than they do about the future of St. Louis. If more people talked about what could be, instead of what used to be, we wouldn't be stuck with things like that unfortunate trolley. This comes with acknowledging the fact that the NAACP put up a travel advisory warning for the state and how we process that. My vision of St. Louis is to lead the state and country with legislation and a cultural attitude that embraces diversity to not only exist, but flourish."

Sitting in clouds of pot smoke at their south-city flat, Glamour explains they see themself as a spiritual leader of drag through glamour, beauty and kindness. They also explain their mission: "I want to drastically change the St. Louis scene." Glamour pauses and considers their words. "I can definitely change St. Louis."

Zeeke's Rebound

A main reason Zeeke left his marriage was that he felt his husband was controlling, so I was concerned when he immediately, and I mean within a week, jumped into a relationship with someone who lived two hours away and seemed far worse.

I've mentioned how Damon had a master plan to change me from the start, and I quickly determined that Judd, Zeeke's new gentleman caller, had similar ideas. Zeeke was to be a gut rehab. Keep his attractive exterior, but change everything that defined him. While Damon masterfully and methodically rolled out components of his plan over time, Judd's execution was anxiety-driven and transparent, and could've probably been spotted even without my 14-year study on the subject. Still, each of their strategies hinged on emotional manipulation, shame and disapproval.

Regarding the polyamorous Zeeke sleeping with anyone else, Judd initially asked for a 72-hour notice. I figured that was to give him ample opportunity to scuttle the rendezvous, or find a way to get to St. Louis.

Zeeke posted a handsome selfie days after they met. He was standing in front of the south-facing stained-glass windows in Villadiva's upstairs hall and the lighting was exquisite. Compliments poured in, which made Judd insecure and territorial. Zeeke removed the photo and re-posted it so that Judd's comment could be first. The comment was a gif reading, "My bae." Subsequently, Judd had ample notice so he could be the first to mark his territory on all selfies.

Regarding Zeeke being a witch, Judd asked him to not mention that to his family, and not wear any jewelry that might identify him as such.

While this was all hard to watch, it wasn't my place. When Zeeke asked for my opinion I would offer it, but otherwise I tried to keep quiet.

One day he vented about feeling constrained.

"It's not going to get better," I said. "This is him on what should be his best behavior, so it's only going to go downhill. The noose will only get tighter."

I again go back to the Damon Origin Story. On our first date he broke down crying begging me not to leave him. Somehow my brain was rewired in that moment to believe my purpose in life was to keep him happy. Zeeke seemed to feel the same about Judd. With a stressed face he would explain he had to travel to Judd's to spend the day watching cartoons in the apartment while Judd worked, because Judd wanted him close by. It was clear that wasn't his ideal way to spend his day off, but he was fueled by a sense of duty. Rather than getting his bearings and processing the end of his marriage, his priority was pleasing Judd. That, somehow, was of the utmost importance.

I understood from experience that Zeeke could look up and find that a dozen years had been sacrificed to this delusion, and I wanted to help him avoid that fate.

Zeeke's Belleville Tour

I was on the porch when Zeeke came bouncing out of the front door, keys in hand, with Judd in tow.

"I'm going to show Judd the Belleville house. Wanna come?"

Most of the time I would have reflexively declined, in part because I think nobody but me knows how to drive, and in part because I don't like being at the mercy of someone else's schedule. I was feeling spontaneous though, and decided to join.

Alton and Belleville were the two Metro East (Illinois side) towns with the largest LGBTQ concentrations. As charming as the historic parts of Belleville were, my passion for Alton and my tendency to compare the two kept me from fully appreciating it.

Zeeke was a fun tour guide, and took us to a 1940s era diner for burgers and milkshakes before making his way down brick streets, past charming Victorians and craftsmen bungalows until arriving at his house, which sat at a dead-end next to a Metro train station.

Judd climbed out of the car with a look of wonderment. "*This* is your house?" he asked, almost giddy. "I don't know what I was expecting, but it's a whole house! You're such a grownup. I don't even know you!"

Unsaid but understood was Judd's bewilderment that Zeeke was holed up in Villadiva's guest room when he had a fine home of his own just sitting there. Zeeke's plan, however, was to sell it. He didn't want the high payments or to be so far away from everyone.

The first floor was comparable, and in some ways superior to Villadiva. It had an impressive foyer, slightly larger dining room and a bigger, better kitchen. It was in essence a single-story house though, with just one room on the second level.

After walking through the house, we returned to the car where Zeeke said, "Let's see what my friend Craig is up to."

Craig was also a witch and someone Zeeke seemed to admire. He called him on speakerphone and Craig invited us to visit.

This is an example of why I don't ride with people, but on this day I was going with the flow as if I'd taken a few hits off a joint. I was up for the adventure.

Craig lived in a more remote town maybe half an hour east of Belleville, and on the way out, as the sun was fading, Zeeke filled us in on Craig's backstory including how brilliant he was, how he came from nothing, earned his MBA and was now wealthy.

We turned down a narrow road and off in the distance through the trees I saw Craig's stately and sprawling Tudor style home, punctuated with bright red doors with big silver lion head knockers.

Twin coach light-topped brick columns adorned the driveway entrance, and as we pulled in we could see a shirtless Craig shooting flames at a big pile of brush. He was a big guy of about 40 with chestnut hair.

"Can I try that?" Zeeke asked. Craig passed the torch to Zeeke, who said, "This is Chris Andoe," while shooting a 5' stream of fire at the brush pile. Craig shook my hand while locking eyes, and I found his confidence sexy. He then led us on a tour of the palatial 5,000 square foot home, beginning with the grounds which included a lake and an indoor pool.

"A gay couple built the house in 1978 so I think they wanted the indoor pool for privacy," he said. "They lived here until one passed away and the other had to go into assisted living. Occasionally a guy will pop in thinking they still live here and hint about wanting to swim."

I thought about how interesting it was that a gay couple built the house and the next owner was also gay, considering the property was in a remote area.

The living room featured twenty-foot ceilings with massive leaded glass windows overlooking the bucolic grounds with their flowering trees.

"I told Chris about the Civil War cemetery down the road and he wants to see it," Zeeke said.

"I'm not ready to go back to that cemetery," Craig replied.

The three of us, sans Craig, walked down a gravel road to the seemingly forgotten patch of weathered gravestones, some of which were toppled.

When we returned to the house, I asked Craig if he'd experienced ghosts from the cemetery.

"There was a man dressed in uniform walking the road trying to figure out how to get in the house because there was a beautiful woman inside, but he couldn't figure out how. I gave him a choice: stay and guard the perimeter or leave, and he left."

Craig and Zeeke had an inside-witchcraft discussion that involved Craig stepping away several times to grab a relevant book, including a thick, leather-bound tome he had written, partially in invisible ink. Not only could I not follow the witchcraft discussion, Craig engaged in discussion the way a short-order cook prepares meals. Several things were happening at once. In the midst of his discussion with Zeeke, Craig handed me a marble on a silver chain.

"Just let the chain rest in your hand," he said as I sat at the massive kitchen island.

He'd engage with Judd, and then Zeeke, before turning back to me and asking a question while observing the movements of the dangling marble.

I mentioned earlier that I rolled with this day as if I had smoked a joint, and while I hadn't, I did eat an edible at Craig's villa. I was already in over my head with the discussion, and that didn't help. Craig seemed to discuss mathematical theory, philosophy and literature while I sat there wondering what the dangling marble was revealing.

Zeeke told Craig we would eventually need to close the portal in the Melrose basement. Craig offered advice as well as some words of caution. He sent us on our way with black pepper and wood strings, which Zeeke knew what to do with.

Gay Men's Social Group

The Gay Men's Social Group had been around for years with little notice, but once the handsome former *Vital Voice* photographer Mark Moore took on a leadership role and retooled the social media operation, it exploded, attracting thousands of members seemingly overnight. The meteoric rise was fascinating, and I'd check in regularly to see what was happening.

There was a mix of new and familiar faces. "There's Jade Sinclair!" I thought to myself when seeing one of our city's most high-profile drag queens.

"I guess I'll do this introduction thing," guys would say as they'd post their initial selfie with a little something about themselves. Of course the more attractive they were, the more likes and comments they garnered. That irritated Ms. Jamieson.

What irritated many others was that it was a group for men, which was somewhat taboo in the age of LGBTQIA inclusiveness. Within that acronym everyone had their own subgroup activities, but the argument against a men-specific group was that cisgender men had been excluding everyone else throughout queer history.

Many of the guys skewed older, and lived on the outskirts of town or at least outside of the traditional gay enclaves. You might even say they'd been put out to pasture, and this group was reminiscent of the classic gay bars they once frequented. Nobody had been clamoring to include many of these men in activities, so I thought it was a great thing.

In the middle of the group's sudden explosion Mark decided its first official event would be a New Year's Eve gala. He decided this around December 1st, so the timeline was wildly ambitious and was greeted with some community skepticism that he could pull it off.

The first drag queen he reached out to was the blue-faced Maxi Glamour. Of course the internationally-known Maxi wasn't available with such short notice, which was the case with most entertainers, but Maxi provided referrals. Mark managed to find three performers and added them to the marketing. The problem: They were all white. That gave those who were already grumbling about the group the ammunition they needed, and they went on the attack with Maxi leading the charge.

Maxi had been on a crusade to diversify the city's stages, which I supported, but considering they were the organizer's first choice, and they referred him to white queens, I thought the attacks were unfair. (Months later Jade Sinclair came under similar fire from Maxi when two regular Black cast members weren't ready to return to the stage after the pandemic shutdown ended, leaving her with an all-white cast one night. Despite my occasional disagreement on their tactics, Maxi's efforts were successful in improving representation, and the city was better off for their work).

Mark deftly navigated the group through the controversy, managing to diversify the line-up, and threw a very successful event.

The group generated so much buzz, drag emcees around town were working it into their banter. Trixie LaRue, who reminded me a lot of singer Carrie Underwood, had the audience rolling one night at Bar: PM with her observations.

"If they leave a heart on your picture, *that* means they wanna fuck you," LaRue said. "I swear everyone is in that group now. Even *Jade Sinclair's* involved!"

New Year's Eve at Villadiva

We had only been in Villadiva for a few days when 2019 rolled in, but after an entire year in the house we felt ready to officially take over the legendary Villa Ray New Year's Eve bash, and Ray welcomed the opportunity to pass the torch.

It would be my sixth New Year's celebration since being back in St. Louis, and the lead-up to the last five celebrations was anxiety-inducing as I had to carefully curate who I could include, since Ray was worried about things getting out of hand. Each year several friends would contact me at the last minute looking for something to do, and I wasn't able to include them. This year, however, we would go all out.

The theme was "Bling," and guests were encouraged to dress in their flashiest, glitteriest ensembles to compete for the 1st ever House of Villadiva Bling Trophy, and our colorful friends did not disappoint.

Emily was among the first to arrive, wearing a shimmering gold dress with an oversized faux fur coat and a tiara. As the party raged, she sent a photo to her mom with the text, "I wanted to be extra for this affair. The theme is 'bling' and everyone is SUPER sparkly and gay, I feel alive!"

I introduced her to a group of friends, explaining how St. Louis got in her blood and she had to return. "When she lived in St. Louis her photograph was in the *RFT* during Mardi Gras—causing her to be known as "the Lurking Lady" because of her mysterious pose in the Opera Box, and she was photographed in *Newsweek* in the middle of a major police protest, and then she returns to Tulsa and it's a media death!" I laughed. "No coverage at all! She missed the drama."

Emily laughed. "I did! I was soooo bored!"

Ms. Jamieson had an aversion to bringing anything to parties, and had gotten by with it for years because I wasn't paying attention. I remember wondering a few times if she'd brought anything, but never remembered to look when she would arrive amid the commotion. When I finally realized she never did, I sought to break her of this faux pas for her own good.

The last party we had prior to New Year's, it was like pulling teeth. The week before the event she had excuses, including being low on cash because she was paying for the post-Dallas bankruptcy.

"The last party was for my birthday and people brought liquor that I didn't take home," she threw out as an excuse, as if it would have been appropriate to pack up the bar after someone threw you a party.

"Well, what should I bring?" she finally relented, baffled and flustered by the entire concept.

"Bring cranberry juice," I replied, and she did. That was a lot of work for some juice, but I was trying to instill good habits..

Bets were made on whether she'd bring anything for New Year's. I told Mac Taylor that after my insistence last time, I thought she'd at least bring a 2 liter of soda. Some thought he'd bring a bottle of liquor, and others thought she'd bring nothing.

When she walked in I could see she was holding something, and tried to discreetly see what it was as I greeted her. She was holding her keys.

Auntie M was in attendance with a lamé-covered baby carriage filled with confetti cannons, of course. He passed one to Kage, and gave one to me.

"Let's shoot them off when the ball drops in Times Square," I said.

"You can shoot yours off whenever you choose," he said smiling, "but this one's for Kage."

Clinton, our DJ, told me that in the playlist he had included one-liners I'm known to say. The voice was that of an elegant Australian man, and he'd begin with, "You're at Villadiva," and then the quote. One of the quotes guests found most amusing was, "You've had a good run."

"When I told Chris that Jasmine was saying she was going to kill herself because everyone was mad she tried to get his dog taken away, Chris said, 'Well, tell her she had a good run," Ms. Jamieson exclaimed after hearing the quote.

In the kitchen, Ms. Jamieson told Kage about having sex with Clyde. She thought he was summoning demons to get people to have sex with him. That would be consistent with what Clyde had alluded to when chatting with Zeeke, who later referred to these as "glamour spells."

"It worked on me, but I felt disgusted afterwards," Ms. Jamieson said.

Kage yelled at her, something about being crazy, but I couldn't hear much of what was said over the booming music. I did hear Ms. Jamieson exclaim, "IT WAS THE DEMONS!"

The Maven dazzled in a purple gown with silver sequins. "A woman keeps trying to talk to me from the basement, but I'm blocking her out. I'm not here for that," she told me before she resumed mingling.

Dallas attended even though he was no longer dating Ms. Jamieson. The two remained friends, and Ms. Jamieson took total responsibility for overspending during their relationship. She was surprisingly upbeat about the whole thing.

I had no grudge against Dallas considering he and Ms. Jamieson were in a good place. Hell, I drove a man to bankruptcy at 19 myself. Me and Kage grew to like him.

At the end of the night Ms. Jamieson got sick from the alcohol and pot, clumsily stumbled towards the bathroom, collapsed and vomited. Dallas, Kage and Marcus crowded in to help clean her up. "Take this towel to the washer," Kage said to Marcus. Marcus turned and tossed it down the basement stairs.

"My husband will have to clean that up now!" Kage said, visibly annoyed. An argument ensued and I approached and stood between them, the two men about the same height and weight, staring eye to eye.

"You made it clear that time we went to eat at Joanie's that you would prefer living in your new place, just you and your husband. I get that," Marcus said to Kage, which disarmed him.

I think Marcus was referring to Kage telling the story of the Clyde saga over dinner, when he jokingly threw out, "Just for the record I don't want to share my husband," which Marcus took as a warning.

"I'm so sorry, I didn't mean to give you that impression at all. I was just saying . . ." Kage tried to explain.

"No, it's cool. I understand . . ." Marcus replied, appearing angry and hurt.

"You two should kiss," I drunkenly contributed out of left field, and they did, as if it were a perfectly rational suggestion. But then the conversation continued as if it never happened. Meanwhile, Dallas was a foot away desperately trying to manage Ms. Jamieson, who was sprawled out on the bathroom floor. "I'm so worried," he said, hands over his face. "I love him."

"Love him as in romantic, or a really close friend?" I asked.

"A close friend," Dallas replied.

Ms. Jamieson passed out, and her listless body was dragged down the hall to the den by Kage and

Marcus. I then sat beside Marcus in the living room to talk about how he was feeling. He reiterated that he knew we would prefer having the house to ourselves.

"When we're out of town, you enjoy having the house to yourself, right?

"Yeah, I do."

"This is no different. Sometimes it's nice having extra personal space, but we love having you here."

I seemed to get through to him.

Ms. Jamieson slept on the floor in the den. The next morning she stumbled out.

"I actually thought I was going to die, like, literally." Ms. Jamieson said, to which I replied, "Well, you've had a good run."

Bullet Bookends: A Day in St. Louis

At 1:38 a.m. I was awoken to the sounds of multiple gunshots right outside. People in the neighborhood always joked about the guessing game, "fireworks or gunshots," but from up close they don't sound the same at all. I could even hear the displaced air. Kage slept through it, so I grabbed my phone and asked Marcus if he was awake. He was. We compared notes, and then I went downstairs to see what I could see. Soon police cruisers arrived, and officers shined lights on half a dozen houses on the block, including ours. I was sitting in the dark when Marcus came down and we exchanged a few words about everything.

"Did you ever hear them that close in Chicago?" I asked.

"Yeah. Been a while though," he replied.

"I'm going back to bed," I said as I walked over and hugged him.

I woke to the news the nation was on the cusp of war with Iran, after Trump ordered an airstrike on Iranian General Qasem Soleimani. That, coupled with my interrupted sleep, put me in a foul mood.

The workday was filled with unusually demanding and labor-intensive customers, and I was getting grief from a few hateful people on the Tower Grove South page who were against talking about the violence. I think some found a certain street cred in not being bothered by it, while others didn't want anything posted that reflected negatively on the trendy neighborhood.

I finally arrived at my last appointment of a very grueling day, which happened to be at the Christy. I got out of my car and began walking when I saw a crowd gathering on the front sidewalk below my old apartment, all staring across the street. A hysterical woman flailed my direction saying someone tried to rob her and then shot her boyfriend. I had missed the shooting by a matter of seconds.

Two police officers approached the man, who was flat on the ground, and unsuccessfully tried to rouse him. An ambulance came, and the sirens seemed to reorient the woman, who turned on a dime and rushed back across the street towards her boyfriend. "No, no, no!" the officers said while holding her back as she cried hysterically.

Amid the chaos of onlookers and over the sound of sirens, two social workers and their client approached to ask if I was there to show them the apartment. This cruel day wasn't about to cut me any slack.

The three had witnessed the shooting firsthand, and while rattled, they were still ready to handle business. The view of the park was normally the main selling feature, but this time I stood at the window with my prospect watching police tape go up, and one of the social workers went back down to see if she could remove her car from the crime scene.

Another prospect in from Chicago, who insisted on seeing multiple listings that day and wore me out with all their questions and eccentric behavior, was also supposed to be at Christy but got lost. As I wrapped up with the social workers, Ms. Jamieson sent a message asking if I was still there. The Chicagoans were looking for the building.

"Please cancel the appointment. The street is closed."

As I drove home, I was rattled in a way I can't recall being rattled before. At the light I checked my phone to see all the reactions and opinions pouring in about the video I posted of the chaotic scene.

The footage showed that someone was on the ground, but not the person's features due to the angle, distance, and the hovering first responders.

"You should remove this video, this is someone's child!" one woman implored, soon followed by, "Why is this still up? And no content warning? Just this triggering loop over and over on everyone's feed?"

That was a minority view, but a grating one after all the blowback from even mentioning gunshots outside my window that morning. What was wrong with people? I was so angry at the People of St. Louis. The ones who were killing people and the ones with all the reasons why we shouldn't talk about it. I poured myself a drink and prepared for my seven o'clock interview with the Maven of Mardi Gras. While that was a big item to tack on to the end of such a day, I knew she was someone who would soothe my nerves. Plus, I had so many questions about the spirits protecting me and the dark entities hovering.

I arrived to her historic townhome on the southern end of Soulard, and as I parked and noticed the twinkling skyline ahead, realized I hadn't given much thought to the higher elevation of this quieter south end of the neighborhood, despite the fact my first St. Louis apartment was on the same street.

I followed her to the kitchen. "This is one of the only places in Soulard with views of the river. You can actually see the riverboats going by, and as someone raised on the river, I enjoy that," she said.

"Where were you raised?" I asked.

"Calhoun County. The only county in Illinois without railroad tracks, since it's a peninsula where two great rivers meet."

"The Wittmond!" I replied. "Calhoun County is one of my favorite places! The owner of the Wittmond gave me a tour of the upstairs after I complimented his 70s Lincoln. I'm very drawn to that area."

"It's the site of the largest archaeological find in North America," she responded. "Sometimes we end up where we are for a reason, because that's where we are supposed to be."

Sitting across from her in her intimate parlor, illuminated by Tiffany glass chandeliers, I interviewed her about the Balls of Mardi Gras, including the one she founded.

Afterwards I steered the conversation back to the unfinished business of our past two encounters, when we were in busy environs subject to interruption. I don't recall exactly how I broached the topic.

She'd previously referred to a paternal figure wrapped around me in protection, as if they were standing behind and over me, wrapping themselves around my shoulders. I said I believed that was my dad, who died when I was 18 months old.

She said he was sad about dying when he did. We discussed the vivid details of the scene the night he died, how mom woke to him dying, how she tried to stick the heart pills in his mouth and how the pills flew all over the bed.

Eyes closed, the Maven heard and replicated the awful hum mom had described him making.

I told her about how close he was to my brother Bill, ten years old at the time, and how my brother Joe, maybe 19, had to pick him up from his scouting trip to tell him dad had died.

"Is he coming back?" Bill asked.

"No, he's not," Joe replied.

"Oh. Something bad always happens when I leave," Bill said.

The Maven looked somber. "He's crying about Bill," she said.

I then broached the topic of the dark entity. I probably should have asked if there was more than one, but maybe I wasn't ready to know.

Is the dark entity here? I asked.

She nodded. "Yes it is."

"Is it human?" I asked.

"No it's not," she said.

"What does it want?" I asked.

"It wants to deliver a message," she said. "But I won't . . ." she replied, seemingly bracing herself against something unseen.

She said the messages were hurtful. Still, I pushed a little more, wanting to know.

"No," she said sternly. "I'm not saying that," she replied, indicating it was not me she was talking to.

She then rubbed her arms to warm up. "Woo! Did you notice how cold it got in here?" she asked. And I did. The temperature seemed to drop by ten degrees.

Her phone chimed. It was a friend waiting for her at Bastille, where I was headed as well. "Would you tell Chris Andoe to stop asking you questions so you can come down here!" he exclaimed.

We hugged and then headed down the hill to Bastille, where we sat at the same long table with a dozen others laughing and carrying on. Both getting drunk off cocktails, shots, and the rich camaraderie of this place.

RFT
RIVERFRONT TIMES

The Maven of
MARDI GRAS

*Vices and Virtues Founder Luann Denten
on Mardi Gras Balls and the Magic of Soulard*

The Maven of Mardi Gras- Riverfront Times cover.
February 4, 2020

Vices and Virtues Founder Luann Denten on Mardi Gras Balls and the Magic of Soulard

So much of my social time is spent in Soulard that it has begun to feel like the center of gravity. It's to the point I feel like Tower Grove South, where I reside, is a far-flung Soulard suburb, and I'm honored when Soulardians leave "the island" to visit, as several did for my New Year's Eve soiree. Chief among them was "Maven of Mardi Gras" Luann Denten, founder of the risqué Vices and Virtues Ball. My New Year's Eve theme was "bling" and she wowed the guests with her glittery, silky ensemble.

I was pouring champagne for the toast, using tasteful but inexpensive flutes due to the number of drunks I was entertaining, but when told by a mutual friend that she was retrieving champagne for the Dentens, I stepped over to the credenza and returned. "This is my finest crystal." I said.

"Yes, yes, that's how they should be presented to Luann!" the friend said, her face illuminated with excitement that I understood I was entertaining royalty.

The Interview

A few days later I arrived at Denten's historic home to interview her about the increasingly vibrant Mardi Gras Ball scene. She asked what I wanted to drink, and then began looking for a specific bottle. In classic Soulard fashion she said, "We have four liquor cabinets, and one in the basement."

Once we settled into her intimate parlor, she explained the inspiration for Vices & Virtues: A 2014 trip to Venice for Carnival. "I attended a series of beautiful events, teas, it's all about pageantry, all about costuming, posing and having a good time" she says.

"Back in the nineties and even later, many of the Soulard krewes had their own balls. There was the Subterranean Ball, Knights of the Purple Haze, Banana Bike Brigade . . ." but over the years, she says, they faded away, leaving only the tony Mayor's Ball—where for $125 a head you can hobnob our fair city's elites.

Denten describes the black-tie Mayor's Ball, which she normally attends, as a status event. "There's a parade of dignitaries, open bars, wonderful buffets, and fantastic performances," she says.

Fabulous as the Mayor's Ball is, it was that trip to Venice that reminded her of how many more events used to compliment it, and inspired her to revive that scene in grand fashion.

Vices & Virtues Ball

"It's very adult. Very high class. Very hedonistic." she says, acknowledging that all that can be *very* difficult to get past the powers that be. Some of her ideas get shot down, like having a buffet served atop the flesh of a beautiful model.

"It's fun. It's a matter of principle that there is something for everyone. High energy entertainment, black tie or full costume: Must be wearing a mask." And instantly my mind went to Stanley Kubrick's

1999 erotic psychological drama *Eyes Wide Shut*. While the ball will not feature the masked orgies that made that film famous, hedonism is the guiding principle. "Hedonism is the pursuit of pleasure, it's self-indulgence" Denten says. "Saliem is our incredible burlesque performer, we'll have Robyn Hearts—who does an exceptional Tina Turner. Our headliner is pole dancing champion Brian Lynch, and of course our emcee is the beautiful Jade Sinclair."

Decadent food offerings are provided by Molly's in Soulard and The Sweet Divine.

Past silent auctions items have been quite indulgent as well, from bottles of Dom Perignon to a mink cape.

The event, going on its sixth year and drawing over 300 revelers, outgrew Soulard's Mad Art Gallery and in 2018 moved to Cherokee Street's Casa Loma Ballroom. "There's no place in Soulard big enough for us, but we do have shuttles to and from Soulard, and then there's the after party at Four Strings."

Pillar of Soulard Society

I returned to Denten's home a second time for another interview, and to see her wardrobe ideas for the shoot. We climbed to the third floor, which had the feel of a costume shop complete with retail-style racks filled with her creations, along with hats, masks and wigs lining the walls. She had me try on a silky, beaded, cream-colored ensemble and then generously offered to loan it to me for the ball. "Isn't playing dress up fun?" she asked.

A native of Hardin, Illinois, which she notes lies in the only Illinois county (Calhoun) without railroad tracks on the count of it being a peninsula, Denten eventually landed in West County, where she raised her children. When her youngest was a sophomore in high school, the Denten's began searching for a more suitable place to live, and they cast a wide net, looking at homes in Maplewood, Kirkwood, Webster, and the Central West End before viewing a few Soulard houses during a driving thunderstorm where at one point they had to step over a live fallen power line. They fell in love. "Soulard is just magic" Denten begins. "It's a place where everyone is accepted just as they are."

Denten keeps busy planning neighborhood activities as part of her role with Soulard Restoration Group, activities which include the Bastille Day celebrations where new royals are crowned and the old ones head to the guillotine. Inspired by two (now deceased) lesbian aunts, she is also an active ally and event organizer in the LGBTQIA Community. That led to her Soulard golf cart entry in the Pride Parade (golf carts are ubiquitous in Soulard, and over forty neighborhood residents adorned theirs for the occasion), and her spearheading the first ever Soulard Pride.

"Luann makes amazing things happen" begins friend Rick Schneider, who has worked with Denten on many projects. "Six years of working closely with her showed me just how devoted she is to elevating not just Soulard, but the LGBTQ+ community as well. Love her or hate her, do yourself a favor and get on board with her shenanigans; it's a fabulous ride!"

Walking me to the door, seeming to bask in the afterglow of playing dress up, Denten followed her goodbye with what I've come to learn is her signature line, delivered with a joyful, Zen-like clarity: "Life is good."

Vices & Virtues Ball: Saturday, February 8

Time: 7:00 pm
Casa Loma Ballroom
Admission: $85 and up

Reflections

In the late 90s I encouraged my childhood friend Francis to move to St. Louis from the small town of Ottawa, Kansas, where his family lived after moving away from Tulsa. With no car and only $20 to his name, his friend moved him in the back of a hatchback. I got him a haircut and introduced him to a wealthy gay art dealer/publisher I knew through my brother Joe, and he hired him on the spot. In the two decades since, Francis became an indispensable part of the operation. He and his wife and daughter had recently moved from the Bevo Mill bungalow behind Trickery to an elegant midcentury ranch filled with fine art in the suburb of Crestwood.

Francis was the closest thing I had to a blood relative in town, and while we didn't see one another as often as we should have, whenever he asked to hang out, I'd rearrange anything to make it happen.

He was inspired to call one day when he was waiting for a takeout order near his suburban home and glanced down to see *The Maven of Mardi Gras* issue on a table.

"The second I saw it I knew it was your work, and I didn't even remember you wrote for the *RFT*," he said.

The alliteration, the older diva, the oiled-up men—mostly of color, the Mardi Gras focus . . . Francis knew me well.

You never know what will impress someone. Kage, for instance, seemed the most impressed when he learned *Delusions of Grandeur* was at the library, and out of all my work over the years, randomly seeing that cover in the suburbs seemed to impress Francis more than anything.

He had some recent triumphs himself, and suggested we meet up. He arrived in a shiny black Porsche, which he had received along with a Rolex watch as his twenty-year bonus. I walked around the car and noticed Villadiva's pointy dormers were reflected on the hood. We really made lives for ourselves in this place.

He drove me to Nadine's where we sat at the bar and laughed.

"I've known this guy since he was too little to come outside to play," I told Nadine.

Turret in Turmoil

Lydia and her longtime store manager Mindy had a falling out a few months before Halloween, their busiest season, and Mindy was in an odd purgatory state. She wasn't actually fired, and she hadn't actually quit, but she was no longer willing to come to work, but was also no longer allowed to come in to work until some vaguely-defined issues were sorted out.

I did not see how that store could survive without Mindy. Lydia was no longer interested or able to be there on a daily basis, but even if she was, Mindy was *infinitely* better with customers. She'd also be difficult to replace, having managed to survive Lydia for decades, for starters, despite their constant bickering.

Anytime I came to the store I'd find Mindy on the antique iron sewing machine making alterations or repairs, a straight pen hanging out of one side of her mouth as she answered a customer's questions. She was the beating heart of that store, and without her, it was doomed.

"I need to be open on Sundays for the next two months. Would you be able to help me out?" Lydia asked. "I know I couldn't pay you what you're worth."

My stomach sank with dread. I was able to relax and cut loose during the Sunday brunches because I was free all afternoon to nap and relax. Sunday was really my only off day.

"Don't worry about money, let's just say it's turret rent," I replied.

I paid the price for that space year-round. I helped her with tenant issues at her rental properties, and even acted as a contractor when necessary. The year before, just before Mardi Gras, she said at the last minute that we might not be able to use the space because the back deck, which we'd use to access the upstairs, was unsafe. I introduced her to a maintenance man I worked with named Kyle, and he agreed to meet her there at 11 a.m. one Sunday morning.

I was at brunch at Nadine's when I got the call.

"Sorry to bother you but I don't know what this lady's deal is and I'm not going to be able to work for her. I came and rang the bell and nobody answered so I waited. About 15 minutes later she finally answered all pissed off and asked why I was late. I said I'd been ringing the bell and she yelled, 'THAT BELL DOESN'T WORK!' Like, how was I supposed to know that?"

The next call was from Lydia. "I'm sorry but I cannot deal with that man you sent. He was late and then he was very rude to me. I'm really upset and I just can't deal with this," she said.

So, that year my turret rent was to be the contractor and pay for all the repairs. I assured both parties that they would not have to deal with the other.

Now, the cost was my Sundays for two months, and not since I was a teenager had I watched the clock so intently at work. Being there was like being a kid in a stuffy relative's house, and I was serving time. I did redecorate the store windows, which was fun, and worked to help Lydia process her anger and frustration regarding Mindy, even creating a "Pros and Cons" list with her in the hopes she would see how critical Mindy was.

Fortunately, Mindy came back. That did not mean I was off the hook for my eight Sunday sentence, just that I would work alongside Mindy. I kept my brunch drinking to a minimum, having the dark cloud of obligation hanging over me, and then I'd walk two blocks from Nadine's to Metropolis

Vintage and Costume, watching through the window, like a kid who was grounded, as friends had fun at Bastille.

Even though I felt it was all worth it to secure our coveted space for our main event of the year, I was wondering if this should be our last hurrah. The price I was paying was only getting steeper.

In the meantime, Lydia and her brother Stan, who helped her with some of her affairs, wanted me to list one of Lydia's rental houses that came vacant. I directed potential buyers their way without listing it, preferring a more casual, arms-length role just because I knew this listing would be time consuming and fraught with landmines. It seemed, however, that I would end up having to list it.

About a month before Mardi Gras 2020 it was time to place the bead order. I called Lydia for the final green light.

"We are preparing to place the bead order and I want to make sure everything is still a go," I said.

Lydia acted a bit like this had come out of nowhere, despite this being our fifth year and despite the eight Sundays I worked in exchange.

"I haven't even been to the store to see what's on the second floor," she began in an anxious, put upon tone. "I have some art deco mirrors that I'd like to sell first."

I took that to mean she wanted my help selling them, or wanted me to buy them.

"I can go inventory the second floor this afternoon," I said in the calmest tone I could summon. "I'll take photos of everything and then come over so we can review them and make a plan for what should be moved."

"This is a lot," she said in a frustrated tone. "There's a lot going on right now and I'm going to have to talk to you later."

After an hour she called back. "I'm sorry, I was overwhelmed when you called. I want you to use the space."

With that, I placed the order. A few weeks later I received the notification that the enormous shipment would arrive the following day. I stopped by the shop to personally let Mindy know.

"Hi Mindy. The bead shipment arrives tomorrow. Here's my number, give me a call and I'll come right over to carry the boxes upstairs."

"No no no no. We're not opening this year. My dad is in the hospital and we're going to be closed. I'm sorry she didn't tell you but Lydia said *nothing* is happening up there this year."

Stunned, I replied "I'm sorry to hear about your dad . . ."

"Sorry she didn't tell you but that's not happening this year," she curtly interrupted, seemingly desperate to shoo me out the door.

I sat in the car wondering what I was going to do. Krewe members had spent money on this event and we had nowhere to go. A very distant Plan B had always been Nadine's, since she had a storeroom above the restaurant, but Auntie M said it would be a difficult option because it was completely full. At this point, however, it was our only hope.

I messaged Nadine: "Lydia completely pulled the rug out from under us, and now the krewe has nowhere to go. Would it be okay for us to throw beads from your second-floor this year?"

"HECK YEAH!" Nadine replied to my tremendous relief.

I notified Auntie M and we managed to reroute the order. The Krewe had been homeless for all of ten minutes.

I understood how Lydia's mind worked. I knew that even though I told her my Sunday hours were payment for the second floor during Mardi Gras, she didn't view things as transactions. I worked for her as a favor because we were friends, and she let me use the second floor because we were friends. The second floor is unavailable so "maybe next year."

It was difficult to be angry with her, understanding her like I did, but I was profoundly disappointed by how little regard I was given by both Lydia and Mindy. No notification, no consideration.

I knew I needed a break from doing Lydia favors, and I certainly wasn't going to list the house. I'd been in regular contact with her brother, and sent him the following message:

Dear Stan,

Thanks for asking me to list Sidney, but I'm going to decline.

I know Lydia is going through a great deal, as is Mindy, but I'm reeling from yesterday.

First of all, use of the second floor to throw beads for a few hours isn't free. Last year I paid for the cost of her back deck restoration, as well as acted as the contractor, and I plugged her and the store in a cover story in the city's weekly paper. This past Fall she asked if I would work Sundays for eight weeks and I agreed to do so in trade for the upstairs. I already work a full-time (and then some) job, plus run a magazine, so this was a sacrifice.

Despite the agreement, based on past experiences I fully understood that nothing is official until we're right upon the event, so earlier this month I called to once again confirm we were still allowed to toss beads because we needed to place the order. She was overwhelmed at the moment and said she'd have to talk to me later. She called later that day, apologized, and said she would like me to use the space. I went to the store to take photos of what was upstairs, and showed them to her so we could make a plan for what needs to be moved. I said I would move everything to the third floor and then return it.

With that confirmation, we collected money from each guest and ordered our bulk beads, which are known as the finest throw beads of Soulard Mardi Gras. Yesterday I stopped by the shop to tell Mindy that the thousand-dollar bead order was scheduled to be delivered, and make sure she had my cell number so I could immediately move everything out of her way.

"No, that's not happening this year. We are closed. I'm sorry she didn't tell you, but she said nothing is happening upstairs this year." Mindy said.

Again, I really do understand the difficult time this is for both of them, but the time to cancel would have been when I placed the call saying I was getting ready to place an order, not the eve of the delivery. There was no acknowledgment of all the hours I put in, or of the humiliation of facing my guests after taking their money. The rug was simply yanked from under me without so much as a thought, much less the courtesy of a call.

I'm not even angry, I'm simply hurt and exhausted, and I need some time.

Best of luck on the sale. Take care.

Lydia left a message.

"We've been friends for too long to let a financial matter come between us. I will pay for the beads, and we can try again next year," Lydia said.

Tone-deaf message aside, I wasn't up for talking to her at the moment, but didn't want to just ignore her either. I went ahead and called, and an assistant answered and said she couldn't come to the phone. "May I take a message?" she asked.

"Yes, tell her Chris Andoe returned her call, and it would be best to connect *after* Mardi Gras."

"Oh, ok" the assistant replied, seemingly startled about the use of Mardi Gras as a milestone.

After Mardi Gras I sent Lydia a card, but didn't hear back from her.

Jesus Walks

In preparation for a Villadiva shindig I repeatedly stressed to our guests that nobody was to park in front of Javier's house. I even had visual aids showing "The No Zone" in red, and a sea of green everywhere else. During a previous event we put out traffic cones at the edge of our driveway/property line, which fortunately worked. This time Javier's car was already occupying the forbidden spot, so that wasn't necessary.

Normally I wore something fun when hosting, so I looked through the sparkly shirts and then remembered that Joe's girlfriend had sent me a Muslim tunic. I had no idea when I'd ever wear it, and decided this time was as good as any. I then donned my latest long black wig, which Kage had used for his Kamala Harris Halloween costume, and voila! I was unintentionally but unmistakably Jesus.

Jesus was a hit among our guests, and then at the height of the festivities there was a knock at the door. It was our displeased neighbor Javier. At some point he left and when he returned, someone was in his spot.

"Let me see whose car it is. We'll get it moved," I said as he followed me around the corner and down the long side of the house as guests watched from the bay window in the den, my wig and tunic blowing in the wind, all without a word of explanation.

Grey Fox Robbed

It was mid-January and we had gone down to Grey Fox on a Thursday night to visit our friends Jack and Sean Abernathy, who were tending bar. Jack and Sean were about my age and were a lot of fun. One thing that amused me about them is how they'd sometimes close down the bar and then head straight to the airport to catch a flight to Florida or Mexico.

Minutes after we left that night, a thin man, possibly in his early twenties, walked in waving a gun. "EVERYBODY ON THE GROUND!" he demanded.

Sean and the dozen or so patrons fell to the floor, and Jack remained standing behind the bar. The man had on a hoodie and a bandana, so only his eyes were visible. Jack emptied the register and the man bolted out the door. From start to finish the robbery took maybe two minutes.

Show Director Jade Sinclair long reminded me of Glenda the Good Witch in how she kind of floated above everything in her protective bubble. She had been in her upstairs dressing room and returned to the main level just after the robber fled.

Patrons were still getting up from the floor when Jade went right to the service area and called for Jack. "I need a shot!" she said. "I'll take a grape bomb."

Clyde's Midnight Reflection

I woke to the following message from Clyde.

You know I just had a random, albeit drunk, thought. Had I been able to keep my emotions under control, and knew how to vent maturely and rationally when I first moved here . . . I would probably be a part of Villadiva, and Melrose 2.0, wouldn't I? It's a fun thought, if only I was different then. Well the old cast is dead and gone . . . I guess now all I can do is support the new members, and create my own story. Still . . . Melrose 2.0 lacks muscle power for protection . . . oh well. I'm sure there's some past cast member who would protect the present cast with all their strength, right?

Clyde elaborated on something he would say several times: praying to God didn't work, but in the basement corner, the demons delivered.

The funny thing though, is I believed in Christianity all my life before I moved here . . . I prayed to "God" for good blessings and help but never got it. Be glad you had happiness in the first place, thank God for what you had, in ending [sic] you had to thank God for your sadness and pain.

But here in this dark corner, I've prayed, and wished for what my heart wanted, and I got results.

Time and time again . . .

So refuse admitting your sexual lust and attraction to me, it's fine, but know this, Zeeke isn't as advanced in his craft as he leads on, and I will have you again Andoe . . . whether in the basement, or in a bar, you will succumb to the lust that exist between us . . . and I can't wait to taste you again . . . :grin:

He followed up the message with a bizarre image.
"That's a sigil," Zeeke said, as he opened his phone to perform a search. "That one is to curse someone with nightmares."

Clyde's Wish for Villadiva

A few mornings later I woke to more midnight messages.

Hehehe, laying back in bed thinking, it's funny how I've lusted over you for so long. I'm a master in the bear world, I can have any bear I want in this city . . . then there's you, who was high or drunk last weekend and posted a gif animation of a spiraling hole, and tagged Marcus "you want in?" Hehe my mind raced that you meant "you want in my hole" and I got jealous at first . . . but thought I was just being hypersensitive. But then you removed the post lol. Showing you had insecurities in it.

In the end I can lust over you all day and night, but in the end you're a 45-year-old man living in a house with your husband lusting over a 25-year-old boy . . . wonder how this will play out . . . I can only imagine what may happen when you come home and Marcus is there, before Kage comes home, and will he ever know? Will Zeeke find out and start to wonder if the things I told him in the basement were real? Ahaha you've painted such a warm picture of Villadiva Chris, but it could crumble at any given second, and I can't help but wonder . . . will this Melrose 2.0 crumble to pieces like the first one? When/if it does . . . who will you blame? The rugby boy, the witch . . . or will you realize it's you, that brings out the worst in people when they start to love you. Time will tell, the campfire has started . . . and I can't wait to watch it burn :)

I replied:

You've wished the worst for me/us for years, that's how the friendship ended: You going public in a video about us being terrible people and then revealing to Thorne you had cursed us. You've boasted to Zeeke about the dark magic you've used on us, told me you sent demons to our home, and indicated you put a spell to cause nightmares.

Regarding your fantasy about Villadiva crumbling after I'm caught having sex with a roommate. If I were fucking anyone in the world but you, Kage would simply join in.

Kage can't forgive because he doesn't believe you've changed. He believes you wish bad things for us. Your nasty message proves he was right and I was a fool to ever believe otherwise.

Clyde begged me to not stop talking to him, and I felt I was in too deep to simply cut him off. He had a history of escalating when ignored, and I thought I should maintain a line of communication to monitor him.

"I'll continue to talk to you on one condition. You have to tell me you understand that this will never be anything more than what it is."

Clyde agreed, but he would have agreed to anything to keep the dialogue flowing.

370

Mardi Gras Opening Night

The Krewe of the Tawdry Turret was now the Krewe of the Lustful Lushes, and we held a Friday night mixer at Nadine's where we took over the north side of the bar area. Many friends of the krewe who wouldn't be there for Saturday's insanity joined us Friday, including The Ladies Who Lunch, Ray, Pauly, and Magali—who bonded with Marcus.

The upstairs Opera Box, which Auntie M radically transformed, was open for tours. Auntie M had spent weeks paying the cooks to empty the space, and then converted it into something like an opulent tent you'd find at the Burning Man festival. The walls and ceilings were draped in shimmering fabric, there was a fountain of cascading pearls, and ample seating.

At the bar I asked for everyone's attention and pulled Nadine over for an announcement.

"When we lost the other space, I sat in my car wondering what the fuck we'd do now. I asked Nadine if we could toss beads here and she replied with an enthusiastic, 'HECK YEAH!' Here's a toast to the wonderful Nadine for giving us a home!"

I'd clung so hard to the turret and was willing to pay almost any price to maintain it, but I now saw this would be a much better fit for us. It felt so good to be welcomed as opposed to merely tolerated. Nadine loved having us there.

Krewe of the Lustful Lushes

Flanking each side of the back gate to our Opera Box were Marcus and his friend Blaze, both strapping men wearing matching black hoodies emblazoned with the word SECURITY across their chests, and armed with a guest list. We weren't fucking around.

Official krewe members who financially contributed received metallic gold wristbands and were allowed unlimited in and out privileges. Non-member guests could accompany a member, but once they were out, they were out. Otherwise, based on past experience, each person who entered would later return with their own freeloading, bathroom using posse.

En route to the festivities, the Maven passed a prominent Soulardian on the street, a Mardi Gras pioneer who had been hearing about our event and decided to check it out. "I was turned away from the party," she said laughing. "The young men were very nice about it though."

As the Maven approached the gate she opened her purse to look for the krewe wrist band, but Marcus, who had been in her *RFT* photo shoot, opened the gate and warmly greeted her. "Your majesty."

Each window of the corner space was filled with costumed revelers tossing beads, and the expansive fire escape landing outside the front windows, which was draped in purple sequin fabric, was our main stage.

Elizabeth Van Winkle, the woman who ran the magazine's social media, stopped by, later saying, "It was such a magical display of well-oiled mayhem."

While the Opera Box had two bouncers, inside the restaurant Nadine acted as her own bouncer. A customer was beyond inebriated, barely holding himself up with a drink in one hand and a hot dog in the other. Nadine told him he was too drunk.

"If you throw away your drink you can stay and finish your hot dog," Nadine offered.

The guy said no.

"Then you have to go."

Again, the man said no. Nadine dragged him to the side door, kicked it open, and pushed him out. He landed on his face.

A moment later she opened the door to check on him.

"Are you alright?"

The man raised his head which was all the confirmation Nadine needed. She tossed the hot dog at him and slammed the door.

Recounting the story, Ms. Pauly said Nadine felt a bit bad about the situation, "but you don't say no to Nadine."

Clyde the Crasher

Clyde had posted for days about how excited he was for Mardi Gras, saying he planned to wander the Sequin Circuit between Nadine's and Bastille. He even wished me luck on my signature event the evening before, so I wasn't surprised when I saw him in the crowd as I was 12 feet above, wearing Pauly's faux fur coat, sunglasses and a gold lamé turban, tossing beads from the decked out fire escape. He was trying to get my attention, but I didn't give him any indication that I noticed him because he was trying too hard, and I had an uneasy feeling something was up.

Maybe fifteen minutes later someone pointed out that he was on the less crowded side street, where our guarded gate was, staring up at the three opened windows with an odd, hopeful smile, much like a child waiting to be let into a birthday party he'd been invited to. It was a heartbreaking sight, and I wondered if crashing the party had been his plan all along, or if he just got swept up in the excitement.

Letting him in was not an option for numerous reasons. First of all, he would have obnoxiously strutted around, intentionally making things awkward for guests who had unfriended him over the years, and then he would have drunkenly cornered Kage and demanded they "fix things." It would have been a shit show.

He locked eyes with one guest he recognized and pointed to the gate, I later learned, but the guest retreated out of his line of sight. Cody, who he'd always been jealous of, looked down and shook his head in disapproval.

It wasn't long before Marcus came up to me and Kage. "I need to talk to you guys. Clyde is trying to come up here. He said you guys invited him."

"No, no, no!" I exclaimed. Kage followed Marcus back down as I continued filling drinks at the bar, and regulating the coming and going from the coveted fire escape. For safety reasons I couldn't allow more than two people out there at a time, and I had to pull people in when they ran out of beads and just wanted to bask in the spotlight. That stage was for bead tossing and putting on a show. Out of beads, you gotta go.

On the back stairs Kage reiterated to Marcus that Clyde wasn't to come up under any circumstances.

"Don't worry about it. He's not getting in, I got you." Marcus calmly assured.

Marcus delivered the news to Clyde, who angrily pointed, "IT WAS KAGE, WASN'T IT?"

"It was a mutual decision," Marcus replied.

With that, Clyde looked deflated. He backed away from the gate and commiserated with our mutual friend Jesse, who was a firefighter and a bodybuilder.

"Jesse really wanted to come up." Marcus later explained. "They had walked up together and Clyde claimed he had been invited by you guys. I said he'd have to call you and have one of you guys tell me. He played with his phone but of course he couldn't really reach you guys. When I came back down, I saw Blaze had just given him a wristband and I explained that people paid for these wristbands to go up there and throw beads and he said 'I paid for one' and I asked when and he said 'just now' and knowing people paid about $100 I asked how much he paid and he said "Forty bucks" and Blaze cocked his head and looked at him and then looked at me like 'Did he really just lie to us?'"

"Jesse was playing on his phone," Marcus continued, "and I was texting him like 'Dude you need to ditch him if you wanna come up.' A minute later a group of about five guys they both knew came out of the gate and as Clyde is saying hello Jesse slides behind them and goes up."

I went downstairs to check on Marcus and Blaze, and came face to face with Clyde when opening the gate.

He was red faced and scowling, and seemed to have a literal fog around him. Despite it being a mild February day, it was like he was in the humid tropics. His glasses were even cloudy.

"It's bullshit you and Kage won't let me up!" he yelled.

"You coming was NEVER part of the plan!" I said as I turned back, closing the gate behind me.

"My biggest mistake was thinking you were a good person!" he replied.

It seemed what left the biggest impression on Clyde were the gold metallic wristbands, which for months he'd work into rants about "the elites of St. Louis." The gold wristbands eclipsed the $50 underwear as the symbol of snobbery.

On the Gay Men's Social Group page, he repeatedly tried to rally people against "community leaders who exclude people." Nearly everyone who responded suggested he focus on his own friends and not what other people were doing. He didn't like that.

The question of whether him crashing the party was premeditated seemed to be answered when someone on one of his men's group posts asked why they didn't see him in the Opera Box. I got the impression he had been promoting his appearance, and may have even told others he would bring them up.

Desecrating Clyde's Temple

Driving down the highway after Saturday afternoon errands, I discussed supernatural topics with Zeeke. "On a scale of zero to 10, how haunted would you say our house is?" I asked.

"I'd say it's a solid 7, but you acknowledge your spirits and acknowledgement means everything" he replied, saying spirits are more at peace when they are acknowledged.

I spoke often of the Melrose basement, but somehow never thought to take him there. I asked if he'd like to go.

"I'm up for adventure," he replied.

"On weekends Clyde sleeps for fifteen hours a stretch. When we arrive, I'll check messenger to see if he's up, and if he's inactive we'll go down."

We parked behind the building and approached. About ten feet from the rear door Zeeke mumbled to himself, "wow, already."

The basement door was noisy due to the rubber weather stripping dragging against the tile floor, and its rusty old hinges. I took my time pushing it open, and thought I heard whispering inside.

We gingerly descended the wooden steps. "It's filthy in here," Zeeke said in a disgusted tone. "And I don't mean the cleanliness. It's the things that go on."

I walked about eight feet in but turned to see Zeeke still standing on the bottom step.

"I'm not leaving the last step," he said, bent over slightly due to the low clearance.

"Oh, come on, seriously?" I asked, still thinking he'd come down. The creepiest part of the basement was a corner behind a big oil tank the size of a horse, and he couldn't see that area from the stairs.

"I'm not leaving the last step," he said again, and pointed towards the bank of gas meters across the room. "I don't like the things in the corner."

Just then we heard the floor above us squeak. Clyde was up. Did he hear us? In a strong whisper I said, "Get out! Go! Go!" and we scurried out while trying to make as little noise as possible. I pulled the door to where it appeared closed, but not all the way for the sake of time and volume.

I wanted to be out of his line of sight as quickly as possible, so rather than running straight for the parking pad, we ran to the side of the building where we stood like two scared juvenile delinquents who were almost caught vandalizing.

We waited for about five minutes to see if Clyde would come out. If he did, the jig would be up because he'd see my car. We seemed to be in the clear, but just to be safe I hopped the chain link fence to get to the car rather than walking to the gate, which was in view of his window.

Our hearts were pounding as we drove up the alley and through the hilly neighborhood. I pulled over to see if Clyde had sent a message, and he had.

So, you know about it. Good.

My head was spinning. What was he talking about? We knew about something in the basement? I then realized it was in reference to an earlier conversation about things Ron Tellcamp had posted about me. He did not appear to know we had been down there.

"I just feel like I've been ravaged, but not in a good way," Zeeke began. "A really strong darkness was down there. Utter darkness without a hint of light is bad."

He said about ten feet out from the door it felt like he was walking towards an industrial oven. "You get this feeling on your forehead almost like goosebumps and then it turns into a burning sensation against your forehead and cheeks, like an instantaneous sunburn."

In his mind's eye he could see about four or five slender apparitions in the corner. "You could feel a sense of acknowledgement coming from them, like they knew I could sense them. Like, 'Oh, a new battery!' They love sensitive people, magically inclined people."

Zeeke thought for a moment.

"They're drinking Clyde like a Capri Sun. He's going to get more and more dangerous the longer he stays there."

Back at the house Kage joined us in the dining room as we debriefed.

"What did you mean about the basement being filthy?" I asked.

"He's cutting himself down there to offer blood sacrifices," Zeeke replied.

"Ms. Jamieson mentioned finding blood spots on the walls," I said. "I see that basement as Clyde's temple. I'm certain he'd be furious to know you were down there."

"It would be like being in his very heart, going in there by force." Zeeke replied. "I hope I never have to go down there again."

Nighttime Field Trip with the Maven

The Maven's husband, Joe, had an award supply business and I went to their Soulard home to select trophies for the Out in STL Influence Awards over martinis.

Since the Maven was always looking for ways to help the community, I again plugged the first ever Alton Pride, which was scheduled for October.

"I'd love to help. When's their next meeting? She asked.

"Actually, it's tonight, in about an hour" I said as we locked eyes.

It was a Wednesday night and Alton was 45 minutes away, but I knew she was up for it.

We enjoyed delightful conversation about many things on the moonlit roads and bridges on the way up, including my love for the town and how I'm pulled to it.

"When I see Alton on the horizon, I feel exhilarated. It's like my soul sings," I said.

"I feel you lived here in another life," she said as we arrived. "It's no accident you were drawn to this area from Oklahoma without knowing a soul."

At the restaurant where the board meetings were held, the conference room was dark. A waitress approached. "Isn't there an Alton Pride meeting tonight?" I asked.

"That was last night," she replied.

As we walked out I said, "Well, now we're free to do whatever we want. Let's explore."

Our first stop was Riverview Park, where I married Kage. I had been horrified to learn a few weeks earlier that the magical cliff where I wanted my ashes spread was now a crater. The older I got the more I realized that permanence was an illusion.

We turned off Bluff St. to Riverview Drive, where a row of stately historic homes overlooked the Mississippi River 150 feet below. We got out when we reached the barricades just before the park. The crater cut through the front yard of the last house, and I could see the silhouette of someone talking with their hands through an illuminated second story plate glass window. I thought about how unsettled they must be.

It was so dark there wasn't much else to see, but the gazebo where we exchanged vows was still there.

We stood at the iron railing at the precipice of the still-intact portion of the bluff, overlooking the wide river as the wind hit our faces. The Maven tilted her head back to breathe it all in. The magic of the moment and the place was not lost on us.

I wanted to show her a pink Second Empire style apartment building tucked away on a quiet street deep in the neighborhood, its long-decaying fountain partially hidden by overgrowth. One sunny afternoon I was showing someone else the neighborhood when I saw an old man sitting alone with his dog in the side yard and stopped to speak with him. I learned the place was owned by a magician, who arrived a moment later.

I stopped the car at the building. "There's a young woman on the porch," the Maven said in reference to an unseen entity. "And she's got so much to say. She's talking and talking. But this town is so full of spirits. There's just so many, and they're all coming out."

The Maven had never been to Bubby's, so we stopped in for a drink. It was a very quiet night, with the owner's husband tending bar and maybe two other customers.

"I feel them coming up from the river," the Maven said while waving her hands in a sweeping motion to indicate movement.

The bartender made a bit of small talk and then I asked, "We're on a ghost hunt tonight. Would you mind if I showed her the upstairs?"

"The lights are out, but go ahead," he replied. "Just be careful."

As we ascended the stairs to the darkened drag cabaret, the Maven said, "There was a lot of violence here. This was a biker bar; it was a rowdy place. Some of the spirits aren't happy that it's a gay bar."

We lingered for some time, standing still at the cabaret bar while she spoke of how strong the energy was. "One of them really wants to speak to you," she said, extending out her hands, which I held.

"Ooh this one likes you. 'I'll make you feel real good' he's saying. He's snuggled up behind you. I'm getting that he killed himself, and he was young and quite attractive. Maybe 25. 'I couldn't face who I was, and you're married to a man!' he said."

After discussing a few other present spirits, the bartender came halfway up the stairs.

"Everything okay?" he asked. This had to seem quite odd to him.

"Yeah, we're coming down now." I replied.

Back in the car we decided to go up the Great River Road. As we were leaving Alton, she said that "they," meaning the spirits, knew she could see them, and that I'm a conduit. Together we woke up every ghost in town.

Alton had a sharp boundary as you left for the River Road. The bright lights cease on cue and then it's darkness, with a tugboat graveyard on the riverbank and then 15 miles of waterfront road lined with limestone bluffs and quiet tiny towns. I'd never been along the road at night, and it was dreamlike.

I planned to turn back at the village of Elsah, 12 miles up, but the Maven wanted to continue. I knew she wanted to cross the river to Calhoun County where she was raised.

The Brussels Ferry was operating. We decided to take it and then drive across the peninsula to the Golden Eagle Ferry, which crosses the Mississippi, returning home through St. Charles. The three other vehicles on the boat were clearly people going home, but we were on an adventure and stepped out to savor the moonlit river as we crossed.

9 p.m. in Calhoun County felt like 4 a.m. There were no signs of life, only narrow roads winding through gentle hills. While in Calhoun, the conversation shifted away from the supernatural to the memories of what life was like for her growing up, where young women got pregnant in or immediately out of high school and were firmly rooted in place for life.

We reached the moored and darkened Golden Eagle Ferry twenty minutes after it stopped service for the evening. Internet service was spotty in the area, so we backtracked uncertain if the Brussels Ferry was still operating, and fortunately it was.

It was a relief to be back on the "mainland" and as we drove through the town of Grafton, I saw a biker bar that looked to be reasonably busy—the only sign of life we'd seen in miles. I considered stopping but it was late, I had to be up at six, but more than anything, I'd already deviated from my routine so much that the rubber band released and snapped me back home. But I regret that we didn't stop. Over drinks we could have taken a deeper dive into the moment, and who knows who else we may have spoken with at that riverside tavern, be they alive or dead.

Morning-After Talks

I was never really in trouble with Kage, which was so nice after being in the doghouse with Damon nearly every day for a dozen years. The closest I'd get as far as disapproval or reprimand would be the morning after Drunk Chris stirred up a whole lot of shit on Facebook. And that was happening more frequently as I was bogged down in a pissing contest with Jasmine and Ron, irritable from responding to their latest accusations.

I would wake on a Sunday morning with that sinking feeling of dread as I began to remember the previous night's posts, and how, being up in my cups at Grey Fox, I relished every bomb I dropped.

I remembered hearing about a woman I always liked posting about me on Jasmine's behalf, and messaging her.

"You do know she's called you a thief for years. Seriously, what's wrong with you?"

And then there were public spats with Ron, back before he blocked all of Jasmine's enemies en masse like an obedient sub.

"Nobody cares about your garbage opinion!" I replied to him, but before I caught the error it read, "garage opinion" which he had a field day with.

Kage would come in with coffee and sit on the bed with a pregnant pause.

"I know, Kage," I'd groan.

"I'm really worried about your recent anger," he'd say.

He was worried for my emotional well-being, but also for the damage I was causing to our social standing and potentially my role with the magazine. In this tribal community, each new person one alienates takes a constituency with them, and in those dreaded morning debriefs Kage would calmly assess the damage reports.

Elizabeth, the magazine's social media director, lightheartedly weighed in now and then as well. In a group chat we'd monitor the attacks lobbed against the publication, specifically my role in it.

Appraising each attacker's sway, Elizabeth would say something like, "Sky has a terrible reputation themselves. All of these people are known to be horrible, so I don't think they're doing any damage. We should be in the clear as long as nobody here decides to drunk post this weekend. Looking at no one in particular."

"I can read between the lines, and assure you I won't let Kage post anything crazy," I joked.

I didn't always remember what I had posted. Ms. Jamieson wouldn't drive in ice or snow, so she was riding with me to work when she mentioned a post I had made weeks earlier about Ron.

"What did I say?" I asked.

"Well, it was totally random. Nothing had been going on that night and then you posted a picture of Jett on a little boy's lap and wrote, 'Anyone who continues to argue this dog is vicious can choke on their own vomit for all I care. Including you, Ron Tellcamp.' You tagged him and everything!"

"Oh my God!" I replied laughing.

"I know! It just came out of nowhere!"

The two of us laughed all the way to work.

"Fuck Ron Tellcamp."

Ms. Jamieson and Her Demons

The following are examples of the posts Ms. Jamieson would make casually referencing the Melrose's demon infestation:

Oh my Gawd. I'm sitting here watching a YouTube video of these guys walking in the Suicide Forest in Japan in the middle of the night and my Google Home Mini, out of the blue, loudly said, "That's my favorite thing to do." My heart is racing. Just moments prior I was hearing a noise at the bottom of my stairs. Fuck.

And,

So, I have a Bluetooth speaker in my shower and I play music every night while I wash my naughty bits. Occasionally, a song I haven't heard in forever will come on and I'll jam the hell out. That happened tonight. I'm pretty sure I sang "I Touch Myself" so loudly that the demons in my haunted-ass basement got aroused.

On that second one I replied: *The basement demons are always on Ms. Jamieson's mind, even when douching her tawdry behind.*

In addition to the social media posts, she spoke nonchalantly to the women in the office about it.

"I told Tina at work today that I have a portal to Hell in my basement and she was like, 'Oh shit!'" he laughed.

It was later revealed that the day the spirits were so active, with the knocking and talking, she had spoken to them in the basement.

"I went down to do laundry and waved at that spooky corner and said, "Hi Demons!"

Malevolent Mezzanine

In preparation for our annual Influence Issue I met with Brandon Reid, who I'd previously interviewed for "Meth at the Melrose." Brandon was highly respected in recovery circles. It was around 9 a.m. on a quiet winter morning and we had the mezzanine of Mokabe's Coffeehouse to ourselves, aside from a solitary man sitting about ten feet behind Brandon. After a few minutes I came to wonder if the man had Tourette's, due to the way he was talking to himself.

As the interview went on, I became distracted, rattled, even, because the oily, increasingly agitated man was looking directly at me over Brandon's shoulder and saying things like, "You son of a bitch, he WORSHIPPED you!"

I tried to stay focused, using note taking as an excuse to avoid eye contact, but each time I glanced up he was staring right at me with a look of rage on his flushed, glistening face as he cursed, and then he repeated, "Gobble gobble! Gobble gobble!"

Brandon was acting as if he didn't notice.

I felt the man was channeling something, and I knew saying so would sound crazy, but the scene was so overwhelming I decided to test the waters.

"The book I'm working on has a lot more paranormal elements . . ." I said in a hushed tone to gauge his response. Maybe he too sensed something dark, or maybe he was interested in the topic.

He politely smiled as he stirred his coffee, quickly resuming his train of thought. I tried my best to ignore the angry words coming my direction, but I felt they were messages from spirits or demons on behalf of Clyde.

I wrapped up the interview as elegantly, and quickly as I could, descending the stairs while the relentless messages cascaded around me as I fled.

Months later I asked Brandon if he remembered that man and his outbursts, and he didn't.

More Trickery Turbulence

At this point Ol' Trickery was pushing 60 and began dating a kid not old enough to drink. Okay, there was some dispute on the age. Ms. Pauly swore he was under 21, others said he was as old as 22. Anyway, the kid took on Trickery's last name on his Facebook profile.

Trickery had me blocked for years and I hadn't seen him since the falling out, but Pauly kept me up to date.

"We were at Just John and Trickery gets right in my ear and starts talking about you. I told him I am not discussing this and turned away and he was totally unphased and just kept breathing all over me about how he had proof of something. I had to get up and move," Ms. Pauly told me over lunch at Villa Ray.

Frank Fontana said Trickery contacted him after seeing photos of us together.

"He messaged me and said something about how you wrote bad things about him and I said, 'Chris and Kage are really good friends of mine, and I value their friendship a great deal' and he replied, 'What about *my* friendship?'"

Frank hardly even knew Trickery. "I was on jury duty once and he pushed to meet for lunch downtown, and after lunch he seemed to be hinting at messing around! That wasn't going to happen," Frank said with his trademark eye roll. "I've had better offers."

The Summer of 2019 I was at the big Pride pool party our friends Giuliano and Josh's hosted every year. They invited the entire community. Trickery walked right up and before I even knew he was there, said hello and opened his arms for a hug. I told him it was good to see him and returned the embrace, thinking maybe all of the bad blood was finally behind us. I did notice weeks later I was still blocked, but I didn't read much into it.

Then his relationship with the young Mrs. Trickery hit the skids, apparently over the elder Trickery cheating, from what I heard. Trickery was insisting his ex remove his last name from his Facebook profile, and for some reason the kid resisted. Tim Beckman, who had been on the wrong side of every conflict for five years, posted to the kid's wall that he reported him for using a fake name, and that it would be best for him if he just changed his name before Facebook pulled his account. The kid relented.

Trickery called Ray to say that me and Pauly were to blame for the breakup, but also told people he was trying to contact me as part of Step 9 in his Alcoholics Anonymous program, making amends.

Trickery unblocked me and sent a message asking that I call him. I wasn't feeling it.

I sent him the following:

Let's recap. After twenty years of friendship, you publicly denounced me because you were infuriated about a joke I wrote for a roast directed at fellow roaster and convicted felon Spike Turner.

Here's an article about the police chase he was in that spanned half of the state, and landed him in prison.

(Inserted a link to the news story).

Mind you, everyone knew that me and Spike were enemies, which is why Tim chose us both to be on the panel of roasters. We were instructed to go after one another. It was the ENTIRE POINT.

The roast was canceled so I shared one of my jokes on Facebook, which led you to come after me for about a week before I even addressed it publicly. That was a LOT of leeway I gave you for your tantrum, which came so much out of nowhere I seriously thought you were in some sort of crisis— why else would my friend of two decades who was all about my book turn so completely on both me and the book? It didn't add up.

I tried to address it privately with you at first, but you deceptively cropped my message and tried to get attention with it as well.

After all that, suddenly I'm to blame for the collapse of your ill-conceived relationship, which is by far the flimsiest and most asinine claim ever leveled against me, and that's saying a lot. You've insisted on trashing me to Pauly when he told you time and again he didn't want to hear it.

It was surprising when you greeted me warmly at Giuliano and Josh's party, but I'm all about letting the past go, within reason, so I happily rolled with it, and will do so again if we encounter one another.

But that's it.

You tried to toss me to the wolves over SPIKE, I assume as some sort of misguided ploy to get attention, and you've poured a lot of salt on that wound since.

There is clearly some deep-seated resentment towards me that goes way back, and flares up like herpes.

I will hug you and say hello at the next party, but I'm not looking for anything more.

Maybe see if Spike's up for a heart to heart.

Working the Runway

Runway was Downtown's glitzy drag bar which catered to a largely straight, mainstream clientele. I was invited to bring a party of six for their soft opening, and it was an evening of glitterati with media and high-profile drag personalities in attendance.

I'd yet to meet the venue's managing partner, Braden Bardoux, but saw the big and tall man meandering through the crowd. When our food eventually came out Cody's entree was missing, and after a full thirty minutes he approached Bardoux to inquire.

"I'm at that table over there and everyone was served a while ago but my food still hasn't come out," Cody said, trying to talk over the loud music.

Bardoux shrugged. "This is just a practice run and everything is free," he said as he looked past and over a hungry Cody.

"Are you going to check on my order?" Cody replied, confused.

Bardoux' eyes narrowed and his brow furrowed. "Why are you yelling? Who brought you?"

I don't think he would have taken that tone with a white customer, although he *was* universally rude. When giving Colin Murphy a tour, Bardoux mentioned how some of the West County women tipped $20 a number. Murphy exclaimed, "I could never afford that!" and Bardoux snarled, "I'm sure you couldn't."

My initial impression was that Bardoux had no business in the hospitality industry.

Since he didn't seem to have any involvement in the outside world, I didn't see him again until Janessa Highland had a housewarming at her sensational 'Drag Embassy' on South Grand nearly two years later. The midcentury modern building was spectacular, with a dramatic curved glass block wall in the foyer, which contained a display case showcasing the crowns of the House of Markstone. On the first floor was a large workshop for Mother Markstone, and a garage. Mother Markstone's private suite was in the plush basement, which featured a bar and ornate antique furnishings.

The second floor was the inviting residence, with contemporary decor and a lavish candlelit buffet. Janessa, only about thirty years of age, had been doing well in her real estate career and Mother Markstone was doing an impressive business creating gowns. I was happy for them, and sitting on the sofa I said to a few guests, "As someone who is interested in the history of this community, I feel like this is a place our historians will discuss years from now."

Bardoux was among the guests, and while saying hello was the extent of our conversation, he seemed affable and I felt like his presence signaled he was venturing out of his cocoon and taking an interest in something other than Runway. Despite my reservations, I decided that rather than renting a mainstream event space for our annual Influence Awards, we would keep our money "in the family." The magazine would sponsor the Miss Gay Missouri America Pageant and hold our awards in conjunction with the pageant at Runway.

The wheels came off before even hitting the road, but unfortunately after the car was already purchased. The fact that Bardoux had been mingling at the Embassy was what led me to believe I could work with him in the first place, but he quickly turned against the House of Markstone, banning them from his venue which prohibited Janessa, a former Miss Gay Missouri America, from participating in the pageant. Jade Sinclair was on the pageant board and even though she and Janessa hadn't gotten along in some time, she objected to Bardoux' ban when the pageant was paying to rent the space. The other board members seemed more hesitant about rocking the boat.

As if the ban wasn't enough, Bardoux posted nasty things about the Markstones on Facebook, including the following to Janessa: *You may have some fooled but you are nothing but garbage.*

Venues treat you very well when you're bringing customers and publicity to their space, but that wasn't at all the case with Bardoux, who twice left me and Kitty sitting when we came to iron out details, including a time we were delivering a $1,500 check. He just let us sit there and never came out.

I'm always curious about backstory, and why people behave the way they do. Queens around town said that Bardoux attempted to be a drag queen years earlier but was no good. I wish I could explain how he fell short, but queens really didn't offer details.

The legendary Alexis Principle, who performed at Runway, did say Bardoux always tried to gossip about drag queens.

"He was always like, 'Alexis why don't you ever call me to dish like Krista does,' and I'm like I'm 50 and I don't have time for that!" she exclaimed waving her hand dismissively as she got animated. "He's not one of the girls! He was always trying to stir things up. Always telling the girls to block someone he's mad at."

I've heard comics say that most comedy club owners are failed comedians, and they treat the talent terribly. Based on the way he allegedly told his entertainers they were all replaceable, it seemed something similar was going on there.

After he twice refused to meet with me, I wondered how I was supposed to make my guests feel welcomed when I didn't feel welcomed myself.

The Best Laid Plans: March of 2020

March 2020 began with final preparations for the Out in STL Influence Awards, scheduled for the 26th. The rollout happened on the 3rd with the following article:

Out in STL Influence Awards to be Held on March 26, Hosted by Miss Gay Missouri America and Benefiting PAWS

A year ago, fashion designer Alicia Markstone was mingling with friends and admiring the skyline views from the penthouse windows of the 612North Event Space on Laclede's Landing. She was there to be honored by Out in STL at our inaugural Influence Awards. But before she could collect her hardware, she got the call no one in her position wants to receive–a contestant at the Miss Gay Missouri American Pageant, happening at the same time, had ripped her gown, a Markstone original.

The MGMA venue, Runway, was in view but still required a hurried journey–in heels no less–across a cobblestone street and several busy thoroughfares, under an interstate, around iron fences, and up a slope. Such is the life of an in-demand dressmaker.

A Community of Creativity and Collaboration

It was an oversight that the events were on the same night, but that got our wheels turning. Out in STL is all about collaboration, so we reached out to brainstorm. The result: Out in STL is the official sponsor of the three-day pageant, and on the first evening MGMA will produce and host our event.

In addition to the partnership with MGMA, we're expanding our collaboration with #Boom Magazine. After working together on the Pride Guide issue for the last two years, #Boom will now contribute select content to our magazine throughout the year, including a feature on MGMA in the upcoming issue.

Our Illustrious Honorees

We'll introduce and honor a dozen individuals who are shaping this community, including Joan Lipkin, who will receive our Lifetime Influence Award.

The other honorees are:

Grayson Chamberlain
Alex Cohen
Christine Elbert
LadyAshley Gregory
Basil Kincaid
Nicci Kincer
James Lesch
Heather Brown-Hudson

Mark Moore
Brandon Reid
Jeff Small

An Evening of Dazzling Performances

Emceed by Tabbi Katt, the reigning Missouri Entertainer of the Year, and Vega, the reigning Miss Gay Missouri America, the event will feature dazzling performances by former Miss Gay Missouri Americas on the iconic Runway stage.

*   *   *

The second week of March was when the ship hit the iceberg, and would take on shocking amounts of water each day.

In December of 2019 there was reporting of a coronavirus pandemic in Wuhan, China, but life in the U.S. was business as usual despite there being nearly 100 confirmed cases in the country as of March 1. By March 9th there were over 700 cases and 26 deaths.

The following is a personal timeline of events as the reality of the situation came into focus.

March 4, 2020: Our neighborhood friend Gary suddenly passed away at 63 after developing what doctors described as drug-resistant pneumonia (My computer went out, and I finished this book using his laptop).

March 12, 2020: St. Louis bans gatherings more than 1,000 to contain coronavirus.

Bubby's closes the drag cabaret indefinitely, since it was the most crowded part of the bar. Various events follow suit.

I emailed Vega. "With everything canceling has there been any talk of canceling the pageant?"

"Absolutely not." Vega replied. "It will go on as planned."

The morning of March 13, 2020: Trump declared a national emergency.

I emailed Publisher Chris Keating asking for guidance on what we should do in the face of the emerging pandemic, letting him know the pageant was still on. He said to stay the course, monitor the situation, but pause on promotion for the time being.

Later that morning my associate editor Melissa Meinzer called. "Has there been any word of canceling? Seems this may not be a responsible time to do this."

March 15, 2020. Colin Murphy writes: "Any talk of postponing MGMA? Hundreds of folks over three nights are starting to sound irresponsible right now."

I replied: "I messaged minutes ago and right now the pageant is still on. I'm weighing options including making it a live streaming event."

Murphy replied that he and his husband Kurt would have to stay home, because they were both high-risk.

The Governor of Illinois announces that all bars and restaurants were to close for dine-in customers. That evening Vega told me the pageant was going to be postponed.

March 17, 2020: St. Louis announces that all bars and restaurants must shut down by midnight on the 19th in an effort to stop the spread of the coronavirus. I formally announce that the awards will be postponed, which was universally assumed. Rather than disappointment, I felt relief because I didn't see how we could work around Bardoux' inhospitality.

March 18, 2020: Gatherings in the City St. Louis and St. Louis County limited to no more than nine people.

The 43-year-old Riverfront Times lays off most of its staff and ceases print operations. *The New York Times* reported on our paper the following week with an image of the stacked newspapers in the window of a closed restaurant.

March 20, 2020: Illinois Governor ordered all state residents to stay in their homes.

March 25, 2020: Colin Murphy's husband Kurt Ross passes away. Because of the pandemic they could not have a proper funeral.

By the end of March there were nearly 4,000 coronavirus deaths in the U.S., and the world was a radically different place than it was weeks earlier, with no end in sight.

Staring Into the Abyss

I learned something was up with the *Riverfront Times* on March 18th when I saw a tweet about a co-worker getting locked out of his company email account. I checked my email, the *Out in STL* website and social media and still had access to everything, which I thought might have been an oversight.

I called the brilliant art director Evan Sult, who had just been laid off. We had many incredible collaborations and as I paced the front porch, I told him it had been an honor to work with him. We toyed with the idea teaming up and creating something new, but we were both paper guys. That would be a challenge.

"If it's only online it just feels like a blog," Evan said.

There were echoes of 2008, and from that experience I knew how quickly things could fall apart. This seemed like it might be even worse, but I felt I was in a much better position to weather it than I had been back then. As turbulent as my public life was, my foundation was built to seismic code. I chose to return to Marquette Realty not because it was the most lucrative or prestigious. I returned because it was safe and steady, and I knew my position would be relatively recession resistant.

My house payment was about half of what it was in 2008. I had a car that was paid for. I had savings and tens of thousands in available credit.

Just as Joe and Ray had been a safe harbor for me, I was in a solid place to be that for others. That would include Marcus, who lost his Soulard bar job due to the pandemic.

Even if *RFT* somehow survived I didn't see how *Out in STL* would. But both did, and most everyone was soon re-hired.

Surviving hard times can bond a team, and I felt it did that for our media empire.

First Lady of Alton Embroiled in International Scandal

As the State of Illinois was shut down, the mayor's wife, Shannon Walker, was caught up in a raid at a Downtown Alton pub-turned speakeasy after a friend spotted her car and tipped off authorities. The story exploded, garnering international headlines and television news reports.

At the height of the controversy Mrs. Walker was often holed up at Steve Potter's historic Alton home, known as "The Potter Palace," where she'd consult with a few trusted confidants during clandestine meetings in the radio celebrity's cloistered garden.

I was tipped off at the time, but didn't say anything. Many months later Steve agreed to talk to me about it.

"I'd known her socially through mutual friends and she had visited when I was entertaining," he began. "She loved my garden and found it to be a safe haven when everyone was attacking her. Of course, she was glued to her phone, and I was sitting right next to her when the story broke on the BBC," he said.

Steve was one of Alton's biggest media personalities and socialites, and an invitation to the Potter Palace was always memorable. Through a second-story closet was a secret staircase leading to a festive party room. In the room was a ladder to a roof hatch leading to a widow's walk.

The Potter Palace was built for socialites so I could see why Mrs. Walker sought refuge there during the darkest days for our kind. Me and Kage sat on the rooftop with Steve one evening, where we could see all the way to the Mississippi. It indeed would be a perfect spot to watch for patrolling police or ravenous reporters.

The Harbinger

In the pricier parts of Tower Grove South it was trendy to not draw the drapes or close the blinds in the evening. Some homes didn't even have window treatments in the foyer or living room. We too left our shades up until the night I saw what appeared to be a human-sized bat flapping about on the front porch. As covertly as possible I went about shutting off all the lights in the front rooms to get a better look, and it was a seemingly intoxicated homeless man struggling with a long rain coat, which appeared to be stuck on his arms. It was not raining.

The oily white man unpacked his belongings and spread them out all over one end of the porch and seemed to be settling in. It would make more sense, I thought, if the house looked vacant or at least dark. I couldn't understand why he chose our brightly illuminated home.

With the pandemic and economic collapse, the flapping shadow at my window felt like an omen, like a harbinger of turmoil. From that moment on we drew the blinds in the evening.

On two more occasions that I know of a homeless person chose our porch as a place of respite. I called the police on the bat-like fellow since it seemed he was taking up residence, but I merely kept an eye on the others, who simply sat for about ten minutes and moved on.

The Maven expressed concern about how charged Villadiva's energy was, with four bold personalities plus Zeeke's card readings. In regard to the readings and the increased activity they generated, she said, "It's not a parlor trick, dear."

Maybe all that energy made the house a magnet or a beacon of sorts.

Distant

On April 15, 2020, the cremated remains of Colin Murphy's husband Kurt Ross were laid to rest. I was haunted by the image of Murphy standing alone, the fields of tombstones as the backdrop, looking at a small table with a rainbow-colored floral display.

Colin and Kurt devoted their lives to this community. Colin had been celebrated as Grand Marshal of the Pride Parade, they were at every event, promoted every cause, and through no fault of anyone this was what Kurt's finale looked like.

My heart broke for Colin.

Commercial Kitchen

I noticed right away that Marcus was a really good cook, and well before the pandemic I made him an offer: I would buy all the groceries if he'd cook enough for the household. It was a great deal for all involved.

After years of sporadically shopping for two I was now buying in bulk at Costco, and the moment I heard that Illinois had issued a stay-at-home order, I messaged Ms. Jamieson: "Please cancel my last two appointments." I then messaged Marcus, who was always home due to his classes shifting to online-only and the bar where he worked being shuttered. "Want to go to Costco?"

Grocery shopping at Costco became something we enjoyed doing together.

At the house, I thought of Marcus as the chef and the kitchen manager. He'd pull everything apart and reorganize, clean, and keep the refrigerator in order.

So many were isolated during this pandemic, but it was impossible to feel lonely at Villadiva. Oftentimes we were in our own corners of the house, Marcus in his room, Zeeke in his, Kage in the den beneath Zeeke's room, and me writing in the dining room, occasionally hearing Marcus walk or set down weights above. We had plenty of personal space, and plenty of space to come together as we'd do for big meals or happy hours at the long dining table.

Four men, three dogs, and two cats. I was grateful for all the quarantine companions.

The Riding Crop

Zeeke was pacing while looking out the front windows. "Judd is about ten minutes out. I bought a riding crop for us to use in play. I'm going to smack him," he said while I filled out the 2020 census questionnaire, plugging in information on the four of us and contemplating how this was the 10th or 11th time census information was gathered on this old house, the number depending on whether a census was taken right after the home was built in 1910.

"So, you like doing the smacking?" I asked.

"Yeah, and I like being smacked too."

Judd arrived in time for dinner, joining us at the table while we discussed the Covid crisis and his experiences as a nurse.

We moved to the parlor to continue our discussion, with Zeeke and Judd cuddled up on the loveseat. It was time to take the dogs for a walk and while we were out, they retired to the bedroom.

Ms. Jamieson messaged.

"Clyde wants me to create a group chat for the three of us. He's got something urgent to discuss."

"No," I replied. We had not been on speaking terms.

Someone at Clyde's workplace was suspected of having the coronavirus and was sent home, and Clyde was nervous about what to do.

He proceeded to talk to Ms. Jamieson about the basement portal, and said he was going down there to close it. From her apartment she could hear him down there coughing, and she was far more concerned about the virus than the portal to Hell.

I had a long day and was nearly delirious as I got out of the shower and made my way to bed. As usual I could hear sports from Marcus's room, but down the hall I could hear what sounded like the clumsiest and silliest S&M session ever.

"Let me turn that ceiling fan off before you whack yourself in the head!" I heard Judd say, followed by a half hour of giggling and chitchat.

Thoughts on Funerals

Contemplating the lack of funerals during the pandemic, I posted the following to Facebook the morning of April 3, 2020:

Of all human rituals, I think funerals are possibly the most emotionally and psychologically important.

The finality of death is hard to process under the best of circumstances, and when we come together to mourn, we're not only mourning the loss of an individual, we're mourning the loss of those we were tied to through them. We're mourning the loss of the world as we knew it.

Everyone is the gravitational pull of their own small orbiting community, and a funeral is an opportunity to come together in grief, find some degree of comfort and closure, and say goodbye to the star we orbited around and, in a sense, to one another.

A funeral is a time when the dead can speak. We comfort by telling the grieving how much the person loved them, something they often said, or by sharing their stories.

When my Grandma Andoe passed, my brother Joe said it felt like there was one less blanket on the bed. The world feels colder when we lose someone, and that final ritual brings the person back one last time, where through their community they can offer one last warm embrace to help sustain us in their absence.

Every person who passes during this pandemic—regardless of the cause—and everyone who loved them is a victim of Covid-19.

When this is over let's do our best to come together to properly mourn each individual.

The Visitor

It was an unusually warm early April evening, more like summer than spring. The windows were open but there wasn't much of a breeze, and everyone was lethargic. Due to the ongoing pandemic, Zeeke was conducting a tarot reading online rather than in person, and while he was doing that Kage and I took the dogs for a long walk through the neighborhood.

When we returned, Marcus and Zeeke were upstairs and we settled into the den to watch television. The dogs ran to the hallway at the base of the stairs and barked the way they would when they didn't know someone well, but short of the way they'd react to a complete stranger. I felt it was Marcus' friend Blaze, because that's how they barked at him, and I saw a brief glimpse of a tall shadow in the doorway before we heard a deep voice seemingly teasing the dogs with a "woof woof."

I expected Blaze to peek in to say hello, but he didn't. And I didn't hear the squeaking of the stairs. I got up and investigated, finding nobody was there. The dogs stopped barking and just stood there looking at me.

I messaged our house chat. "Did either of you have a visitor just now?" but neither of them did.

Zeeke said he had been astral projecting with his coven, but he didn't think that would have caused anything.

"When I was sitting at the dining table doing the reading, I felt like I saw a 6' tall grey figure standing in the archway to the coat room," he said.

I sent the Maven a message about what had occurred.

"A positive spirit. Could be a visit, could be a message. Could be signifying a journey or transition," she replied.

Our chat faded as I prepared for bed, and then I decided to send her the only photo I know of that shows our whole family, as we were only whole for 18 months. I sent it without comment.

"Do you notice the leaning pose of your father? She asked. "Toward and around."

"Is he familiar to you?" I replied.

"Yes. His hand is open and seems to be pointing."

"He was all about having a new baby. More so than mom," I said.

In the photo he was beaming like a headlight while mom looked like a deer in the headlights.

"He is the only one really smiling." After a few moments she followed with, "He feels cheated. He did not want to go."

"Is he always with me, or does he divide his time with others in the family, or can he be several places at once?" I asked, but at that exact moment she replied, "How precious that he remains with you, you are a very lucky man."

Seeing what happened with our messages she replied, "So funny how those were concurrent. What do you have of his? He said you have something put away."

I said I had his watch somewhere in a drawer. I didn't wear it because I wasn't used to wearing a watch and am always afraid of losing jewelry, since I tend to take things off.

"Sleep with it. If he is visiting, it may be quite clear."

I did, and dreamt he was always around, but was just out of sight, as if in the next room or garage, and I kept noticing helpful things he had done.

Return of the Rogue's Gallery

After about a month of the coronavirus shutdown everyone was in serious need of grooming. Zeeke mentioned finding a barber to come to the house, and one Thursday he notified me that the forbidden cuts would be going down at 7 p.m. He asked if I was in.

For nearly twenty years, during the times I lived in town, Francis' wife Edie had been my stylist, and I cherished our time together for that hour every month. But she was closed, so was it okay to have some dude cut my hair in her absence? It felt like adultery.

My mangy locks were too much to bear, so I said I was in. Zeeke spread a big sheet over the living room floor, placing a swiveling stool with a red vinyl seat in the middle, and then we waited.

At 7:15 Zeeke said, "I messaged him at 6:15 asking if we were still on and he said yeah and that he'll likely be here before seven."

I continued editing a piece about Lesbian Awareness Week for *Out in STL* as time continued to slip away.

"I'm going to make you find the barber next time," Zeeke said around 7:45, as he began to pack away the makeshift barber station he had set up.

"I don't know why people are so flaky," I replied.

Just after 8pm me and Kage were settled in the den when I heard a knock at the door. "That must be the barber, Zeeke," I yelled.

I heard Zeeke greet the man and let him in, and then excuse himself as he went upstairs to retrieve everything he had just packed away. I got up to offer the barber a drink. I walked from the kitchen to the dining room and looked through the scalloped archway to see what looked like a backpacked homeless man facing away from me, casing the room.

"Can I get you . . ." I began as the man turned around. It was Menashe!

"Hello Menashe," I said, stunned.

Menashe began to say the word "Hi," but it became a garbled "I didn't know this was your house" as he nervously looked away and I retreated to the kitchen.

He looked rough, at least 15 years older than he should.

I went to the den, closed the door and told Kage who was in our living room while at the same time typing the information for our group chat.

"Wait . . . no? No? Really?" Kage sputtered.

To the chat I simply opened, "Menashe is in our living room."

Nobody believed me.

Kage stood at the cracked door to the hall and when Zeeke walked past he called to him. "Pssst. That's MENASHE!"

Zeeke was puzzled, not knowing anything about our history with him. "What's the issue? I don't know . . ."

"He cannot be in our house. He has to go!" Kage insisted.

Sitting across the den I said, "Just let him cut his hair."

I didn't feel right putting Zeeke in an awkward position, and even though Menashe didn't seem like the same person due to the addiction, he was someone we once cared about a great deal, and someone who once cared about us.

Kage said, "Do not leave him alone and do not take your eyes off of him."

As Zeeke returned to the living room to get situated, I tried to discreetly grab my wallet off the buffet. Me and Kage sat in the den with the television off, ear hustling and reporting to the chat.

Sitting on the floor and peeking out of the inch gap between the mahogany door and the frame, the two were just out of sight but I could hear bits of the conversation over the buzzing of the clippers.

"She said we need to be social distancing and I was like, I've been to seventy-five orgies since this all began!" Menashe exclaimed.

Everything about him was so foreign from the person we once knew, the person who planned our wedding, cutting fresh flowers from his garden and the gardens of Alton friends for the reception. The best way I can describe it is when someone becomes a zombie in the movies. It's a sickly version of their shell, but the soul is gone.

Not everything was foreign, though. Menashe reiterated the same talking points about his estranged husband Dan that he'd been reciting for five years. "I never told him I was going to be exclusive," along with how abusive Dan was, etc.

"Is that who you're running from?" Zeeke asked. "I sense you're running from someone."

Seemingly startled, Menashe mumbled and then changed the subject.

After the haircut Zeeke offered him a beverage (my earlier offer had been aborted) at which time Menashe spoke about his deceased mother before Zeeke mentioned being a witch.

"Oh yeah I'm a witch too," Menashe replied. "I lived in New Orleans for a year and learned Haitian Voodoo."

After the chatty Menashe left, we sat with Zeeke to debrief.

"He had a heaviness to him, sort of a weight. His mind kept buzzing, very paranoid, talking about how his exes threw his stuff away and how he got in a few fights with people. He was nuts. When he left it felt like the air re-entered the room," an exhausted Zeeke said. "I just hope he didn't take a lock of my hair. I'm going to soak in the tub with Chinese Wash, holy water and Devil's Vinegar," he said, explaining that the concoction breaks magic, cleanses and protects from bad magic.

"Why do you think he'd want to harm you?" I asked.

"It's not necessarily about harming. It could be persuasion or seduction, or if he is trying to harm it's because of my connection with you."

Considering Menashe was definitely not in New Orleans for a year, we were all skeptical of his voodoo claims. Still, we all felt depleted after his departure.

"What was your story with him?" Zeeke asked while standing beside the staircase.

"He planned our wedding and was a very close friend, but sided with Clyde and Rick and then got a meth addiction." Pointing to the framed "Meth at the Melrose" article on the wall, I said, "Here's the story."

"Wow," Zeeke replied. "I really did bring back the classic Villadiva rogues gallery!"

Ms. Jamieson Finds Her Niche

Selfie-focused gay Facebook groups were popping up like weeds, and Ms. Jamieson was frustrated that only the young, fit, white guys were getting attention. In one of the bigger groups, she posted, "Let's see the guys with average bodies, let's see men of color, let's see everyone who's not getting the attention on here."

The thread exploded and raged on for a week.

I was thrilled, because Ms. Jamieson had a habit of beating her head against the wall and trying to guilt and shame everyone into changing, but this time she found a constructive workaround, and it was a hit.

"You should start your own group," I told her.

"You think?" she replied.

"Yes. You've clearly tapped into something here. There's an interest."

She started a group called, "Guys Next Door," and she found managing it enjoyable and fulfilling—and did those bad boys keep her busy! Below are some of her "housekeeping" posts:

Hi guys! Please keep FB community standards in mind when you post things. There was a post on here from last week that I did not even see that FB removed because it went against their standards. It was a pic of someone getting rimmed. DO NOT POST PICS OF SEX ACTS ON HERE EVEN IF IT DOESN'T SHOW FULL NUDITY. Facebook can shut this group down for things like this. I don't want to have to approve every post before it's posted or have to remove group members. Thanks and have a great day!

Morning guys! Facebook has been removing photos left and right in this group that "violate" their standards, so here's a couple of more things not to post:

1) photos containing cum, even if the photo doesn't mention that it's cum, and even if a penis isn't shown.

2) photos containing ass that shows the crack/balls.

The Benevolent Brunch Floozies

The Maven wrote to me concerning the men at Soulard's St. Peter & Paul Shelter.

> *I have a new project (aren't you surprised!); the homeless guys at Sts Peter & Paul are kept in that shelter 24/7 except for smoke breaks. Can you imagine? They really have nothing. I made masks for them & now I am looking for 28 people to 'adopt' a guy; they are going to submit a simple wish list' -low dollar items- Socks, underwear, games, books, etc . . . want to adopt a shelter guy?*

I worked with the homeless and formerly homeless population for years in San Francisco, yet when reading her message, I still had the classic hobo visual of someone who was homeless as a way of life. Regardless, I was more than happy to sponsor someone.

Each person requesting help wrote a letter, which the volunteer coordinator then sent to the sponsors as a package. We were to read their stories and select the ones we would help.

I was only a few notes in when I came to an articulate letter from someone who had moved to St. Louis from Chicago after the death of his partner, and found a job he loved at "the wonderful Nadine's" just before everything shut down, which he hoped to return to.

My whole demeanor changed, from "Let's see who I'll sponsor and then get back to the task at hand," to "This is one of our people and we need to help him!"

I shared his letter with the Brunch Floozies Chat and was floored by the response. Everyone was on board instantly, He had one of the longer wish lists, but we knocked everything off of it and kept going. A tablet was ordered, work shoes, shirts, and the next day Frank Fontana handed over a brand-new prepaid smartphone. Gift cards from $50 to $250 were also donated by group members.

Many of the items still had to be shipped, but I wanted to get him the phone and gift cards right away. I packaged them in a small Rubbermaid tote, writing on the top, "From the Brunch Floozies @ Nadine's, with more to come," and left them with the shelter manager.

Nadine hadn't known about it. With her revenue at zero for a month and counting we didn't want to make her feel pressured. She then received the following message:

> *Hey Nadine, I am a little speechless because I just got back and there was a package waiting for me from "the brunch floozies at Nadine's" with a real phone and some other stuff . . . which is the nicest gift and gesture ever . . . plus my flip phone I showed you is almost out of the prepaid minutes. I am just so grateful for you and Dre and the job and everything. And I know you will not take credit for anything but just know I am beyond words thankful for your kindness and I will hunt down these "brunch floozies" and somehow thank them! haha*

"She was at a loss for words," Frank began, reporting on the talk they had when she called to ask about it. "And that's not easy, you know, 'you have no idea.' She was so thankful, and she said she just couldn't believe how wonderful this was, and she said she thanks everyone from the bottom of her heart. She was amazed at the generosity, and she can't wait for everyone that has not met him to meet him."

Kage Claps Back

Jasmine and Ron Tellcamp recruited a former JJ's bartender named Lee Gustin to publicly attack us, which wasn't difficult since he had a vendetta against me for six years.

The twinks (young and often pretty guys) from the Grove began flooding into JJ's late Saturday nights, and some of them were mocking and insulting the bears. I'd written about it in the hopes of initiating a conversation and educating them, but Gustin was adamant that the piece was an attack on the club. He reached out to me personally, and out of respect for him I removed the piece altogether.

He's a chief reason I stopped doing that. The few times I've removed a piece simply to placate someone, they were total dicks about it and presented the removal as if they had my severed head on a spear. Rather than saying "thanks man," or even simply dropping it, they spun the removal as vindication that the article was faulty. My piece about the way some twinks were behaving at JJ's was accurate, and did ignite the conversation I intended. One of the main offenders reached out and apologized to someone he'd insulted.

Since all that went down Gustin jumped on any opportunity to throw shade. He cheered on both Clyde and Menashe when they went on the attack, and he was all over Ron Tellcamp's hate threads, including one where Ron said he'd be fine if I killed myself. On Ron's posts Gustin mocked me for not finding success in New York. This coming from a guy who was only in San Francisco to be a third to a pair of sugar daddies.

I was told Jasmine had a short-lived public post about how much she loved Gustin a few days prior, so I knew something was in the pipeline. Sure enough, when a member of the Brunch Floozies randomly shared the years-old "Dustin Does Dallas" article, Gustin chimed in:

Be wary of sharing anything from Andoe. He's as much a sociopth [sic] and an abuser as Mitchell and doesn't need a platform.

He'd posted similar things in the past, but "abuser" was new and clearly Saccharine Sisters inspired. I was never in the market to antagonize him so over the years I would either let it slide or reach out to him to try to resolve his issue, but get no reply.

Everyone knew Kage was the good cop to my bad cop, so on the rare occasion he snapped on someone, it was noticed. And on this day, he showed up with guns blazing. He posted the following to Gustin's comment:

Shall we recap?

You hate Chris because of a story he wrote, which he removed out of personal respect for you.

Since then, you've cheered on everyone who has ever come after us, including someone who's meth addiction caused a loss of all his relationships, someone who tried to get our dog removed from our home to save face, and someone who literally put a blood curse on us in a drunken rage because he couldn't have us.

403

So, who is the real sociopath?

BTW: It takes a real lack of self-awareness to mock Chris for not making it in NYC when he thrived in SF for 8 years, a city you only survive in at the pleasure of two sugar daddies.

Unfortunately, you can't read facial expressions in a thread, but Gustin still revealed clues that he was thrown off. His first comment was only Kage's tagged name, indicating that he hurriedly tried to react and failed. He then tried to deflect with an, "Oooh she mad," which was undercut when he removed his original comments altogether and blocked us.

Our whole lives are pushback, so it's easy to forget many skate by without dealing with opposition, and fold like a house of cards when faced with it.

Jasmine's Devils Come for Christine Elbert

Christine Elbert's life was an open book, so when she went to her favorite coffee shop, the sex-positive Shameless Grounds, she'd post in advance in the event a friendly face wanted to join. That habit, unfortunately, also benefited her Saccharine Sisters stalkers.

One afternoon Christine was enjoying a conversation with several friends when two members of Jasmine's Poison Potluck Posse took a seat at the neighboring table. One was the person who hatched a plan to go after Christine's professional licenses months prior. After a few minutes Jasmine's pawn approached the manager to complain that Christine was engaging in an anti-Trans conversation that made them uncomfortable.

Everyone there knew Christine well and didn't buy it.

But Jasmine's minions weren't done.

Christine had withdrawn considerably from the social scene to avoid Jasmine drama, but during the pandemic she began posting uplifting videos on Facebook Live. These simple and cheery videos drove Jasmine up the wall and rattled her like nothing else. Inexplicably, she was convinced they were all about her.

She even messaged Christine directly over text.

Hello. I almost went live, as a reaction, but I've been working on that so I decided to take the advice of a few and give this one more try since you apparently just went live about me.

Nobody who watched the videos would find anything even vaguely about Jasmine in them.

And what is a Jasmine message without a threat? She went on to offer Christine one final chance to talk to her before going public with what she claimed were damning screenshots and voice recordings.

When that failed, she released the hounds.

In one of Elbert's videos, she discussed taking back slurs that have been used against the LGBTQ community and other marginalized groups, and rattled off a few. A full 24 hours after the video was posted, about a dozen hostile people Christine didn't even know descended on the Facebook video to condemn her for using hate speech. One said they were emailing complaints to her employer, and another threatened violence.

I had enough. I had tried very hard not to feed the beast, but it was time to speak out. On April 27, 2020, I posted the following:

What many don't know about Christine Elbert is she's been dealing with a crazed stalker for over two years now. Someone who has people follow her into restaurants and try to get her thrown out, threaten her livelihood, and as recently as tonight—triggered by her happy videos—threaten her safety. I simply want to stand as a witness and say that I see it. I stand with my friend Christine.

This spurred numerous messages of support.

Former parade director Ellen Vanscoy felt partly responsible for Christine's situation.

"You don't know my story with Christine but she probably saved my life years ago," Vanscoy began. "When Jasmine was first starting to try and get sober it was Pride season and of course she was always around me. I actually tried to be supportive because I had been there years before. In trying to help her reach out to others who might be good support I said, 'You know, Elbert would also be someone good for you to reach out about sobriety.' I had no idea what I set off then or how deep her monstrous traits would go."

I've often thought about retiring from public life, and during low points I've even wondered if I did more harm than good. Then I'm reminded of this city's sinister underbelly and realize that stepping aside would mean looking the other way while good people were thrown to the wolves.

Kage's Knockout

Jasmine was clearly relishing the attacks on Christine, and appeared to be feeling cocky and loose. She even trolled Ms. Jamieson, which was unusual, and we heard she was leaving both of her primary Facebook accounts open simultaneously. Such carelessness left her wide open for having one reported.

Kage had a fake profile that was friends with her older profile, allowing him to report the newer account as an impersonation if he caught it when both were active.

"I was pissed off about the attacks on Christine and the trolling of Jordan," Kage explained. "At that same time, she kept saying she was going to sue us once the courts reopened, which was bullshit because they were open. Early one day I saw both profiles were up, and I tried to report one but she pulled it before I could, but later they were both up again and as soon as I reported it the super-secret new account was gone and I was purged from the old one. Clearly she was purging her list in response to being yanked."

Trivial as this maneuver may sound, in Jasmine's world this was comparable to a rival gang shooting up her block.

Jasmine knew that someone had to be a friend in order to report the second profile. Her anger and paranoia consumed her. Gone were the gloating posts and in their place were regular warnings that she'd purge anyone she deemed disloyal.

Many on her friends list didn't actually know her or engage. They were just there to watch the perpetual shitshow for as long as they could until the inevitable culling.

Intent

One thing I picked up from being around Zeeke and his associates was the concept of intent being at the heart of witchcraft, meaning to cast a curse, for example, one needed clear intention.

"I've been thinking about the time I told Shawn Adams he was bound to Clyde, and would own anything Clyde did going forward. That really stayed with him. Even though I knew nothing of witchcraft, I think I cast a spell in that moment.

Zeeke agreed that was a possibility. "Humans are inherently magical; witches are just the ones who realize it."

Catching up with Colin

About a month after the passing of Kurt, Colin called to thank me for checking in on him and for the modest financial contribution I made.

He shared intimate details of Kurt's final moments. He felt fortunate that they had been in a good place in their relationship, and that he was with him at the end. But the grief was overwhelming.

"I wouldn't wish this on my worst enemy," he said.

It was around 6 p.m. and I was sitting on the front porch waiting for a storm to come in that was still an hour away. I did my best to shift into neutral and allow him to lead the conversation, which I think is a skill I was only recently developing. I've over-managed in the past, thinking about what I was going to say next as opposed to really listening, and worrying too much about silence.

Colin spoke at length about how unexpected and sudden Kurt's decline was. He spoke of finances and logistics, what the plan was with the house. He spoke of feeling Kurt's presence in a very tangible way.

He seamlessly shifted to how community businesses and institutions might look after the pandemic was behind us, a topic on which I could more competently engage. We spoke of old days and the dens of debauchery—from Faces to the adult arcades in Brooklyn, Illinois.

"We would go from Magnolia's to Faces, which closed when the sun was coming up, but by then the Front Page would begin serving Bloody Mary . . ." he began.

"The Front Page was on Menard?" I asked.

"Yeah, and after a few drinks there Clem's would open and we'd spend all day and early evening and then it was time to go back to Magnolia's and then to Faces again having never hit the bed!" he said.

"I can honestly say I've never done anything like that. I've stayed out all night, but not two nights straight. I love sleeping too much," I said.

"I don't know how we all did it," he replied.

We then talked about the adult bookstores in Brooklyn.

"Crossing that rickety old McKinley Bridge, with potholes big enough you could see the Mississippi . . . there was such a feeling of anticipation going to the East Side," I said.

"One night the Black woman who ran Fantasyland was watching Titanic downstairs—this was the 90s—and the only way she could watch it at her desk was to pipe it down from one of the porn booths. Someone accidentally pushed a button and messed it up and she yelled upstairs, 'Don't push any buttons I'm watching Titanic!'

"Then we all started making a game of it, trying to mess it up. She was yelling, 'STOP IT YOU FAGGOTS I'M WATCHING TITANIC' and then that music comes on really loud, "Near, far . . ." and we all start singing to it, drunk off our asses," he laughs.

"So, what the hell is all this Jasmine business?" Colin exclaimed. "I read that entire thread and you all look like lunatics! Nearly everyone on that thing was best friends with her just months ago!"

I caught him up to speed the best I could without bothering to defend how I was coming off to the community. We returned to topics of "then," "now" and "what's next."

Colin was 50 and I was 45, but those five years didn't seem to mean much anymore, particularly on that call. We were two seasoned old friends with a lot of history discussing our shared love of this complicated place.

"I'll get off here. I'm sure I've bored you to death by now," Colin said.

"Not at all! I think this is the best conversation we've ever had!"

And I believe it was.

This House is Clean

Clyde had been posting pictures of porch parties at his new boyfriend Gervais's house every weekend when his boss's gay son, who got him the job, mentioned the parties were irresponsible, especially since someone at the factory tested positive for Covid. Kristin commented, "He's right you know," and got the full wrath since Clyde couldn't very well go off on the boss's son. The full wrath being an angry vague post about social shaming and then blocking her.

It had to be incredibly frustrating to want to flaunt a brand-new social life just as being social became taboo.

Clyde's boasting was useful when we were working to schedule a time for Zeeke and Rachel to seal the portal and reverse the curses he had cast.

Our evening began in the Villadiva dining room where Rachel, who arrived with her partner, met Zeeke for the first time. I wondered how they'd get along, but within minutes they were cheerfully playing Show & Tell with their paranormal and witchcraft collections.

Our field trip began with the Samurai Sword murder apartment, where we only turned on the foyer light. Rachel made a beeline for the bathroom where she sat on the edge of the bathtub exactly where the body was found, and, dowsing rods in hand, began asking yes and no questions. The rods were responsive to every question asked.

Zeeke, Rachel and her partner all said they came face to face with a gargoyle-looking demon perched high in the bedroom closet. I did not want to see it face to face, but I hoped to catch it on camera and so I took a series of photographs.

"Ooh it does *not* like that," Zeeke said as the flash blasted the closet.

"This is where he slept, and they talked to him all the time," Rachel said. "They did a number on him, they convinced him he was the Antichrist and fed on those delusions. They told him to kill."

We then went to the Melrose and parked in the back, where Ms. Jamieson met us at the car. She led us to the basement where Zeeke drew a big chalk circle of protection on the floor and carefully arranged his tools of the trade.

Rachel pointed to the stone wall Ms. Jamieson found Clyde staring at the evening he said he couldn't escape the basement.

"That's the portal." She said as she pointed, and then turned to us. "He's looking to sell his soul for power and influence, but he doesn't realize he no longer owns his soul."

"They want something more from him. They want him to help them get other people," Zeeke replied.

With salt, candles and a crystal, Rachel and Zeeke worked to seal the portal.

"There's so many of them," Rachel said.

While nothing was visible to the naked eye, my phone was picking up dozens of orbs flying in all directions.

"We're about ready to bury the nail," Rachel said.

Burying the nail was the final step in reversing the curse.

It was about 9 pm. on a Saturday night, so people were out and about walking dogs, heading to Friendly's Bar, and even parking a car on the street and going inside a Melrose apartment—and there

I was on the ground digging a hole with my spade in one hand and a cocktail in the other while Kage stood close by using his phone's flashlight. We must have had an air of confidence because nobody seemed to pay us any mind.

The group assembled at the hole, and Rachel dropped in the rusty nail along with the quartz crystal used for trapping the negative entities Clyde summoned, salt, and the remains of the candles used to seal the space. When the narrow but relatively deep hole was filled it was hard to tell where it had been.

Everyone went upstairs to cleanse Ms. Jamieson's apartment and discuss the night's events. I had only been in his place once or twice since he and Dallas split up a year or so earlier, and noticed how his cute apartment, which was such a wreck during the relationship, was once again neat as a pin.

Rachel said the house was clean, but that she wanted to return at a later date in order to banish Clyde from the Melrose altogether.

Civil Unrest Hits Villadiva: Night One—
Facebook Status, Monday June 1, 2020

Anyone who has visited Villadiva knows not to park in front of our neighbor's house. We stress that on all invites, and have even put out orange cones at the property line during events as a reminder.

The guy is tough AF. We got off on the wrong foot, but I grew to appreciate how he maintains order around here.

Anyway, last night a store across the street was looted. People were running everywhere and a car pulled in front of his house to load up.

"Don't even think about doing that shit in front of my house," he told them.

They moved.

The unrest was in response to the murder of George Floyd by Minneapolis Police. Night one had been intense, but was nothing compared to night two.

War Zone

I was housesitting at Villa Ray during the 2014 Ferguson uprising, and had just gotten in from work when the neighbor rang the bell. The straight, quiet white man was in his sixties, and had been a solid neighbor of Ray's for years. Despite all my time there, however, we'd only exchanged a couple of nods.

"I know Ray's gone, and as we've seen from last night, if things fall apart around here, we'll be on our own. Nobody is coming to help us. Here's my number if you need it. I've also got an extra gun if you want it."

I wasn't worried at the time, and had even been on the ground in Ferguson the night the verdict was read and the city burned. I wouldn't truly be afraid of civil unrest for another six years, until 2 a.m. the morning of June 2, 2020.

I woke to endless gunfire right outside the house, yelling, the screeching of tires and the roaring of engines. I jumped out of bed and looked out the side window to see cars speeding through and out of the parking lot, and people running.

Picking up my phone, I tried to see what was going on. There were fires downtown, four officers were shot . . . I came downstairs to find Kage sitting in the fully-illuminated den with the venetian blinds raised. I hit the lights and closed the blinds.

"Turn on the news, try to see what's going on," I said.

Meanwhile I checked to make sure the front and back doors and storm doors were locked. I returned to see Kage looking at a weather report.

"This might be an earlier broadcast," he casually said.

"If there's no news turn it off!" I snapped.

I kept pacing. I saw light coming from under Marcus' door and as I approached, Zeeke crawled out of his own room to avoid any bullets that may come through the window.

"Marcus, do you have a gun?" I asked. I'm not sure why I thought he did.

"No, I don't," he replied.

I turned to Zeeke. "Do you have a gun?"

"We kept one in the nightstand table at the old house but I don't have it here," he replied.

"We'll need to barricade the doors," I said.

Directly outside was pandemonium and no police in sight. I thought back to 2014 and Ray's neighbors' words about being left to defend ourselves.

Every few minutes we'd hear sirens in the distance, and then they would fade out. Looters were stashing things beneath Kage's car in the driveway, people were running through the decommissioned alley behind the house. Even our macho neighbor was staying out of sight.

In the middle of the scene at the shopping center was a slender, upper-middle class looking blond white guy, maybe 25, and two friends standing at the lot entrance just watching the show. They weren't hiding behind anything, either. The main guy was standing right on the curb as looters loaded up their cars and drove past. One jovial woman yelled out her car window, "Y'all go get you some shit!"

The gun fire quieted and it began to dawn on me that the people seemed to be focusing only on the stores, not houses, cars or bystanders. Even the active shooter had been aiming at the sky while doing figure eights in the lot. Strange as it is to say, the mood was joyful, celebratory.

As one man finished loading his old Grand Marquis and said goodbye, the blond guy replied, "Have a good night. Stay safe."

"I'm going to nickname him 'the Looter Liaison,'" I said.

Another neighbor walked up with his dog and visited the Liaison, and then I noticed neighbors across the street sitting on their porch watching the scene as well.

The vibe downtown had been far more volatile, and the next day I saw posts from friends who lived in lofts down there reporting men dragging a safe from a store and shooting the lock. They also posted about the fires and teargas.

It seemed everything in our shopping center, aside from Aldi and the dollar store, had been looted. The following day nothing was open and most of the dozen or so retailers were boarded up.

"It makes me sad and concerned," Kage said. "I enjoy having those shops there, and wonder if they'll come back."

The mayor set a 9 p.m. curfew.

Six years earlier I was in the streets when things went down, and now I was peeking through blinds in terror. I wondered what that was about.

The Shakedown

Even the pathetic crowd who followed Jasmine had to notice that her storylines never went anywhere. One she doggedly promoted for nine months was that she had a major lawsuit against me and Kage in the works, and she even solicited money so she could print her 884 pages of evidence.

"Is this Jasmine a crazy person?" an elderly man named Walter asked Frank Fontana one day. Walter lived in an assisted-living facility, but was active on Facebook and sometimes Frank would bring him to our gatherings at Nadine's.

"I'd only commented on her posts here and there and then she wrote asking me to block Chris Andoe. She said I never show an interest in her problems, and then said she's raising money for a lawsuit. I don't have any money! How should I handle this?"

I reached out to Walter.

"I had to unfriend her," he began. "At first she sounded alright but then she was really freaking me out with her messages. That's when I reached out to Frank for advice. The last straw was when she started asking for money and really weird favors. Was she supposed to be in rehabilitation of something like that?"

"Oh wow, she asked you for money?" I inquired.

"Yes, but what really concerned me was when she claimed she had to do some 1,400-page dissertation for an officer and asked for money to make all the copies of texts that her enemies had sent her. That's when I started asking around and discovered how many enemies she has made in her lifetime. Then I realized something was really wrong. Apparently, she has a very vivid imagination."

My initial thought was shaking down the elderly represented a new low for the Saccharine Sisters, but I guess it was on par with demonizing a puppy.

Poser Jasmine

With racial injustice front and center in the national conversation, of course the shameless and exhausting Jasmine decided to pose as a leader of the Black Lives Matter movement. Aside from her stint as the chauffeur and sidekick of the felonious bar photographer Spike Turner, she seemed to have had little involvement with people of color in the course of her thirty some-odd years.

With so much of the conversation being about whites calling the police on people of color, I remembered multiple instances where she threatened to call the police on Kage. The first was when her then-landlord circulated the photo of her passed out on the stoop, at which time she vowed to have Kage classified as a sex offender even though he wasn't there and obviously had nothing to do with it. She'd threatened to press trespassing charges against him, and when she located a fake profile of Clyde's on her list, she publicly announced that Kage created the profile and that she had notified the police.

For someone who built her entire brand on being against the police she incessantly boasted about having her own assigned uniformed detective at her beck and call. She'd slide from "Fuck the Police" to "Ultimate Karen" and back with zero self-awareness, and her unsophisticated audience seemed equally oblivious to the incongruent messaging.

In the midst of her BLM rebranding, one of her close friends made a racially clumsy post tying his heavily-tanned skin to his support for the movement. She found this quite embarrassing and instantly disavowed him. Then she bizarrely claimed he had actually been *my* friend all along. I don't know if I'd even met him in person.

The manic machinations continued with her dredging up ancient screenshots from several different and unrelated chats, and hobbling them together as proof that I was a rapist. This only served to reveal that her anxiety-inducing screenshot game was now running on fumes. It was her shoddiest work to date. Still, it needed to be addressed.

The morning of Tuesday, June 9, 2020, I posted the following to social media:

A very disturbed individual who for months has told her sad little audience she was on the cusp or suing me is now posting cropped and altered screenshots purporting to prove that I was fired for having sex with a subordinate. Just like everything she says, she's simply making things up.

There is not even a kernel of truth to what she's saying.

She's also claiming that someone who is embroiled in scandal for a racially insensitive post is part of my group. Though she's famous for her weaponized screenshots, she failed to post one single photo of us together. The fact is I don't personally know the man, and she's hugged up with him in dozens of photos.

I've often said I can't stay angry at crazy people. I can get fire-breathing mad, but it blows over. I'm far angrier at those who have enabled and fanned the flames of her insanity, and that anger is durable. I know who you are and I won't forget.

And for those pathetic enough to buy her fantastical tales about a lawsuit, when you sue someone there is a thing called discovery, look it up. That's where the fun would begin, and believe me, I would love it.

The thread grew to nearly two hundred comments, including from co-workers spanning the past twenty years, all expressing astonishment. Mac Taylor cleverly posted a series of memes created from photos of Jasmine with the man who made the racially offensive post, each with the caption, "Where's Chris Andoe?" That caption worked especially well on a photo of them looking off into the distance while hiking.

For happy hour that evening I went down to the corner with Kage and Zeeke, and after a call with Joe, I decided to go on Facebook Live. Zeeke sat beside me and was a great addition, riffing on my comments and making appropriate facial expressions.

I titled the video, "Jasmine's Rape Accusation."

"Hi everybody. This is my man Zeeke, we're sitting here having some drinks, and it's been a big day. As a lot of you saw earlier, the craziest person in town, Jasmine, today decided that I am a rapist. That I've been raping people. That I was fired from a previous job for sexual misconduct. She is, uhh, I don't know. The thing is, every time she does something insane, the responses I get are, 'You should ignore it. You should ignore it. Yeah, she accused you of rape but you should ignore it because she's crazy . . .'"

Zeeke chimed in: *"Rape is not one of those accusations you can ignore!"*

I continued: *"You guys are . . . people ask a lot of me, you know, I mean this is somebody who tried to get my dog taken away, is accusing me of rape, is saying I was fired for sexual assault, and everyone's like, "Oh you need to keep quiet about it" and it's like, you know, I don't know. It's not reasonable. It's not a reasonable request. The people who are investing so much in telling me to be quiet should be getting help for her, because I want you to stop and think about this: She accused me of raping people today. Let's let that sink in. I'm raping people.*

"What proof did she have? She had some doctored screenshot, that had nothing to do with anything. But everyone is like, "But she's crazy so don't.." No. Someone accuses me of rape I'm going to talk about it. And meanwhile she is making Christine Elbert's life a living hell. She has people following Christine Elbert into restaurants, she had people follow Christine Elbert into Shameless Grounds and claim she was engaged in offensive conversation and try to get her thrown out.

"And so, she is fucking out of control, and there is no lawsuit. That's why I'm using her name because she's lying. She's saying there is going to be some big lawsuit. There is no lawsuit. There will be no lawsuit."

Zeeke backs me up, shaking his head and mouthing "No lawsuit."

There was no rape, there was no firing for sexual assault and there will be no lawsuit she is batshit crazy, ok? I'm just being serious; I'm keeping it real with you guys because I don't know why everyone is walking on eggshells when she is going around being such a destructive force in this city. But you guys do what you're going to do, ok? But this is what she's doing, she is a nightmare. And now she's trying to connect me to her best friend who made racially insensitive comments, meanwhile she threatened my Black husband with the police numerous times. She is a nightmare, ok? I don't really care how you're taking this. It doesn't matter to me, because if you want me to sit here and not answer accusations that I'm out here raping people, you're a fucking idiot. Ok. That's all I have to say on this. Bye."

The video racked up about 1,400 views and a few hundred comments in the first 24 hours. To my amazement the feedback was 100% positive. People who had said nothing for a long time offered support, and her followers, including her manservant Ron Tellcamp, were dead silent.

Funeral Invitation

Zeeke's favorite grandmother died of lung cancer at the beginning of the pandemic, so plans for a memorial were postponed for months. Once the funeral was scheduled Zeeke made plans to attend, and since his soon-to-be-ex-husband Jeff knew his grandmother, he planned to attend as well.

It would be Zeeke's first trip home in nearly four years.

His mother knew about Judd, but requested that Zeeke bring him another time. She felt it would be an uncomfortable time to meet. When Zeeke explained this to Judd he replied, "Can you double check? Can you talk to her and try to convince her? Can you talk to your brother and have him convince her?"

"It's a funeral. I think it would be a weird time to meet the family."

"I just wanna be there for you and I'd really like to go," Judd replied.

The following two weeks were stressful for Zeeke as he felt he was caught between Judd's demands and his mother's wishes. Each day Judd would ask if he'd gotten the green light. "Did you talk to your mom? Did you talk to your brother? Can I go?"

As the date approached, it became clear to Zeeke that Judd was in denial that the trip would take place without him, until a few days before when he said in a resigned tone, "I'd like to at least see you before you leave."

Judd arrived at Villadiva around bedtime, and the following morning said, "I have this cough and I feel warm. I need to go to the V.A. to get tested for coronavirus."

They quarantined at Zeeke's vacant Belleville house while they waited for the results. Me and Kage smelled bullshit.

Judd was neurotic about Zeeke going on that trip without him, and the timing of all this was questionable to say the least. We suspected he either knew he was sick before coming, or that he wasn't sick at all.

"Does Judd feel bad for being the harbinger of pestilence?" I texted.

"Sort of." Zeeke replied.

During their days in Belleville Judd walked Jeff's dog through the neighborhood and seemed more or less okay. Finally, two tests in a row came back negative, and Judd went home.

Sitting in the Villadiva dining room, I asked Zeeke if this meant he was going to the memorial.

"No, I'm staying here," he said with a forced half-smile.

"If you leave right now you can still get there. Even if you missed part of the service you could spend time with the family," I urged. "These events are important."

"I've already missed part of it. I'm just going to stay here."

Looking straight into his eyes I said, "You don't feel like you *can* go."

Zeeke didn't answer. He didn't need to.

The Mug

Zeeke had a much higher sex drive than Judd, and completely different sexual mores. It seemed the two were engaged in a tug of war over which one's lifestyle would rule the day. Zeeke was open about being polyamorous, and pushed the envelope with play dates. Judd would give in a bit, but then try to reel him back to a more monogamous arrangement—even though Judd was also on the apps and swapped nude pictures and flirted.

It was starting to occur to Zeeke that he was newly single and was living in the city surrounded by fun gentlemen callers. He was getting fatigued with Judd's restrictions and turmoil. When he brought home one of the sexy models who was pictured on "The Maven of Mardi Gras" cover, I sensed the end was near.

He told Judd about the model and then Judd began asking questions about who else he'd been with. Zeeke prided himself on being truthful, so he told him he had slept with Kage.

Zeeke messaged me at work to tell me Judd was upset, and that he was asking people around town about us.

"His drama will engulf us all," I replied.

Honesty was noble but I felt thrown under the bus. I didn't know what their arrangement of the moment was or what he told Judd or when, but if he slept with Kage knowing it would be a problem, I felt he shouldn't have done it, or should have kept it to himself. Now it was on my plate to deal with.

"Here's the deal going forward. If you can't or won't bury your turds like any common house cat, then stop fucking around."

I was especially frustrated because this came exactly a week after Jasmine's ridiculous stories that I was a rapist, meaning that in one week I was involved in two sex scandals that did not spring from me actually having sex.

"Is this what middle-age is for me? Sex scandals without having sex? That's like the calories without the cake or the hangover without the fun night out," I vented to John Kreisel.

Zeeke sought the counsel of several friends, including me and his soon-to-be ex-husband Jeff, and then contacted Judd to say it simply was not working out. Judd was blindsided and livid, demanding that Zeeke return his belongings in person that evening. A 240-mile round trip.

I tried to get Zeeke to wait, but he said he had things he wanted to retrieve. I also think he wanted resolution.

"He's still calling the shots. He doesn't get to do that anymore. I'd just mail him his things and write off whatever you left there because it's too soon to go. The Jell-O needs to set," I said to no avail.

I figured when Zeeke arrived Judd would get inside his head and they'd end up back together. Instead, Judd sat on the sofa with a girlfriend from work and basically ignored him as he packed up. Zeeke got away surprisingly easy.

Too easy.

Judd fumed for weeks, posting passive-aggressive comments everywhere, sending bitter diatribes to Ms. Jamieson and angry messages to people including Kage, "I'll never forgive you for ruining my happiness."

He blew up Marcus' phone asking for help talking to Zeeke, even after Marcus told him he was in Chicago visiting family and there was nothing he could do.

"Am I going to be in the book?" Judd asked me. At that time, I had no intention of including him and told him as much. By the time I realized he was going to be another one of the house's permanent detractors, he had blocked me.

The message to Jeff was the one I found the most bizarre in that it seemed to reveal he felt his six-month rebound with Zeeke outweighed the decade-long marriage with Jeff.

Listen—I resent you and Zeeke discussing our relationship.

You're his (soon to be) ex-husband. He said he did it because you're a neutral third party?

You. Are. His. Not. Even. Ex. Husband. Yet.

I resent it.

Jeff responded: *K*

Debriefing at the dining room table with Zeeke and Kage, I replied, "I could have spent days crafting a masterful comeback that would have fallen short of 'K.' Absolutely brilliant."

Walking back from the kitchen carrying a white coffee mug with a drawing of Judd's face on it, Zeeke asked, "What are we going to do with this?"

It was a strange thing to have in the house to begin with, and his expression in the drawing was oddly serious.

Inspiration struck instantly. I grabbed a black sharpie from my cup of writing utensils. "May I?"

"Yes, please" Zeeke replied.

I drew a big talking balloon with the quote, "I RESENT IT."

Breakup Master Class

Once a week I stopped by Magali's to take out her trash and clean the litter box.

With outings canceled due to the pandemic, she would ask for updates on how everyone was doing.

"Zeeke broke up with Judd, and I had to teach him *how* to break up!" I exclaimed.

"He didn't know how to break up?" Magali asked in astonishment. Breaking up was her specialty. She had been a wild young woman who didn't want to be tied down, and had broken many hearts.

"I coached him a bit with Jeff but that one was easy because it was mutual, so it was mostly just moving past the fear. I don't know if he'd ever broken up with someone who was going to fight it," I said. "If so, it has been over a decade. It was an entire class complete with notes, props and role play."

And it really had. Zeeke sat on the sofa in the parlor and I handed him a bag of flour.

"This is the baby, and by baby, I mean all the expectations and obligations you're currently saddled with. The core of the break up is the handing off of the baby. You're not going to give him warning because he will be prepared to refuse the baby and will be armed with his talking points and manipulation tactics."

While Zeeke sat nervously, I used the big round coffee table for the battle plan.

Setting a folded index card reading, "Now Single" on the farthest edge of the table, I explained, "This is where you need to get to, and the shortest route is a straight line. He will try to pull you off course with distractions," I said as I placed cards reading, "TRAP" elsewhere on the table. "He's going to lure you with insults about your character and anything else he can think of. When he does what will you do?"

"Well, I'll just . . ."

"You reply 'I'm sorry you feel that way,' and continue making a beeline for the exit. The baby will have been handed off, and you will officially be done. If he breaks down, you are not the person to comfort him in that moment. That's what close friends are for, not the person who just broke things off."

After that we had role play, and I think I deserve an Oscar for my role as Judd. I hurled objection after objection, but once he mastered the, "I'm sorry you feel that way," I felt confident he was battle ready. Especially when he finally refused the baby I tried to hurl back at him.

Like a champ.

Mid-June Weekend

It was an ideal summer evening and I was sitting on the front porch with Marcus. He and Kage had a drunken and heated argument the previous weekend, and Marcus had been quiet since, but had also been working long hours—Zeeke got him hired on at his workplace—and doing his college coursework. On Wednesday he sent a message asking if we could talk on Friday, which would be his next day off. When I heard him stirring upstairs, I sent a message telling him I'd be on the porch.

I fully expected him to tell me he was moving out.

Sitting beside me, Marcus calmly explained his side of the argument. One part that hurt him was Kage saying he was ungrateful, which Kage didn't remember.

"He said I was ungrateful and that's not true at all. If not for you guys, I could've ended up on the streets, especially with the Covid shutdown and not having any money. You guys never made an issue of it, always shared food. And then Zeeke got me the job, which I'd been trying to get for years and that would have never happened had I not been here."

Taking this in I replied, "I'm sorry that he said that. He's never said anything like that to me, and we certainly don't feel that way. We love having you here. I was in bed and heard much of the argument, but I thought I'd do more harm than good by coming down. I thought you might feel ganged up on, and that it was best to let you two work it out. I didn't realize how hard Zeeke was taking it, though. I think it triggered his anxiety."

I continued, "I think there can be value in an occasional argument. In this case you were able to see that there can be a disagreement, and it won't change the way we treat you or threaten your home. I've been in situations where one disagreement blew up everything. Once I wrote for a website and raised one objection to an assignment, and found myself locked out. And I tend to be closer with those I've had an argument with at some point."

The conversation shifted to current events centered around the Black Lives Matter movement.

"I had it good in Chicago and I didn't really see racism, or at least I didn't realize it like I do now. I look back and can see examples of race and class divisions, but I didn't really notice it then. It's been heartwarming to see all these people out in the streets."

"We're witnessing a major cultural shift. For years there have been horrifying examples of Black people being unjustly killed. John Crawford buying a toy at Walmart, Tamir Rice playing in the park, and it never shook the national consciousness for some reason. Now it finally has and I think we are going to see profound change."

A big fancy car with the windows down stopped in front of the house. "Hey girl we're going to Grey Fox!" a man yelled.

"Well go on bitches! We might stop in!"

As the car pulled away Marcus asked, "Who was that?"

"Oh, I don't have my glasses on. No idea."

Marcus made a startled expression and then laughed.

I was due to meet the Maven at Bastille, and Marcus said he wanted to join. He and Kage sat in the back seat to have their first face-to-face since the argument while I drove the ten-minute stretch up the meandering Gravois Avenue. It was a very easy and sedate conversation of quiet explanations.

As I approached Bastille, I saw the Maven holding court on the sidewalk with friends sitting around in a big oval. We hugged and I pulled up a few chairs, and then I saw my friend Anthony Jackson, whom I long said had the best smile in St. Louis.

I filled folks in on my history with Anthony. "When I was homesick for St. Louis, a montage would flash through my mind of what I missed, and Anthony's smile was always one of those images. To be out and greeted with that smile . . . it always filled me with joy."

Just about then Juan, the former Mrs. Trickery, wandered up to greet us. I introduced him to everyone, and Anthony spouted off when hearing the name.

"Trickery! Girl she a mess!" he exclaimed with his booming sandpaper voice. "We was at a party one time and I was taking a piss and she saw my dick and pulled down her pants and tried to sit on it right then and there."

"Oh, wow I've got to hear this story," I replied.

"That *IS* the story. I was like naw this ain't happening."

Lydia's turret windows were illuminated. She used to only illuminate them for Halloween and one day Peyton asked if I'd see if she'd keep them illuminated year-round. "It really enlivens the intersection," he said, and when I told her of the request she agreed. The lights were green, but I'd also seen them in orange and red. I wondered if me and Lydia would ever speak again.

Across Russell Boulevard from Lydia's shop was the home of the owners of Grey Fox. I pondered how despite frequenting their bar I had never had a conversation with them, and probably couldn't identify them in a line-up. Soulard gossip sometimes involved their younger third.

A chair opened up next to the Maven and I took it.

"I had a dream about you," she said. "You were ahead of me in a long hallway and I had something I wanted to say but I couldn't catch up with you. How have you been?"

"I feel like I've turned a corner on several fronts. I'm making tremendous progress on the book; I think people have finally seen through my main detractors. I'm also less afraid than I've been in my entire life. My earliest memories are of being terrified by the ghosts in my mom's house, for instance, and I've always been uneasy there but now I plow down that dark hallway like it's nothing. Like I'm daring them to do something."

"Because you can, dear. You have that power."

After a few minutes the Maven said, "I love Villadiva, but you really need to be in Soulard."

"Do you know how much I paid for that house? I couldn't afford anything in Soulard."

"Tower Grove is lovely, but you're away from the river, you're away from the limestone caves, you're away from the spirits and you're away from the energies . . ."

A burly man approached and said hello, and the Maven introduced us, saying he moved to Soulard from Fort Lauderdale for work. We had been preparing to go to a quiet back room for a reading, and invited him to join us. After I read an excerpt involving Soulard, the Maven was in the middle of complimenting it when she looked startled, and then caught her breath.

"I just saw Peyton's face right there," she said. "He was smiling."

Marcus came in and took a seat beside the Floridian, and I could sense there was a mutual chemistry. As we got up to go back out, Marcus said to me, "That guy is hot."

Joe, the Maven's husband, was ready to go and had pulled up in their golf cart. Of course, it was going to take her at least ten more minutes for all of her goodbyes. I approached Joe. "I'm trying to be a good wingman for my roommate. Would you drive him and the Floridian around a few blocks?"

Joe seemed a bit puzzled by the request but agreed. I approached the guys. "C'mon, we're going for a golf cart tour of Soulard."

They both sat on the back of the golf cart, talking about their respective hometowns and their thoughts on St. Louis. When we pulled up to Bastille the Maven was ready, and we hugged goodbye.

I told Marcus we were going home. "Are you just going to take an Uber back?" I asked.

"Yeah, I'll take an Uber," he replied.

World's Best Wingman.

Marcus spent the next two nights with the guy, and on Sunday morning I was sitting at the dining room table drinking coffee with a shirtless Kage and Zeeke. Marcus walked in from his night out in a black cap, black shorts, and a tight bright white tank top that accentuated his muscular physique.

He was telling us about going to JJ's last night and running across Clyde.

"As Clyde was leaving, he said, 'I still remember you not letting me into that party.'"

Clyde and the Closed Portal

Clyde had already been seeing a highly-respected man in the bear community when Zeeke and Rachel closed the portal in the basement. It took him three weeks to notice the large chalk circle drawn on the floor during the ritual, which meant he hadn't been hanging out down there. An encouraging sign.

He asked Ms. Jamieson about the circle and she played dumb, positing that it may have been the cable company who was there for a new tenant.

It was a very slow Thursday night at Grey Fox, on the cusp of 4th of July Weekend. The audience for the drag show ranged from two to ten as people wandered between the bar's two sides, and to and from the patio. Jade Sinclair put on the same show as if the room were packed, except with much more audience engagement between numbers. On this evening she walked table to table taking selfies with everyone's phones.

Kage went home early, and I decided to check in on Clyde for the first time in months, which meant unblocking him. He replied that he had a story to tell me, but he seemed reluctant to discuss it over text. I told him to open the back common door and I'd meet him there.

I walked down the hill and descended the stairs to find him cursing Ms. Jamieson's temperamental dryer as he turned knobs and slammed its door a few times. There was a single overhead bulb partially illuminating the cobwebbed space, and the energy down there was innocuous in a way it had never been.

"Oh, you surprised me," he said.

He looked good, with his dark beard and more confident posture that made him seem two inches taller than I remembered. He seemed bright and put together.

He wanted to talk to me about health news regarding Rick, our former Melrose bad boy. I didn't even know they were still in touch, but he nearly cried as he spoke of him as if we were all still close.

I couldn't shed a tear over Rick considering all the irreparable harm he intentionally caused. Not long before this exchange, Ms. Jamieson sent me before and after photos of a young guy Rick got hooked on meth, and the image of his scab covered face was seared in my mind.

In the basement I kept my opinions of Rick to myself.

Clyde spoke of his boyfriend in the way one would speak of a beloved spouse. There was a lot of "we" and "us." He didn't exhibit any of the lustful or emotional energy towards me that he had in the past.

"It doesn't seem like there's anything down here anymore," I said.

"No there isn't," he said as he surveyed the surroundings. "They're all gone."

For the first time since before the curse I felt Clyde had positive intentions. Just as I felt his demons were gone, I felt some demons inside me were gone as well.

The last time I had overwhelmingly positive thoughts about Clyde I believe I was under a spell. There was something artificial about it, a masking of all negative memories and a glow around everything positive. This was different. I knew every flaw and hadn't forgotten our incredibly messy history, but I felt a kinship in that journey. I felt forgiveness and I felt humility.

If I'm being self-critical, I had originally selected Clyde the way a casting director would select someone for a part. Clyde, by contrast, came to St. Louis to find family in the deepest sense of the word.

Even when we were warring, he still saw me as family, just as he saw Rick. Dysfunctional as it is, he saw me as family when he was casting curses while drunk on liquor and anguish.

"I know Kage will never talk to me again and that's okay," he said, although I knew he was heartbroken.

But it seemed Clyde had finally found the sense of belonging he'd been missing since the Melrose imploded years earlier, and I was happy for him. We hugged warmly and then said goodbye.

Angel

Zeeke hit the scene with zeal once fully unencumbered by Judd, bouncing from one fun outing to another. He seemed so light, effervescent and carefree. And the gentlemen callers were flocking.

Judd threw shade wherever he could on various Facebook posts, telling his story of betrayal and how the House of Villadiva was dead to him, but nobody seemed to bite and Zeeke was having far too much fun to notice.

My strategy was to not give Judd any oxygen.

"Judd's itching for a fight. Just seething," said someone in a group chat I was part of. "Judd said 'I don't even know if I want to be part of the St. Louis community,' and I was thinking, 'She doesn't even go here!'"

Kage brought me coffee in bed one Saturday morning. "Zeeke had an early reading downstairs and now they're in his room," he said with a scandalized cringe.

Adamant he was sticking with his plan, Zeeke would repeat, "I tell them all I don't want anything serious. I'm going to be single for a year."

One of the guys he was seeing was Angel, Rick's disastrous longtime on-again, off-again boyfriend. Angel said he understood Zeeke wasn't in the market for anything serious, but that didn't stop him from executing an impressive courtship.

Zeeke still stressed to us that they weren't a couple, all while seeing Angel multiple times a week, staying the night, and even driving him to a doctor appointment.

When the two were photographed in a downtown rooftop pool on the 4th of July, Ms. Jamieson took note and sent me a message.

Ms. Jamieson: "So are Zeeke and Angel a thing now?"

Me: "Seems so."

Ms. Jamieson: "Interesting."

Me: "I think Zeeke is destined to be in back-to-back relationships."

Ms. Jamieson: "It's funny because he asked me on a date and then that never happened and then he got with Judd and now I still never went on a date with him and he's never came to cleanse my apartment like he said and now he's shacked up with Angel."

Me: "Angel has been quite persistent. Shown up with little gifts, coffee."

Ms. Jamieson: "I'm a little salty. It's stuff like that that makes me go from a good mood to a bad mood. I keep getting passed over and it sucks."

While careful not to make things worse, I attempted to convey that things happen as a result of work and persistence, not taking a number and waiting for a turn.

Me: "Like I said, Angel was ON IT. Zeeke told him he wasn't up for anything serious and he said ok, but then left gifts at the door, surprised him with dinner. It was a full-on courtship."

Ms. Jamieson replied, "Ugh."

Like with Judd, however, it seemed to me Angel's master plan was to have something more exclusive with Zeeke. At 1 a.m. one morning Angel sent a message that things weren't working out because they wanted different things.

Zeeke felt rejected.

"This isn't a rejection. It's a negotiation," I replied.

The Melrose disapproved of Angel back when Rick was with him, and the remaining cast still thought he was bad news. The memories of the terrible fights he'd have with Rick were as fresh as ever. Fights that would get Rick banned from bar and end up with Rick in the psych ward with slit wrists. But knowing the reality of who Rick really was, me and Kage were open to the possibility of having misjudged Angel, and we were willing to give him a fresh start.

"I don't trust him any farther than I can throw him!" Ms. Jamieson said, and it turns out her intuition was based on more than sour grapes. Webster, a friend of Angel's, told Zeeke that Rick and Angel never stopped having sex. This was essentially confirmed when, during an argument over the phone, Angel said, "Rick is coming over."

When Zeeke and Angel walked into a neighborhood restaurant and saw Rick, Angel pushed Zeeke out the door. "I'm afraid Rick will start a fight if he sees us," Angel said.

Rick and Angel had been bonded by chemistry and chaos for years, and I could see that lasting until death. Unfortunately, Zeeke was under Angel's spell as well.

Everyone Loved Cody

While one end of the expansive dining room table was my desk, the other end served as a communal dining area for Zeeke and his gentleman caller du jour. When that was Judd, they were constantly eating delivery, which seemed awfully expensive. And then I learned Zeeke was normally paying for it which made my cringe all the harder to hide. Angel earned far less than Judd but was much more generous, so he normally bought their meals.

Since I was working on the laptop, Zeeke and the gentlemen would converse as if I were in a completely separate room, or maybe like I was the stranger at the next table at a restaurant. But when Zeeke was eating alone he was very chatty, and one evening the topic turned to Cody.

"If the timing was right, I'd be with Cody right now," Zeeke began.

He stopped just short of saying Cody was the love of his life, but that was the impression I got from the discussion.

I think many of Cody's friends were in love with him.

Exchange with Gervais

About two weeks had passed since my clandestine basement meeting with Clyde. That felt like ages ago in the wake of the runaway pandemic, which seemed to have ensnared Zeeke. I opened my email to find a message from Clyde's boyfriend Gervais, which read:

Chris,

Currently you and I have no drama or bad blood between us and frankly I would like to keep it that way. I'm certain you know Clyde and I are in a relationship. I understand you made a late-night visit to Clyde's basement Friday, 7/3/2020. Clyde has shared with me the past nature of you and he and you and he and Kage's relationship. He has explained to me in detail the nature of your relationship. I know about the witchcraft, the spells, the demons in the basement, the darkness, the restraining order and why and how you have the keys to his apartment complex.

Clyde's character was damaged pretty badly by all that has occurred between you and your husband in our small community and he is rebuilding his life that his Mother intended for him to have in the city. If you truly care for Clyde and his happiness on any level leave him be and respect his current relationship and allow him to rebuild his life. As gentlemen I am requesting you respect our relationship and make no further visits to his basement.

We both hold a level of respect in the LGBTQ Community and I would rather not have any drama between us or tension towards each other considering we may be seen in some of the same circles. I hope we have an understanding.

Sincerely,
Gervais

I responded:

Gervais,

I believed in ghosts since I was a toddler, but I never knew anything about curses until he began casting them. Since then, I've had a wild ride.

On May 2nd a psychic medium and her team visited the basement and sealed the portal. July 3 was an opportunity to see for myself if that ominous place really was different, and I now feel confident that the May 2nd effort was a success. That is good news for all of us, especially Clyde.

Our story is widely known but that doesn't mean it can't have a happy ending. I have no problem putting the basement behind me for good.

Below is an excerpt I wrote about that night.

Take care.

I attached the story "Clyde and the Closed Portal."
Gervais responded:

I appreciate you taking the time to respond. I have a question: Did you arrange for the psychic medium and her team to come to the basement and close the portal? Was Clyde present when this occurred? I also appreciate you sharing the details of your meeting 07/03/2020. I'm glad we are able to be respectable and cordial as gentlemen. I wish you the very best of success with your book and I hope it's release is therapeutic and healing for you and your family.

Kind Regards,
Gervais

I replied:

Gervais,

I did arrange for it. My employer owns the building and my friend and co-worker Ms. Jamieson lives upstairs from Clyde and shares that basement. Ms. Jamieson's apartment was plagued with paranormal activity, and I had been told that in addition to getting my home blessed by a priest, which I did, the portal needed to be closed.

Right after the original curse Clyde's bird died and my dog got a tumor which led to his death. During the second round in the Fall our cat had a stroke and is now disabled. I also heard my name being called from the bottom of the stairs when I was in the bedroom and nobody was downstairs (one of the dogs heard it too).

I understand this all sounds like pure madness, and I haven't ruled out the possibility of coincidence, etc. but Clyde believed in what he was doing down there and I became a believer too. (I do not at all believe he intended to hurt the pets. I think those were unintended consequences).

Several times I mentioned getting help to close the portal and he'd sometimes agree, sometimes adamantly disagree, but most often preferred a DIY approach which I had zero faith in. I thought it was better to go down there without telling him so he wouldn't interfere. Getting one expert was tough and if he derailed us it would be nearly impossible to get her back.

Mediums have told me that Clyde needs to be blessed by a priest. That is not my business but I know you love him and want what's best for him. Communing with demons is corrosive to the soul, as I'm sure you can imagine.

I can tell you are nourishing for him and it sincerely brings a tear to my eye. He was for a time a very close friend. We didn't know he was falling in love and when we tried to redirect him everything fell apart. We moved him here when he had a boyfriend who was supposed to come too. We really thought he was a cool guy and wanted to help him set up a new life, just as we had done for Ms. Jamieson and others.

Everyone knows the most sensational aspects of our shared story, and sweeping it under the rug for 50 years wouldn't erase memories. Instead, I think context and a vindicating, humanizing resolution is the way to move forward. I want readers to see that we all did some wild things but it's all over and we're thriving.

Chris

Gervais replied:

I didn't think he had any knowledge of it. It appears it may have worked. Thank you.

Actually, it doesn't sound like pure madness. My family is Creole and Native American and we are from New Orleans originally. I won't go into my family's history. I will just say I'm very familiar with the spirit realm. When Clyde and I first started dating I told him he has a dark spirit attached to him. He told me he practiced Wiccan. He was extremely concerned about what I heard about him or what might be said about him. He kept asking me what have I heard and honestly, I had not heard anything about him. He divulged to me what he thought I might hear that could possibly cause me not to want to continue to date him. It wasn't a turn off because I know my own faith and power.

I too also offered to get the entity/portal out of the basement and he declined the offer. Hence why I asked did Clyde know about it and was he there. I believe that he believes that dark magic gives him power. I've told him if you're cursing others you are only cursing yourself. Be careful how you use your "power." That holds true for any religious faith. If you seek darkness, darkness will find you. If you seek light and enlightenment, light and enlightenment will find you.

I'm sure he does need to be blessed by a priest. He has opened himself up to be a personal portal for demons to come forth. Clyde came from a very prejudiced town as I'm sure you know and I believe he had so much hurt and anger built up that he sought out the wiccan faith and in doing so he became drawn to the dark aspect of the faith believing in its power. This is just my own personal assessment. I do love Clyde. I will support him, encourage him and redirect him towards the light and away from the darkness in every way I can. In the end he has to have the desire to live in the light and not the darkness. Living in the light requires as much work as dwelling in the darkness. The choice is his to choose.

I feel Clyde's hurt and anguish deeply. I'm thankful to be able to empathize and understand his pain and that he has an outlet that he is able to communicate his feelings. Sometimes even the best intentions go awry and don't work out as intended. You were the catalyst to help him get established here. I'm certain he will always have gratitude towards you. In the end he is living in a big city, that was he and his Mother's desire and it's up to him to determine how he wants to live and what he wants for his future. The racist, prejudiced people of Anna win if he continues to hold and carry the bitterness and anger in his spirit and dwell in the darkness. Rather than living his best life and leaving all that ugliness behind him.

May the release of your book be therapeutic and healing and I wish you all the success and happiness for you and your family.

Best Regards,
Gervais

After reading the last letter, Zeeke messaged from upstairs. His fever was nearly 103. He needed a ride to the hospital.

Getting Affairs in Order

Zeeke sat in the back passenger seat and I had all the windows down while driving him to a hospital in an affluent part of town. I'd made the mistake of taking Magali to the city's main emergency room one evening, where we waited for hours as gunshot and accident victims rolled in. This time, I selected a quiet hospital.

I felt certain they'd admit it him, but within two hours they had diagnosed him with bacterial pneumonia and discharged him. Because he disclosed he'd already been tested for coronavirus a few days before and was awaiting the results, they didn't test him.

While writing in the dining room I could hear his relentless coughing upstairs, and sometimes vomiting from the bathroom off the kitchen. When he had some energy, he'd shuffle around a bit in a black mask and a thin charcoal grey bathrobe, which accentuated his gaunt and tattered appearance.

I was a child during the early, and I'd argue the worst days of the AIDS crisis, but the news images were seared in my mind, coupled with the many plays and movies which depicted those days. This pandemic felt a bit like a version of that. Particularly how quickly people could die.

Death was something I spoke of more often than others in my age group. I think that's because of how young Dad was when he died. I'd maintained a life insurance policy since I was 27, and on more than one occasion went over the details of it with Kage. Still, I was worried he wouldn't know how to manage in the aftermath of my death, and that was more urgent now that sickness visited our home.

I contacted our sister-in-law Jenna to fill her in on what was happening, and sent her the life insurance information.

"I'm afraid Kage will freeze up if something happens to me," I began before explaining the policies and what I'd like him to do with the money, which included paying off Villadiva and visiting a financial advisor.

"Oh wow. Okay. Please keep me updated in regard to your health and your roommate's health. I'm sure everything will be okay, but please keep me posted. I have lots of love for you and Kage and you don't have to worry, I got your back."

If something happened to us both, Donald in Oklahoma City was the contingent beneficiary on one of my policies. I told him my brother Bill would take the dogs, and asked him to get Magali to her family in Miami, and get her whatever she needed. The second policy would go to our families.

It was an interesting exercise, thinking of how to prepare and care for those you love after you're gone, and who you trust to carry out your wishes. It puts things into perspective.

Don't Come Home

When Zeeke's results finally came in on Monday July 20, I messaged Marcus. He was in Chicago but I knew he was heading back soon.

"FYI Zeeke's results came back positive."

"Oh man. Is he home now?"

"Yes. When do you get back?" I asked.

"Midnight. So, we need to all stay home I guess? Or can I still go to work?"

"If I were you I'd stay elsewhere. You haven't been exposed."

"Are you feeling okay?" Marcus asked.

"We feel okay so far, but once you've been in the house you have officially been 'exposed to the coronavirus.' Weeks of your life would be sidelined because you're supposed to quarantine."

"Okay."

"Let us know what you need and we'll retrieve it."

"How long will you have to be isolated?"

"Here's the problem," I explained. "Fourteen days since contact. We remain at Day Zero as long as he's sick. There's no end in sight. I'm so depressed."

"Oh man. This sucks. Of course I don't want to get sick but the moment you or Kage starts to feel bad I'm coming back."

Because Marcus was a quiet and private person I sometimes wondered where I stood with him, despite Zeeke saying he spoke highly of me. Quiet and private are not what I am used to. While I had no intention of calling on him if we succumbed to the virus I was moved by his words.

Day Zero Chat with Tom Choinski

The guideline was to quarantine for 14 days after being in contact with someone who had coronavirus, but since Zeeke was actively sick we were effectively living at Day Zero every day, and that was wearing on me. I was preparing for bed when my friend Tom Choinski, the Bostonian, reached out. He, along with "Ladies Who Lunch" Michael Lonergan and Frank Fontana had brought us food and regularly checked in.

"How's it going?" he asked.

"Pretty depressed. Otherwise, me and Kage are still healthy. Zeeke may be a bit better but still very sick."

"I'm so sorry! I want to do something to cheer you guys up."

"Create a vaccine and a cure."

"Ok but it's gonna have a lot of frozen corn because that's all I got," Tom quipped. "I go through cycles. Had one earlier this week."

"Was anger involved?" I asked.

"No, typically heartbreak."

"I get so angry at Trump's enablers. And voters."

"When I was in college my first group of friends were not your typical college group. Half of them were in AA. I learned that people sometimes need to hit rock bottom before rising back up. Sometimes they don't rise back up and don't make it. In many respects Trump supporters, or even friends who don't take this seriously have to go through the same cycle. Not that I'd forgive perfectly capable persons of reason with economic means who still won't wear masks. It's been a struggle. Yet I see our mutual friends also out every weekend with friends doing nothing to help. Do I get angry? Do I write them off? Do I just seal myself in a tower and let Darwinism take its course because I'm fortunate enough to have that option?

"You *are* moving to a tower," I replied.

Tom and his partner were selling their sleek Midtown condo and moving to the 31st floor of 100 Above the Park upon completion in the coming months. The daring building, which critics said resembled everything from stacked cups to a magazine rack to an origami sculpture, was designed by the world-renowned Studio Gang Architects and faced Forest Park in the Central West End.

"What's depressing you?" Tom asked.

"Layers, from the national runaway pandemic to the limbo at home. We are at Day Zero, every day."

"We're both social people, although for me that's Yang, and stay at home antisocial me is Ying. Limbo has made it tolerable. Although the entire St. Louis experience for me has been a form of limbo. In another universe I'm avoiding people on Cape Cod. Although ironically there they are in a scientifically supported phase of reopening. Much of my Facebook feed comes from that alternate universe. I see it every day."

"How much longer until you return?"

"Four years. It's like I'm in a successful sitcom and I'm only in Season 3."

"Things will get more interesting."

"Hell, we've fired the cast and gotten new writers twice already! The tower is reboot three? Four? My time here has been so adrift."

Poor Tom had a turbulent time in St. Louis already. Three years after moving from blue-bubble Boston, Tom's experiences in St. Louis were what he described as "a mix of wild success and heartbreaking disappointment."

The hardest part was adjusting to what he perceived as St. Louis's unique 'division culture.' His first apartment was on the Delmar Divide, Delmar being the thoroughfare that divides some of the region's wealthiest and poorest areas. One block east was one of the city's most exclusive gated communities, made notorious by the gun wielding McCloskeys. Two blocks north, the famous *Meet Me in St Louis* house, now a ruined lot as a product of racist redlining practices. Three blocks east, the last remaining Planned Parenthood abortion clinic in Missouri and frequent headline-grabber on the national news as the state tried to shut it down.

His new city had divorced its county over a century ago and reunification was largely hampered by class division. He couldn't drive more than a few blocks without encountering literal roadblocks designed to keep non-residents out.

In a city full of social activism, he saw conflict among those who should be natural allies; the fact that the city has two competing LGBTQ Pride Festivals on the same day was one example.

And now two sides of the friend group he'd hobbled together—one side anchored by Ron Tellcamp—were at odds over a crazy woman he never met.

Trying to offer some encouragement, I said, "You're hitting your stride, pandemic aside."

"Actually, I agree with you. I've always likened this city to Ancient Rome around 600 BC. The city has a large footprint but its population has shrunk. It's a village inside a city. It's no coincidence I run into the same people all the time like a badly written soap opera."

"My book will be a brilliantly written soap opera."

"I just want to be cast as Susan Lucci."

Reflecting on the AIDS Crisis

In 1991, at sixteen years of age, I began hanging out at Tulsa's gay park along the Arkansas River. When my friends loitering around the picnic tables would see a solitary gay man ten or twenty years older, we found it terribly sad, and would vow we'd never be that guy.

"If we're thirty and alone let's just marry one another," we'd often say,

Although we saw the ravages of AIDS on the news, and I think we all figured that's how we would die when the time came, we still had no real grasp of how the pandemic ravaged the generations before us. While any teenager would likely see thirty as old, what we were seeing really was unique. We were seeing men who had lost their tribe.

Having so much downtime during the coronavirus pandemic, and with Zeeke, who had been young and healthy ten days earlier, fighting for his life upstairs, I found myself thinking of the early days of the AIDS crisis. Of course there is no real comparison when you consider the stigma, the criminal indifference among those in power, and the sheer hopelessness around an AIDS diagnosis. But even as limited as the comparisons were, it was enough to spur me to imagine those early years in a less abstract way than I had before.

That also spurred a memory of a man who was an occasional guest at Villa Ray in the 90s. I was about 23 and he was probably in his early forties. He wasn't the most pleasant person to begin with, but when the alcohol hit he came completely unhinged, angrily wailing about his partner who had died of AIDS. Ray's longtime companion Manny would lead guests to the front parlor while Ray unsuccessfully attempted to console him in the kitchen. I hadn't thought of that man in ages, but his rage made more sense to me now than it did back then.

I had far, far less to be angry about, but I worried about succumbing to my anger all the same. Not about the pandemic, but about those who had been getting under my skin by attacking my family.

Damon once told me that optimism was my super power. I couldn't let circumstances or my enemies diminish that.

Unworthy

For as long as I knew her, Jasmine understood that she was not seen as credible. Many first came to know her as the felonious Spike's messy sidekick and would never view her as anything more. That's why she obsessed over bolstering her claims with screenshots. But weaponizing private conversations only cemented her reputation for being messy, regardless of whether people believed her evidence. And in 2019, when she became the head of her own pop-up house and went all in on bearing false witness, even her receipts were deemed suspect.

Once she exhausted many of the sycophants she earned from her Pride stance, her sphere of influence was largely limited to Ron and their little group of shut-ins. The screenshots, once viewed as her vast arsenal, were now only useful for obtaining yet more hollow validation from her echo chamber. When a friend passed away, for instance, Jasmine's Facebook tribute would be centered around screenshots purporting to prove that the deceased—who was publicly silent on Jasmine's interpersonal conflicts in life—actually sided with her in all her sundry feuds (who does that?). But even those comments weren't the proverbial smoking gun, but were the kind of garden variety, "girl you got this" pep talks you might offer a stranger on the bus.

One of my oft repeated quotes is from a pastor I heard at Metropolitan Community Church of Greater St. Louis in the late 90s: "If you hold two pennies close enough to your eyes, they'll block out the entire Grand Canyon."

For me, Ron and Jasmine had become those pennies.

For his part, Ron almost seemed to go into hiding. Gone were the hot-headed hate threads about the dog and quips about me failing in New York. No more memes taunting Kage for being sad, no bizarre remarks about me killing myself. Instead he dutifully offered an endless supply of validating comments on Jasmine's redundant posts, which people would sometimes send to me along with links he shared which seemed to blame Christine for triggering Jasmine, thus causing her to react poorly.

Two mutual friends, one whom I hadn't spoken to in years, separately reached out in an attempt to negotiate a secret, discrete truce between me and Ron that would not involve an apology. Basically, the very deal I had offered after he first turned against me, Kage and the dog—somehow swept up in her insane tale that Jett was vicious and that we adopted him for spite.

"Ron publicly and resoundingly rejected my offer for civility," I began. "He relished rejecting it. Since then, he lent his credibility to Jasmine's wild claims about my family, and validated her Christine fixation. Ron needs to understand that he is not entitled to my civility, and should *never* expect it."

Writing really is like therapy, and after rehashing the tedious Ron and Jasmine stories it occurred to me that what I resented the most, aside from their cruelty to Kage and harassment of Christine, was just how uninteresting the two were. While not their plan, they got to me in part because there was little literary or entertainment value to their trolling. Nothing noteworthy or clever. Even Trickery had comedic value, and seemed to have an innate sense of timing. He'd go quiet for a year and then briefly resurface with some trademark treachery and then fade out again. It was kind of fun. And he more or less stuck to a plotline, ridiculous as it was. I was the villain who sabotaged all his relationships (and I later recruited Ms. Pauly as my partner in crime!). That's succinct. People can grasp and follow that.

Now, contrast that with:

Me somehow getting away with serial sexual assaults in this town for ten or twenty years without so much as a peep about it from the community;

Adopting her vicious dog for spite in order to defame her by implying he was a good dog;

Me harassing Jasmine to the point the police department of America's most dangerous city was focused on her case *and* roped in the FBI;

A slam-dunk civil suit with 884 pages of evidence was in the works, based on Facebook shade. A suit that waited on the court to reopen when the courts were open. A suit that hinged not on money for an attorney, but on raising money for photocopies. A suit teased and hyped for nearly a year and then just forgotten;

That I lied about a blood curse that was admitted to in writing, with photographic evidence, in a court of law;

My ex-husband in California was collaborating with them.

A known friend of Jasmine's who made a racially clumsy joke was actually *my* friend all along, despite Jasmine being in numerous photos with him on hikes and at get togethers, and zero evidence of me spending time with the man.

Or how about the convoluted case against Christine Elbert? Someone who allegedly triggered Jasmine to the point of insanity by ignoring her, yet simultaneously stalked her to the point she aggressively chased Jasmine down Arsenal and stared her down in coffee shops. How can you sadistically ignore someone *while* stalking them? Talk about threading a needle!

As a storyteller Jasmine and Ron's endless parade of shitty stories tortured me like a drop of water to the forehead every sixty seconds 24/7. And when their flimsy storylines fell flat, which they always did, they'd just slink away from them like they'd never rolled them out at all, without the least bit of self-awareness about what all the dead-end accusations and abandoned plotlines did to their chances of making something, *anything* stick in the future.

I resented that he and Jasmine were ruining the book with their insufferable monotony. And I considered Ron to be especially odious because unlike Jasmine he knew better. She manipulated him to destroy his brand, hand over his credibility for her to piss away in a matter of weeks, and then his pride kept him from doing anything but doubling down.

But my adversaries were big. My adversaries were people who fooled entire metro areas with their scams, convinced police that I was a suspect in a hostage standoff, and wrote deranged letters to my media rivals from prison. My adversaries made headlines for high-speed chases across the state. My adversaries had shocking revelations. My adversaries led to calls from reporters in megacities seeking my quotes and resulted in me hopping on last-minute flights. And my adversaries managed to send fucking demons to my hallway to call out my name. Jasmine *barely* qualified and her drama split the community in two and rocked the Mayor's office. Now my biggest adversary was Jasmine's cowardly manservant who was playing possum? Spike's sidekick's sidekick?

No, that wouldn't do.

It was time to sweep Tellcamp into the dustbin with Ol' Trickery and the other forgettables. Who the fuck cares what she says? Especially post-Jasmine.

And just like that, I gained perspective and had a sense of closure. More importantly I stopped taking the bait.

The Alleys of Grey Fox Hills

One early summer evening, pre-pandemic, I decided to stay home and clean while Kage went down to the corner.

I carried out the recycling and thought about how the decommissioned alley behind our house was like a country road in the middle of the city. It required mowing, but still had patches of busted concrete and asphalt in sections, gravel and dirt ruts in others. I had to hike down it to get to the dumpster on the main alley below, which was inconvenient but didn't bother me.

As I descended, I could hear laughter and Kage getting high pitched—as he was prone to do when excited—while telling a story on the Grey Fox patio which was thoroughly obscured by a forest of bamboo and an ivy-covered crumbling brick wall.

Looking up I could see the illuminated penthouse atop the art deco South Side Tower a few blocks over. The penthouse was home to a leather daddy and his tribe, and featured a sprawling terrace. It was a goal of mine to see and write about it, but it had yet to happen. Looking down the main alley to our street I could see the steep steps leading to the charming cottage where the elderly previous owners of Grey Fox still resided. I met them at a block party and even though they lived across the street from the bar and could see down into the patio from their porch, they hadn't been inside since they sold it many years earlier, and inquired about what it was like now.

There was such a village feel to this rolling corner of the neighborhood, which I dubbed "Grey Fox Hills." It sometimes felt everyone lived here, it was so dense with homosexuals, and there was a camaraderie. These were people who wanted to have fun. Tough, diverse personalities who weren't quick to frighten.

One night at the Grey Fox we were invited to the after party of a young guy who lived around the corner and had a framed tax form in his home proving he'd earned $80,000 one year showing his impressive penis online. He was a character and reminded me of an earlier incarnation of Rick, the former Melrose bad boy, in how jovial he was. He couldn't sit still.

The last Saturday of July, 2020, a couple three blocks over posted a photo of their lovely backyard drenched in the golden evening sunlight with the caption, "Only missing friends."

After tossing that week's recycling in the dumpster I noticed the quiet. No music or laughter. Covid had swept through and impacted many in our orbit, from Zeeke to the Abernathys—our favorite Grey Fox bartenders, and even the guy with the $80,000 penis.

I wondered when things would return to normal.

Geoff Story

The first *Out in STL* feature, written by the interim editor Nicholas Phillips, was about documentary filmmaker Geoff Story and the priceless footage he found of a 1940s gay pool party. The piece went viral and the story was later picked up by major outlets including *The New York Times*.

In 1996 Geoff attended an estate sale in a mansion facing Forest Park, not far from the manor made internationally infamous when the McCloskey's shouted and waved guns at Black Lives Matter marchers. Geoff found the reels in the attic and bought them not knowing what they were. He later learned the palatial home belonged to a once-prominent gay couple, and went about the years-long task of identifying and making contact with the surviving men in the footage.

I'd put Geoff in the top three of community historians in town, along with Steven Louis Brawley and Ian Darnell of the St. Louis LGBT History Project. He had a special interest in elderly drag queens, creating a film about one, Gene Dawson, AKA "Miss Gina," and taking an apartment next to the world's oldest performing drag queen, Bonnie Blake, for a project involving her. The second-floor studio was above Bonnie's antique store on scrappy South Broadway, sandwiched between the LGBTQ bars Hummel's and Bar PM.

One Sunday Geoff visited Villadiva to pick up a few signed copies of *Delusions of Grandeur* for his coterie of aged queens and treated me to a screening of his riveting film about Miss Gina. It included stories about legendary midcentury nightclubs where black and white, straight and queer mixed when that was unheard of. Back when St. Louis was still among the largest cities in the nation. There were also tales of violence, including one about Miss Gina being left for dead in an east side ditch (Miss Gina liked rough trade).

In one scene, Bonnie Blake sits down with Miss Gina, who was nearing the end of her life. Miss Gina was warm and familiar with Bonnie, who was polite in return, but didn't seem to really remember her. Geoff explained that Miss Gina hadn't been an entertainer like Bonnie. She was likely sitting in the dark while Bonnie performed in the spotlight.

"Is Bonnie sentimental?" I asked Geoff. "She strikes me as tough."

"Not so much, I think," he replied.

As I sat down to write about Geoff for the book a month or so later, it occurred to me that I never asked him when he rented the South Broadway apartment or why. Geoff actually lived in a cavernous, elegant and meticulously decorated row house, circa 1864, between Downtown and Soulard.

I sent him a message to inquire.

He invited me to visit the apartment the following Sunday, and sent a photo of a carefully placed mannequin head sitting on a mauve velvet armchair that was probably from the seventies or early eighties.

"Right now it's full of mannequin heads."

Geoff said he bought two heads from Bonnie's store and since then she'd hide new heads around the apartment when he wasn't there.

"Do you recall asking if Bonnie was emotional?" he asked.

"I believe I asked if she was sentimental."

"I saw her cry for the first time yesterday. Her last sibling, Sue, just succumbed to Covid. She's considering moving and selling the shop. She's sad and anxious after this. Nobody comes to the store anymore."

Sunday With Geoff Story

The following Sunday morning I sat an acceptable distance from the ninety-something year-old Bonnie, who was at her big wooden office desk at the front of her crowded shop, while Geoff stood close to the opened door. The large, deep store was overflowing with all kinds of knickknacks, lamps—including a delightfully gaudy candelabra with crimson shades, and a variety of furniture.

She had been in that location since the 70s. I thought about how when something has enjoyed a long run, it felt like it would never end. Since that store "had always" been there, it always would be. In my 40s I was beginning to see what an illusion that sense of permanence was. This special place, the store, the apartments above, the little row of queer businesses accompanying it, was not long for this world.

Geoff understood this far better than I. He was in a mad scramble to locate and interview people in their eighties and beyond for his documentary, particularly those with ties to the historic film reels, and then Covid put everything on ice. He mourned the time wasted. He had sat on these reels for years before inspiration struck, and infinitely more people were alive when he first acquired them.

When Bonnie first opened the door to the space her store now occupied, it was the 40s and the space was a bar.

"I came here to go dancing," she said.

She had owned nearly every building on the block at one time or another, and her late sister had a store of her own a few doors up.

Geoff took me up a flight of stairs to the second floor, where there was a long, wide hall which was decorated with art, including a water color of the very block we were on with its dormered row houses and ornate iron balconies. The hall featured inviting seating areas with doily covered end tables and antique lamps. Several doors were to our left.

"Bonnie combined these units for her own apartment," Geoff said as we made our way to the end of the long hallway. He pulled out his keys and opened the door to a sunny, tidy, and clearly unlived-in apartment with high ceilings. The furnishings, while sparse, reminded me of something old people would have had when I was a child, including the mauve chair, mint green vintage sofa and proper coffee table. The apartment, the furniture, the neighboring nightclubs, it was somewhat reminiscent of David Lynch's *Blue Velvet*.

Through the ivy-covered windows to the north, I could see the large backyard and patio of Hummel's, the hardscrabble lesbian-owned bar next door.

"How long have you had the apartment?" I asked.

"Six months," he replied. "I thought the interviews would be more natural and organic if I was close by."

I assumed we would settle in for a while, but the apartment felt more like a set. Geoff never sat down. I asked if he ever stayed the night there and he said no.

"She charged $500 a month, but when seeing how little I was here she said, 'How about we knock that down to $250."

It was clear the two had gotten quite close. If I lived to be that age and had someone who wanted to hear and document my tales, I know I would be happy.

I asked about the third floor and he agreed to show it to me. The light faded as we approached the slanted staircase with its thick antique banister leading up to a door with a four-pane window.

"She found one tenant dead right here. He was sitting upright on the stairs, like he had gotten winded and sat down," Geoff said.

The vacant third floor apartment was charming, with French doors, a large front window with lace curtains, and a sweeping arch between the kitchen and living room. It seemed it had been vacant for some time. Back downstairs, Bonnie told me two guys had once occupied it for fifteen years.

I perused the store and found a decorative New Orleans plate for $4 and handed her the money. "Go find another you like and you can have it," she offered.

Geoff had tried to prompt stories from her with some success, and while she wasn't especially talkative that morning, she seemed tickled by our attention.

Bonnie wasn't soft. She was a veteran with thick hands who had sometimes run with mobsters while in drag in the 40s and 50s.

"These girls today are so dainty," she laughed. "I see them fluttering back and forth out here . . . we were never like that."

Geoff had given her my book and said she'd remark, "That girl sure did move around!" in reference to my adventures.

"I'd say, 'You know Chris is a man, right?' and she'd reply 'Oh I know, and she sure did like to move around!'"

Geoff thought for a moment. "I'm sure she refers to me as a girl, too."

Nadine on Ms. Pauly

Sitting at the bar with Geoff, Nadine chatted us up. "Covid really swept through Bastille. They shut down for two weeks! Lisa West got it. I talked to her today and she's slowly recovering."

Ms. Pauly took leave when Covid hit months earlier, and Nadine asked if I thought she would ever return to work.

"I don't think so," I replied.

"I don't either. I asked Ray and he said, 'I think Pauly is settling in to quarantine.'" Nadine recalled.

I've mentioned Nadine and Pauly's Grace Adler - Karen Walker dynamic. Nadine was wistful contemplating the end of an era, but her humor was intact.

"I know he doesn't do the best job. He's not the friendliest. People don't always get all their food. But he was there for me."

Meltdowns at the Melrose

"Clyde messaged me last night saying the portal was open again and it was all his fault," Ms. Jamieson told me at work first thing one morning. "What's interesting is he is owning being a witch now, which was something he always downplayed."

"I noticed that too," I replied.

Jasmine had been saying the story of the Satanic curse was false as a way to undercut my credibility, seeming to forget it was all immortalized in court documents and wasn't even disputed by Clyde. Rather than being charmed by the effort, Clyde, who thoroughly detested Jasmine, was mortified that anyone might think he'd joined her house. He was proud of his manly, dangerous and rugged image and knew being aligned with the Saccharine Sisters Support Group was not on brand.

Clyde posted, "Let me make something clear. I practice witchcraft, not bitchcraft."

I did not mention to Ms. Jamieson that Clyde had messaged me as well. In the late-night note, he wrote:

"It's opening back up and I can't stop it. It's affecting me and Jordan. He messaged me wanting to fuck around. I told you before you have a darkness that follows you, and it guides your hand in everything you do. So stop, please."

"Your glamour spells must be making Ms. Jamieson horny. It wasn't my doing," I replied, receiving no response.

That evening Zeeke posted a picture of himself with his arms around Angel. It had a high-school sweetheart vibe, like Zeeke was the star quarterback and the smaller Angel was the head cheerleader.

It triggered Ms. Jamieson.

"Can I ask you a question?" Ms. Jamieson asked Zeeke over text, followed by questions regarding why he dated both Judd and Angel after once mentioning taking her on a date. "I feel I've been passed over twice!"

I was at my spot writing and Zeeke was at the head of the table reading the messages while eating toasted seaweed, clearly exasperated.

"Didn't you have the same issues with Marcus?" Zeeke snapped.

Ms. Jamieson had a rendezvous with Marcus but felt he ignored her afterwards and was in a huff about it, vaguebooking daily while also grousing to our group chat. "Well, it's been 23 days since I sent him a Merry Christmas message and no response," she'd fume.

Marcus indicated he liked Ms. Jamieson but had gotten busy with school. When he took note of the bitter vaguebooking, it gave him pause.

Answering Zeeke's question, Ms. Jamieson simply replied, "Yes."

Looking over at me, Zeeke rolled his eyes. "The Melrose is a minefield right now."

The Opportunist Strikes Again

It had been five years since my then-friend Dickery saw an opportunity to slit my throat for a few minutes of attention, and he stayed true to form when giddily posting that, "Someone who lives with a local gossip queen," had MRSA (flesh eating bacteria) and had been to JJ's Saturday night.

I knew that Zeeke had a brief scare when sores developed under his arms after recovering from Covid, but within an hour the doctor determined it was a mere yeast infection. I sent him the Trickery screenshots and then called him. He was out to dinner with Angel.

"You need to think about who you talked to in that first hour and determine who spread this," I told him.

"Okay, I'll be back to the house in about half an hour," he replied.

Meanwhile I went on Facebook Live to clear the record.

"I'm on here talking about things that should not be discussed, but it's critical because dirty Ol' Dickery had decided to, like he always does, that guy jumps at any chance to get attention, so now he's targeting Zeeke, because Zeeke lives here.

"As most of you know Zeeke had coronavirus. The entire house was quarantined for weeks. Many people brought us everything we needed during quarantine. Zeeke has fully recovered except you do get a lot of, um, complications. So on Sunday he had something under his arm, and again I feel so gross even having to talk about this because it's not right. He had something under his arm and his first thought was, 'Is this MRSA?' you know, 'Is this something really bad? So he went to Urgent Care, got it checked out and it was a yeast infection. Again, I resent that I have to talk about this, but it was a yeast infection and he noticed it on Sunday.

"So pathetic Ol' Dickery gets on Facebook and says someone with MRSA was at JJ's, as if our bars aren't having a hard enough time right now. It was a lie. He doesn't care that it was a lie because he's a pitiful, pathetic person. Just because he dates guys young enough to be his grandkids doesn't mean he has to be at their maturity level. In fact, those kids are a lot more mature than he is.

"Zeeke Harris does not have flesh eating bacteria. He had a simple yeast infection that's already cleared up. He didn't know about it until Sunday. And the reason I am talking about this is because TRICKERY could get JJ's shut down with all his rumors, so I needed to address it. So, sorry I had to talk about someone's personal health but that's where we're at."

While I was recording, Kage determined how this got out. The leak was from Zeeke. In a moment of frustration, he posted a status about how he might have MRSA. Kage messaged to remind Zeeke he had made that post, at which time he removed it.

"He's unsophisticated about living in the city," said Kage, who himself had a long and painful learning curve beginning with Rick's Melrose betrayal and extending to the more recent Saccharine Sisters attacks.

"It's like when he announced he had coronavirus without giving us a moment to absorb it and plan our response," I replied.

Zeeke walked in and handed me his fungal infection diagnosis so I could post it. "Angel is waiting in the car because he thinks you're going to yell," he said.

I had never yelled at either of them, but he had mentioned Angel was afraid of me.

What's rich about Trickery calling me a gossip queen is that he was the biggest and least accurate gossip in town. For instance, he regularly told his friends that I was the writer behind the raunchy Penelope Wigstock and Penny Gosling characters, when playwright Donald Miller had been outed as the writer by Spike via Gassy five years earlier. The very Spike he turned on me for.

His own friends would try to explain this to him, but he was adamant.

"No, no. I have it on reliable sources that it's Andoe."

A few months later he posted to one of the gay groups that he had been single for 10 years. I posted to my Facebook:

Someone in town has often claimed I'm the reason all his relationships ended over the past 5 years, but now he's on sites claiming to have been single for 10 years. I guess that means I'm exonerated.

Roth

I threw shade over the topic of Trickery's young boyfriends mainly because he blamed me for the demise of his relationships, and I generally just enjoyed shading Trickery. But I actually had no real problem with age differences and found it inspiring that gay men of all ages were deemed attractive as of late. That certainly hadn't been the case when I first came out. A gay man's shelf life was short.

Among my friends, none inspired me more in this area than Roth, a 60-year-old tattooed, masculine brunch regular who always had the best-looking younger companions. They weren't Trickery-style barely-legals, but were often in their late twenties or early-thirties. Roth also dated Cody for a time.

Me and Kage were in New Orleans for a debaucherous festival called Southern Decadence, and found ourselves on a block full of St. Louisans. Among them was a tall Black guy I had found attractive since I first laid eyes on him in 1997, and the man was standing in the street crying because he had slept with Roth the night before but Roth didn't want anything serious. I think I handle aging pretty well, but there's always the concern of one's attractiveness waning. The thought that I could possibly have an incredibly sexy guy decades younger crying over me at sixty was motivating.

Roth was a free spirit, and lived near the beach in Florida for a few months at a time. His wandering ways weren't conducive to serious relationships, but he seemed okay with that. And I think he enjoyed the variety.

Whenever Roth said he'd join us for brunch we just planned on him having +1, so we were surprised one day when he greeted us in the street by himself.

"You're traveling solo today? We're always expecting to see a handsome gentleman caller with you!" I said.

"Yeah, I normally have one, and I take them all to meet Nadine."

Zeeke's Initiation

The day after the Trickery turmoil Zeeke walked into the den where I was reading, and took a seat by the bay window to debrief.

"Why would Trickery come after *me*?" he asked.

"Because you're part of the house," I began. "The house goes back generations. It's a lineage of friends traced back to Ted & Lenny, who lived above the legendary nightclubs of Gaslight Square and frequented the same haunts Bonnie Blake did in the 1950s; of Ray, who had his own booth at the disco Herbie's in the 70s, and who welcomed me to his dinner parties and famed New Year's Eve events in the 90s, and it continues with you taking up residence at Villadiva.

"Trickery was part of the house until melting down over the joke I wrote about Spike for Tim Beckman's roast in 2015. Since then, he's alienated everyone including Ms. Pauly after trashing me every time he was around her, and then accusing her of being my co-conspirator in breaking up his latest May—December relationship.

"He's told people I ruined his reputation and social life. He's the ultimate opportunist, and when he heard the MRSA rumor, he saw an opportunity for some payback. But each time he comes for me it goes terribly for him. He's nothing if not the perfect foil."

I felt that Zeeke was beginning to better understand that he was part of something much bigger than himself, and that his place made him a target for total strangers.

Bonnie's 92nd

Sunday Funday at the scrappy Hummel's Bar on South Broadway didn't get going until about 3 p.m., but at a quarter till one I was enjoying a Bloody Mary alone in their backyard gazebo while looking up at Bonnie Blake's ivy covered building next door. The bushy vines which engulfed the three-story brick wall were cut back around the two side windows to Geoff Story's second-floor apartment, but they were working to retake that territory.

After the cocktail I made my way next door for Bonnie's 92nd Birthday Party, which Geoff was filming for his documentary. Bonnie was dressed sensibly in a short blond wig, flowery grey blouse and black slacks, and was surrounded by about ten friends and family members.

"How does it feel to be 92?" Geoff asked her.

"It's okay. You can't fight it," she replied, smiling.

Family members said Bonnie's store became the living room during events, and it certainly had that feel. When Geoff stepped to the side to adjust his camera, he updated me on his other primary subject and muse, Gene Dawson, AKA "Miss Gina."

Gene was dying.

"I didn't know if they'd let me in. The nurses there are great, they are mostly Bosnian women and they know me. They weren't sure if he wanted visitors because his light was off, but they came back and said I could go in. He was clearly a dying person, shriveled up to the size of a child. He reached his hand out and I reached out towards him without making contact, doing the distance thing. I said, 'I have to follow the rules,' but thinking about it now, I should have touched him. He's dying. He said 'I just want to die,' and I told him his stories would live on because of the work we did together, and he nodded."

Geoff was holding it together remarkably well for someone who had just experienced that heartbreaking goodbye. I thought of the other goodbyes he'll have to face after becoming so close to these elderly icons.

Sitting next to Bonnie, I asked how she met Ted and Lenny, the patriarchs of my house. It's a question I had wondered about but failed to ask.

Overhearing the question, Bonnie's sixty-something niece asked "How are Ted and Lenny?"

"Well, Lenny passed a year or so ago. Ted is adjusting and is grateful for Ray and Pauly, who look after him," I replied.

The woman, who had just lost her mother (Bonnie's sister) to Covid sat silently for a moment.

"I loved Lenny. That's who I'd talk to when we'd all go out to dinner. Bonnie had Ted and I had Lenny."

"Did you know Grandma?" Bonnie asked.

"Yes, I did," I replied.

"Grandma" reminded me of an older Rod Stewart and ran a bar called Grandma's Rainbow's End where Sensation later was, and then moved down the street and opened a bar called Grandma's, which looked like a grandma's living room and was probably furnished by Bonnie. Grandma was a riot and could have me laughing to the point I couldn't breathe. He was also a generous person who often had buffets of food out at no charge.

"Ted and Lenny came in there and we hit it off. They knew all the people and places I did, but we didn't meet until then," Bonnie said. "Then" being around the mid-2000s.

After sandwiches and cake Bonnie decided everyone should go next door to Bar PM. I told them I would go first and make sure we had seats. It sounded like a party as the loud music could be heard from the street, but when I opened the door there was only one person at the bar: my friend Salam.

Salam greeted me warmly and we had much to catch up on since we hadn't seen one another since the pandemic began six months earlier. He was impressed that me and Kage did not get sick while taking care of Zeeke.

Speaking of Zeeke, he said after the breakup Judd vowed to expose Kage as a homewrecker.

"I said, 'but Zeeke's poly and you guys were open,' and he said, 'But we had rules! And started to explain all the rules and I just glossed over and dropped it," Salam laughed.

Our deadbeat former roommate Niles also came up.

"It's so weird I ran into you because just today he asked if I still talk to you guys and I said we sometimes chat over Facebook and he was like, 'Eww.'"

Geoff, Bonnie and the group shuffled in and took their seats alongside me, but I think the music was too loud for their tastes. After one round they returned to the shop.

A large man walked in and sat as far from us at the bar as possible.

"Hey, come join us!" Salam said to the man.

"Naw I'm good," he curtly replied.

"That's my boyfriend," Salam said quietly. "He never wants to go anywhere or do anything, but he somehow found me here."

Despite the bizarre situation, we continued a lively discussion for another half hour as the man glared. We discussed the music Salam had been working on with a London-based producer, the book, and what it's like dealing with a partner with depression, i.e., the man at the end of the bar.

"He's probably going to break up with me now," Salam said, not sounding overly concerned.

"Accept it as your Get Out of Jail Free Card if he does," I replied. "There's no reward for staying another twelve days or twelve years. He'll hate you when it's over regardless."

The man soon got up and walked past us and out to the patio.

"I'm taking this as my Get Out of Jail Free Card," I said as I hugged him goodbye, grateful to avoid the awkwardness of passing him on the way out.

I walked through the opened door of the shop where Bonnie and about six friends sat. Bonnie seemed really happy, with a big smile on her face. I wished her a happy birthday and said I was heading out.

"Are you going home with that guy?" she said pointing in the direction of Bar PM. "He's cute!"

Flipping the Script

I find it pompous to describe someone as a fan, but it really fits when it comes to Randy, a guy I would run across at Bar PM and Grey Fox. He loved to sidle up and complement my writing, talk about my first book, and tell me who should go in the next one. And he had a lot of suggestions. Most were about guys who were once prominent but lost everything because of their drinking or drug use.

"He lost his job with the city, burned every bridge and is now a recluse. Nobody has seen him in, I don't know, five years" he'd say.

He also loved stories about Gassy, the hothead who moved down to Memphis shortly after my evil surprise at his clandestine birthday bash.

"He's a nut. I think he's running from the law, myself," Randy said.

When he wasn't peppering me with leads, he was talking about his quiet, masculine husband's impressive dick. "Oh, it's huge. He's a total top and I don't mind," then looking me in the eye and using his hands to communicate the size, he'd mouth expressively, "Huge!"

One early evening on the Grey Fox patio, after fifteen minutes of story ideas, Kage quipped, "Chris could write a whole book about your suggestions!"

The conversation eventually shifted to travel, but dick was still involved.

"We flew to Manchester because we were really into soccer boys."

"Were? That shit doesn't go away," the normally silent husband chimed in across the table without looking up from his phone.

"They're hot as fuck. Of course, they don't have teeth, though. That's how you know they are locals."

"That's not true," the husband interjected.

When the husband went in to get a drink Randy unloaded about how much the man was getting on his nerves since the Covid layoff.

"He does nothing all day. He won't even go to the store," Randy lamented.

"Well at least he gives you the good dick," I said.

"Actually, I'm giving the dick now," he said dryly as he sat expressionless. "He flipped."

The Brick

The crumbling back wall at Grey Fox was a constant topic of conversation on the patio. Trees were growing out of it. Water poured down the inside when it rained. The mortar was completely missing in many places. I worried it would collapse and the bar would shut down for good.

I always asked people in the position to buy a bar, like Sean and Jack Abernathy—who worked there, if they'd buy it. I was attempting to plant seeds, just as the bird droppings planted seeds in the wall's busted crevices.

A friend said the owner was out there one day, so he brought it up.

"When are you going to do something about this back wall?" the friend asked.

"There's nothing wrong with this wall!" the owner replied.

The friend then walked over and pulled a brick from it and held it out as evidence.

"Put that back! You're not supposed to pull a brick out of a wall!" the owner said.

"You're not supposed to be *able* to pull a brick out of a wall!" the friend replied.

Frank Fontana's Birthday Poem

He's a lady of leisure living in one of the fine villas of Pasadena Hills, and tossing items into a stranger's cart is how he gets his thrills.

He presents more new cars than The Price is Right, and spoke up when someone started a Zeeke rumor for spite.

At first blush you might find him as discreet as a mouse, but he said 'PENIS' ten times at Chris' Pancake House.

You might also assume he's mild-mannered, or maybe you've been told, but he's been spotted on the shoulder of I-70 with a man in a choke hold!

The famed Villadiva Dining Room, where we entertain the tramps, features his former table, and his two elegant lamps.

He's famous for his delicious cakes which always stop the show, but don't ask him to bake one for someone he doesn't know.

Police at Javier's

"Hey Chris!" Javier shouted as I got out of the car one afternoon. He was strutting towards me, clearly agitated. Gesticulating towards his car in the street, he continued, "The neighbors down the block, they hit my car when they were parking and then called me the N-word. They called the police, who are talking to them now. They're saying I threatened them. Can I have them come talk to you to vouch for me?"

His eyes were bulging and bloodshot, and he had an air of desperation I had never seen in him before. He was anxious.

"I'm so sick of that goddamn word," he said.

"Sure, I'll talk to them," I replied.

I really didn't think they would want to speak to me since I was not a witness to the incident, but about ten minutes later Marcus came in.

"Javier is asking for you. Guess he wants a white person to vouch for him," he said sarcastically.

I could see two officers in the decommissioned alley talking to Javier and his wife, who were standing on their elevated deck. I walked to the back fence where a Latino officer who seemed thrust with the ordeal turned to me.

"There was an altercation with the neighbors down the block. They said he's a nuisance. Have you had problems with him?" he asked.

Javier and his wife were both pleading their case with the other officer who had their attention. I was able to speak freely.

"Javier keeps order around here," I replied. "He's gruff and abrasive but I miss him when he's not around. He was away for a few weeks once and a dozen kids were throwing debris over the fence. I knew they wouldn't have done that if he'd been here," I replied.

I don't know what occurred between Javier and the neighbor, but I imagine Javier was being Javier. Warts and all I had grown to value his contribution to Grey Fox Hills, and was glad I could do a solid for him in return.

Prior to this incident Javier avoided eye contact and didn't regularly acknowledge me. But after that he always greeted me by name. A few weeks later, one sunny Sunday morning, I was walking up the alley when he yelled from his deck, "Hey Chris! I'm having a birthday party back here next Saturday at five and I'd like you guys to come. We'll be grilling and playing dominoes. I'll be 52!"

"Great! I'll be there!" I replied.

An Evening with the Three Mrs. Greeleys

Jasper Greeley was Cody's infamously hotheaded ex. I say ex, but they were still married only because Jasper, who was living in Colorado or Utah (He moved a lot and I couldn't keep track) always had an excuse for not signing the papers.

We had a small shindig at Villadiva for Marcus' going away, and it was a total fluke that *three* Mrs. Greeleys were in attendance. Twan, who was the most intoxicated at the party, had been with him beneath the turret that fateful 2017 Mardi Gras when he threw a beer can at Cody. Greeley later broke Twan's arms. Then there was Travis, who was with him for quite some time and seemed to be the best at calming him. Travis was on the *Maven of Mardi Gras* cover, and months earlier had a one-time rendezvous with Zeeke.

When our stockpile of wigs came out, Travis put on a full show that, minus wardrobe and make-up, was ready for any drag stage in town. He was definitely the most gender-neutral of the three, and he had a dancer's body and choreographed moves. A wigged Miss Jamieson attempted to be his backup dancer, but wasn't ready for prime-time.

I don't know if Twan was normally an angry drunk, but he was a bit salty with Travis, several times saying, "You slept with him while we were still together!" but later hugging him and saying, "I don't even care about all that." Then, repeating it all again.

Twan asked for a tour of the house, and when the two of us got to the bedroom he tossed me on the bed, sat on my waist and held my arms back. "You are everything a Black man wants in a man," he said.

He was really strong but I somehow managed to make him laugh and wormed my way out from under him. He later threw up on the front lawn, all over his cloth mask.

Cody was interested in marrying Jake, and a few days after the event he sent Jasper another message asking about the papers. Jasper responded with a photo of his face covered in blood, with a big gash across his forehead. He had fallen down a mountain. He then sent another photo from his hospital bed where his latest partner, a young, smiling Black man, was hugged up with him.

"Just able to get back to messages. Yes I definitely want this matter taken care of, not avoiding you, had a serious accident. As you know I live a life of very high activity than not many people can. When I'm able to give this matter more attention I definitely will. You and Jake are fairly sedentary so please take the initiative to expedite as much of this as you can, and be as proactive as you can instead of the reactive measures you've displayed in the past. I will reach out when I'm able. All the best to you guys."

Cody replied, "I'm glad you're ok. You are a very lucky man. Believe me when I say nothing would give me more satisfaction than serving you divorce papers on that hospital bed. I was hoping that accident would knock some sense into you. Guess I was wrong. Bye, Humpty Dumpty."

It seemed to annoy the fuck out of Jasper that people enjoyed their lives in St. Louis, as if everyone in his hometown should instead follow his adventures and shower him with adulation. About once a year he'd go on an angry bender where he'd stay up all night either posting insults to the celebratory photos of St. Louisans, or sending them nasty messages, normally telling them they were fat. I got one of those, along with most local guys I knew.

Marcus Moving On

It was challenging to wrap my mind around the finality of Marcus' last moments at Villadiva as he loaded up to move home to Chicago. Even though I knew from the beginning he was just passing through, emotionally there was a feeling of permanence, irrational as that was.

Many of these pages were written from my spot at the table while the chandelier crystals would occasionally rattle and the ceiling would creak from his movements in his room upstairs. Those creaks were comforting.

Me and Kage carried box after box and then there was nothing left but the furniture I excitedly bought in preparation for his arrival. We had felt like we were expecting a new baby when he told us he was moving in, and I dropped everything and went furniture shopping.

Marcus hugged us as he carried the last bag.

"It started with Beef and Beans and turned into all this," I said, referencing his Instagram handle and how we became acquainted.

He came back in to get a blanket out of the dryer.

"One more hug," Marcus said as he gave me a kiss on the cheek. "I love you. You guys have done so much for me."

The House of Villadiva sent Marcus home better than we found him, and I was proud of that. Zeeke helped get him a transferable job with benefits, Frank helped him get his first car . . .

Watching him drive away in that car was much harder than I expected. Kage cooked breakfast while I sat down to write while the emotions were still fresh.

No sounds from above.

The Columbus Statue

The Christopher Columbus statue was finally removed from Tower Grove Park, which set off ripple effects that would change the face of LGBTQ St. Louis.

It all began with a debate over the removal of the statue on the Facebook wall of Just John manager Kareem Lahai-Pumagoi, 28. A guy opposed to the removal was far outnumbered on the thread, and so he tagged another gay Republican, Bruce Roider, for support. Bruce was a bodybuilder in his early forties who somehow attracted a large and fervent online following of horny housewives from far and wide, which he'd mobilize against his enemies.

When Bruce himself was hammered on the thread, he called Just John co-owner John Arnold and furiously demanded Kareem be forced to apologize or be terminated, otherwise Bruce vowed to have his legion of followers bombard the bar with bad reviews.

The unflappable John Arnold essentially told him to fuck off.

Bruce then switched gears, targeting legendary entertainer Krista Versace's coveted perch at Runway, since she defended Kareem. In that original thread Versace alluded to Bruce's HIV status in a remark about how she would expect him to be more compassionate. When the argument escalated, she called him out for (allegedly) being a sex worker. Bruce and his followers went to Runway owner Braden Bardoux demanding she be fired for disclosing his status.

A glaring problem with that claim was Bruce had been in more than one magazine discussing his status. Still, Bardoux folded. .

I tended to steer the spicier content away from the magazine to my private label. I strove to make *Out in STL* bigger than me, which is why we'd often cover people I didn't know or maybe some who I didn't get along with. I didn't want to be seen as weaponizing the platform.

I decided to cover the Runway controversy on my blog.

Gay Republicans Cancel Krista Versace—chrisandoe.com

I've joked privately to friends that Krista Versace is our own Elektra–the villainess diva on *Pose*. She's a bitch and always has been, but she's fierce and she's ours.

Yesterday Versace was fired from Runway after a handsome gay Republican with a large social media following accused her of bullying him and disclosing his HIV status and past drug use. The post where the exchange took place, which was on Just John bartender Kareem Lahai-Pumagoi's wall, has been removed. I haven't seen images of the comment and it seems images haven't been produced.

"I never said he had HIV. I said he was a drug addicted porn star prostitute and has had his virus for over two decades, something he's publicly talked about," Versace said in reference to the man's interview with POZ Magazine.

"I hate to see it," begins longtime follower Mac Taylor upon hearing of Versace's termination. "Krista is a bitch but a bitch you enjoy. Like an Alexis Carrington. I remember she had on this baby blue jumper once, sipping on a glass of white wine at the back bar at the Complex. I stopped and told her, mid sip, that the blue was a really good color for her and without missing a beat as I walked on toward the bathroom, she yelled back at me 'ANY COLOR!'"

According to bartender Kareem Lahai-Pumagoi, the same gay Republican behind the campaign against Versace has been viciously targeting him over his support of Black Lives Matter for some time. On a since-deleted post where Lahai-Pumagoi shared numerous screenshots, he writes: "This dude is trash. So obsessed with clout chasing. His narcissism knows no bounds and I love how he's attempting to intimidate me by blowing up my IG and Facebook page. It's harassment and you have zero power over my life."

I'm withholding the name of the gay Republican and his known Trump supporting associates at this time as I wait to see a fuller picture of what occurred in the coming days. I don't condone mocking someone's status, period. As far as being bullied, though, it's hard to see someone as a victim when they love trolling "libtards" and using their sizable following to harass people of color.

Knowing that Kareem Lahai-Pumagoi seems to be next on the gay Republican hit list, it's important for the community to be vigilant. In St. Louis especially we've seen cancel culture co-opted by narcissists time and again to advance their own self-interests.

*　*　*

(Yes, that last line was a swipe at Jasmine and her followers.)

An Open Letter to the House of Bardoux' Katherine Newman

The focus on Runway and Bardoux ignited a much larger conversation about the way Bardoux treated people, with former employees and even customers coming forward with complaints.

Runway cast member Katherine Newman had left the Markstone's Drag Embassy to join Braden Bardoux, and went on Facebook Live to say all of the accusations against Bardoux were false. That spurred an impassioned reply from Mother Alicia Markstone.

Mother Markstone had known Katherine since they were in their teens, and their tumultuous journey went from the Ozarks to decades in Florida to St. Louis. In the Facebook post, Markstone wrote:

Katherine Newman, As I watched your performance tonight I was actually saddened by your life. For the 35+ years I've known you, you have continually destroyed not only me but everyone you have come in contact with. Thrown me to the trash so many times to get what you want I have lost count. I didn't want to forgive you this time but you sat on my couch and said, "I have changed a lot. I'm not that horrible person anymore." I gave in because unlike you I am good. I was good enough to sew for you for nearly free. All the way up to the minute you lied about everything and frantically moved out because I was "evil." Well the week before you did this I was okay enough to make you 7 costumes for New Year's Eve. For free. Yep, that's evil. You knowingly took the side of someone that did me horribly wrong. You let him be so mean and cruel to me, because he could give you work and be your meal ticket. But you have done this my entire life to me. You have never been good to me, you have always used me. Had me put in jail for something you were responsible for and threatened my ability to get HIV medicine. All the time. You have been run out of every place you've ever lived because you are evil. I was still afraid of you until I realized that I lived in a city that sees you're evil too. I am proud and you can no longer hurt me. I have reclaimed my strength that you have stolen from me over 35 years.

Community Reacts to Runway Controversy

The community was outraged by the firing of Krista Versace and the various reports of mistreatment, and organized a protest outside of Runway to call for Braden Bardoux' removal. Virtually all of Runway's big-name entertainers quit in solidarity. The club brought in a queen from New York, and largely filled out the cast with lesser-known performers from small surrounding towns.

Chuck Pfoutz took things a huge step further, alleging Bardoux sexually harassed him. In a blog post he dubbed Bardoux, "The Harvey Weinstein of St. Louis."

Chuck's involvement in the protest effort created an uneasy alliance because some in the Trans community had been feuding with him for some time. They had managed to cancel his trans-focused fashion show at Soulard's Mad Art Gallery, and in turn Chuck took credit for canceling the lightly-attended Monday night show of two of the performers who targeted him.

Protest organizer Simone Shasta reached out days before the rally to gingerly tell me that some said they didn't feel safe with Chuck in attendance, and they planned to ask him not to attend. Chuck was a petite little computer programmer and it was hard to imagine anyone being afraid of him. I then learned that the head of the effort to ban him was one of Jasmine's minions who followed Christine Elbert into Shameless Grounds and then tried to get her banned. The Banning Bandit!

"Has anyone asked that I not attend?" I asked.

"No," Shasta replied to my amazement.

Braden Bardoux was villainous enough to unite the drag houses of St. Louis in closing down the street outside his establishment in protest. Nearly fifty people, mostly entertainers, attended the Sunday morning demonstration, including Jade Sinclair, which surprised me because she wasn't known to be in the fray. Simone Shasta, a community leader for decades (despite some ethical scandals) did a remarkable job leading the group along with her beautiful drag daughter, rising star Chasity Valentino. Mother Markstone commandeered the bullhorn for a time, rallying the crowd, and of course Krista Versace was marching.

When people were invited to speak, me and Cody stepped forward and I told the story of how he had been treated that first night, and how that set the tone for what we'd see going forward. Because Runway was a "community" business, I, like many others, overlooked a great deal. For me, that included overlooking the mistreatment of one of my dearest friends when deciding to hold an event there, which I deeply regretted.

The Banning Bandit didn't even participate, but I was amused to see Chuck peeking out from behind a traffic light pole at the corner, live streaming the marchers from a distance.

"Chuck! Is that you?" Zeeke yelled down the block as Chuck ducked out of view only to peek out again moments later.

Bardoux' Backlash

Several of the high-profile queens were targeted at their day jobs in the weeks after the protest. Janessa Highland's real estate office was bombarded with unrelenting bad reviews from fake profiles, as well as accusations she was racist. But Simone Shasta's position with a prominent AIDS healthcare nonprofit was targeted more overtly.

"He went to them about my involvement in the protest," Simone relayed. "And they had my back, but I need to not rock the boat because if he went up the chain to corporate, they might not be able to protect me."

With Simone Shasta neutralized and others fearing retribution, plans for future protests collapsed. It appeared Bardoux would comfortably survive without making any changes in the way he operated.

The community moved on.

Sixth Grade Flashback (Facebook post)

I was in the sixth grade taking my seat in the front row when a boy pulled a girl's hair in the back corner and got into it with another girl who came to her defense. I rushed to get in the big middle of it, and when the bell rang the wiry middle aged science teacher demanded I come to the front of the class.

"What were you doing at the back of the classroom?" she barked.

"Joey pulled April's hair and . . ." I began before she cut me off.

"You are not the defender of the girls!" she said as she began a screed about how I seemed to believe I was, and how I was always involved in situations.

I don't remember the exact words because she sounded like Charlie Brown's teacher at that point. Of course I was the defender of the girls! This was crazy talk!

I'd forgotten about the entire episode for thirty years, until one morning when my mind was preoccupied with how to handle someone who was targeting Janessa Highland at her real estate job. Suddenly there's the recovered memory of that sixth-grade lecture about how I'm not the defender of the girls.

I'm still not convinced, though.

Served

~~~~~~

I was on the patio of Grey Fox for a meeting with Kitty when activist and performer Chasity Valentino called.

"I was just served with a lawsuit from Braden Bardoux! You're mentioned in it, and *Out in STL*, *Riverfront Times*, and Chuck Pfoutz are named."

Suing the community when you're already a pariah in the community seemed like an odd choice for a business owner, but it was also exciting. After many months of dealing with Jasmine and Ron's sloppy and mundane trolling I would never again take a quality storyline for granted.

I sent the suit to Keating and *RFT* Editor in Chief Doyle Murphy. Both thought it was ridiculous.

Cody called in the middle of the revelation. "Greeley fell off a mountain," he said.

"Oh my God. Is he dead?" I asked.

"No, he's got a gash on his head and is in the hospital, but he'll be fine."

"Okay. Well, *Out in STL* is being sued by Braden Bardoux! I'll have to talk to you later."

Authentically Weird

My sister-in-law Tracy, who was Emily's mother, sent a package back with us when we visited Tulsa over Labor Day. Emily came over to retrieve it, and sat down at the table for a drink.

Her current living arrangement was reminiscent of the Melrose. It was only three blocks south of our old haunt, and about three blocks down the hill from us. At the Melrose Opal lived above Emily, and now Emily lived above Opal and her boyfriend. They also befriended the other tenants.

Opal had grated on her nerves at the Melrose, but absence made her heart grow fonder, not just for Opal but also the city in general. On the topic of Opal, Emily brought up the couple next door to the Melrose who Opal had three ways with. She met them while smoking on the front porch, and I'd forgotten all about that chapter.

"The guy was into BDSM but was *really* bad at it. Opal said it was the most disappointing thing ever. But she enjoyed sex with the woman. The couple split up, he moved out and the woman got with a new guy and they are leaders of a Marxist, Leninist, Maoist cult."

"Do they still live next door to the Melrose?" I asked.

"Yeah they do, and they're always at Black Lives Matter protests trying to recruit. The ex is constantly trying to hit me up online, and that's never going to happen."

The last time Emily was at Villadiva she brought her cousin, who was raised in Tower Grove South, and it turned out her cousin had been in our house as a child. I was already Facebook friends with her cousin's mother.

"Your mom sent me photos taken in the house, along with stories," I relayed. "Her friends who lived here were also an interracial couple who had similar experiences with ghosts and the difficult neighbor," I relayed.

Emily complained of how boring life was during quarantine, but was grateful to be in St. Louis during the pandemic as opposed to Tulsa.

"Like you always said, this city gets in your blood," she said. "Austin and Portland try really hard to be weird as part of their branding, but St. Louis is authentically weird. It's weird without trying."

"You should start joining us at Grey Fox," I said. "We're there once or twice a week."

"That sounds fun! I have a friend who lives across from the Grey Fox and I was walking by one day and heard your voice from the patio," Emily said to Kage. "I yelled through a crack in the fence and you rolled your eyes and kept talking."

"Oh, I didn't know that was you!" Kage replied.

Months later I saw that an abandoned building around the corner on Gravois was tagged with messages in support of Chairman Mao.

Illuminating Memory of the Melrose Walk of Shame

Clyde randomly sent me the following memory about the time a guy named Brad came over for one of our infamous after-parties, and made his way through the Melrose:

I was doing some tidying up before work and I was checking my corner lamp, and thought about lighting.

I recall after Brad and I left your and Kage's place we headed to my place so he could sober up a bit, he then left my place shortly after to go to Ricks, and never returned, until the next day to get his phone charger. I remember telling you about the exchange and you randomly asked, "Do you have indirect lighting or just overhead?" I said "overhead," you sat down on your couch and so overly forlorn said "I can't stand overhead lighting, I bet that's why Brad left, because you have overhead lighting" and it was so melodramatic yet dry I couldn't help but be like "It's not that big a deal" to which you said "Lighting is everything!"

I haven't thought of that for a while but it tickled me just now lol.

I sent him gifs of interrogation scenes. "If overhead lighting wasn't bad, they wouldn't torture suspects with it."

My relationship with Clyde had to be the most unusual of my lifetime, and it was about the only big thing me and Kage didn't agree on. I was careful not to push the topic because I had no logical argument for suggesting we restore the friendship. I myself didn't understand my fondness for him, and even posited that I was under one of his spells, which he denied.

Ours was a friendship of incredibly frank late-night discussions. I told him I worried for his soul. I even worried for my own by associating with him.

He fashioned himself as a protector of me and Kage, and attempted to assure me that would even be true in death.

"Those demons don't work for free. They are tending you like a rancher tends the herd. You will have no free will in death. They will own you," I warned, but he dismissed those concerns.

Even though he got messy around Mardi Gras 2020, he didn't really go for the jugular. And I respected him for not joining forces with Jasmine and Ron. I once joked to friends, "Doesn't it say something that he would summon Satan himself to fight me, but joining forces with the Saccharine Sisters was a bridge too far?"

Of course, it's not that he really thought Satan was less extreme than Jasmine and Ron. He just found Satan to be far cooler.

My only plausible explanation for my fondness of him despite all that happened is that I found him interesting, and as you've read, I'll roll with a lot for a good story.

I told him as much one night, and he took offense. I replied, "The fact I find you interesting should be a compliment. Most of those who hate me do so because I *don't* find them interesting.

Zeeke's Birthday Poem

Before living here with all of our shenanigans and jokes,
I only knew you as the good-looking guy who was friends with Stokes.
Offered you the guest room when you were going your own way,
And didn't imagine you'd like it so much you'd stay.
You went from a log cabin deep in the woods,
To a place where gun-shooting looters run off with the goods.
From a place where wild animals would appear on the forest floor,
To where drag queens on the corner leave the audience begging for more.
From where nobody knew how to find your abode,
To wear friends waved hello, down our street as they rode.
From where living a private life was simply a breeze,
To where our detractors accuse you of spreading disease.
What was so foreign months earlier has become your norm,
And I'm glad you found your home in the eye of the storm.
Happy birthday!

The Senators Greet Caesar

The energy was inviting and lively on the patio of Just John as we celebrated the release of our September issue under the string lights shortly before sunset. Our slender ad rep Kitty was unusually bubbly and in full host mode, which made sense because Just John was her home bar—or her second home.

Elizabeth VanWinkle wrote an incredible story covering 70 years of LGBTQ biking, which included an interview with 92-year-old Betty Neely, who had been riding since she was fifteen. A new and uncertain writer, I was proud of Elizabeth for the excellent work and I sang her praises to her small entourage.

Betty was a character. Aside from using a rolling walker she seemed to be healthy, and her mind was sharp. She was warm and animated when talking about the scene over the years, and when the topic came to the east side, I asked her about mobsters.

"I used to work for Buster Wortman in the 50s and 60s," she said, referring to a notorious gangster who lived in a house surrounded by a moat. "He had affairs and if one of the gals started trouble, I'd deal with her."

Colin Murphy was in attendance and I was happy to see him. He sat at our table chatting about various things, including this book, which he had read a draft of. He got choked up when talking about Kurt's mention.

"I am beyond honored at the way you spoke of him," he said.

"Just stating the facts," I replied. "He was the Jackie O of St. Louis."

About fifteen minutes later he pointed to the magazine on the table.

"I'd like to revisit talks about coming together," he said in reference to merging *Out in STL* and *#Boom,* something me and Keating pitched to them at the beginning, at my suggestion. At that time, I offered to bring him on as my equal. He and his team would run the news and digital operation, and me and Melissa would retain control of the print product.

"There's too many players right now. The writing is on the wall and we'd be stronger working together," he said.

I was excited to hear that, and told Kitty the news.

"Oh, I know," she replied. "And [former *Vital Voice* publisher] Jimmy wants to be involved too."

This was strange. It seemed things were in the works I was unaware of.

I mentioned to Colin, who was several beers in, that Jimmy was seeking to be involved with the magazine. When I said something about "folding in *#Boom*" he replied, "No this wouldn't be folding us in. I'd be the editor in chief. I've earned it. They want me, Jimmy and Lovett to run it. They're not happy with your personal blog. If you don't believe in something enough to post it under *Out* you shouldn't post it."

I was floored, but also drunk so my reactions were muted and delayed.

I approached Kitty to ask her about it.

"Keating offered me an ownership stake and I decided my dream team would be to bring Murphy and Jimmy on board," she said, indicating there would still be a role for me. "But I haven't heard anything more about the ownership stake and don't know if that's even happening."

I was calm but pointed in my remarks, telling her we had lost business because clients were unhappy with her, including Bar PM, but I never went behind her back about it because we were a team. "You clearly didn't share that sentiment."

She was wide-eyed and seemingly desperate to rationalize the situation.

"People are always complaining that you put your friends on the cover . . ." she began, and I knew exactly where she got that: her top drinking buddy Alan, who Darin Slyman long blamed for many of *Vital Voice's* problems. Alan seemed to assume anyone on the cover he didn't know was my personal friend.

"ONE close friend was on the cover," I interjected in reference to Cody in the turret three years earlier (Auntie M and the Maven were on *RFT* covers). I pointed towards Elizabeth, who had been on a cover. "Elizabeth was a critic that I recruited and cultivated as a writer. I had never met her until her issue was out. The vast majority of people on the covers are people I didn't know."

"If you don't know them nobody else does," she replied, indicating that the cover should be reserved for A-listers as defined by her Just John coterie.

"They are all people with compelling stories in the issue," I replied. "If I'm being pushed out, I'm at least asking for full marketing for the book in the March issue."

That segue wasn't my smoothest, but I thought we should get down to the brass tax and cut all pretense. She had conspired to push me out of something I had built, and I offered to leave elegantly despite all that in exchange for book press.

Colin Murphy walked up to the two of us. "I feel since I'm part of this I need to . . ." and I don't remember what more he said, just that everyone was repeating themselves, including me, and Kitty seemed shaken. The entire unfolding scene was like the time the Trump Administration attempted to handle a North Korean missile launch from the dining room at Mar-a-Lago while dozens looked on. There were layers of people engaged, including a worried Kage, a shellshocked Chuck Pfoutz who repeated, "This is bullshit. You worked so hard to build this for the community. They can't do this to you," and Alan, who attempted to convince me to drop my conditions.

I returned to my table and Colin followed. "Why in the world would I leave my own company to work for Keating?" he said, as if he hadn't just talked of merging. "Why would I work somewhere I could be fired," he said while beginning to sob. "I will not take that position. We've worked so hard to be friends again. You've gotta believe me. I'll make a pact right now. I'll post it to Facebook right now!" he exclaimed while punching his screen with his thick fingers.

"No, don't do that," Kage said as he gently reached over and touched Colin's hand. "That will generate a lot of questions right now."

Colin slid his phone into his pocket.

Meanwhile, a good-looking guy several of my friends were regularly sleeping with, including Zeeke, started making out with me right there in the middle of the drama while Kage nonchalantly played on his phone.

"This is scandalous," I said. "We need to stop."

We would stop for a minute, tops, then he'd lean in and kiss me again, until I repeated that we were causing a scene.

"Literally nobody is looking," a member of our party said dryly, seemingly tired of my hints of a bloodthirsty paparazzi on the then-dark and sleepy patio.

I woke at 3 a.m. and wrote Keating asking for clarity on the situation. I was tired and hungover, but I felt somewhat peaceful about whatever the outcome would be. As betrayed as I felt, I was also kind of delighted by the literary value. I had just presented Jimmy with an Influence Award, and I'd been regularly checking in on Colin in the wake of Kurt's passing. I ran a story of Colin's in the magazine, and I had offered to share the platform with him from the very start. What a cutthroat move! What treachery! I felt like Caesar in the Theatre of Pompey.

Colin texted me first thing in the morning.

Well I'm hung over as fuck. How did we leave things last night? My mouth and drinking without my keeper aren't ideal. Ugh.

When I got to the office I replied.

Colin,

It was an evening of shocking revelations, and overall I'm feeling adult and sophisticated about it. Business is business, but there's no getting around that it was a stunning betrayal from many directions, all concocted by Kitty and her drinking buddy Alan. It's also embarrassing to be the last to know.

I have no plans to unfriend anyone involved or get messy, but at the same time I won't pretend the story is anything different than what it is. Everything came to light and it's my story to tell. You know how much I love a good story, and this is quite a plot twist.

We will be ok in the long term, but I would like some space to process everything. I'm waiting for a response from Keating, and if Kitty's plans really are in the works, I will hold no ill will should you decide to run the magazine. I'm incredibly proud of how far I've taken it, and want to see it continue.

Chris

He promptly replied.

Chris,

I have my own entity and business and legacy and will not under any circumstances take that job. I like being my own boss and they'd stab me in the back eventually as well. I haven't been out in the community conspiring. This was brought to my attention about a month ago in one of my rare patio outings. I'm all for combining forces but maintaining autonomy of my own business, if that's at all possible, so left it open to discussion. Didn't mention anything until you said Jimmy was wanting some buy-in at OUT IN STL and then I knew they had the knives out for you and felt I needed to tell you. Again, I'm not interested and wouldn't accept. In the end, I'm glad it's out, so to speak, but I'm unhappy how it happened. I probably should have said something the moment something was said but it was drunken patio talk. I'm not the bad guy here. Just a pawn in a hatched plan amongst folks who are the ones doing this. Again. I want to focus on myself and #Boom. I hope you believe me. And I really want to cultivate our friendship. I feel rotten but also a bit of a victim in the whole thing and you have every right to be pissed.

I felt sorry for Colin and knew he was remorseful. I didn't want to add to his current struggle, but at the same time I wasn't in a place to pretend all was fine.

A few hours later he posted the following to his Facebook:

I have a rock-solid moral compass and when something doesn't sit right, I'll eventually speak to it. Last night was one of those complicated situations. I was complicit but not guilty. Yeah, this is vague booking and it'll all be fine. But I feel lousy about last night. I need to quit going "out" solo as it always ends up a mess. I miss my ballast. I miss Kurt.

My feelings about Colin's involvement were of course tempered by what he was going through, but also by the grace and forgiveness he and Kurt had shown about things I wrote in *Delusions of Grandeur*. Colin had a great sense of humor about the book, and even said he was proud to be in it.

It turns out Keating knew nothing of the coup d'état, and said he was "blown away" by the tale. It seemed Kitty confused profit sharing with ownership, and ran with it. Jimmy told others he had no knowledge of it either.

My position, for the moment, was secure.

Getting on With It

It took me almost a week to become depressed about the coup plot because I was on an adrenaline high. It then set in that in every direction were no-win situations. Kitty and Alan were never going to stop, which would make running the magazine miserable and more knives in my back inevitable. If Kitty left, however, she'd likely take Pride and some of our biggest advertisers with her.

I knew the end was near, which would mean saying goodbye to the team I nurtured for three years, at least in a working sense. But I was proud of our masthead and what we created. *Out in STL* began as a tiny seedling and I kept detractors from stomping on it, giving it a chance to grow. It grew to viability, and now some of the very people I'd been protecting it from were plotting to take it. The fact it had value three years on was a testament to our team's work.

Just as those in Jasmine's camp held their fire to allow for my coverage and attendance of the Runway protests, the queer establishment did something similar while the magazine got established. Two factions on opposite ends of the community saw that I was useful for a time and a purpose. In the case of the establishment, meaning those on the boards, those calling the shots from the patio of Just John, my error was mistaking a hall pass for a meaningful alliance, or for belonging. I definitely felt that I had been rolled.

But there probably was a certain wisdom to the plan to usher me out before my next book. For three years I colored between the lines, to the best of my ability, but the impending book release signaled a coming storm. A return to classic Chris Andoe controversy. The Runway protest was seen as a precursor.

A bird removes everything soft from the nest when it's time for its young to fly away, and in reality, without knowing it, they were doing me a favor. They were keeping me from getting comfortable.

I long viewed *St. Louis Magazine* as the pinnacle of local print media, and now I had the drive to see if I could get my foot in the door. In addition to her work with *Out in STL*, my colleague Melissa had written for them for many years, and offered to introduce me to Deputy Editor Amanda Woytus.

I was a little surprised at how helpful Melissa was because since she was such a reserved person, I never knew if she even liked me. I was appreciative that she thought enough of me and my work to make an introduction.

With my reply to the introductory email, I included this manuscript. The next day Amanda replied, beginning her message:

Hi Chris, thanks so much for reaching out. I had to absolutely tear myself away from your manuscript. I would love to talk to you as well.

I called to speak with her, and she said she was happy to have me as a contributor.

Writing for *St. Louis Magazine* would be like a homecoming of sorts. In addition to Melissa, Nick Phillips, the man who recruited me to run *Out in STL,* was also there.

I had yet to decide whether to continue running *Out in STL* as well, if that was even an option anymore, but either way I was comforted that Villadiva's Hall of Fame would continue to expand, regardless of the community's sinister machinations.

Musings at the Monocle

Janessa Highland was the Monocle's show director, and one Thursday night I invited Darin out to see the House of Markstone perform. I felt a kinship with Janessa because we'd been on the similar trajectories. For her, she went from the "Queen of Controversy" pariah to being crowned Miss Gay Missouri America, and then was excommunicated by that very system shortly thereafter.

An irony of the night the coup plot was revealed was that was the night I felt I was initiated as a native. There I was, hosting an event in what I once referred to as "the belly of the beast," where the House of Alan long plotted my demise, when Colin Murphy told me of the whisper campaigns against Runway. Pageant owners were quietly conspiring to never set foot in Runway again, in part because of the frivolous lawsuit against *Out in STL*.

"Not until the Runway controversy have I truly felt like an insider," I said to Colin. "The whisper campaigns are the secret language of the locals, and were always against me. Now, they're backing me up."

"Well, you've lived here a long time now," Colin replied.

Moments earlier he said he wanted to join forces, which seemed like quite a triumph. I think I enjoyed a good half-hour of feeling like an insider before the curtain was yanked back in epic fashion.

As I mentioned, Janessa had been on a similar ride. And then there's Darin. Most everyone, including me, had migrated away from him after he wound down his media empire. But when the rug was pulled out from under me, it was Darin I called in the middle of the night. He was someone who could relate, and despite the shade thrown at times, which was aimed at the magazine, but which I took personally, in that moment on the patio it was clear that Darin was someone who had never wavered in his support. Boards demanded he fire me from *Vital Voice* for years and he was unphased. Highly unusual in this risk-averse community.

And he had sounded the alarm all along that things were not as they seemed.

The Monocle was *in* St. Louis, but not *of* St. Louis. Founded by accomplished men from Southern California and Chicago, it aimed to give LGBTQ St. Louis something better, with world-class entertainers including film and television star Coco Peru, who was a dear friend of one of the owners, and who told me that the club's top-notch systems and amenities rivaled the best cabarets in the world.

As you can probably imagine, the community resented it. The craft cocktails were too expensive, the shows originally weren't free. Somehow, though, the Monocle endured.

Before the show, Janessa joined us at the bar, which was partitioned with tall plexiglass due to the pandemic, and I thought, "What a perfect setting for the three of us. All non-natives. All resented in certain circles for trying to elevate standards. We *are* the Monocle!"

Mother Markstone, acting as emcee, later gave me a shout out from the stage.

"Chris Andoe is here. He's a great person to know, *IF* you're on his good side. If you're not, God help you!"

Three years of going outside of my comfort zone and doing business with former foes was a good exercise. I am richer for it. And there are people I made amends with who I believed would remain good friends. But there was nothing like the kinship of being with one's own people. Sitting at the bar with those two lightning rods, everything felt right with my soul. I was at home.

Shuttered

Our corporate attorney was baffled by the lawsuit, and called to find out what he was missing. He wasn't missing anything. There was zero substance.

On September 27, 2020, I was tipped off that Runway was closing, and I posted the following Facebook status, leaving out names to avoid adding meat to Bardoux' case.

1. June 16: Christopher Columbus statue gets removed from Tower Grove Park.

2. Gay conservative upset about removal. Weighs in on the thread of a popular bartender to say so.

3. When outnumbered 99 to 1, gay conservative tags another gay conservative (I'll refer to him as GC #2) to help.

4. When GC #2 gets his ass handed to him, he calls the bartender's boss and threatens to bombard him with bad reviews unless the bartender is fired. Bar owner tells him to fuck off.

5. GC #2 switches gears to target a legendary drag queen who defended the above bartender. That business owner (referred to as BO #2) immediately caved. Queen was fired.

6. Community was upset about the mistreatment of the performer, and the way others had been treated before. Most performers quit in solidarity.

7. Public Relations #101 would be for the business owner to stop, address concerns, and work on making amends. Instead, BO #2 files a lawsuit against those who spoke out. (Pending)

8. September 27: It appears the business is shuttered, meaning the last night of operations was 90 days after firing the performer.

And it all began with a statue being removed in Tower Grove Park.

*   *   *

Sadly, though, the Monocle was soon to follow.

The Tireless Mole

After my public departure from *Vital Voice* in 2015, I allowed my enemies a week to celebrate and then reappeared with an interview with movie and television star Coco Peru on AMERICAblog.com. Now, with rumors circulating that I was soon-to-be-out as editor in chief, and with a frivolous lawsuit pending, I had a similar opportunity with *St. Louis Magazine*.

I had two options, the first being to play it safe. The mere fact I was writing for them was vindication enough, after all. The second option was to roll the dice. Revisit the very subject that (undeservedly) landed *Out in STL* and the *RFT* in court.

I chose the latter, pitching a piece about the state of local drag in the wake of closures and Covid. I highlighted four venues to see socially-distanced drag, and showcased two performers, one being Braden Bardoux' nemesis Krista Versace, pictured elegantly reclining on a gold throne.

Her introduction opened as follows:

When the iconic Krista Versace was let go from Runway, not only did big names follow her out in solidarity, dozens shut down the street in protest. It may not have been the night the lights went out in Georgia, but the venue did go dark 90 days later.

In retrospect I don't think anyone was surprised to see me published in *St. Louis Magazine*. My confidence was briefly shaken by the coup plot, and I needed validation from a new team. But the effort to replace me was based on those I chose to cover and on my controversies. Not my talent.

With that in mind, I'm glad that I chose to come right out of the gate doing what I do, which is telling the story of my community. While few were surprised, I imagine Braden Bardoux was. He would learn his efforts to silence me were akin to a game of Whac-A-Mole.

Help from Hermes

On a Thursday night me and Kage went down to Grey Fox and Zeeke soon joined us, coming straight from work. Zeeke admitted to having sex with Angel the night before, days after again vowing they were done for good after Angel broke it off for the fourth time. Angel would tell Zeeke he didn't find him attractive, and then after a day or two would send Zeeke photos of them together and talk of how much he missed him.

"He's admitted he's intimidated by your looks and how people react to you. He's trying to erode your confidence so he feels more secure," I said. "It's emotional abuse."

Standing beside me at the bar, I noticed Zeeke had popped a blood vessel in his eye.

"I did it during magic," he replied. "I was concentrating really hard."

Kage proceeded to lecture him about his choices while I instead focused on friend and bartender Jack Abernathy, who was discussing he and Sean's palatial new Italianate home in Lafayette Terrace, blocks from Villa Ray and doors down from both Jimmy Eden and Jade Sinclair.

"Oh!" I said as I swung back to Kage and Zeeke. "Jimmy Eden said Rick was arrested."

"I had a hand in that," Zeeke said. "I made a deal with the god Hermes, who is the god of mischief, communication, magic and commerce. I already have a deep relationship with him and I asked him to do something about Rick. He has a special relationship with gay men, he's the only god I'm aware of who doesn't have a wife, and he's really androgenous. After that Angel flooded my inbox about how he couldn't stop thinking about me no matter how hard he tried."

"Certainly Hermes has a return window!" I exclaimed. "You have a god on hand to help you land a man and you asked for help landing *Angel*? That's like asking a car god for a Mazda!"

I shook my head and turned back to hear more about the new house. When I later told Ms. Jamieson the story, she said, "I need to know the details of how the deal with Hermes was made. It's integral to the plot development!"

"You'll be down in the basement like, 'Hi Demons. Does anyone here know Hermes?'"

Ms. Jamieson laughed. "You're not wrong!"

Angel was the weirdest and most unsettling little person. Late one weeknight, after I was already in bed, he kept drunkenly running up and down the stairs and for some sadistic reason he pulled Troy's injured leg, causing him to howl in pain. Kage was still up and told him to leave the dog alone. He then pretended he'd left Villadiva when he was actually hiding behind the bathroom door for half an hour. He jumped out to scare Zeeke, which stirred the dogs and woke us up.

It wasn't just me, Kage and the vestiges of the Melrose who couldn't stand Angel. He somehow enraged a total stranger at Grey Fox to the point she tried to tase him.

During their 8th or 9th break-up, Angel seemed to blame us for them not instantly getting back together. He sent Zeeke a rambling message which included the following:

I'm ready to call them out online. Chris thinks he's on a throne and people respect him so much, but I truly believe people are just afraid to share their true thoughts. How are you so loyal to them? I hope you get out of that house soon.

Angel had stopped denying he found Zeeke attractive, but he had kicked him out for various reasons including spilling a can of Sprite. Our mutual friend Webster told us he'd fucked around with Angel immediately after "the Sprite incident."

"Then I spilled coffee and had to leave myself," Webster said. "Angel has a low tolerance for spillage, apparently."

Zeeke's Premonition

One afternoon Zeeke sent an ominous message: "I feel like someone is gunning for you, so I'm making you a protective necklace Mr. Andoe. I just woke up with a sense of urgency to get you something productive."

I asked Zeeke if he thought it was Runway owner Braden Bardoux.

"I dunno. But I'm having major league anxiety about it."

"Getting any visions of what they're after? Money? Reputation? Safety?" I asked.

"I think Braden is the spearhead of this. I think I may have to turn to hard-core spell work to deal with him."

I then reached out to John Kreisel, who replied: "Honey, my anxiety has been way out of control. Especially yesterday."

"About me?" I asked.

"I have not learned the ability to know who. I just feel that someone, or many in my life are in danger. So that would include you. You were heavy on my mind last Friday. Actually, all last week. I meant to reach out but each time I picked up the phone to message something would happen. And by danger, I mean anything that could harm, physically or especially emotionally."

"I think it's Braden Bardoux. Runway closed and I posted about it."

"I don't know him. But the name just turns my stomach. He is holding a huge grudge against you. And the 90-day timeline that you published was succinct and on point. We really do express ourselves best through writing. You have a tribe that has your back. But please, be careful. Not meant to scare. Just to inform. Evil is trying to silence the voice of those looking out for others."

John sent a photo of Bardoux that he had just pulled up.

"He has an ugly aura around him. Like a bile green color."

When Zeeke came home he handed me a black velvet pouch with a necklace inside.

"It is a piece of black tourmaline that was concentrated in frankincense smoke and blessed by the 4 directions elements, and charged with protection. The way you take care of your charm is every Sunday wash it under cold water and let it air dry, and I would also leave it outside under the full moon, which you could do tonight!"

"What's the significance of tourmaline?" I asked.

"It's a black stone. And it's known for its ability to ground out negative magic."

I began wearing it regularly, along with my dad's watch. In our bedroom I also had a crucifix and rosary beads from Kreisel's husband. I was amassing quite a collection of protective items.

About the watch, the Maven said dad brought it up whenever he'd come to her, to the point she seemed to find it comical.

"He's always saying, 'I told you about the watch!'" she laughed.

Unpacking Dad

I spent my life feeling like I didn't have a father. I felt inappropriate even referring to him, since he was someone I didn't remember. The biggest gift the Maven gave to me was a sense of connection.

It wasn't long after meeting her that my brother Bill gave me Dad's watch out of the blue, which I kept in a drawer until she told me to wear it. After I told Joe about my experiences with the Maven, he sent me photos of Dad holding me. We began speaking of him more often, and Joe would remark on our behavioral similarities, which was something I'd never heard.

One October evening in 2019, after a week of hearing what sounded like a bird chirping from the bookcase in the den, I found a tiny frog in a houseplant that had been outside for the summer. I contacted a wildlife center to ask if it would be okay going back out so late in the season, and they said it was too late. I brought it to their facility to stay over winter.

When I told this story to Joe, he said it reminded him of a story about Dad. He found a baby bird, and worked to care for it and nurse it to health in our garage. "It didn't make it, and he was really down about that," Joe said.

Dad died of his second heart attack, and the story was that after the first, he said, "I'm not afraid of dying." I grew up hearing this story regularly, and I subconsciously internalized that to mean he didn't care if he died. He didn't care if he left me behind. The pain of that wasn't something I was aware of, but a cold numbness.

At 45, with the Maven's prompting, I unpacked all of that for the first time.

"He didn't want to go. He fought it. He felt cheated," she'd say.

Looking at the photos it's obvious that was true. He beamed with joy. He loved me so much, he never did leave.

Mom had many old relatives when I was a child and I recall the hospital visits when they were dying. Each one of them spoke of long-dead relatives coming to see them. I find it so comforting that at the end of life we might not only be surrounded by our living people, but also by those that have gone on before us. I believe Dad will be waiting for me and I don't think he will be a stranger. I think all of those memories and emotions from our 18 months together will come flooding back.

He must have been happy to know the tiny frog survived. It was the policy of the rescue to return animals to where they were found whenever possible, so the following Spring it was returned to the grounds of Villadiva.

Ms. Jamieson Shapes Up

After a health scare, Ms. Jamieson fundamentally changed her diet, and began doing yoga. She lost 56 pounds, going from 225 to 169, and looked incredible.

"I can twist myself like a fucking pretzel," she said.

The Farm

It was the strangest thing. Gay guys around St. Louis were buying RVs. The reason, I soon learned, was the new clothing-optional gay campground in Franklin County, an hour outside of town in the foothills of the Ozarks.

It was called SIRenity Farm, and was all the rage. It featured a fun pool area, lake, cabins, camping sites and of course RV spots. Many guys were going out there every weekend.

I contacted the owners and they invited me and Kage out for the day. We invited Cody and Jack to come along and had a lovely afternoon swimming and visiting. Kage instantly embraced being nude, and Cody warmed up to it after half an hour.

I asked owner Dennis Duncan if he had any problem getting his campground approved.

"Franklin County has had a nudist colony for many years, so there was some precedent. We've had no problems at all."

Our brunch regular, The Queen of Camp, was there and was thoroughly sold on the place. She had moved from North County to South City's Bevo Mill a year or so earlier, and was initially delighted to be so close to all the gays. It had been hard to get anyone to go to North County, but now she was filling her basement for monthly sex parties—except during tax season, when she was too busy.

Unfortunately, the newness wore off for both her and her waning pool of tricks, and she grew disenchanted with the South City scene.

"These vipers down here . . ." she'd begin when expressing her frustration about her flaky and backbiting former tricks. But she was all about the Farm.

On the tour upon our arrival one of the highlights was "the Happy Camper," an empty retro RV that was open to anyone. As the four of us were leaving at the end of the day, we decided to take a peek inside and there was the buck-naked smiling Queen of Camp with a gentleman caller.

"Aren't you guys coming in?" she asked.

A few months later I posted the following poem to the Queen of Camp's wall.

She's a fun and lovable tramp,

Known far and wide as the Queen of Camp.

She's been seen on the Price is Right and even on Wheel. She hangs with Vanna White, keeping it real.

Orgies fill her basement because that's how she relaxes. They only pause when she's busy with taxes.

A bit disenchanted with city queens for which she's lost her affinity, but she sure loves the Happy Camper down at SIRenity.

Happy Birthday!

2020 Catches Up with Us

On Sunday, October 11, I received a message from John Kreisel out of the blue.

Please let me know you're okay. I'm a bit concerned. Love you, friend.

I replied: *We have coronavirus.*

I wondered if Zeeke and John Kreisel's premonitions and anxiety were over us getting coronavirus, or if yet another shoe would drop. Fortunately, ours were mild cases, but we worried about taking a turn for the worse, and the possible long-term implications.

One evening while we were ill, close to bedtime, I was on the sofa in the den and Kage had just stood up from the dining room table when we heard a single, angry bang on the wooden front door. It was so loud and ominous that we didn't initially answer, but instead peeked through the windows for several minutes.

We found the storm door still locked, so nobody could have even reached the wooden door.

I remember Marcus' most unsettling moment at Villadiva involved the front entrance. He was cooking dinner and heard the door open. He walked into the hall to see who was there and found the door locked, and stood dumbfounded trying to make sense of the situation.

After digesting our own experience for a few minutes, I walked towards the basement to rotate laundry, and found all the lights were off. Kage hadn't done it, and I never turned them off during laundry.

Zeeke saged and blessed the house when he got home that evening, and all was calm.

The Maven seemed to think being sick was a factor. "Vulnerability and depleted emotional faculty, which is double nasty!" she said. "You are a divining rod."

Clyde's Nightmare

I was not connected with Clyde on Facebook, but he followed everything I posted and would engage with me about it. One late October Friday evening, Kage was stuck at home as he awaited his negative Covid test result. I decided to share a few excerpts from this book online, including the story about the time Clyde had sex in the middle of one of our parties at the Melrose.

"It was actually me who said, 'Quiet in the Peanut Gallery," he wrote.

In Clyde's memory the bear discreetly mentioned that the chatter was distracting, so he shouted to us. Memories can be imprecise so it's possible.

Years later I ran across that bear at a busy Starbucks. I was there to meet a big potential client but there were no seats available. The bear noticed me and greeted me warmly, and when I told him of my predicament, he kindly offered me his table. I landed the client.

After sharing the Peanut Gallery story to Facebook I posted the one about Ms. Jamieson talking to the basement demons.

Clyde messaged again. "This book is going to destroy me all over again, isn't it?"

I simply replied, "no."

He had been aware that I was writing the book since I first met him in Carbondale, Illinois more than four years earlier, and knew that almost anything could be in it. When it was important to him that something not be included, he'd request that it be off the record. Once, he asked if he could tell me a supernatural story off the record and I said no, so he didn't tell me. But I have honored every such agreement. As we approached the publishing date his anxiety would grow, along with the anxiety of half of Queer St. Louis.

But still, I knew "no" was an overly-simplistic answer. A more accurate answer would have been that I believed he would go through phases of emotions concerning the book, ending with a peace about it.

As a kid I remember Grandma Andoe and her husband Chester would sit at opposite ends of the dining room table playing solitaire, and how odd I found that at the time. Now it was common for me and Kage to sit at the table on our computers, which wasn't much different.

While engrossed in our online activity we heard what sounded like a crate being dragged along the basement floor. The dogs heard it as well, and ran barking towards the back of the house, where the basement doors were located.

"What was that?" I asked Kage.

"It sounded like something being dragged across the floor downstairs, but also kind of like a growl," he replied.

Despite believing in the paranormal, we lived on a busy block and I thought there was a reasonable chance the sound was coming from outside, regardless of how much it sounded like it was right below us.

I woke the next morning to more messages from Clyde, which came in just after 1 a.m.

So, for once I decided not to drink tonight when I came home from work to do some laundry. I went downstairs to put a load in and I heard the most scraping sound behind me. It was like a smooth dragging across the concrete, but in short spurts. I took a deep breath and turned to the corner and said, 'be at peace' and turned back around. As I did I felt dizzy and lethargic. I got my laundry as best as I could and came back upstairs as fast as I could. I started hearing voices as I closed my back door. Now I'm laying in my bed up in my cups trying to drown out the whole ordeal. I'm done thinking I can quell whatever it is down there. Nothing I do ever works. You told me before a few times you had dreams of me laying in the basement and shadow creatures were latched onto me feeding on my body and I said 'it's fine.' I just get overwhelmed. It's silly to type out endless descriptions of what I'm going through to you, only to get short three or four word replies from you, but I get it. You keep me at arm's length for a reason. I thought about this today, I keep reaching out to you because I see you as a father figure, I don't mean that as disrespect but rather a sign of high respect. I dunno what I'm trying to say right now but it's like a spell has been broken over me lately and I don't see you as a sexual object of my own obsession anymore. But anyway I should leave you be, sorry for blowing up your messenger.

I replied that we had heard something similar coming from our basement. He didn't comment on that, but instead spoke of bad dreams.

"What happened in the dream?" I asked.

"Me wading through an ethereal swamp-like area trudging through mud, coming across large creatures lurking past me as these human sized ghoulish creatures surrounded me and started biting my neck and tearing out chunks as blood flowed down my body and pulling me down to my knees. Pulling me down I could feel the pressure and hands pulling me down."

"I think it's a valuable dream because those demons aren't your friends. And when you die, they certainly won't be."

"I'm tired of being hurt and having no way to retaliate. At least this magic wields a result."

"So, who are you retaliating against with magic?" I asked.

"No one it just seems I wield results more so than I ever have before."

"Results implies you are using magic against people. I think you said more than you intended."

"The last person I did was you."

"So, you won't turn against the demons because they retaliate against me?"

"No Chris, you're jumping to conclusions. I just feel like I can make a difference. I always make things worse even with the best intentions, Magic isn't always dark either, and I'm not exactly up in here hexing people and cursing enemies and laughing at their misfortune. I don't know what I'm trying to say, this all sounds like nonsense. I know. I should go back to bed. I am not casting spells or anything on you or your circle, and haven't for a long, long time, you need to understand that. You thinking I am by saying, 'I think you said more than I intended to' makes me want to take a gigantic step back from you."

"You have to do what's best for you. I've always been direct in our discussions."

"I can't be hurt by you again, even if it's not your intent. I'm going back to bed; I don't feel well. Enjoy your weekend and rest of your day please."

One week earlier we had heard a pound at the front door, and now we were hearing a sound from the basement that was echoing at the Melrose. The premonitions Zeeke and John Kreisel were having, the feeling someone was coming for us. I had suspected everyone but the most obvious suspect.

Sidewalk Sale at Nadine's

Geoff Story couldn't pass up a good junk sale, and Soulard was having one. All proceeds for the items sold at Nadine's went to the St. Louis LGBT History Project, and Geoff asked if I'd like to meet him there.

Nadine had been clearing out her upper two floors, which made me nervous. I was seeing a trend of my Baby Boomer friends breaking camp and heading to Florida, and I wondered if she was up to something similar. She worked awfully hard, often running the kitchen as well as socializing with the customers. She deserved to cash out and rest, but for selfish reasons I wasn't ready. I was also getting hints that the Maven might be eying an adventure.

Frank Fontana was selling his baked treats out front, right beside the history project's Steven Brawley, who was selling retro items from antique books to shirts from a long-defunct leather club.

"That's Carl Nixon," Frank said while nodding towards a bald man of about sixty looking at the merchandise a few tables over. "He posted the other day that he was voting for Trump and if anyone didn't like it they could unfriend him and fuck off. So I unfriended him. I saw him walk up and nodded, and he just ignored me."

"Frank, will you show Carl where the map to the other sale locations is?" Nadine shouted down the sidewalk.

Carl approached and Frank barely turned around. "It's there," he said in a deep, grouchy tone completely out of character, which I found amusing.

Sitting at the bar with Geoff, we discussed our respective projects. He showed me several loosely related film clips, including one of Bonnie Blake.

"How many films are you working on?" I asked.

"Therein lies the problem," he laughed. "Three. Do you see your book becoming a screenplay?"

"I could see that. I'd have to pare it way down to make it work," I replied.

"I think your next project should be fiction, and should involve your character being murdered and the reader or viewer trying to determine who did it and why."

"That would be incredible. So many have motive!" I began. "A distinguished older gentleman I know who owned a city block downtown once told me, 'I know people who were killed for revealing less than you have.' I've been subjected to everything from lawsuits to a Satanic blood curse, but nobody has killed me yet. If they do, let it be known that I had a good run."

I could possibly picture Clyde snapping in the heat of the moment, Braden Bardoux putting out a hit. Jasmine's friends once assaulted a woman outside of Grey Fox, not on her behalf, but maybe she could gin up some violence. But the very next day a main character I'd almost forgotten about came back into focus. Maybe he was why Zeeke and John Kreisel were having anxiety that someone was plotting against me. Or maybe there was such a critical mass of folks sharpening their knives.

Dustin Mitchell Plots Vengeance

"So, Dustin's brother got a hold of me last night," began Lacey, the former Mrs. Dustin Mitchell. "He wanted to warn me that Dustin was trying to get paroled in December, which we already knew. He told me Dustin sent him a letter going on and on about how he was going to ruin our lives once he got out and that he had filed a lawsuit against us, the same one I had dismissed over a year ago. He has, apparently, still learned nothing. His brother knew that Dustin is facing charges in Missouri, but Dustin denied it when he confronted him. Their mother died in August and, apparently, her dying wish was 'for Dustin to stop this foolishness.'"

"Do you think he'll get released?" I asked.

"No, I don't think he will get out. He's a parole jumper. What the Parole Board told me when they asked for a statement regarding his application was that he was on parole in Missouri when he came to Texas, meaning he was not supposed to leave the state. With him having committed two new offenses in jail, and Destiny and I both having had to contact the warden's office to request they check his mail before it goes out because he had sent threatening and harassing letters from the prison, and the history of jumping both bond and parole, plus the standing extradition from Missouri courts, the odds of him getting early release are slim."

"This anger has been enduring. In the past his anger would blow over like a summer storm," I said.

"He's angry that it was implied that he is a predator. He is. He absolutely is a predator. You realize that the lot of us are basically a support group, right? Surviving Dustin Mitchell."

Lacey later messaged me with an update.

"Dustin has been placed on 'serve all' status by the Texas Parole Board. His last parole application was denied on 11/10/2020 and they changed his status to indicate he is not eligible- ever- for early release."

His sentence was to end in 2025.

Halloween 2020

October felt like a year. We had been sidelined with coronavirus for half of it, and we were literally counting down the days until the election on our kitchen calendar. Defeating Trump consumed me, and Halloween, in my mind, was nothing more than an annoying distraction.

It was on a Saturday, and at the last minute I decided to dress as Jesus (lazy choice because I had everything already) and go down to Grey Fox. Mitch, the nice-looking blond guy who a year earlier spent the fateful weekend with our then-roommate Niles, was there in a leather harness, and was unusually chatty. At the end of the night, I noticed him sitting half asleep at the bar by himself.

"I don't think you should be driving. Would you like to sleep at our place?"

"Oh, can I?" he lit up.

He walked in and collapsed on the sofa in the parlor, not wanting to put in the effort to climb the stairs to the guest room. I covered him with a blanket, held a glass of water while he took a few sips, and then attempted to help him open his phone, which he'd forgotten the passcode to. The screen was full of notifications from goddam Ron Tellcamp and I shook my head, thinking to myself, "Thirsty bitch. That's never gonna happen."

The next morning, I made him coffee and sent him on his way. (Soon he'd no longer need to worry about driving to and from the Grey Fox. He rented a room from the guy with the $80,000 penis.)

Over brunch with Frank Fontana at Nadine's, we discussed how moved Marcus was that the Floozies sent him housewarming and gift cards. He had just gotten his own place in Chicago.

At 2 a.m. that morning, Marcus wrote to the Floozies:

I have no words.

I don't know what I have done to get great people in my life, but this . . . I'm lucky, I'm grateful.

Thank you, all of you. I sit here as I receive this mail and think . . . why and how do I have this? It's not the money. It's the thought. I'm gone away from each one of you, but y'all are here.

Right in my hand, a card that says "You are so amazing" . . . to someone who is trying not to fall apart. You guys kept me whole.

After brunch I came home to write, and then I got in my car to head to Tom's new place in the Central West End's striking new skyscraper. Before pulling out of the driveway, I glanced at my phone.

"I just heard about Jimmy Eden. So sad."

Jimmy, who was central to the "Meth at the Melrose" feature, apparently died of an overdose. The death should not have been a surprise, but my stomach dropped nonetheless. He had become a fixture in my inbox, always sharing an update or something cultural. He really enjoyed being in that article, and I was comforted by the notion that he knew his words would live on in this book. The lessons, the quips, the shade.

At Tom's I helped unpack while taking breaks to savor the stunning skyline views from his 31st

Floor windows. From that elevation the city somehow appeared to be more urbane, with all of the Central West End and Midtown towers marching towards Downtown, yet smaller because you could see almost the entire region.

Looking down, I could see the roof of the infamous McCloskey Mansion, and directly behind that, the synagogue where Emily was photographed for *Newsweek*. A few blocks over was what appeared to be a miniaturized intersection of Maryland and Euclid, where my book signing was held. To the far left I could see almost to Alton. Straight ahead was Downtown, with the Arch front and center. The bluffs where Belleville rests were on the horizon. I thought about where John Kreisel and Jonathan Batchelor's home was, and then my eyes followed the bluff 20 miles south, where me and Kage watched the solar eclipse with Joe. The Climatron, a geodesic dome housing the rain forest at the Missouri Botanical Garden, was visible, so I knew Auntie M and Magali were immediately to the west of that. They had the exact same house number, just a block apart. Due to the trees, I couldn't see Villadiva, but I could see the nearby South Side Tower, and past that, the twin steeples of St. Anthony of Padua Catholic Church, which I admired daily from our kitchen window. Off to the south I spotted the soaring arched top of the Jefferson Barracks Bridge. It always seemed so far away, but there it was anchoring the south end of this village I called home. This place where I saw friends in every direction.

Back at the house, where Kage had been napping, he wondered what Rick and his camp would have to say about Jimmy's passing.

"Regardless of what they say, through my book Jimmy will have the last word, and it will be enduring," I replied.

Late Sunday night Clyde weighed in as expected, offering condolences yet seeming to take indirect credit for the death.

"My condolences for you losing a friend. But he had quite a bit of darkness in his ledger, it was only an amount of time before his lifeline was cut short. I find it unsettling that the life of someone who I actively hated died on such an empowering night for witches, when I made no active prayers or thought of ill will. I guess Karma and Hecate work well together."

"Whatever bad karma you think he has, you have to know Rick's is a million times worse," I replied.

"I've no doubt. I no longer clutch to the idea of Rick being good, nor did I ever. But he did stick by me when everyone else rallied against me, and I'll never forget that in my entire life. As for Eden, may he get his just rewards in the next plane."

For the record, Rick's aim was to stay out of the Melrose conflict, but Clyde eliminated that option by exposing his betrayal of Kage. He was then only left with the choice of siding with Clyde or with nobody. But I wasn't in the mood to pick at that scab. I was annoyed enough about his comments concerning Jimmy.

The next morning, he had more to say.

"My biggest regret is not having the chance to confront him in person for shit posting about me when I never did a thing to him."

I reminded him that he did plenty of trolling, especially about the drug relapses. That pissed him off, leading to a rant about "A-list fags" making a saint out of Jimmy, and how he hoped he burned in Hell.

Wherever Jimmy went after leaving us that Halloween, it had to be satisfying to know his enemy was tormented over him getting the last word.

Performance Art

What a cast of enemies whose stories intertwine: Spike, Jasmine, Trickery and Ron.

I was cursed with Jasmine because of my vindictiveness towards Spike, and Trickery was exiled from the house after casting his lot with Spike during what would be Spike's high-water mark, seduced by a social media frenzy that turned out to be the very last time the Grove would rally around its once favorite photographer before he fell into obscurity. And while Spike was one bookend of the Jasmine chapters, Ron was the other.

There was a year or two—after Spike was no longer a Grove celebrity, but before his 2018 drug arrest after an 85-mile police chase—that he was relegated to the dark corners of Boxers 'n Briefs, the all-night male strip club on the East Side which was bottom rung of the queer community's bar scene. It was during that period of time he sent me a lead on a story about himself. That's not the first time something like that has happened with a former subject. What some don't understand, but Spike did, is this is all a show. The public hysterics, the protestations. It's performance art. If someone didn't enjoy the stage, they'd simply step away from it.

I've long said, "If you think people don't like when I'm writing about them, wait until I stop."

Even though Spike had been my enemy, albeit a largely forgotten enemy, when making his pitch, he trusted I wouldn't pull a Tellcamp and immediately betray his confidence. It's not how things are done in this ancient city. Just as whisper campaigns are the language of the locals, private asides and clandestine back-channel communications are respected, providing they are handled respectfully. There's a code.

Violating that code made Ron the enemy I least respected, and making fun of Kage during a dark moment made me loathe him like no other.

By the Fall of 2020, when I no longer answered every one of Jasmine's accusations, I remained the star villain in her story. Much like Trickery, a deflated Jasmine tried to keep her dwindling audience invested with increasingly fantastical tales about the horrible things I was allegedly doing to her.

On the topic of Ron Tellcamp, before I stopped responding to he and Jasmine's trolling, I had a definition added to Urban Dictionary:

Tell Camp: *When you block someone and then trash them by name on social media. Known as the most underhanded form of shade.*

Ron managed to get the definition removed in a matter of days, but not before I ordered coffee mugs from Urban Dictionary featuring the definition. When he was telling people he suspected that Zeeke cursed him, I posted a photo of Zeeke drinking from that mug.

The House of Villadiva did not curse Ron. He did that to himself, just as I did when making that original Devil's Bargain with Jasmine in 2014.

As aside about Boxers 'n Briefs, it was one of several queer establishments to shutter in 2020 and when it did, I asked my Facebook friends to share their favorite stories about the place. Among the wild tales was one about a stripper who bent matches around his nipples and set them ablaze.

Too many to count involved being hit with hard dicks, including this one from well-known radio personality Taylor J.

"On my most recent visit a dancer slapped his penis on my hand. On the way home, my hand started to itch and burn. Hand to God."

"Hand herpes?" I replied.

"Afraid so."

Fortunately, she was joking about the herpes.

I don't want to leave anyone with the impression I'm looking down on Boxers 'n Briefs for being seedy. While it was seedier than the local bars I frequented, when I was in the mood for seedy, it wasn't nearly seedy enough for my tastes.

I've seen some shit.

Eyeglasses

It was Sunday morning and I couldn't find my glasses. I'd lost another pair months earlier, and the only backup pair I had left had been a parting gift from Damon days before I left California. At that moment everything between us was very civilized, and he was downright giddy about his beautiful gentleman caller. The glasses had been expensive, but were more than six years old and were so loose from wear that they'd fall off my face when I looked down.

I went to the optician in the shopping center next to Villadiva and selected new frames.

"How quickly will they arrive?" I asked.

"Two weeks, most likely," the salesperson said. "Rush delivery doesn't work anymore, with all that's going on with the Post Office."

In advance of an election where Democrats were pushing mail-in voting, Trump appointed a Postmaster General who was deliberately sabotaging the agency. Sorting machines were being scrapped, overtime was eliminated, and post boxes were removed. People weren't getting their medications on time, and live chicks were arriving on farms dead.

Before my new glasses arrived Zeeke walked into the dining room to find me wearing the pair I had lost.

"Where did you find them?" he asked.

"The front yard," I replied.

Jimmy Eden Postscript

Almost two weeks after Jimmy's death, the fellow AA member who told me of his passing followed up with an update:

Hello Chris. Thought you might like to know about Jimmy. I just checked. He was cremated and taken back to Arizona. I did hear that he died from a heart attack. Apparently his family has a history. No drugs were found in his system. He died clean.

Apologies of the Dead

I worried that I spoke to the Maven too much about her gift of being able to communicate with the dead, which I found endlessly fascinating—and in the case of dad, healing. I feared I was being inconsiderate, and possibly a bore, so I normally did my best to hold back. But one Saturday evening she brought up a neighborhood man who passed away, who had been a thorn in her side for years. He was against everything she proposed for Soulard and fought her constantly, but was now reaching out to her from beyond the grave.

I was sitting beside her in her dining room, along with a straight couple, when she brought him up, which I took as an opening.

"Are there any spirits around now who want to talk?" I asked.

"There always are," the Maven said as she closed her eyes for a moment.

"There's a child, and he passed not long ago."

A woman at the table began sobbing.

The Maven had been a therapist, and was predominately wearing that hat as she sought to comfort her. She relayed a message or two from the other side, all while keeping a calm and reassuring posture.

I felt terrible about steering events in that direction. And worse so when the woman and her companion stepped out, and the Maven, who had been positively serene in their presence, momentarily broke down. She had vividly experienced the child's passing.

When everyone sat back down the conversation returned to the Maven's recently-deceased neighborhood nemesis. The man apparently regretted his actions in life.

"He's always around trying to apologize. Go away!" she said waving her arm back and forth in a shooing fashion.

"Are apologies worth less when they're from the dead?" I asked.

"Oh yes!" she replied.

Many of us think of ghosts as novel. We have television shows about hunting them, homes they're known to inhabit have a draw. But what I was coming to realize is there was nothing more common than disembodied spirits. What's novel is being alive. This brief, golden moment in the sun.

We need to make the most of it, and deliver our apologies while they're still worth their weight in gold.

The Egg Tree

Ms. Jamieson told Zeeke she needed his help.

"That portal seems to be fully open. I'm being woken up at 3 a.m. by a voice in the corner of my bedroom that sounds like a man on a walkie talkie. Plus, I'm having a lot of very sexual thoughts about Clyde again."

Zeeke agreed to stop by after work to cleanse her apartment. I said I would like to join, and after some thought, Kage decided to come too.

In Ms. Jamieson's boudoir, Zeeke unpacked sundry items from his big black case, and burned sage and rang bells as part of his ritual.

"I'm obsessed with this floor," Zeeke said while on all fours looking under the bed. "When was he last here? I'm trying to figure out if he did something to the underside of the bed."

Ms. Jamieson said it had been months.

"His bedroom is directly below us," I said.

"I don't think he's containing his activity to the basement. I think he's doing things down in his apartment."

Zeeke handed Ms. Jamison an iron nail on a chain to wear around her neck. "That's Southern root work and hoodoo," he said.

He then took eggs from the refrigerator and rolled them over each of us, from our heads to the bottoms of our shoes. He said whatever was attached to us would be absorbed by the eggs.

He ran an egg once over Ms. Jamieson, then Kage. When it was my turn, he indicated he was picking up a heavy energy and then paused when he was nearly done, saying, "I'm giving you some extra," as he began making a second round. "You know," he began, not as a question, but as an indication of mutual understanding, "a lot of people hate you."

He then cracked each egg into a glass of water to read it. Ms. Jamieson's egg was the cleanest. Kage's was cloudy, and mine had an unusual attachment that reminded me of a fetus on an umbilical cord.

"Now we need to throw them on a tree, which will ground them," he said.

I followed Zeeke, opening the front door for him while Kage and Ms. Jamieson watched from the balcony above. Ms. Jamieson had the biggest and best balcony at the Melrose, which she used the least. That might have been the first time she had stepped out there all year. Zeeke tossed the eggs against the base of a tree near the curb.

Zeeke felt that nothing was specifically aimed at Ms. Jamieson, she was simply impacted by the amount of supernatural traffic downstairs. "There's so much activity that it spills out and contaminates her space. Think of a roach infestation. I think what's in Ms. Jamieson's bedroom corner is like a spiritual cockroach."

Late the next evening both Ms. Jamieson and Clyde took videos of an epic ninety-minute meltdown another tenant in the building was having. The middle-aged white man began his loud tantrum on his balcony, where he cursed and tossed everything over the railing. He went to the middle of the street where he continued to yell and curse, before picking up the broken wooden chair he'd tossed and beating it against the very tree where Zeeke had grounded the eggs.

After half an hour he returned to the tree to continue beating it.

Clyde stepped onto his porch, and the man, who I knew personally as heterosexual, approached him.

"I'm tired of this body. I've been alone for eight months and I could really use the company. What are you doing?"

Clyde passed on what seemed to him like a sexual advance.

"He seems like someone who might kill me after sex," he laughed to Ms. Jamieson afterwards.

Ms. Jamieson, for her part, thought the demons and the glamour spells had impacted the man. She believed the spiritual cockroaches were spreading, and Kage agreed, saying he felt that was why our downstairs neighbors at the Melrose fought so much, and why Rick went downhill with his drug use.

I felt I owed it to the guy, whom I'd known socially for years, to tell him he may be influenced by something paranormal. I believe he was intoxicated during our online exchange because he was abrasive, and was oddly suspicious of my motives. Despite my requests that he keep our conversation confidential, he posted the following to the Tower Grove South Facebook page late that evening:

I'm being told unwholesome blood rituals are being conducted in my building. I say whatever floats your boat. All life is horror, and no one scares me.

I was furious, and told him so. Nothing online got past Clyde and I knew this was going to open such a can of worms. The man deleted the post, and amazingly I got lucky for once. It escaped Clyde's notice.

The Election of 2020

After polls showing Joe Biden ten points ahead, half the nation, including us, had 2016 PTSD on election night as Florida easily fell to Trump and there was no good news on the map.

Magali sent me a text that I could not make out (I had dropped off celebratory bourbon earlier that day), so I gave her a call. She was despondent about the results in Florida, and how it was the Cuban vote in Miami that destroyed Biden's chances there.

"This is why I don't want to live in Miami!" she exclaimed. "I'm Cuban and I know that the Cubans are more racist than anyone! They don't even care about the kids in cages!"

I made my final post of the evening at midnight:

Since we will not know much else tonight, I'm going to bed, but first I will say this:

This is not a cafeteria. You cannot accept some of Trump but not all of Trump. If you voted for him, you endorse ripping nursing infants from their mothers. You endorse grabbing random women by their genitals. You endorse mocking Gold Star families and calling our war dead "losers and suckers." This is who you are.

It defines you and it always will.

With that, I stormed upstairs. Zeeke stood in the doorway to his room.

"Do we have a new president?" he asked cheerfully.

"No. I can't," I said as I waved him away.

In the darkened bedroom I shook out the blankets as Kage walked in.

"Can I give you a hug?" he asked.

"No. I'm a black hole right now and I don't want to pull you in."

Surprisingly, I managed to get a few hours of sleep, but woke at 3 a.m. when Kage crawled into bed. I told him I was getting up for a bit.

"Hey," he said as he grabbed my hand. "I want you to know we're in this together. Don't be afraid of impacting me with what you're going through."

I sat in the den, which was only illuminated by the television and the street light, and watched the news. Many states were undecided, but it was looking ominous.

Would this break me? More importantly, would it break the back of the nation? How could it not? It certainly appeared to cement who we were.

I didn't know what to do with myself. I didn't think I could sleep, but there was no point staying up. I recalled a brief scene from *Titanic*, when all the lifeboats were gone and rather than being out amidst the chaos, an elderly man held his crying wife in bed while awaiting their fate.

I went upstairs to Kage.

Waiting

Days of waiting ensued as mail ballots were counted, and hope began to appear.

Thursday evening, I posted the following:

Four years of unparalleled corruption in our nation appear to be coming to an end.

Foreign interference, sex crimes, family separations including babies in cages, grotesque nepotism, the worst public health crisis in a century—grossly mismanaged. Vulgar and childish insults of war heroes and Gold Star families. Institutions decimated. An average of 50 verified lies per day. White supremacists celebrated. A Post Office so maliciously sabotaged that all across the country crates of chicks arrived on farms dead.

Four years of our country being absolutely humiliated by this horny, childish thrice-married failed casino operator who pays off porn stars and ran a scam University and scam charity—an absolute clown of a man who cheated CHILDREN WITH CANCER. A man so compromised he basically kneels before Putin.

It's all almost over. And we will stop at nothing to make sure it never happens again. We will never forget those who enabled this.

Meanwhile, a once self-righteous GOP, who long proclaimed to be the party of "family values," finds itself morally bankrupt after absolutely debasing themselves in service of their gluttonous god who partied with Epstein and who shits on a golden toilet.

It's important to come together for the greater good, but reconciliation will never involve validating Trumpism. This chapter will be seen for the abomination it was, and that will only become clearer in time.

A grateful and heartfelt thanks to everyone who fought to end these dark days.

We find ourselves weaker, sicker, poorer with vastly diminished credibility in the world. But soon we can rebuild.

I felt certain the race would be called by Friday, but after the polling errors, the media was extraordinarily cautious. I went to bed irritated, and Saturday morning went out to meet a man who wanted to list his house. As I was finishing up, Kage called to tell me the networks were finally calling the race for Joe Biden.

Exhilarated, I shared the news with my potential client, who fortunately wasn't a Trump supporter, and hurried home. Kage gave me a big hug, and then I settled in to watch as people celebrated in the streets across the country.

A clip was run of someone with Down Syndrome running up to Biden a year or so earlier and hugging him. Biden greeted that person with such sincere, warm kindness, and the sight led me to break down and sob. Biden was a good, decent man, and I was overcome with relief that he would lead the nation.

Freed Bandwidth

We watched Biden's victory speech that Saturday evening, popped champagne and pulled out the fine crystal we'd last used for the Maven's New Year's toast. Joining us in the den were our friends who hosted the huge Pride Pool Party each year, Giuliano Mangiore, who had lived across the street from me and Damon a decade earlier, and his partner Josh Abbott, who used to hang out with Ms. Jamieson at the Melrose. Afterwards we went to Grey Fox to continue the celebration.

At the end of the night, neighborhood friends who had advertised their restaurant in the magazine brought up an issue they had with Kitty, and then one mentioned her disdain for me in a moment of drunken candor.

I hadn't heard from Kitty in almost two months, and it appeared we were in a game of chicken, each seeing how long the other would wait until making the first move. As a result, the magazine was moribund. The only thing active was social media.

The next morning, I woke with an electoral afterglow and with freed bandwidth. I was glad I hadn't done anything impulsive in the wake of the coup plot revelation, but after weeks thinking about it, I still knew it was time to move on.

After coffee I spoke with my colleague Melissa, and even though we'd both be writing for *St. Louis Magazine*, it still felt more like a goodbye than I expected. It was a goodbye in the sense that this project had been our baby, and together we labored over it for years. That feeling carried over with the writers, including Elizabeth.

"So, I don't have a boss now, huh?" she asked.

I told her she'd be reporting to Melissa, and that I would be happy to continue helping her to develop as a writer. I still felt a bit like I was abandoning her, though.

I sent my resignation letter to Chris Keating and *RFT* editor Doyle Murphy, and then posted a simple public announcement along with photos of many of the magazine covers.

After three great years I have stepped down from my role as editor of Out in STL, and will now be writing for St. Louis Magazine.

This has been an incredible experience. I'm grateful for the wonderful team I've worked with, and am proud of what we built together.

The sadness and the sense of loss were deeper than I expected, but I didn't doubt the decision. Rather than introducing the community to itself, I would introduce the region to the community through *St. Louis Magazine*, and introduce the world to the community through my books.

And hopefully I'd be less distracted by politics for a few years.

Deadheading the Mums

It was sunny and 74 degrees, warm for a November day, and I was on the porch deadheading the mums when the phone rang. It was Lydia. It had been roughly eight months since we last spoke, and she didn't bring up our falling out, which was fine. She simply began talking about her relief that Trump lost, and about her health.

The conversation turned to how more Soulard residents her age were moving out. The Baby Boomers who ran things for so long, one by one, were pulling up stakes and selling their homes and businesses.

As I pulled off the fading blooms, I saw many buds ready to flower. I wondered if that was also the case for Soulard.

A 2020 Thanksgiving

In January of 2011 me and Damon were liquidating our life in order to return to California. Our lovely home, two blocks from Villadiva, opened its doors for buyers to peruse our things. Things we had so lovingly collected and assembled. We needed to pare down our treasures to what could fit in one small sedan.

It all broke my heart. I didn't want to leave. And at the end of this big move, we would arrive at a rented room in someone's home. Damon was uncertain about the comped apartment that came with my job, since it was in a building housing formerly homeless people, so I arranged for us to initially rent a room in the suburban home of a friend of mine. The thought that at the end of all this sacrifice we would be in someone else's space was one more depressing layer.

I've moved countless times, but I thought of that time as "the mean move." There was none of the joy or excitement, and regardless of how I lowered my expectations, I'd have to lower them more. Everything about it felt cruel, including the weather. The night before we left, an ice storm came through and I slipped several times while carrying things to the car.

Finally, when we were getting ready to pull away, I needed to jettison one more box of treasures that wouldn't fit. I'd parted with everything except for these most special items, but this hateful move demanded more.

2020, in many ways, felt like an entire year of that mean move. Friends passed away. Influence Awards, Hawaii trip to see Kristin, New Orleans trip: all canceled. The Spring Tulsa trip was nearly canceled when Zeeke's boyfriend Judd had the Covid "scare." I had to let go of the magazine. I was quarantined while Zeeke was sick, and then months later me and Kage were sidelined with Covid. And rather than an expected repudiation of Trump, an election where more Americans voted for him than in 2016.

So many disappointments and reduced expectations, but I was proud of my resilience.

When Thanksgiving came around, I decided to not go to Tulsa. I loved that tradition, and felt me and Kage were probably the safest people to be around since we likely had immunity, but I didn't want to risk mom's health. Instead, we'd host a small gathering at Villadiva.

That scaled back plan was like the final box of treasures I tried to fit in the sedan. After a week where I spent hundreds shopping, was on my hands and knees cleaning the woodwork and on ladders polishing chandelier crystals, it was Thanksgiving Eve and as I walked past Zeeke's bedroom door he flung it open.

"Guess what! I have a 102 temperature."

His delivery was odd, but I think for him it was like ripping off a Band-Aid. Kage took him to Urgent Care, and I notified our guests that Villadiva Thanksgiving was canceled.

Zeeke was diagnosed with an upper respiratory infection.

After handling so much so well all year, this got to me. I'm sure it was the cumulative impact of the pandemic, but I was feeling low. I'm not good at feeling sorry for myself, and in this instance I was not only depressed about the dinner being scrapped, I felt guilty for being depressed about it. I felt guilty for being frustrated with Zeeke. I felt guilty when thinking of the hundreds of thousands of families who lost someone. I hate canceling, and felt like I was letting our friends down.

Tom Choinski, who was to attend our dinner, instead invited us to his and his husband's place. Just the four of us Covid survivors. It was sunny and the views were as spectacular as ever. I had paid my niece Emily to prepare the meal, and everything was delicious.

"Had Biden not won I can't imagine the state I'd be in right now," I said at dinner. "The expectation of getting Trump out, and my book project are the two things that made this year bearable."

We came home for a nap and then met the fun people of Grey Fox Hills at the bar. Everyone was jovial and warm.

At the end of the night, the guy with the $80,000 penis was trying to make a move on someone, and his overt efforts caught everyone's attention. Jack Abernathy was standing across from me and I said, "I heard he's too easily distracted to have sex. He'll stop two minutes in and go play with the stereo for the rest of the night. I think he's got ADH . . ."

"Oh, he's got all the letters," Jack interrupted.

We came home and played on our phones before going to bed. We'd oftentimes spread out, with Kage in his corner spot in the den and me in the dining room, but I had decided to sit in the parlor and Kage took a seat beside me. We laughed and visited with one another, and I ended the day thankful.

Belated Pride 2019 Debrief with Terry Willits

At the end of November 2020, this book was essentially written and the first third had been edited. As I revisited the stories it occurred to me that there was one main mystery I hadn't gotten to the bottom of: Who on the Pride Board concocted the plot to convince protesters that Homeland Security was taking over security for the parade?

Since Jasmine left, the Board was surprisingly leak-proof and my efforts to get answers from current and former members proved unfruitful. I thought about which Pride volunteers might speak to me, and reached out to Terry Willits, who I should nickname "Ol' Transparent Terry" because he's remarkably direct, maybe more so than just about anyone I've ever met who wasn't drunk, and Terry doesn't drink. I invited him to Villadiva on a cool and overcast Sunday afternoon, where for hours he affably answered every question I asked without hesitation.

Terry, who had designed and constructed Fancy Slovak's award-winning Pride floats for years, volunteered in 2019 because he wanted to make sure the event's Trans inclusion efforts went smoothly. He said his role was to be a liaison between MTUG and Pride St. Louis.

"Around that time Jasmine was turning against the Pride Board and was talking bad about them, and was trying to get her clutches into MTUG," Terry began. "I don't know why she was so focused on the trans community other than Christine was a mother figure to young trans guys. You know with Jasmine everything goes back to her Christine crap."

Terry indicated that many in the Trans community expected there to be no officers in the parade, period. "Jasmine definitely oversold a banning of police officers, which had never been part of the official plan. She was also taking full credit for keeping them out."

When the uniform ban was reversed in that mayoral press conference, Terry said dozens of community members gathered at MTUG Headquarters. Some were crying, some were making signs, and some were agitating.

A radical, non-trans contingent was also present, and they were known to carry weapons to protests.

"I always saw my role as Sayer's voice of reason. Everyone was deciding what to do, and the thing with Sayer is he always seeks consensus. I told him, '*You* need to make a decision on behalf of the community. You have to decide. We will have kids marching and they will be in harm's way."

Terry said Sayer responded, "I don't even want my own kids there," and one of the more radical activists said, "Maybe it's time some of these little white kids see a gun drawn now and then like Black kids see all the time!"

"I'm not in," Terry announced. "You want a big old riot but this is not the right way. You're putting all those Trans kids in the line of fire."

Terry went to the Pride Board to tell them what was being planned, including the details of Jasmine's plot to provide protesters with official Pride shirts and open barricades. Jasmine later told Terry she didn't know how they found out.

"We agreed to meet for coffee and she brought one of her Trans guys because, you know, she can't do anything by herself. I admitted I was the one who told them."

Both Jasmine and her friend expressed outrage and astonishment. The young companion said he couldn't believe Terry would betray friends.

"First of all, none of us have ever been friends," Terry told them. "I was just involved to serve the community."

After that Jasmine blocked Terry.

"Who came up with the plot to convince protesters that Homeland Security was taking over due to the terrorism threat?" I asked.

"Dennis Gorg," Terry said in reference to Pride's former compliance director.

Terry notified MTUG, believing the story was true, and when learning the truth, he felt betrayed that Gorg, a longtime friend, used him to disseminate false information. Terry publicly called him out on Facebook, and Gorg resigned within days.

Fancy's passing brought Terry and Jasmine together again because Terry was a dear friend of Fancy's and Jasmine had a garage full of Fancy's belongings. Jasmine unblocked Terry and invited him over for coffee so they could coordinate the distribution of the items.

"We sat in her kitchen and she asked if I spoke to you. I told her I had never met you face to face. She said you had turned against her and adopted her dog for spite, like that's anything functioning adults do," he laughed. "But later in the conversation she said she had to get rid of the dog because it was shitting on the floor and her landlord would be mad. Her stories were all over the place, like she can't keep track of her own lies."

Their conversation then, of course, turned to Christine Elbert.

"Jasmine said Christine only goes to Hartford Coffee because she knows Jasmine goes there, and that Christine sits and stares at her."

Hartford Coffee was blocks from Christine's, and a mile from Jasmine's.

"She said one day she left Hartford because Christine was there stalking her. She went to the park to drink her coffee, and Christine was behind a tree watching her! She also said there's no reason for Christine to ever drive past her house. She lives on a major street right next to the gay supermarket! It's crazy."

Regarding Jasmine's claims of having to print 884 of pages of evidence, Terry exclaimed, "Print!" and shook his head. "I'm sure the FBI's Cyberbullying Department can open digital files."

All of Fancy's belongings were cleared out, and a few months later Jasmine again blocked Terry.

"It was immediately after me and you both commented on one of Christine's threads."

Terry was concerned for Ron when he learned his old friend had become close with Jasmine. "Ron is one of my oldest friends in St. Louis, we go back thirty years. I talked to him before my [transition] surgery, and we used to always go to karaoke together. The thing is he's susceptible to manipulation when given attention, and he can get really intense," Terry began. "He can be the sweetest man, but . . ." he trailed. "Jasmine is the wrong person for him to hang out with."

"Jasmine is good at forming instant bonds, and she makes people who've never felt like they belonged feel like they are part of a house," I replied.

"That would be Ron," Terry said, concerned. "It seems she has a revolving door."

Terry seemed to feel like Ron was the victim in the Saccharine Sisters dynamic, while I thought Ron was just as bad for Jasmine as she was for him.

When all of the 2019 Pride maneuvers went down, I, like Jasmine and MTUG, felt Terry was a turncoat. I can be just as blinded by the tribalism as anyone, and as I sat across from him, I felt regret. I thought it must be lonely for him to buck the tribal system and stand completely on principle.

One time I publicly disagreed with Terry, and that's when he wrote a piece that gutted Chuck Pfoutz like a fish. I think the way we both handled it was a model for how things should be done, though. I gave him a heads up that I disagreed with his take and would write a rebuttal. He respected that, and neither of us took any of it personally. We even collaborated after that.

As our clandestine meeting was drawing to a close, Terry sat in disbelief about all we had discussed, particularly around the 2019 Pride Parade. "So much was happening at that time. It was hard to keep track of it then, and it's nearly as hard to put all the pieces together now. I'd almost forgotten some of it."

As Terry prepared to stand up, Jett, who had been on his lap for the latter half of the visit, licked him on the cheek.

A week later I had a call with Sayer to confirm his quote in the story. He didn't recall hearing the comment about pulling a gun, but said overall it was an accurate accounting of events.

"I do want to say that I like Jasmine and she's been very good to us," Sayer noted before discussing his experiences and feelings about the 2019 Pride fiasco.

"Dennis Gorg called to warn me about Homeland Security's involvement. He was careful with his words as if he was being recorded, but I believed him and I feel bamboozled."

Sayer said he wanted terribly for his folks to have that mile-long standing ovation after years of feeling ignored and dismissed. He felt gay white men on the Board and in the community robbed them of that.

"And if they tried to offer it again, I don't think we'd take it."

Matters of the Soul

"Well, it looks like Ms. Jamieson might have sold her soul to Satan," I wrote to Jonathan Batchelor and John Kreisel.

Despite the cleansing Zeeke performed, things at the Melrose had only deteriorated. Tenants in the unit below our old place had a massive street melee in the middle of the day, at least twenty people involved. Ms. Jamieson had been up in her window recording the whole thing and sharing the footage. I was leaving the market next to Villadiva when I saw an ambulance enter the neighborhood, and I knew exactly where it was going.

One of the people in front of the Melrose pulled out a gun and shot it.

Ms. Jamieson had been depressed for weeks, and had neglected basic household chores like dishes during that time. She sent our group chat the following:

So, remember how I jokingly asked the other day if I were to sell my soul to the devil for beauty and shit if there was a proper protocol? Well, that night I was feeling kinda ugly and I was in a bad mood and I may have said out loud "Ok Satan or God, whoever grants my wish first gets my soul" out of frustration. Well, I swear after that, I started getting these hot men hitting me up, as well as after I posted my THOT pics. I hope I didn't inadvertently sell my soul to Satan lol.

"Whoever grants my wish first? That's not how any of this works!" I exclaimed. "God isn't a genie in a bottle!"

We really shouldn't have been surprised, though. Clyde boasted that the demons gave him results, and even Zeeke had used a spell on Angel. We knew Ms. Jamieson was paying attention to both situations, and had made several cracks about taking similar extraordinary measures.

Kristin, who didn't even believe in any of this, was frustrated and exclaimed, "Jordan, you live over a HELL MOUTH!"

I asked Zeeke about it while at my computer in the dining room.

"She did it of her own free will," Zeeke said, explaining that he thought it was irreversible.

Jonathan and John, however, thought there was hope. I reached out to Jonathan in particular because of his role as a deacon in the church.

Jonathan replied, "Well every sacred mystery, blessing spell good and bad needs words *and* action. If there was no action then it is a moot point. Did Ms. Jamieson act on it?"

"I don't know what act there is other than vocalizing it," I replied.

"Those are the words. My thought is if he acted on it, like had sex with his spewing Grindr account, then he would be toast," Jonathan laughed.

They suggested she abstain from sex for 45 days.

"She certainly wouldn't turn good sex down," I laughed. "Yeah, if I told her the only way to save her soul would be to turn down good sex, she'd take her chances."

"I'd steer clear of those that have come forth since her declaration," John replied, and Jonathan offered to bless her with holy water.

Meanwhile, Clyde messaged about seeing a shadow person in his apartment, and said he was sleeping so much better at his new boyfriend's place.

"I kind of wonder if the presence is affecting all here. Jordan told you about the shooting and fight of one of our neighbors. Then there's the dude that threw his chair off the balcony."

In our group chat we discussed how bad things had gotten for even Clyde to acknowledge it.

Kage asked Ms. Jamieson if she'd had any tricks over since the 45-day suggestion.

"One person but he doesn't have a job or a car and rode 2 miles on a bike so I don't think that counts," she replied, indicating she could have easily gotten him without help from the underworld.

Kage gave her hell, no pun intended. After some back and forth she said they actually didn't have sex.

"Literally his penis did not go in my mouth and my penis did not go in his hole."

"Notice she didn't say he didn't blow her," I yelled to Kage, who was in the den, from the dining room.

Kage pushed her for that clarification, and she said no sex happened whatsoever.

I also had another spiritual matter to discuss with Jonathan. Magali's best friend Jazz, the woman who joined us at the Cliff House and the next morning was waving goodbye on the sidewalk outside of the Cadillac Hotel, had passed away and Magali, who was raised Catholic, wished to light a candle for her.

Jonathan invited us to Saturday Mass. "You should seriously take up a career as a religion coordinator," he laughed.

After the Mass, which took place outside for social distancing, he took us inside so Magali could light the candles, and he showed us around. John left us for a meeting with Father Marek, who had blessed our home a year earlier. John had just told Jonathan that day that he decided to become Catholic, which was a surprise to us all.

I had spent very little time in the section of North St. Louis where St. Stanislaus was located. The impressive brick building dated to the 1890s, but everything around it had been recently redeveloped.

"What's interesting to me is how the city rose and fell all around this church several times," I said.

The urban fabric that was built contemporaneously with the church, which was a Polish neighborhood, had been cleared in the 50s to make way for the infamous Pruitt-Igoe housing projects, 33 massive 11-story communist block style modernist buildings which were demolished with explosives in the mid-1970s. The attractive new neighborhood around the church was at least the area's third incarnation.

I thought about Jonathan's comment about being a religion coordinator, and I do think I tend to try to nudge people towards their chosen or necessary path. A central concern about Zeeke's ex Judd, for example, was the feeling he was only pretending to support Zeeke's spiritual practice.

On the ride to dinner after Mass, Magali said she'd recently rediscovered her faith in order to survive the Trump years. I hoped she would start attending St. Stanislaus regularly, and thought about how beautiful it would be if honoring the passing of her best friend led her to an entire community.

And always contemplating the way things intertwine, I thought about the San Francisco—St. Louis connection to the evening's encounter. I first met John when I overheard him mention St. Louis on a San Francisco patio. Magali lived in San Francisco at the time I met him, and we were all at the St. Louis church to honor a San Franciscan.

The following day was cloudy and about 50 degrees. Kage had an activity planned, and I felt called to Cahokia Mounds. I packed up the three dogs, and as I arrived the sun came out. We had the woodland and pasture trails to ourselves, and as I wandered the grounds, I thought about how that place was spiritual for me. It's where I went to commune and recharge.

The dogs darted in and out of the woods, took in all of the new scents, and ran across the fields.

In one of the Maven's most vivid dreams about me I was in a pasture surrounded by dogs. "So many dogs," she said at the time.

If that's my afterlife while I await Kage's arrival, a never-ending afternoon at the mounds with all my life's dogs, I shall be quite satisfied.

Loose Ends

As 2020 drew to a close, loose ends were getting tied up and other stories had updates. For starters, the United States Supreme Court rejected a ridiculous Texas suit to overturn the vote in four states, which *The New York Times* reported effectively ended Trump's hope of reversing the election in court. And speaking of lawsuits, Chuck was getting his list of witnesses together for his defense against Braden Bardoux, and Dustin Mitchell somehow managed to get his suit against everyone involved with the "Dustin Does Dallas" feature, which had been dismissed in October, reinstated.

Lacey sent me a photo of the notice which I shared to social media, writing: *I appreciate that he actually filed paperwork, unlike a local nut who claimed to have a lawsuit in the works for nine months while raising money for photocopies.*

Lacey assured me the suit would go nowhere for numerous reasons including the statute of limitations and the unlikeness of him getting all parties served across four states by late January (which proved to be an accurate prediction). In regards to the outlandishness of the suit, she added, "Please recall that in the lawsuit he outed Destiny as Trans and accused me of murdering Riley."

Riley was her boyfriend who had committed suicide.

Clyde's new relationship (things with Gervais ended amicably months earlier, and he'd been dating a redhead) was progressing nicely and it seemed his desire to reach out to me had diminished a bit as a result, which was healthy. He shared he was a bit nervous about just how well things were going, and I advised him to let his gentleman caller take the lead. In the past things had soured when Clyde rushed them, but I believed if he'd simply retain a confident and relaxed posture all would unfold to his liking. After a few rounds of advice, he asked if I'd consider officiating their wedding, should that day come.

"That would be quite a plot twist worthy of our soap opera!" I replied.

"My first St. Louis crush marrying me. I do admit it's rather racy," he laughed.

In Oklahoma City, Shane Morter was finally charged with unauthorized removal of a dead body more than six months after the infamous wheelbarrow incident, and it was all over the local news. He'd also lost his foot to diabetes.

His longtime best friend Floyd Martin, who no longer spoke to Shane, blamed meth for his downfall. In a Facebook post "The Mayor of Gay OKC" wrote:

Something I need to publicly say and please don't put a bunch of wheelbarrow jokes in the comments. That is not the intention, nor is this post the place for it.

Shane and I used to be best friends. I will always appreciate the crazy and hilarious times we had and trips we took. I miss that Shane. I am sorry that meth has taken our friendship, his quality of life and in this case, the dignity of a dead guy. I wish him nothing but the best, but it is sad. I can't deal with him at this time, and I hope something good comes his way.

People, I have always been a proponent of whatever makes one feel good temporarily, and that includes recreational drugs, but meth is a bitch. If it doesn't kill you, you will spend the rest of your life trying to stay off the shit or regretting what you did while you were on it. I have seen it too many times.

It was a message so many in the gay community needed to hear. I could easily see Rick or Menashe in a similar situation.

Barb, the "What's that smell" gal from Tramps, called to tell me Shane Morter had reached out to her, and that he had zero remorse.

"It was a tough call. I mean, yeah, he's a piece of shit, but we were friends at one time. I was super honest with him. I told him I make every joke I can. I said he'd do the same if roles were reversed. He actually cackled and said, 'Darling, you are so right. We are both *so* bad. I'd ruin you.' So, basically, he's reenacting *Party Monster*. He acts like nothing happened but some inconvenience. It was, seriously, really hard to hear."

"Did he say anything about what it was like when the guy died, or about the body being there over the following days?" I asked.

"He legit acted like he was put out. *Very* Michael Alig. Like, that entire mentality. Now that we have a face to the victim it's way fucking worse," Barb said.

"It's very sobering," I agreed.

The victim was only 32 and had a wife and a daughter. In an article that spared no gory details, Oklahoma City's paper of record, *The Oklahoman,* reported: *Oklahoma County sheriff's deputies found the decomposing and maggot-infested remains on May 6 under a box spring by a white couch.*

They also reported that the victim's wife died of an overdose later in the year. When Barb asked Shane who the victim was, he dismissively replied, "Some fucking privileged Edmond fuck with daddy's money."

Edmond is an affluent suburb of Oklahoma City.

"Chris, he literally thinks he's done nothing wrong," Barb continued.

Speaking of drugs, Rick's luck was finally running out, and I couldn't help but wonder if it was due to Zeeke's curse. He'd risen to the top of the queer drug game and seemed to always skirt repercussions, but was now out of money and facing hard time.

"He can't afford his legal fees," my source said.

"I thought he was awash in cash," I replied.

"I thought so too. He probably miscalculated and overstocked and wasn't able to sell enough quickly enough."

Back in Grey Fox Hills, the bar began work on the crumbling back wall. It seemed to be going at a snail's pace, but about 20% of the bricks had been tuck pointed and I hoped whatever work they wound up doing would at least buy us some time.

The final loose end was about the Maven. I had been concerned that she was planning to break camp. She did sell her three-story home, but she only moved around the corner to a more manageable first-floor flat. It was raining that Friday evening when I went to see her regarding a Mardi Gras piece I was working on for the February issue of *St. Louis Magazine*. Chuck joined us because he was going to produce a Vices & Virtues Mardi Gras fashion show for her, and the three of us took deep dives into both Soulard machinations and those of the city's LGBTQ community.

The Maven had young gay neighbors, only 22 years old, who she wanted me to meet sometime soon and mentor. They were new in town and intimidated.

"I was 22 when I moved to St. Louis, right around the corner from here. And I'm about the age Ray David was then," I said, contemplating.

The conversation was oriented to the future, which was comforting after my suspicion she was planning an exit. She wasn't going anywhere, and we had much to look forward to.

Christmas at the Embassy

In early December Janessa Highland had to wait in line to get into Just John, which she said never happened when out of drag. Up in her cups, she made a federal case out of it with a Facebook post in which she tied the indignity she suffered with that of drag queens in general, as well as women, people of color and the trans community.

The bar responded like white blood cells on a germ, and their thread exploded as their patrons condemned her. When Janessa roused the next day, she composed an elegant apology for the ordeal. Unfortunately, the bar's thread continued to rage.

Such situations in this town are always rife with hypocrisy and double-standards. If St. Louisans deem one to be weak or nutty, they'll often carve out a massive exemption and basically give that person carte blanche for their outrageous behavior without any demand for so much as an apology. A perfect example is how there wasn't a peep from bar owners or employees when Ol' Trickery posted that someone (Zeeke) was running through their bars with flesh eating bacteria, which would have been a devastating claim if believed. Even Tim Beckman, who long owned a bar, came to his defense.

On her public apology I commented: *You've proven you are capable of doing two things 99% of those in this community aren't: Admitting fault and weathering a good Ol' St. Louis pile on. This town gives a lot of leeway to those they feel are weak, but they descend on you because they think you're strong enough to take it. And they're right.*

The House of Markstone's Drag Embassy held their 2nd Annual Christmas Party on Sunday, December 13th, which was a scaled down affair due to the pandemic. Me and Kage donned our sparkliest ensembles and enjoyed an intimate candlelit evening with the Markstones and other colorful entertainers.

"I always say if me and Janessa had a baby it would be Chris Andoe," the bosomy Mother Markstone said while holding court. "He has my grandeur and her mouth."

Later in the evening I sat beside Janessa on an antique settee in her hunter green study. We discussed Braden Bardoux' lawsuit, and her near-certainty that he was behind the efforts to destroy her livelihood.

"I had to go before the Missouri Real Estate Commission. I had to have several meetings with my brokers. It was not fun. Back in Springfield we'd pull some shit but we never went after someone's job. There were lines you didn't cross," she said. "I know he could say his business was targeted, but he'd already fired Krista and tried to keep her from working again."

After firing Krista Versace, Bardoux posted a laundry list of things he claimed she said about every queen in town. Notably, the list was not comprised of screen shots, because if those things were being said I can guarantee Bardoux was saying more than his share right along with her.

"In this town they'll go after anything and everything. They'll even try to get your pets removed," I replied. "And if they don't have a leg to stand on they'll just lie."

The subject turned to how Bardoux bought an east side flower shop for Katherine Newman to run since she wasn't welcomed on any stage anymore. One year earlier the petite and elegant Katherine, wearing a simple and meticulously fitted red dress, had given the embassy tour, but within weeks had defected to the House of Bardoux.

"It seems odd that he'd continue to target the community while having his own business that could be targeted in return," I said.

"Have you seen Katherine's arrangements?" Janessa asked. "You'd be better off going to a supermarket florist. That's a dumpster fire that will burn itself out."

I spoke about the book, and gaming out strategies on how to handle attacks from the detractors. Janessa suggested capitalizing on any controversy.

"And you do so much for people, way more than you realize. It's time to call in some of those favors."

I had long ago stopped expecting reciprocity. For example, when Tim Beckman's exit interview blew up, I fell on the sword and tried to take 100% of the blame to shield him and Sensation. I thought that would have at least been a bonding moment, but instead he'd subsequently taken the side of anyone who was against me for the next five years, including Clyde, Jasmine and Trickery. (His rationale was that he's always for the underdog).

But when someone would pull through for me, they do it *spectacularly*. From putting me up at Villa Ray to getting Kage a good job with travel benefits to bailing me out of the Fiat fiasco with a $10,000 check. I decided I should focus on those instances, and not dwell on the situations that left me disappointed.

The "calling in favors" advice did spur me to spearhead an effort to raise the $2,500 needed for Chasity Valentino's defense in Bardoux' lawsuit, which was accomplished in a single weekend. I believe he targeted the young, underemployed Trans woman of color because he thought it would be an easy win. That he could make an example out of her. I was thankful for my friends and proud of the community for coming together to get it done. Everyone from Clyde at the base of the Melrose to Tom Choinski atop the Central West End's highest skyscraper donated. Many pitched in as little as $5, which added up. Hell, even the miserly Ms. Jamieson pitched in $25!

Expecting

Josh, a main character in *Delusions of Grandeur*, was not mentioned in *House of Villadiva* until now, and that alone indicates he was a success story. He was 18 and I was 36 when I took him under my wing shortly after he arrived in St. Louis. A straight, redneck kid from rural Missouri, we were opposites in most ways and he was unpolished to say the least. A perfect example was when he was lamenting his girlfriend's poor personal hygiene. His mother called in the middle of the conversation and they had a nice exchange, but when they were getting ready to hang up, he thought of an important question to ask her.

"Uhh, Mom, wait a second," he began, his brow furrowed and his voice deep and sincere. "Is it normal for a woman's vagina to smell like some nasty tuna?"

That would pop into my head at random moments and I would laugh like I did the first time the line was delivered.

I got him his first apartment, went with him to open his first bank account, taught him how to write a check and helped him navigate countless situations. A decade later he was a hardworking married guy with a happy little girl. We'd talk every other month and meet for a meal maybe once a year, and it really did feel like he was my adult son. I'm proud of the man he's become.

The times it goes bad are more interesting to read about, as some bottomless pit paints the house as the bag guys after we got them set up, adopted their unwanted pet or gave them a car. But even some of those people eventually come around. I've been guilty of ingratitude myself. I was ungrateful for all my Oklahoma City boss did for me, but realized it and worked to correct the record. We humans pretend our decisions are based on logic but we're emotion-driven animals. We make messes, but those with character go back and try to clean them up.

At the end of 2020, Amanda Love, a drag queen I knew in Tahlequah, OK, population 17,000, told me about an 18-year-old bisexual kid named Max who was about to be homeless. Over brunch at Nadine's me and Kage announced we were "expecting."

"Oh my God, not again!" Magali exclaimed with her head in her hands. The rest of the table shared the sentiment, but softened when I showed his photo. Something about putting a face to the story.

Nadine was using a back table as a desk and I asked to speak to her. She was someone always trying to help those down on their luck, hiring homeless people and ex-convicts.

"I can use him as a porter and pay him $11 an hour to start," she said.

It was a more somber and serious discussion than we normally had. I was asking her to sign on in an effort to change someone's life. I think the solemn mood was because the kid was in a bad place, we had a big task ahead of us, and the odds were it wouldn't work. Still, together we'd challenge the odds.

I should mention Josh, who I discussed at the beginning of this story, was Nadine's favorite character in *Delusions*.

So, on December 31, 2020, we prepared a room for a desperate kid who was due to arrive on a bus in a couple of days. A kid referred to me by an Oklahoma drag queen. It all felt exactly like how our story would go.

Mama's Gonna Move You Uptown

Amanda Love had taken the 18-year-old with special needs under her wing shortly after he arrived in Tahlequah, having run away from his abusive mother back in a tiny Michigan village. Amanda, in many ways, became his new mother.

She didn't have much to offer him, she didn't have a car or even have heat in her home, but she was his advocate and used her social media network of gays to search for a better place. It was reminiscent of Reba McEntire's "Fancy"—minus the prostitution angle—how Amanda sent Max to live with strangers in a desperate attempt to give him a shot in life. She scraped together $20 so he had food on his journey, and he headed off to the closest Greyhound Station thirty miles down the road where we had a ticket waiting for him. Destination: St. Louis.

"I feel like we're expecting a baby," I told her.

"I feel like I'm losing one," she replied.

The bus arrived around 11pm on a cold Sunday evening and I picked him up from the station, which was 50ft below an elevated interstate downtown.

"I've never lived in a city this big before! Oh my God!" Max exclaimed.

He was a tall and nice-looking Native American with a baritone voice and positive demeanor. We hadn't even turned off of the old cobblestone street by the bus station when he told me of his horrific life-long history of abuse.

At the house Kage had the dogs sequestered in the den. After showing Max his room, the one Zeeke first occupied before upgrading to the larger dormered twin of ours, I suggested he sit in the parlor and meet the animals. Troy could take months or even years to warm up to someone, but loved Max instantly. Max would develop the closest bond with Jett, though.

I was home for lunch on Monday when Nadine messaged to say she was available to meet him. He'd been in town for all of 13 hours, and was in his room playing *Call of Duty* on the television Frank Fontana had sent. His door was open and from the top of the stairs I said, "Nadine is available to meet with you now if you're up for it," and he nodded and eagerly jumped up to get ready.

He came downstairs sharply dressed in black pants and a button-down shirt.

"Would you button these?" he asked, arm outstretched, in reference to his cuff buttons. "I can never do it."

Walking into the closed restaurant, I made the introduction.

"Well, he's too well-dressed to work here!" Nadine joked.

Me and Max sat at the bar over coffee while he filled out the application and Nadine updated me on the upstairs renovations she was working on. She then mentioned Lisa West, the Bastille regular and gal about Soulard who organized Peyton's memorial, and said something about her being a hospice nurse.

"She's a hospice nurse?" I asked, surprised. "It's so St. Louis to engage in dozens of conversations without even asking what one does for a living."

Nadine asked Max to join her at a table on the other side of the restaurant. I couldn't hear much, but knew she was asking tough questions, including inquiries as to why his last job didn't work out. After firmly laying out her expectations she offered him a position.

"I've never gotten a job so fast in my life!" he exclaimed upon leaving.

Having seen the way our enemies came for people's livelihoods, I was relieved he'd be working for someone with the fortitude of Nadine. But I was most comforted by the knowledge she genuinely cared for her employees.

He loved working there, proved to have a strong work ethic, and was excited about all of the kitchen training.

"My mom didn't let me do anything in the kitchen," he said. He also said Nadine's was the first job he'd had where everyone was nice to him.

Two of the most rewarding experiences of my life were when I had the privilege of showing Josh, and years later Kage the Pacific Ocean. I had a similar and maybe even more profound experience when showing Max the Arch. Somehow, he'd never even seen a photo of it.

We drove him across the river to an observation deck where the triumphant Arch loomed large over the skyline. Max stared at the sight before him with a look of tranquil exhilaration and wonderment. I sensed he was awakening to the fact that he was looking at *his* city.

On our outing we also took him to the Zoo, which was his first zoo visit in a decade. During our first days together, I wanted to cry thinking about the abuse and deprivation he'd suffered, and I did cry while writing this story.

I wrote to Amanda with an update, and then asked if he liked hugs.

"I'd like to hug him, but I know some people don't like them," I said.

"He hugged me all the time," she replied.

With that, I stopped by his room and hugged him goodnight.

State of the House

I remember how formidable the doors of Old St. Louis looked when I walked past them as a newcomer in 1997, behind iron fences and atop limestone steps. They were tall, weathered, imposing and shut.

Had the wide door of Villa Ray not opened up for me back then I surely wouldn't have bonded with this place like I have. Ray welcomed me into the house, the tribe, the dynasty. The houses of St. Louis are notoriously closed, but for generations ours has welcomed outsiders more than most, just as it welcomed me as a broke kid who just blew in from Oklahoma. A closed house would have far less turmoil, but also less vitality and passion.

Rightfully, there has been much analysis and lamenting about how closed the city can be, but little if anything has been written about what it's like on the other side of the doors, where friends are your chosen family and where they will be there for you through your darkest days until your final breath and beyond. Dark days like those of an abandoned and solitary Mother Markstone before being lifted out of impoverished retirement, brought to St. Louis and spectacularly relaunched at the helm of the Drag Embassy. Or like those of Magali when she knew she had to leave her expensive city, but didn't know where to go. Or like those of Fancy Slovak, whose community would join her for one last spectacular bash at the sunset of her life.

Beyond, as in, perhaps, retiring your office, or busting out your ashes for a closing number, ala Midnight Annie. A Geoff Story may immortalize you in film during your final months, or a Lisa West might just drag the mayor to the podium at your memorial. Or maybe your tribe will communicate with you beyond the grave via a Zeeke or a Maven.

Being part of an enduring house is like being in a secret garden, and as you've read in these pages, those who leave the garden often spend their years searching for a way back in, but the spell is broken.

As of this writing I find myself in my mid-forties, and life is more fun and fulfilling than I could have imagined. I enjoy counseling and mentoring. I enjoy developing talent. I enjoy planning for the future of our diverse and intergenerational house as we continue to welcome new people. And I relish being part of my community.

Hours after Marcus left for Chicago, Cody walked into the drag cabaret and sat beside me. I hadn't expected him. He lived 45 minutes away and he's a man of few words, but he was present because he figured I needed it. Kage wasn't a drag enthusiast, preferring to socialize at the bar or on the patio, but he took shifts beside me as well.

I remember the loneliness of pre-internet Tulsa as a gay teen, looking for signs of life as I roamed the desolate streets in the middle of the night. I thought of that once when atop San Francisco's Buena Vista Hill, looking down at the city and thinking it looked like a model train set. "Nobody from here could know the loneliness I've known," I thought at the time. I had a similar feeling when overlooking St. Louis from Tom's 31st Floor apartment, but felt a much deeper connection because the people behind those windows and under those roofs weren't ephemeral. They were as rooted as the large trees lining the streets. They had traditions that spanned decades and bonds that were magical. Out of everywhere I've traveled and lived, I've been the least lonely in St. Louis.

I'm driven to tell the story of this place, and telling such a story runs counter to the private and secretive culture, riling up the tribes and causing constant turmoil. For years I wondered what Ray David thought of all of the controversies I've found myself embroiled in. Even before me our house had always been bold, but I feared I gave him acid reflux. I'd long been afraid to ask.

I got my answer when he treated me to an exquisite birthday dinner at one of the city's finest restaurants. I was turning 45, and the topic turned to how at times it seemed everyone in town was fired up over something I said or wrote.

Ray raised a glass. "When you're bad, you're better."

Drama is not the aim, but is a byproduct of having entanglements with so many people. Even after all that's been thrown at us, the House of Villadiva continues to do what we do. The beads are still tossed. The events are still produced. Opinions are still offered. New people still arrive in the storied dining room to share their intimate thoughts. And most importantly, new faces are still welcomed into our dynasty. This city has a number of fine houses, some of which may condemn us at times, but when they're being targeted by this town's ruthless underbelly, we're often who they turn to.

As long as one is breathing, they are also exhaling. As long as our doors are open and our house is running as it should, there will be drama. There will be someone who didn't get the coverage they wanted, or the invite they felt they were entitled to. There will be someone who's upset that their sinister plans were exposed or thwarted, or that their bad behavior wasn't validated. And since this is all theatre, there will be those whose story simply needs a villain to spice things up.

The cursing and dragging of our name simply demonstrate that we continue to withstand it all, and that we're still at it. The drama isn't a sign the House of Villadiva is weak. The drama is a sign the house is strong.

Fin

Acknowledgements

I'd like to thank all those in my life who allowed me to share their stories, with a special shout out to Ms. Jamieson. In the past five years I gave her many lectures about oversharing over social media, but her openness to letting me tell her story was a real gift to me and to the readers. I'd also like to thank Clyde, who was also surprisingly sophisticated about this endeavor.

I've been honored to collaborate with the talented RFT Art Director Evan Sult on the various magazine and newspaper features, and I appreciate him taking an interest in this project and doing amazing work on the cover.

Most of the photographs featured were shot by Theo R. Welling, who is also a world-class talent.

Three of the people who helped me the most with this book are people I've never met face to face, and they were also helpful with my first book, *Delusions of Grandeur*.

Robert Julian, author of *Postcards from Palm Springs*, has consistently given the tough feedback one finds hard to come by in the polite Midwest. I credit him for critical changes I made to *Delusions of Grandeur*, and I appreciate him making time for me again six years later.

Crystal Hubbard is the award-winning author of *Catching the Moon*, and I'm incredibly moved that she volunteered to take time from her own work and family to edit both of my books.

And Paul Emery of New York. Paul has been a friend and a champion, counseling me through difficult times and motivating me consistently. There were moments I wasn't even sure if the book was interesting, and he was who would turn me around.

On the other end of the spectrum, my childhood friend Marsha Sioux performed a final edit days before going to print, and having a brand new perspective and fresh eyes proved invaluable. And how interesting that the fresh perspective was from a friend who knew me so long ago. As a young teen I entertained her on Saturday evenings, serving her soda in stemware, talking about ghosts and carrying on. At my core I'm definitely the same person.

Finally, I've been able to flourish creatively because of my kind, loving, cuddly, fun and supportive husband Kage. He's such a radiant light in my world, and this book is dedicated to him.

CPSIA information can be obtained
at www.ICGtesting.com
Printed in the USA
LVHW071655130521
687360LV00009B/193